Making Boys and Girls

»Substanz«

marta
press

Ulrike Schneeberg

Making Boys and Girls
in Picturebooks with Monsters

Marta press

Die Deutsche Bibliothek verzeichnet diese Publikation
in der Deutschen Nationalbibliografie.
Detaillierte bibliografische Daten sind im Internet abrufbar unter
http://dnb.d-nb.de

Besuchen Sie uns auch im Internet:
www.marta-press.de

1. Auflage Juni 2016
© 2016 Marta Press Verlag Jana Reich, Hamburg, Germany
www.marta-press.de
© Umschlaggestaltung: Niels Menke, Hamburg
unter Verwendung eines Bildes von © Henrik Drescher
Printed in Germany.
ISBN 978-3-944442-43-3

Contents

Acknowledgements 11

1   Introduction 13

    1.1   Research questions and hypotheses 14

    1.2   Research context 18

    1.3   Response 26

2   Theoretical Approaches 35

    2.1   Monsters, children and children's literature 36

Introduction 36

Monsters from an adult culture perspective 39

From antiquity to the Enlightenment era 42

Monsters in fairy tales and moral tales – the long 19th century 49

Nonsense and fantasy – The late 19th and early 20th centuries 53

An explosion of meanings and media – the 20th and 21st centuries 58

Picturebook child and picturebook monster 64

    2.2   Gender, children and children's literature 77

Introduction 77

Who does the 'making'? – Picturebook monsters from a social constructionist perspective 79

Creating queer spaces – queer theory and psychoanalysis 90

3   Methodological Approaches 103

3.1   What is a picturebook? Some formal considerations 104

Narrative content 105

Narrative mode 106

Dual audience 107

Historical and geographical location 107

Material parameters 109

Distinction from other print media with similar characteristics 111

3.2   Overview of the corpus 112

The number coding: thematic patterns 115

Icons and abbreviations 119

Some counting 119

The authors' biographical background 120

Editions, publication dates and publishing houses 123

Verbal coding and visual coding regarding protagonists'
            gender 123

What is a main protagonist in a picturebook? 128

Dividing lines between categories 129

Selection process 130

Historical patterns... 130

Quantification as a research method.................................... 131

3.3   Analytical concepts for reading picturebooks 133

Finding focus... 133

Focalization 136

Conclusion... 145

4   Picturebook Analyses 147

4.1   The monster under the bed 148

Introduction 148

'Little Red Riding Hood' 151

'The Monster and the Teddy Bear' 154

'Hungry! Hungry! Hungry!' 166

Queering 'Little Red Riding Hood' via 'Hungry! Hungry!
         Hungry!' 178

Conclusion 186

4.2   Marriage, monsters and maidens 187

Introduction 187

Marriage, fairy tales and feminism 188

'Princess Smartypants' 194

'Outside Over There' 204

Conclusion 215

4.3   Outsiders: sissies, freaks and foreigners 218

Introduction 218

Ugliness as disability: 'The Big Ugly Monster and the Little
         Stone Rabbit' 223

"Funny foreigner types" – racialized otherness 233

Sissy stuff – gender norms and deviances 243

Conclusion 252

4.4   On raising monsters. Erhm: children. 255

Introduction 255

The evil child: 'Bad Habits!' 260

The competent child: 'Where the Wild Things Are' 277

The child as king: 'The Boy Who Ate Around' 294

Conclusion 316

5   Conclusion 321

Works Cited 329

Acknowledgements

My sincere gratitude goes to my PhD supervisor Prof. Dr. phil. Eva Boesenberg, who welcomed me as a new PhD student in addition to the very large number of students she was already (and still is) supervising. Eva regularly inspired me to change perspectives, to readjust my thematic focus, and to maintain academic rigour while nuancing my arguments. She introduced me to Babette Cole's *Princess Smartypants*, a picturebook without which my project would have been very different, if not incomplete.

I wish to thank my colloquium, whose members (PhD students and staff alike) accompanied and commented on my project for nearly five years. Their feedback proved to be one of my greatest motivations to continue working on, altering and often rewriting parts of my thesis. I particularly cherished the opportunity to contribute talks on my ongoing work at the Annual Students' and Graduates' Conference in front of an international audience in 2011 and 2012 respectively. In addition, I want to thank Prof. Dr. phil. Martin Klepper for accepting to be my second reviewer.

I am very grateful to the *Studienstiftung des Deutschen Volkes*, which provided me with a generous doctoral stipend from January 2011 to December 2014. Without this scholarship, the present study would never have been completed. The many workshops and conferences offered by the *Studienstiftung* to their scholars proved at least equally valuable as the financial support I was granted.

Many thanks go to my friends and family, who never tired of sharing their enthusiasm and fascination with my research project. I especially want to thank (in no particular order): Naomi Tiley for giving me *POG – Or, the Monster Who Was Afraid of Children* and for reading, commenting and proofing the chapter "Marriage, monsters, and maidens;" Maria Mocanu, for her spirited encouragement and her hilarious side-comments, for our lively electronic exchange and for reading, commenting and proofing part one and the chapter "The monster under the bed;" Jamie Pallas, for sharing a childhood treasure with me, *Not Now, Bernard*, which considera-

11

bly fuelled my thinking on picturebook monsters; Fredi Wenzel, for reading, proofing and commenting on the chapter "On raising monsters," and for listening patiently and compassionately about my worries and woes whenever there was the need for it; Kathrin Wittler, for providing such thoughtful and constructive feedback on the chapter "Monsters, children and children's literature;" Sabine Hiller, for pushing my theoretical reflections into the practical and professional realm of early childhood education; and Linus and Clara Schneeberg, for challenging my assumptions about what they found funny or scary.

Finally and above all, I want to thank Mo Becker, my partner in everything that matters, for unconditionally supporting and encouraging me, and for helping me with his acute, critical mind and technical skills especially in the very final stages of this project.

1   Introduction

1.1   Research questions and hypotheses

Monsters are ubiquitous in children's cultural artefacts. Monsters romp through movies, they populate video games, they adorn children's clothing items, and they represent the mischievous and wild side of a global market for children's consumer products that is contrasted by hyper-feminized and sanitized dolls, such as Barbie and Disney Princess. Children's literature appears to be just another site where the figure of the monster-child, or the child-monster, thrives. In picturebooks,[1] typically marketed to children aged four to eight, the strong presence of monstrous characters may reflect a synonymous use of the words '(young) child' and 'monster' in everyday speech. The suggested affiliation or even interchangeability of monster and child in picturebooks is particularly perplexing when compared to the regular relationship between monster and human character in artefacts of 'grown-up' culture, which is one of opposition and characterized by a sense of danger that threatens the very essence of humanity. Some of the most influential theorists of the twentieth and twenty-first centuries (and many more lesser known scholars) have argued that understanding a culture's monsters is of paramount importance to understanding what it means to be human in that culture. But while the field of monster studies in the humanities is thriving, at the point of writing this nobody has given the omnipresence of monsters in children's culture and, more importantly, the markedly different relationship between monster and child, any sustained thought. Apart from isolated articles that conceptualize monsters in predominantly psychological terms – and even those mostly in passing – there is virtually no scholarly literature on the topic.

If monsters in fictional narratives for grown-ups must be read as an antithesis of what it means to be human, what is at stake for children, whose fictional representations, as a rule, *bond with* and *befriend* monsters? Their humanity? To complicate the matter, the

---

[1] Rather than writing it as two separate words or hyphenated – both versions are more frequent than my own use – I agree with David Lewis and others that writing it as one word underlines the interdependence of words and images upon one another – as well as the necessity to analyze the picturebook as a whole (Lewis 2001: xiv).

child protagonists' gender in picturebooks with monsters is, in an overwhelming number, male. Thus the implication of a natural affinity to monsters is not based on children as an entire and undifferentiated group, but on male children alone. This observation suggests that monsters in picturebooks function primarily as a narrative support for the construction of 'the male child. Those girl characters that do play a principal role never quite fit the grid. Their relationship with monsters or their identification *as* a monster is never as assertive, affirmative and harmonious as boys', but instead reminiscent of the ways monsters are used in grown-up culture. Thus, the preliminary hypothesis that monsters in picturebooks are used for the positive construction of boys does not hold true for girls. Despite increased awareness of gender stereotypes and discrimination based on notions of gender difference in children's literature studies, reporting more diversity and equality in publications of the past decade, the gender stereotypes present in picturebooks with monsters seem to support a far from overcome sexism where boys colonize the same semantic field as monsters – but in contrast to monsters in adults' culture, picturebook monsters are studded with flattering and becoming attributes such as playful, creative, resourceful and humorous – and where girls, in their process of maturation, dissociate themselves from any friendly relations they may have entertained with a monster. Picturebooks are often described as many children's first contact with a printed medium that is supposed to teach them about the world and about themselves. But what is it exactly that picturebook makers, editors, sellers and buyers think children should learn about being boys and girls? Monsters in picturebooks present a perfect gateway for offering answers to this question, both with their explanatory power about what is human in fictional narratives for grown-ups and their highly gendered usage in picturebooks.

In the course of writing this dissertation, I have gathered a text corpus of sixty-five picturebooks with monsters, all published in English-speaking countries in the last fifty years, with the aim to detect thematic patterns that help clarify my research question. As a result, I have established four larger thematic fields that are based on the high number of publications that follow one respective field or theme and that are based on the relevance for this project: (1) fear of monsters, (2) strong/independent female characters in relation with monsters, (3) monsters as outsiders, and (4) monsters within parenting strategies. Due to the absence of research on monsters in children's literature and culture the theoretical body of my project is extremely interdisciplinary and oriented to answering three questions: What are the respective concepts of 'child' and 'monster' in children's literature and everyday life in the past and the present? What gender- and queer-theoretically oriented viewpoints within children's literature studies already exist? And what formal or theoretical language can I use for the analysis of the picturebooks? The large number of different disciplines that have contributed to offering answers to the first question made my own attempt interdisciplinary and complex, since theoretical approaches include children's literature theory, childhood studies (mostly anchored in social history), gender studies, feminist and masculinity studies, psychology, pedagogy and critical discourse analysis (following Michel Foucault). Finding tools to answer the second and third questions was easier, since there already exist an established research community devoted to gender issues in children's literature and a small but respectable number of publications in the field of picturebook studies. In addition, I made use of Gunther Kress and Theo van Leeuwen's semiotic work *Reading Images – The Grammar of Visual Design* (Kress and van Leeuwen 2010.) With these theoretical and analytical foundations, I analyzed two to three titles in detail for each of the four thematic groups mentioned above. The remaining titles of each theme group served as points of comparison and reference, usually to indicate that certain observations are likely to be patterns rather than exceptions.

One possibility of conceptualizing monsters in children's culture is to deny them their status as monsters, as Rolf Parr does in a short section of an essay that was published in *Monströse Ordnungen* (2009). Because these monsters are always friendly and harmless, he claims, they are only "misrecognitions of non-monstrous figures as monsters" (Parr 2009: 26 [my translation]). The limited selection of his examples (one picturebook and three animated films) may be responsible for Parr's own misrecognition of all those monsters in picturebooks that maintain their subjectivity as monsters and that do not turn out to be common household objects, as in his one picturebook example. Denying these figures their monstrosity on the grounds of their friendliness leads to an unnecessary paradox: if these fictional creatures that are clearly labelled as "monsters" in the narratives themselves are not actually "real" monsters, then what are they? Parr's refusal to read these figures as monsters seems to me only meaningful insofar as the detection of one of their most striking characteristics is concerned, namely their general friendliness that is incompatible with monstrous character- istics in narratives for grown-ups. Why not simply granting mon- sters in children's culture a different semantic composition from those in adults' culture?

Indeed, approaching the phenomenon of friendly monsters for children from a perspective that acknowledges their difference and that simultaneously keeps in mind the interpretability of monsters as anti-markers for (adult) human subjectivity leads to more pro- ductive questions than simply putting monsters in picturebooks aside as irrelevant for the discussion: if, in monster narratives for adults, the human protagonist needs to distance him- or herself from the monster in order to protect their humanity (or, more spe- cifically, those features that mark them as participants of the domi- nant group), and if in contrast, in picturebooks, boy protagonists regularly and to their advantage associate themselves with mon- sters, does this mean that their humanity is at stake? Do picture- book makers contribute to the perpetuation of the image of the (male) child as savage and wild? How do these monsters' friendli- ness, loyalty and humor fit into this reading? Why is it that the overwhelming majority of principal characters in English language publications – be they monsters or children – is male? And not only that: why are the very few female principal characters por- trayed in such strikingly different relationships with monsters or with their own monstrous identity?

Monsters in children's culture are anything but marginal. And yet there seems to be absolutely no research out there that does more than acknowledge (or, in the case of Parr, contest) this fact, let alone answer any of the above questions. Considering that mon- sters in adults' culture are used by scholars in order to tease out the meanings and definitions of the culturally dominant group(s) of humans, the lack of comparable undertakings in the field of chil- dren's culture is significant. It seems only reasonable to me that monsters in picturebooks can reveal, to attentive readers, funda- mental aspects of dominant Western images of male and female children; in other words, that they can be used for interpretation and analysis in much the same way as in fictional narratives for adults. I hope that this research project may be a beginning. A beginning in acknowledging the relevance of monsters for reading children's culture and a beginning of awareness of the blaring discrepancies in the representation of male and female characters in monster picturebooks. Having framed my research question and my initial hypotheses, I am now going to provide a cursory overview of the theoretical background for this study, lay out my approach and offer a roadmap for the reader.

1.2   Research context

In the first paragraph, I claimed that there is, up to this date, no academic writing about monsters in picturebooks. This statement needs to be qualified: there is no research about the pervasiveness of monsters in this medium as part of a phenomenon that permeates all of children's culture and about the associated questions of gendered subject constructions of child protagonists. There are, however, a handful of journal articles and numerous longer passages in monographs that address monsters in picturebooks implicitly. This is mostly due to the fact that many children's literature scholars and most, if not all, picturebook scholars write, at one point in their career, more or less extensively about Maurice Sendak's *Where the Wild Things Are* (1963). While the wild things as central characters of this picturebook are usually discussed to some degree, they are not necessarily interpreted with respect to their function as monsters nor are they connected with monsters in other picturebooks. Thus, many pieces of research are devoted to the formal or structural analysis of the interaction between words and images, such as works by Schwarcz (1982), Roxburgh (1983), Arakelian (1985), Moebius (1986), Nodelman (1988), Perrot (1991), Sipe (1998), and Nikolajeva and Scott (2001), testifying to the artistic accomplishment and innovation of this picturebook classic. Other approaches to *Where the Wild Things Are* include psychoanalysis and art history (Poole 1996), post-colonialism

(Shaddock 1997), pedagogy/psychology (Galbraith 1998) and discourse analysis (Stephens 1992, Keeling and Pollard 1999, Nodelman 2008). For my interest in how monsters are used for the construction of male and female protagonists in picturebooks, the discourse analytical approaches (that reverberate to some degree also in Shaddock's and Galbraith's articles) are the most inspiring as they emphasize the roles of ideologies, knowledge and power, and ultimately work to expose the hidden agency of adults in the literary and visual construction of child characters with the example of *Where the Wild Things Are* and, in the case of Keeling and Pollard, of one other monster picturebook (Henrik Drescher's *The Boy Who Ate Around*). Apart from the limitation of these academic discussions about monsters to essentially one picturebook, they often only mention the monsters in passing, without conceptualizing them as influential ideological interventions that shape picturebook readers' perceptions of girls and boys.

Although children's literature scholars have up to this point never theorized the impact of monsters on the construction of male and female child protagonists, one of their central concerns is of course how children's literature constitutes 'the child.' After all, the main protagonists in children's literature, as a rule, are children. Another important layer is added by the most pervasive definition of children's literature by its essential characterization by an age imbalance with inherent tensions between its targeted child readers on the one side and its adult creators, editors, distributors and purchasers on the other side (Nikolajeva 2010: 8; Stephens 1992: 3; Nodelman 2008: 85). This makes children's literature studies a plausible point of departure for my investigations. One of my first encounters with children's literature theory was John Stephens' *Language and Ideology in Children's Fiction* (1992), one of the first academic works drawing attention to the underestimated impact of children's literature on the formation and consolidation of socio-cultural values and beliefs in large parts of society. Stephens writes that "[…] all developmental paths [by that he means the most pervasive pattern in children's fiction of a child protagonist's maturation process] are ideologically constructed, involving conformity to societal norms, and it is important for anyone concerned with children's fiction to develop an awareness of the processes and ends of this construction." (Stephens 1992:

3f.) In many ways, Stephens' request – if I may call it that – became fundamental for my dissertation project since I set out to unravel the gender-ideological implications of the colorful and ever-so-harmless-looking picturebook monsters. For the question of how concepts of 'the child' are reflected in children's literature, historical accounts exerted a great influence on my own thinking. A number of articles in Peter Hunt's edited volume *Children's Literature – An Illustrated History* (1995) and Fiona McCulloch's comprehensive *Children's Literature in Context* (2011) deepened my insights into the interrelatedness of socio-historical conditions with the reflexive nature of children's literature itself. These authors trace a major shift in the construction of 'the child' in children's fiction at the turn of the nineteenth century from "the child as biologically, intellectually, or socially primitive," mirroring ongoing ethnological rhetoric about 'the savage' at this time, to the child as always already integrated into society as a human being, albeit still "awaiting the education that would transform them into civilized adults" (Briggs 1995: 168). The idea of transformation from 'savage' to 'civilized human' is particularly revealing because of its omnipresent recurrence in my corpus. Furthermore, I credit Kimberly Reynolds' *Children's Literature in the 1890s and the 1990s* (1994) for providing the historical evidence for another important shift that took place at the end of the nineteenth century: for the first time in history, the production of children's literature became a highly gendered affair.

> In the early and middle years of the nineteenth century most children's literature was intended to be read by both boys and girls (think of the *Fairchild Family*). By the end of the century, however, there began to be increased anxiety about what was happening to the familiar patterns of manly and womanly behavior. On the one hand, women were agitating for social and legal reforms which would give them more independence; on the other, men were struggling in their attempts to govern the country and rule the empire effectively. Children's literature was one of the most obvious and influential ways of reaching the next generation and trying to correct what seemed to be failings in the way understanding about appropriate behavior for both sexes was being transmitted. The result was that images of masculinity and femininity in children's books began to be more ex-

aggerated, and books began to be written and marketed with gender very much in mind. (Reynolds 1994: 30)

Rather than having dissolved into meaninglessness, this gender segregation in children's literature and culture has been flourishing more than ever in the last decades of the twentieth and in the beginning twenty-first centuries – a situation that the picturebooks with monsters unfortunately help to confirm. Other scholars such as Perry Nodelman (2008) and Andrew O'Malley have considerably raised my awareness about the power of children's literature to "disseminate and consolidate [dominantly white] middle-class ideology" (O'Malley 2003: 11). Their research opened my eyes to the overwhelming and almost exclusively white and middle-class settings of the picturebook stories. Only one out of sixty-five titles represents human main characters with a visibly non-Caucasian heritage. The boy and his grandfather in *Anh's Anger* (Gail Silver and Christiane Krömer 2009) are both illustrated with an Asian physique. While I believe that cultural, racial and sexual diversity in picturebooks cannot be encouraged enough, the fact that these two Asian(-American) protagonists are used – by a white writer and a white illustrator – to praise the benefits of Buddhist meditation opens up complex issues of racial and cultural stereotyping, however positive these may be. But what happens in picturebooks with only monster characters? Of course, one of the advantages of using monsters as main characters in this context is their ethnical indeterminacy. Nevertheless I would argue that, through the mediation of middle-class values, even in those books without any human characters 'whiteness' is always implied.

Because children's literature reflects norms and values of the time and place in which it is situated I also turned my attention to sociological and anthropological accounts of childhood. Chris Jenks' *Childhood* (1996) provides an excellent overview of contemporary sociological approaches to childhood that the author links with their historical origins. In Jenks' publication, I found a striking number of paraphrases or definitions of 'child' and 'childhood' that, taken out of their context, perfectly match some definitions of 'monster' that I have encountered. For example, Jenks writes that

[...] the child is familiar to us and yet strange, he or she inhabits our world and yet seems to answer to another, he or she is essentially of ourselves and yet appears to display a systematically different order of being. [...] the very possibilities of difference and divergence contained within childhood, understood either as a course of action or as a community, present a potentially disintegrative threat to sociological worlds. [...] Childhood constitutes a way of conduct that cannot properly be evaluated and routinely incorporated within the grammar of existing social systems. (Jenks 1996: 3, 12)

It is precisely these intersections of 'child' and 'monster' that I was searching for in the theoretical literature. Although the extracts just quoted are exceptionally explicit in this respect, I found a few other passages with implicit parallels to certain aspects of monster theories. Thus Adrian James and Allison James' article "Changing Childhood in the UK: Reconstructing Discourses of 'Risk' and 'Protection'" (2008) pick up on Jenks' suggestion about the perceived socially disruptive potential of children; a quality that is also attributed to monsters. Heather Montgomery (2009) recalls the anthropological-historical parallels between children and savages, who were also frequently conceptualized as monsters, and that I have already mentioned above. For the largest part, however, childhood studies – be they historical, sociological or anthropological in orientation – are clear of allusions to monsters.

Although one of the tenets of children's literature theory is that this body of texts reflects changing images of 'the child,' which arise from the multidimensional relations between actual children and actual adults, the explicit inclusion of pedagogical theories into the discussion is marginal. In fact, none of the works just cited critically engages with the academic field of pedagogy beyond the observation that children's literature and pedagogy are closely connected. There is, of course, a large branch dedicated to empirical research and the development of concepts and criteria concerning children's literacy, literary tastes and abilities, and related topics (e.g. Arzipe and Styles 2003; Chang-Kredl 2013: 174-190; Doonan 1997: 53-72; Graham 2000: 61-67). Furthermore, one of the most renowned journal publications in the field, *Children's Literature in Education*, also attests to a general acknowledgment of the importance of educational ideas for the development and analysis of children's literature. Nevertheless, I have found that there is little, if any, engagement with pedagogical theories – in contrast to most other humanities and social science disciplines. For example, the modern founders of pedagogy and their enormous influence on the practice of education today, like John Dewey, Maria Montessori, Erik Erikson or Jean Piaget, never appear to figure in children's literature criticisms. Perhaps one reason why I noticed this lack of pedagogy in current theorizations in other disciplines so late was that these pedagogues' ideas of 'the child' are as far removed from 'monster' as one can imagine. But this is only so at first glance. Working with the picturebooks that I have grouped into the theme of parenting strategies made the link to these pioneers in education more visible to me, albeit by taking a detour via popular parenting blogs and recent popular science publications in Germany, such as by theologian and educator Bernhard Bueb (2006) or by psychiatrist and psychotherapist Michael Winterhoff (2008), both emphasizing the importance of discipline and obedience and a corresponding image of the child as tyrant – a term with easily traceable links to 'monster.' It could be argued that some of the picturebook monsters in my corpus symbolize this backlash in popular education against reformist views of education that conceptualize the child as complete and competent (Juul 2011) or as the human being par excellence (Montessori 1938).

As one might expect, 'monster studies' are neither as established nor as voluminous as childhood studies, which are themselves still a relatively new academic discipline. The more recent cultural theoretical publications on the topic, such as Jeffrey Cohen's *Monster Theory* (1996) or Joachim Geisenhanslüke and Georg Mein's *Monströse Ordnungen – Zur Typologie und Ästhetik des Anormalen* (2009), all refer to Michel Foucault's series of lectures in 1975 that were transcribed and later published under the title *Abnormal* (1999) as the foundation of present monster theories. But literary and film studies, too, at least implicitly recur to Foucauldian ideas: Jack[2] Halberstam (1995), Paul Goetsch (2002),

---

[2] In my bibliography I have listed Halberstam's books under Judith, which corresponds with the name given in the respective publications. In my text, however, I use Halberstam's chosen name Jack (Halberstam 2012: np).

or Joseph Andriano (1999). Cultural anthropological studies, on the other hand, compose their research primarily of historical texts and Freudian psychoanalysis and less of theory, such as Leslie Fiedler's *Freaks – Myths and Images of the Secret Self* (1978) and Stephen T. Asma's *On Monsters – An Unnatural History of Our Worst Fears* (2009). Regardless of their academic orientation, all these authors exclusively examine texts (in the widest sense of the term) that are located in the cultural space of adults.

In summary, my aim in studying this literature was to establish links between concepts of 'child' and concepts of 'monster' from Antiquity to the present. I am aware that this is a massive time span, and I want to stress here that the brief sketch I offer in chapter 2.1 should be read as a rough historical guide that highlights some of the more important literary landmarks for the development of children's fiction with monsters, with the aim of tracing changing ideas about monsters and children in literature with a special focus on those areas in which both concepts have overlaps. My intention in outlining the theory I have used for chapter 2.1 was to carve out the academic fields that have tackled the question of what 'the child' is, or what 'the monster' is, respectively. In the chapter itself, I try to merge the two thematic complexes into one. Because the literature on these topics involves so many different disciplines that influence and fertilize each other, the introductory overview I have provided here hopefully contributes to the clarity of my approach.

My historical outline of overlaps of the concepts 'child' and 'monster' leaves gender mostly out of the discussion. The first reason for this is that children have only started being considered as gendered subjects in academia with the onset of second wave feminism. Nancy Chodorow's *The Reproduction of Mothering: Psychoanalysis and the Sociology of Gender* (1978) is often cited as emblematic for this rising awareness. Feminist readings of women's position in society in the 1970s and 80s lead to a dead end when children and picturebook monsters are concerned. They simply cannot be compared. For example, Julia Kristeva's *Pouvoirs de l'horreur* (1980) became influential for the feminist criticism of psychoanalysis because it develops the idea of connecting the mother with the abject. The abject, in turn, is associated with disrupting the social order, being situated between object and subject – a definition that touches many points in definitions of monsters in adult culture, but that has nothing in common with monsters in children's culture. In other words, the intersections of monster discourses and female gender within feminist theories cannot be transferred to conceptualizations of children. The second reason for disregarding the thematic complex of gender in the short historical outline is its centrality for my overall thesis: it requires a chapter on its own.

Why is it that hardly any female characters in picturebooks entertain an assertive and harmonious relationship with monster characters? What images of boys and of girls are being constructed through the portrayal of friendly and empowering relationships between almost exclusively male characters and monsters? These principal questions fuelled my research. Being a newcomer to children's literature studies, I set out to identify the major viewpoints of gender- and queer-theoretically oriented research in this field. Not surprisingly, a lot of research done in this context draws its inspiration from psychoanalysis (Rose 1984) and, almost as a logical consequence, is increasingly influenced by gender studies and queer theories (Flanagan 2008; Pugh 2011). Another orientation within this research body is loosely based on Foucauldian discourse analysis and might be called social constructionist (Reynolds 1990; Stephens 2002; Toomey 2009). There is a third orientation within this thematic complex that represents itself as strikingly unaware of any gender theoretical developments of the past thirty to forty years, maintaining that girls and boys are, as a matter of fact, essentially different and, therefore, need different literature to further develop their "natural gender identity" (Allen 1999; Huck 2002). I came across a number of articles and chapter sections where Freudian (and sometimes Lacanian) psychoanalysis is used, sometimes without even making it explicit, for uncritically attributing certain characteristics of picturebook protagonists to girls or to boys respectively (e.g. Reed 1986; Nikolajeva 2010: 171). Although psychoanalysis seems to be used increasingly with a deconstructionist objective it often simply functions as a conventional justification for making gender essentialist claims. For this reason, I also offer a critique of the use of psychoanalytical concepts for the interpretation of literature, including picturebooks, that is based both on methodological and on ideological objections in chapter 2.2. I conclude this theoretical overview with the question if picturebooks with monsters might, in fact and perhaps unwittingly, epitomize this third, essentialist, viewpoint.

Finally, the third theoretical complex that contextualizes my project, chapter 3, deals with those aspects of picturebook theory that explain the formal selection criteria for my corpus. Here, I concentrate on Perry Nodelman's *Words about Pictures: The Narrative Art of Children's Picture Books* (1988), Maria Nikolajeva and Carol Scott's *How Picturebooks Work* (2001) and David Lewis' *Picturing Text: Reading Contemporary Picturebooks* (2001). Because of the relative straightforwardness of this section I abstain from unnecessarily lengthy explanations in this introduction.

1.3   Response

In this final introductory section, I am going to visualize in some more detail the individual parts of this project, which constitute my response to the current research situation – or, rather, its lack – of 'the monster' in children's culture and, more specifically, children's picturebooks. On the previous pages, I have outlined my theoretical approaches, drawing from a wide range of authors and disciplines. To recapitulate, the guiding questions for chapters 2.1 and 2.2 will be: Can the contemporary use of 'child' and 'monster' as cognates (in private and media language, and in the production of consumer goods for children, including picturebooks) be traced back in Western literary history? And: How is gender theorized within children's literature studies? While the second question requests little more than a straightforward review of existing research on this topic, the first question calls forth a highly selective and multi-disciplinary outline. This outline suggests several points in history where the term 'child' and some aspects of 'monster,' such as wild, savage, or violent, were conceptualized closely together. The late nineteenth century appears decisive for current conceptualizations of these terms in several aspects. Firstly, at that time the anthropological rhetoric that paralleled 'the child' with

'the savage' was established and, despite its subsequent dismantling by more progressive anthropologists, retained a certain momentum. Secondly, for the first time in its history, children's literature became gender segregated by producing genres that were ex-
pressly designed to address either boys or girls, according to the
ideological values that were deemed essential for girls and boys
respectively (physical aggression, high rationality, independence
and emotional control for the boys and future rulers of the empire –
child bearing and family care, love and domesticity for the girls
and future mothers of the next generation of rulers). This division
may be at least partly responsible for the exclusion of girl characters from fictional narratives with monsters.

Publications of picturebooks with monsters of the last fifty
years, at least, seem to support this idea: Because monsters are
traditionally associated with characteristics prominent in boys'
fiction it seems more 'natural' to populate picturebooks with male
heroes and male monsters. Yet, while the cast in contemporary
monster picturebooks corresponds to the dictum of late nineteenth
century children's literature, there is an undeniable shift in the
prevalence of values that are deemed important for today's (male)
children. Courage and independence are still high up in the list, but
so are humor, politeness, creativity, affection and care – while
physical prowess, rationality and emotional restraint have mostly
disappeared. Can picturebooks with monsters then be seen as an
early school that promotes the making of the new boy? What about
the girls? To what extent do these picturebooks contribute to the
construction of gender as a binary system that considers 'male' and
'female' as identity categories? And in how far can the picturebooks of my corpus be used to integrate a view of gender as performative, based in a series of actions, rather than in any perceived
'essence'? In the subchapter 2.1.7, which follows the literary-
historical outline, I offer a preliminary definition of the contemporary picturebook monster that addresses precisely these questions.

Before moving on to the interpretations of individual picturebooks in part 4, I use part 3 to   consider some methodological
questions that proved important for this project: What are my selection criteria? What titles does my corpus contain and what are
the categories used for structuring this corpus? And, finally: Which
analytical tools were used prominently and why? In many respects,

this methodological/analytical part already offers some ideas for my central research task, namely to find a way of making sense of my voluminous corpus of sixty-five titles. Are there any patterns? Are there recurrent motifs or themes in which the monsters are central? How exactly are the characters distributed in terms of gender and age? How many single heroes are there as opposed to siblings? Does it make a difference? Are the monsters always essentially good and harmless, as Rolf Parr claims? Considering that the few female characters that exist seem to be largely represented according to old-fashioned sexual stereotypes (dependent, domestic, passive, meek), are there any female main child characters that represent similar values to their male counterparts? Do the monsters in these books have different functions? Finally, and again, are there overarching clusters that might illustrate some first answers to these questions?

Reading and rereading these picturebooks, zooming into details and zooming out to get hold of the larger frame, establishing categories, dismissing some, retaining others, I eventually centered my analysis on the following four themes, discussed in the respective chapters:

Chapter 4.1: The monster under the bed. This chapter is about the fear of the monster and contains twenty-three titles. This is the largest group in my corpus. But in spite of the many titles there is very little plot variance: a single male child faces his fear of monsters, or one particular monster, and learns that with the help of humor, politeness, care, loyalty, creativity, innovation and wit – the emphasis may change from book to book – he can overcome his fear and, often, gain a good friend in the monster. This made it easy to choose one book that is representative for this pattern for close analysis: *Hungry! Hungry! Hungry!* (Doyle and Hess 2004). Some books play with this pattern by a role reversal of monster and boy, making the monster the character that is afraid of humans, but the message stays unaltered. The overt pedagogical question is: how do we teach our children to deal with unknown and sometimes scary situations or with a real child's actual fear of monsters? My expectation – as a parent but also simply as a thinking adult – is satisfied by these story patterns: The child characters learn that it pays off to engage with their fear, that successful strategies that involve curiosity, courage, wit, and so on, are character- and confidence-building. But what about female characters? Among these twenty titles, there is only one in which a single girl protagonist is confronted with a threatening monster: David McKee's *The Monster and the Teddy Bear* (1989). Unlike any of the male children, this girl needs her Teddy, who transforms into a giant superhero, to deal with this monster. She is represented as meek, passive and ultimately helpless. The monster here is also the only monster in this group that is unambiguously evil. In my analysis of these two exemplary texts I argue that the blatant sexism in McKee's book may be extreme but is indicative of a general tendency in picturebooks with monsters: female characters are not only underrepresented but their representations also often correspond with regressive sex stereotypes, while male characters, as in *Hungry! Hungry! Hungry!*, seem to contribute to an image of a new kind of masculinity.

Chapter 4.2: Marriage, monsters, and maidens. This chapter is about strong female characters and their relationships with monsters and contains six titles. But are there any female characters at all that could be read as role models on the basis of their self-confidence and bravery? Yes, there are two: Princess Smartypants, who is the heroine in three picturebooks by Babette Cole (*Princess Smartypants* 1986; *Long Live Princess Smartypants* 2004; *Princess Smartypants Breaks the Rules* 2009) and Ida in Maurice Sendak's *Outside Over There* (1981). In this chapter, I focus on *Princess Smartypants* and *Outside Over There*. The protagonists' relationships to the monsters and the role of the monsters as protagonists themselves are atypical in both books. In *Princess Smartypants*, the monsters are mere household pets whose important role in getting rid of the annoying prince is nowhere acknowledged. And in *Outside Over There*, the goblins are insidious and genuinely terrifying kidnappers. An underlying theme in both books is marriage – and this surprised me since both heroines seem so independent and freedom-loving. The fact that romance is entirely absent in stories with male human main characters further contributes to my impression that however independent a girl may want to be she still needs to position herself toward others' expectations of her to "stop messing about with those animals and find [herself] a husband", as Princess Smartypants' mother puts it. Two other titles slightly alleviate this impression. John Fardell's *The Day Louis*

Got Eaten (1988) and Pat Hutchins' *The Very Worst Monster* (1985) both feature active and successful girl characters, but they both have to share their success with their younger brothers. It is perhaps significant that all six publications (with the exception of the two follow-ups of *Princess Smartypants*) date from the 1980s, a period when picturebook makers' awareness of gender equality issues may have been particularly sharpened by the feminist movement at the time.

Chapter 4.3: Outsiders: sissies, freaks and foreigners. This chapter contains fourteen titles. The picturebooks in this group all negotiate the question of who represents the social center, which is synonymous with particular norms of appearance and behavioral performance, and who is delegated to the margins. Another way of putting this is to ask who sees and judges whom and by what standards is the inclusion of the 'other' enabled or prevented by the dominant group? Traditionally, monsters occupy the margins of such theoretical constructs. In monster fiction for grown-ups, where this motif is probably the most dominant, the most frequently used marker for alterity is race, which in turn is deeply imbued with cultural practices, and also, but often less explicitly, intersects with gender and class. In the picturebooks, race and ethnicity only constitute a small proportion within the overall theme of otherness. Gender deviance and failure to conform to aesthetical norms of appearance (to the extent that this failure leads to social disability) are two further motifs that I examine in this chapter. For each thematic complex, I analyze one picturebook in greater detail: Chris Wormell's *The Big Ugly Monster and the Little Stone Rabbit* (2004) – ugliness/disability; Colin McNaughton's *Have You Seen Who's Just Moved in Next Door to Us?* (1993) – racial discrimination; and Angela McAllister and Allison Edgson's *YUCK! That's Not a Monster!* (2010) – gender deviance. In order to form a picture of the representation of male and of female characters within these contexts, I make numerous extensive cross-references to other picturebooks in this group. Drawing comparisons and establishing contrasts between representations of masculinity, femininity and monstrosity make visible that being a monster excludes certain character traits and modes of behavior that correspond with essentialized femininity. The two only heroines in this group of books either have to compromise their sense of selfhood in order to be included by their monster peers (*Mostly Monsterly* 2010) or they are expelled from the socially dominant center because they lack the stamina, aggression and meanness that characterize members of the in-group (*Beegu* 2003). While the inclusion of female 'others' can only be described as failed or incomplete and the integration of racial 'others' is by and large represented as illusory regardless of gender, male characters whose gender performance or whose aesthetic appearance deviates from the norm are represented as successful in expressing their subjectivities. This observation must be linked particularly to the conclusion of chapter 4.1 where I suggest that books about the fear of monsters ultimately promote an image of a new masculinity, albeit one that is addressed primarily to members of the white middle class.

Chapter 4.4: On raising monsters. Errhm: children. This chapter is about the use of monsters as parenting strategies. The eighteen titles of this final chapter all make explicit the question of how best to raise our children. In many respects, this fourth group addresses one of the overarching themes of children's literature, including the picturebooks discussed in the first three groups. The picturebooks in this group can be clustered around three dominant parenting attitudes: authoritarian, authoritative and permissive. This classification is based on a publication by psychologist Diana Baumrind (1967) that scholars of parenting still refer to today. Particularly the books that I ordered into the authoritarian category pose the question – because of their use of irony and humor – of the credibility of the apparently underlying message: children are literally little monsters and can only be brought under control through severe disciplinary measures such as threats and corporeal punishment. Two of the three books in this category represent a pair of siblings (boy and girl in both cases) who are not individualized beyond their names. I argue accordingly that gender in the context of education is irrelevant in these two cases. But in the third case, *Bad Habits!* (Babette Cole 2004), the protagonist is a single female child. The fact that this is the only protagonist in my entire corpus who is regulated and corrected to such an extreme degree – even compared to the pairs of siblings in the other two books of this category – is indicative of a culturally reinforced incompatibility of girls and monsters. This becomes all the more graphic in contrast to the other two categories. The stories that represent an authoritative parenting style all share the focus on harmful emotions. I suggest that this concentration on emotional or mental states such as anger, envy and worry is based on the idea of a child-centered pedagogy that always assumes a motivation for a child's unsocial behavior. Being familiar with these progressive educational convictions, the educator's role – in most cases here: the parents – is to provide the child with the necessary confidence and freedom to find a solution to their emotional conflict. I illustrate this idea with Maurice Sendak's *Where the Wild Things Are* (1963). In this final chapter again, I find striking that the only girl character in this group is also the only character who does not find a solution to successfully deal with her harmful mental state (excessive worries) by herself but needs the help of an adult. The permissive parenting attitude is reflected most colorfully in Henrik Drescher's (1993) *The Boy Who Ate Around*: the parents only play the role of dummies while the child is king and completely takes over. For their implications with power and the state, I use Mikhail Bakhtin's concepts of the grotesque and of carnival.

For the close analysis of the picturebooks, particularly of the interaction of text and images, I find certain narratological and visual semiotic concepts and tools particularly helpful: focalization/perspective; the second person address/demand pictures; and finally the double voiced discourse that has its origins in feminist narratology and that I adapt to the dimension of age difference – rather than gender difference. In using these concepts, my attention is always directed towards the representation of the child characters in relation to the monster characters and, in a second step, towards the possibility of two different kinds of implied readers (child and adult) that are embedded in the text. This second orientation proves particularly problematic because it rests on assumptions and ultimately on the attribution of certain properties to child readers (for example: naïve, unskilled, fond of bodily humor) versus adult readers (knowledgeable, experienced, sophisticated). One common way to approach this problematic is to conduct surveys and field work with a significant number of real children and real adults, to establish categories according to which their answers would be assessed, and so on. In sum, this would amount to a pedagogical or psychological undertaking that would constitute an entirely different research project – one that by far surpasses the time and the resources I had available for this project. At the same time, however, I cannot simply ignore what is an established debate in children's literature theory and, particularly, picturebook theory: the existence of two different audiences, how they are coded, and how they should be assessed. I side with Perry Nodelman here: "While I can't describe how a 'real child' understands children's literature – or even how real children do – I can certainly use my knowledge of reading and textual practices to attempt a description of how the literature works to affect its implied readers – the child readers constructed by its texts." (Nodelman 2008: 87) I could have chosen to incorporate my own children's or their friends' reaction to some of the picturebooks into this project, but I did not because, first of all, such an approach demands a solid methodological groundwork that would explode my cultural studies perspective, and second and more importantly, I find the significance of individual children's responses to some picturebooks highly questionable in relation to my research questions. They have at best an anecdotal entertainment value. Of course, my own interpretations of these picturebooks are ultimately no more than an elaborate response by a white, middle-class and female individual. My angle on these texts is not only influenced by the social context in which I am situated but also by my experiences as a mother of two small children. But by interweaving my subjective and highly personal readings of these books with other individuals' readings of the same texts and with theoretical contexts, I position my interpretations within this network of scholarly debates around the question of gendered subject positions of child characters within children's literature.

2   Theoretical Approaches

2.1 Monsters, children and children's literature

Introduction

In today's children's consumer culture, there are few characters or motifs that hold their ground as successfully as the monster. Unlike the princess and the warrior-hero or villain,[3] the monster as a generic figure has not yet been turned into a global monopoly. And yet it is a recognizable and undeniably popular figure with recurring traits and features that offers an identification foil for children in the West. The story picturebook is one location where the monster prospers particularly well. In addition, picturebooks conceptualize like no other medium in children's culture the interdependence of children and adults. While it is true for all products of children's mass culture that they are created, produced, marketed and usually purchased by adults, there are hardly any other media that equally address child and adult consumers through a fictional story. In part three, I will look closely at the formal composition of picturebooks, present my corpus and discuss some analytical approaches. For the present chapter, the picturebook as a specific text type is only relevant insofar as it both creates and reproduces child-monster-adult relationships that are also constituent but less visible characteristics for monsters in other consumer products for children. More accurately, it is not 'the picturebook' that creates 'the monster,' but rather adults active in the picturebook business (writers, illustrators, editors, publishers, purchasers) who contribute to the creation of an enormous amount of individual books with

---

[3] Since the installment of the Disney Princess brand in 2000 'the princess' as a consumer product for children is more or less owned by the Walt Disney Company. The warrior-hero or warrior-villain is dominated by Star-Wars merchandise, owned by Lucasfilm, which Disney bought in 2006, and Marvel franchises such as Spiderman and Batman. Retail sales of the bestselling entertainment character merchandise in North America in 2011 made Disney Princess the number one (making 1.6 billion US Dollars, and 3 billion US Dollars globally), beating Star Wars (with 1.5 billion US Dollars number two), Peanuts and Marvel's superheroes. (Cf. Goudreau 2012; Orenstein 2006).

individual monsters that, despite their quantity, have common characteristics. In this sense, the monster picturebook is anchored in and stabilizes a discursive phenomenon that describes 'the (male) child' and 'the monster' in terms of correlated and occasionally identical categories.

But when did the conceptual convergence of monsters and children begin? What were the social circumstances that made this development possible? And how much do contemporary images of 'child' and 'monster' have in common with their historical precursors? My primary objective in this chapter is to look back in time in order to single out literary occurrences where the concepts of 'monster' and 'child' had any significant relation. I realize that this is a problematic enterprise, partly because both terms are extremely volatile and subject to changing paradigms of knowledge, and partly because it risks exploding the thematic focus of this project. On the other hand, the detailed analyses of the monster's functions in chapters 4.1 to 4.4 do require an overview, however brief, of the frameworks, image traditions, and themes that established and helped stabilize convergences between 'the monster' and 'the child'. Hence, the following pages are intended as an important background for my interpretations of individual contemporary picturebooks as well as a basic prerequisite which outlines and anticipates the specifics of my corpus selection. Amongst other aspects, the following overview will highlight that the concept of 'child' upon which I built my corpus is a recent one, suggesting that the representation of 'child' and 'monster' as friends and associates that is so common today would not have been possible or thinkable in the past. However, first and foremost, this overview is the result of my search for literary texts containing monstrous figures (mostly, but not exclusively) within the canon of European children's literature. If German and other non-English texts appear to dominate this account, this is due to their enormous impact on the development of English-language children's literature.

One reason why both 'the child' and 'the monster' continue to fill scholars with fascination is their resistance to definition. This resistance increases noticeably the longer the historical time span that is examined. Nevertheless, monstrous figures in literary texts which were intended for children, or which children were exposed to just as adults, yield valuable information about origins and conceptual changes of the contemporary picturebook monster. While there is an abundance of scholarly literature about monsters in fictional narratives for adults, including some veritable monster theories, no one, to my knowledge, has ever attempted a literary-historical survey of 'the monster' in relation to childhood or 'the child.' Despite the ubiquity of monsters in children's culture and a thriving scholarship on children and childhood across various academic disciplines for at least the past ten years, the strong bond between these two cultural signifiers has at the point of writing this thesis not yet been studied in any detail or depth. Considering the purported explanatory power of monsters for the elusive essence of humanity, I claim that monsters in children's culture have a comparable share in that power by serving as fictional vehicles that attempt to reveal something important about what it means to be a child in contemporary Western societies.

But of course, the picturebook monster does not exist as an unconnected signifier, floating directionless through contemporary cultural space. It has roots from which it has developed into its own monster sub-species. For this reason, a historical overview is indispensable for this project – notwithstanding the risk of incompleteness or inaccuracy. Before I start my journey with the bestiaries of Antiquity and the Middle Ages, I will begin my explorations with some theoretical considerations about monsters originating in adult culture. These considerations will provide a useful reference for historical monster concepts just as they will clarify in what respects monsters in children's picturebooks diverge. Historical concepts of 'the child' as well as the history of children's literature will necessarily be touched on, but my focus here is on 'the monster' as a literary figure in texts read or otherwise received by children. My historical sketch will end in a presentation of the picturebook monster's most striking and recurring characteristics.

Monsters from an adult culture perspective

In contrast to picturebook monsters, monsters in fictional narratives for adults are by definition fundamentally opposed to humans. If humans want to preserve their humanity they must keep the monster at bay. In order to stay human it is essential to establish clearly dividing characteristics and to erect a border that is ideally impenetrable. For these reasons, the monster in adult culture has frequently been theorized in terms of negativity. For Georges Canguilhem, whose *La connaissance de la vie* hugely influenced Michel Foucault's thoughts on normalization and governmentality, "the monster remains the living example of negative value" (Canguilhem 1992: 172). Rasmus Overthun paraphrases this premise as follows: "Monsters may consist of parts that we [humans] are familiar with, but they construct forms of negation [...] Monsters are negative beings" (Overthun 1999: 50). Jack Halberstam, writing about monsters in Gothic fiction, elaborates on Canguilhem's notion, asserting that monsters "produce the perfect figure for negative identity. Monsters have to be everything the human is not and, in producing the negative of human, these [Gothic] novels make way for the invention of human as white, male, middle class, and heterosexual" (Halberstam 1995: 22). With regard to the friendly bond between children and monsters in children's culture, should Halberstam's summary of threatened characteristics of being human be complemented with the attribute 'adult'? In other words, does the representation of monsters and children in children's culture question the status of children as human?

Since Plato and Aristotle, monstrosity has been conceptualized in four dominant discourses: aesthetics, natural history (later medicine), law, and morality (Parr 1999: 20). In monster theories (and social practice), these discourses often merge, the ugly, the deformed, and the disabled (whatever this means in any given culture or social milieu) being discussed or perceived as signifiers for moral depravity, criminal intentions, or some other kind of hegemony-threatening otherness. The Latin etymology of the word *monstrum* may rarely be present among most contemporary consumers of monster fictions of any kind, and yet it literally points to "that which reveals," and "that which warns." Departing from this original meaning, Jeffrey Cohen, in his introduction to *Monster Theory – Reading Culture*, claims that "[the] monstrous body is pure culture. A construct and a projection, the monster exists only to be read: [...] a glyph that seeks a hierophant" (Cohen 1996: 4).

The most prominent way to read monstrosity in theoretical debates from the 1970s until now centers on notions of otherness in terms of race, sexuality, gender and class (Cohen 1996; Hintz 1999; Halberstam 1995; Foucault 2003; Asma 2009). Michel Foucault, in his lecture series from 1974–75 which appeared in a printed edition in English under the title *Abnormal* in 1999, paved the way for conceptualizing monstrosity as an effect of governmentality, which, according to Foucault, spurned social movements labelled as 'healthism' that mask mechanisms of normalization and self-disciplining. While monsters, through negation, serve the purpose of defining human normality, they are also and paradoxically essentially elusive. As Cohen pinpoints:

> The monster is the harbinger of category crisis. This refusal to participate in the classificatory "order of things" is true of monsters generally: they are disturbing hybrids whose externally incoherent bodies resist attempts to include them in any systematic structuration. And so the monster is dangerous, a form suspended between forms that threatens to smash distinctions. (Cohen 1996: 4)

Overthun aptly assists, classifying the monster's relationship to order as ambivalent. While, on the one hand, monsters represent the breach and the incommensurable outside of every order, they are, on the other hand, its constitutive ingredient (Overthun 1999: 52). Joseph Andriano sees the monster as "a signifier of the fantastic [...] [taking] on meaning for us as a way of bridging the gap between humanity and animality" (Andriano 1999: xiv f.). Halberstam formulates the monster's hybridity in yet another way: "The monster itself is an economic form in that it condenses various racial and sexual threats to nation, capitalism, and the bourgeoisie in one body" (Halberstam 1995: 3). Omar Calabrese, at last, considers the monster as combining a plethora of symptoms of a postmodern zeitgeist, including indeterminability, fragmentation, the dissolution of the canon, carnivalization, constructedness, the nonpresentable, and hybridization (Calabrese 1992: 93f.).

40

At least one of Calabrese's key words strikes a chord when thinking about monsters in children's literature, and that is "carnivalization." Coined most notably by Mikael Bakhtin in his groundbreaking *Rabelais and His World*, carnival seems at first glance the least dangerous and the least threatening – and thus the most appropriate, certainly the most amusing and diverting – element of monstrosity to feature in children's fiction. In carnival, laughter replaces horror and monsters are comically subversive rather than seriously threatening. The king's power is ridiculed, but only over an authoritatively regulated time-span: that of carnival. The child in a picturebook, making the monster his ally, could be argued to parallel Bakhtin's fool by rebelling against adult order and, contained within the book covers, establishing his own carnival. Indeed, many children's literature scholars who comment on Maurice Sendak's wild things – up to this day the only literary monsters that attract regular critical attention – refer to Bakhtin's idea of carnival (e.g. Stephens 1992: 135; Keeling and Pollard 1999: 142).

It is their outward friendliness that leads Rolf Parr, one of the very few scholars outside the field of children's literature theory to comment upon this topic, to deny monsters in children's culture the status of *actual* monsters, since they do not actually represent a type of monstrosity, but rather temporary misrecognitions of non-monstrous figures as monsters (Parr 1999: 26). His examples include one children's book in which the monsters turn out to be common household objects, and three films, two of which are whitewashed versions of originally literary texts about genuine monstrosity (*The Hunchback of Notre-Dame* (1996) by Disney, loosely based on Victor Hugo's Gothic-Romantic epic from 1831; and *Shrek!* (2001) by DreamWorks, even more loosely based on William Steig's picturebook from 1991, a parody on chivalry romance aimed at adult knowledge and adult humor). The third film, *Monsters, Inc.* (2001) produced by Pixar, is the only one which features monsters that were actually and originally created for children. Unfortunately, Parr does not further examine his thesis, but simply insists that friendliness and monstrosity – or does he mean: children and *actual* monsters? – are mutually exclusive. The fact that Parr's claim is little more than a passing comment can be considered as representative for a general lack of interest in or awareness of the critical implications of monsters in children's cultural artifacts in the humanities at large.

If conceptualizations of monsters in adults' culture have one common denominator it might be this: monsters symbolize an inherent threat to human social law and order, where 'human' is synonymous with white, middle-class, male, and healthy. The attribute 'adult' is never explicitly mentioned, or even just implicitly alluded to. But excepting some few side comments which usually discredit children's monsters' relevance for cultural and literary criticism, the monsters under discussion in these theoretical texts are figurations of *adult* 'otherness,' where concepts of 'child' play no role. Furthermore, the scholars whose ideas on monstrosity I have fragmentarily introduced here generally concentrate on the 19th and/or 20th centuries. At the same time, (childhood) historians argue that the separation of spheres – private and public, feminine and masculine, but also child and adult – only started emerging in the 19th century (e.g. Steedman 1985: 75; Coontz 1992: 128f.). An interesting question arises from these observations: Apart from the past fifty to sixty years, where there ever any ideas about monsters that directly or indirectly affected the way people thought about children?

From antiquity to the Enlightenment era

Children's literature as it is known today is a recent phenomenon that only started taking shape two hundred to three hundred years ago. Before children had their 'own' literature, they were exposed to the same stories that adults read, but mostly told each other. Although I could not find any evidence – probably because there isn't any – that real children read or listened to Antique and Medieval accounts of monstrous beasts, I assume they did, for example when an aiodos or rhapsode (a professional performer of poetry and song) recited the adventures of Odysseus defeating the Cyclops, or of his encounter with the cannibalistic giants, the Laestrygonians (Rieu 2003: xi). Ancient Greek mythology is home to many more monstrous creatures, such as the Sphinx, the Minotaur, the Gorgons, or the Centaurs, and the stories in which they played a central part were performed in front of large audiences. Natural histories, the most well-known ones stemming from Pliny the Elder and Aristotle, referred to travelers' reports, for example from Ktesias and Alexander, further contributed to keeping collective imaginings of monsters alive and extremely relevant to Greece's and later Romes' political self-image as an imperial superpower that annexed, subdued and dominated the culturally and racially 'other.' Bestiaries were developed and made it easier for the imperialists to assert their own humanity as not only different but superior to the many monsters that populated the rims of the various empires in the history of Antiquity. The initially unfamiliar and hence unrecognizable creatures were classified and ordered into knowable monstrous threats that corresponded, in part, to specific monstrous races.

Medieval bestiaries adopted and enhanced many Ancient monsters (the Blemmyae – headless creatures with their faces in their chests; Cyclopes; Kynokephaloi – dogheaded people), and added some of their own, such as the woodwose – wild furred men living in the forest, related to the faun and the satyr. Isidore of Seville's list in *Etymologiae*, book XI, "and that of every other medieval monsterologist, is heavily influenced by Pliny the Elder's *Natural History*" (Asma 2009: 297). One problem that the Ancients did not have was, of course, how to reconcile the existence of monsters with the perfection of God's creations, "because, if God made matter, then he must have *wanted* these monsters to exist" (ibid: 75 ff.). A central question was whether monsters possessed a soul and were consequently capable of redemption. Augustine answered this question with astonishing tolerance: "Whoever is anywhere born a man, that is, a rational mortal animal, no matter what unusual appearance he presents in color, movement, sound, nor how peculiar he is in some power, part or quality of his nature, no Christian can doubt that he springs from that one protoplast [i.e. the first formed human; *my addition*]" (Augustine *City of God*, book XV, 8; qt. in Asma 2009: 81). Augustine determined rationality to be the only relevant factor that decided whether anyone was eligible for immortality via 'the soul.' Meanwhile, conceptions of the 'monstrous races' in medieval European societies were alive and well; they were very much based on "distorted and stereotyped perceptions of people – or

43

sometimes of simians – from other regions and other cultures (Asians, Africans, and later Americans)" (Burke 2004: 25) and hence they fulfilled a concrete function.

It is impossible to establish with any certainty to what extent children knew about these monstrous races. Disregarding for a moment the many critics of Philippe Ariès' famous claim that "in medieval society the idea of childhood did not exist" (Ariès 1979 [1962]: 128), I would argue that the overall absence of a concept of 'the child' is one of the reasons for the extreme paucity of historical evidence of what stories actual children were exposed to. Scholars at the time had very clear convictions and elaborate categories of imaginary creatures, but according to Ariès, they did not think of their children as a group needing special labelling, care, or treatment. Childhood sociologist Chris Jenks sums up Ariès' radical thesis as follows:Up to and including the Middle Ages it would seem that there was no collective perception of children as being essentially different to anyone else. People populated the world but their status was not established in terms of their age nor their physical maturity. (Jenks 1996: 63)

Although it has met with much thoughtful and well-researched criticism (e.g. Linda Pollock 1983, De Mause 1976), Ariès' *History of Childhood* remains influential, especially with regards to contemporary critics' awareness of the constructed nature of childhood. Whether or not children existed as a distinct and visible category in the Middle Ages, by the end of the European Renaissance and early Enlightenment era they certainly did. What I find even more exciting is that there is evidence for this thesis in the form of "the first children's picture book," as the subtitle of *Orbis Sensualium Pictus* ("The world of all perceivable things in pictures") is translated into English. The book was first published in 1657 as a bilingual (Latin and High Dutch) text and alphabet book by Czech educator John Amos Comenius, and soon became a popular text book all over Europe. *Orbis Pictus* opens with a dialog between a teacher and a male pupil, in which the former explains to the latter what to expect from this text book and what to learn in which order. Once the letters of the alphabet are mastered, the pupil is to study pretty much everything of importance and relevance in his world. The variety and breadth of things and topics covered is impressive: God, the world, the elements, anatomy,

CXX.
The Society betwixt Parents and Children.

Societas Parentalis.	
Married Persons,	*Conjuges,*
(by the blessing of God)	(ex benedictione Dei) sus-
have *Issue,*	cipiunt *Sobolem* (Prolem)
and become *Parents.*	& fiunt *Parentes.*
The *Father,* 1. begetteth	*Pater,* 1. generat
and the *Mother,* 2. beareth	& *Mater,* 2. parit
Sons, 3. and *Daughters,* 4.	*Filios,* 3. & *Filias,* 4.
(sometimes *Twins*).	(aliquando *Gemellos*).
The *Infant,* 5.	*Infans,* 5.
is wrapped in	involvitur
Swadling-cloathes, 6.	*Fasciis,* 6.
is laid in a *Cradle,* 7.	reponitur in *Cunas,* 7.
is suckled by the Mother	lactatur a matre
with her *Breasts,* 8.	*Uberibus,* 8.
and fed with *Pap,* 9.	& nutritur *Pappis,* 9.
Afterwards it learneth	Deinde discit
to go by a *Standing-stool,* 10.	incedere *Seperasto,* 10.

Fig. 1   *Orbis Pictus* (Comenius 1658)

skills, crafts and trades, animals and plants, customs and games, theological and military concepts, geography and astronomy. Further, there are three separate chapters that explain the peculiarities of the relations between different groups of people: "The Society betwixt Man and Wife," "The Society betwixt Parents and Children," and "The Society betwixt Masters and Servants." The parent-child relationship is described in the same matter-of-fact tone as all the other topics (fig. 1).

The text goes on to say that the infant is suckled with the mother's breasts, gives a short list of things infants do (learning to speak and walk, play with a rattle) before they are old enough to get accustomed to piety, labor and chastisement for misbehavior. It defines children's duty to their parents as reverence and service, but also the father's duty to gain the family's sustenance. Of course it is not just this chapter but the very fact that this is one of the first books intended for children that indicates that by now children were thought of in different terms. Worthy or needful of special textbooks, these children were nevertheless not shielded from what today would be understood as 'inappropriate' information. For example, a chapter on "The Tormenting of Malefactors" lists "Thieves," "Whoremasters," "Murtherers and Robbers," and "Witches." The description of how these "malefactors" are tortured according to their classification is explicit: hanged, beheaded, "either laid upon a *Wheel*, having their *Legs broken*, or fastened upon a *Stake*," or "burnt in a *great Fire* [...] some before they are executed have their *Tongues cut out*, or have their *Hand*, cut off upon a *Block*, or are burnt with *Pincers* [...] *Traytors* are pull'd in pieces with four *Horses*" – each means of torture or death is neatly rendered in the illustration above, clearly marked with corresponding numbers. Another topic that in children's books today is highly censored, although it has lost nothing of its relevance, is warfare, which Comenius subdivides into several chapters, including "The Camp," "The Army and the Fight," "The Sea-Fight," and "The Besieging of a City."

Were there still any monsters around in Comenius' time? Yes, there were! Intriguingly, Comenius slips in "the Dragon – a winged serpent, killeth with his breath" and "the Basilisk, with his eyes" into his chapter on "Serpents and crawling things." The section "crawling vermin" funnily includes "the book-worm," and I find it difficult to imagine how people even 350 years ago would not chuckle at this passage. In contrast, the dragon and the basilisk may well have been thought of as real, living beings. One chapter is titled "Deformed and Monstrous People" (fig. 2):

> *Monstrous* and *deformed* people are those which differ in the Body from the ordinary shape, as the huge *Gyant*, the little *Dwarf*, One with *two Bodies*, One with *two Heads*, and such like Monsters. Amongst these are reckoned, the *jolt-headed*, the great *nosed*, the *blubber-lipped*, the *blub-cheeked*, the *goggle-eyed*, the *wry-necked*, the *great-throated*, the *Crump-backed*, the *Crump-footed*, the *steeple-crowned*, add to these the *Bald-pated*. (Comenius 1658: 56)

XLIV.
Deformed and Monstrous People.

Deformes & Monstrosi.

Monstrous and *de-*
formed People are those
which differ in the Body
from the ordinary shape,

Monstrosi,
& *deformes* sunt
abeuntes corpore
à communi formâ,

Fig. 2   *Orbis Pictus* (Comenius 1658), detail

It is difficult if not impossible to imagine a similar picturebook for children today, depicting and naming physical impairments in humans, how people in our contemporary world fight in wars, die or are mutilated, or enlisting explicit and detailed information of how people suspected of terrorism are tortured or how exactly murderers in many parts of the world are executed – much less military or crisis-ridden concepts or practices are taboo in children's books, just think of death, burials and mourning. Just as death and burial feature in *Orbis Pictus* so do practically all other aspects of life, even theological – and of course heavily biased – reflections on different world religions and abstract concepts, such as patience, justice and humanity.

With respect to the inclusion of all areas of knowledge, *Orbis Pictus* is representative of all texts intended for children until the 1770s, consisting primarily of textbooks for private tuition, spiced with fables and moral exemplary tales (Ewers 2006: 131). This seems to be a strong indication in favor of Ariès' claims, at least as far as the imparting of knowledge is concerned. In this respect, learning about human 'monstrosities' was considered just as important as learning about any other observable phenomenon in the world. Children were to grow into useful, industrious and pious members of society as quickly as possible. Of course, the emphasis lies clearly on male children. Literate girls and women at this time were an exception, schools were for boys only, and since *Orbis Pictus* is a school textbook, the implication of "the first children's picture book" is obviously 'boys,' further reflected in the chapters "Races" (about popular running games played by boys) and "Boys Sport" (about other outdoor games played by boys). Girls, apparently, do not play, and women's role in society in this book is reduced to childbearing and nursing. What I find interesting with a look forward to how monsters in children's culture function today, is that the chapter on "Deformed and Monstrous People" abstains from any explicit judgments – safe for the word "Monster," which in itself carries moral philosophical connotations. Thus, as I have pointed out before, the Latin *monstrum* is cognate to *monere*, meaning "to warn." In this humanist picturebook, especially with respect to the many Christian themes that are dealt with, this warning may have been intended as an illustration of "God's wrath," the physical deformations as "symbol[s] of vice" (Asma 2009: 13). It is also possible that, quite to the contrary, the prosaic representation of human impairments anticipates the medical discourses on monstrosity in the centuries to come. Considering Comenius' pioneering role as an educator, such a perspective seems likely. The textual evidence alone, in any case, only allows for speculation on this account. However, one observation can safely be made: in contrast to the chapters on Judaism and "Mohametism," whose followers are unmistakably described as deficient and inferior to Christians, the chapter on physical impairments does not establish a dichotomy of 'us' versus 'them.'

As an early Enlightenment textbook, *Orbis Pictus* may well have shaped philosophical Enlightenment ideas about 'the child.' With its "emphasis on the role of reason and progress, [the Enlightenment movement] [...] regarded children as having great potential for intellectual development" (McCulloch 2011: 9f.). John Locke's *Some Thoughts Concerning Education* (1693) was a major influence on the transforming perception of children, particularly in relation to education and the environment. Monsters as imaginary beings must have had little value in these new educational concepts.

> Reason rather than the fear of punishment was stressed as it was argued that the trust of children could be won by kindness and reason at certain stages in their development. Childhood was viewed positively and youngsters were not preoccupied with sinfulness, particularly as most were religious skeptics during the Enlightenment. (Ibid: 10)

Jean-Jacques Rousseau's *Émile, Or on Education* (1762) as a pre-Romantic treatise further sculpted and developed these notions, but it also embraced religion again. Education is presented as an almost exclusively male endeavor and the chapter on Sophie, Émile's female counterpart, primarily serves to make clear that man and woman are not equals. Thus, women are ideally "passive and weak," "put up little resistance" and are "made specially to please man" (Rousseau 1979 [1762]: 358). There is an interesting passage in the sequel *Emilius and Sophia; or, the Solitaries* where Rousseau continues the stories of the now married couple. In this particular passage, Sophie' adultery – described in terms that suggest that she was drugged and raped – causes Émile to exclaim that "Sophia an adulteress is the most odious of all monsters; the distance between what she was, and what she is, is immense. No! there is no disgrace, no crime equal to hers" (Rousseau 2010 [1783]: 31) 'Monster' here carries connotations of (female) sexual immorality; expressed through acts committed by adults who are debauched and depraved and as such completely opposed to the pristine innocence that particularly male children represented to Rousseau.

Monsters in fairy tales and moral tales – the long 19th century

In line with their religious skepticism and their eradication the notion of original sin, the Romantics essentially formed the concept of the innocent child, which is still a very dominant one in contemporary Western societies. Thus, William Wordsworth affirms in the poem "My Heart Leaps Up When I Behold" from 1802 that "the Child is father of the Man," (qt. in McCulloch 2010: 10) meaning that the child is closer to God since he [sic] is nearer to his time of birth and has therefore insights which adults can learn from.

> The Romantics believed in the intrinsic goodness of children: if they become sinful it is not because they are children but, rather, because their educators have not nurtured and developed their natural goodness. The child was regarded as a seed or young plant that had to be nurtured and this happy state was viewed with painful nostalgia from the adult perspective, which was seen as a shift away from the intimate relationship with nature that only a child has immediate access to: revisiting childhood was the only way to maintain a link with that time. (McCulloch 2011: 10)

Not without reason, then, is the era of Romanticism often paralleled with the discovery of childhood, a conceptual development that is reflected in the literature. Coveney specifies: "Until the last decade of the eighteenth century the child did not exist as an important and continuous theme in English literature. Childhood as a major theme came with the generation of Blake and Wordsworth" (Coveney 1967: 29). If we look at contemporary children's literature, the originally Romantic values of childhood are still very much present.

With the Grimms' literary stylization of a centuries-old oral tradition of fairy tales arrived a body of stories that made it into the canon of (Western) children's literature. Although regularly wrought with magical motifs, monsters as they were heretofore known from bestiaries and natural histories are a marginal appearance in the *Kinder- und Hausmärchen* (1812), consisting only of a few dwarves and goblins. Of course, there are many figures that represent a form of moral monstrosity: all the evil, but often beautiful, stepmothers/witches, for example. One other bestial figure that continues to fascinate scholars and is often discussed with reference to 'monstrosity' is the Wolf in *Little Red Riding Hood*. As I elaborate in more detail in chapter 4.1, the many versions of this story that existed before the Grimms wrote down theirs explicitly dealt with a young woman's sexual maturation. In 1812, the Wolf as a monstrous sexual predator can perhaps still be recognized in his outline by astute readers (or readers familiar with the genesis of this fairy tale), but the Grimms did put in a lot of effort to turn the former brave and cunning young woman into a naïve and helpless little girl – presumably so that it can be enjoyed by the Romantic, 'innocent' child, too.

Folk tales, fables and schoolbooks were the most prominent forms of text with which children before the emergence of the children's books industry came in contact (Avery 1995: 1). There existed many tales of goblins and changelings, but only three are present in the Grimms' *Kinder- und Hausmärchen*, one of which explicitly deals with the problem of how to get rid of a changeling (*Die Wichtelmänner*). This tale was an inspiration for Sendak's *Outside Over There* (1981) which I discuss in detail in chapter 4.2. As records of recurring child exchanges, child abuse, and infanticide indicate, tales about changelings and goblins carried with them a very real and unsettling connection to life at that time.

> The cruelty to which suspected changelings are subjected in folktales makes it clear why the perpetrators of this harsh treatment sought the symbolic approval of their community. In the Grimms' accounts alone, we learn of changelings being thrown into water, beaten severely with a switch, left unfed and crying in an open field, or placed on a hot stove. This list of ordeals can easily be expanded by consulting other changeling tales from throughout northern Europe. (Ashliman 1997: np)

Folklorist Ashliman refers to court records all over Western and Northern Europe up until 1900 as evidence of numerous cases where children were tortured and murdered on the grounds that they were believed to be changelings (Hartland 1891: 121-122; Piaschewski 1935: 141-146; both qt. in Ashliman). The supernatural beings in these tales, often elves or goblins, have monstrous qualities in that they possess the cruelty to kidnap healthy human children and replace them with changelings – usually ugly, dumb, staring 'copies' of the original child. Of course, a "changeling with a thick head and staring eyes who would do nothing but eat and drink" (Grimm, third tale of tale 39: "The Woman whose Child They Exchanged") is no less, but rather more, monstrous in effect than the goblins. The atrocity that lies within these acts of abuse and murder is represented through an image that holds 'monster' and 'child' as distinct and not to be confused categories. A child with impairments, genetic or acquired through infections, risked losing her status as human and becoming a monster that, following the 'logic' of the tales, had to be tortured in the hope of making the goblins return the 'real' child to the parents. At a first glance, such a concept of 'monster' could not be further removed from today's monsters in picturebooks and other entertainment products for children, but as I suggest in chapter 4.3, there are three titles in my corpus in which the monster can be read as representing disability. Although these books have nothing in common with folktales about changelings and despite the lack of human characters (and consequently, an absence of the opposition between 'healthy' versus 'disabled,' this changes nothing about the fact that the principal (monster) protagonists are ostracized because of their monstrous appearance, which is described in terms of ugliness and repulsion.

The nineteenth century not only produced the image of the innocent child as an integral part of Romanticism but, as part of Evangelical movements in Britain and the United States, also popularized stories which "depicted children as either being very good or very bad" (McCulloch 2011: 11). The good ones usually died at the end, but not before they had converted and saved the bad ones from sinful misbehavior. Very different from sentimental literature, yet containing a similar sense of moral condemnation of 'bad' behavior, Heinrich Hoffmann's *Struwwelpeter oder lustige Geschichten und drollige Bilder* (1845) or Wilhelm Busch's *Max und Moritz – eine Bubengeschichte in sieben Streichen* (1865) could be referred to as portraying (particularly male) children as 'naturally bad' and in need of severe punishments. As contemporaries expressed concern about "imaginary beings" in fairy tales (Avery and Kinnell 1995: 69), the talking Wolf as an effective means of education was replaced by the evil tailor who cuts off Konrad's thumbs in "The Story of the Thumb-Sucker" (Hoffmann), or even more common: children's bad behavior is eradicated by 'natural consequences,' such as the corn mill that grinds Max and Moritz to death or the fire that reduces Harriet (in German it is Paulinchen) to ashes. Monsters as fantasy creatures were only to enter children's literature properly in the latter part of the nineteenth century, namely in fantasy writing.

Nonsense and fantasy – The late 19th and early 20th centuries

The notion that encouraging children's vivid imagination by providing them with fantastic creatures and unrealistic scenarios was slowly giving way to quite the opposite conviction: that fantasy and inventiveness are treasures of childhood and should be honed and cultivated. The first work of fantasy for children has been attributed to E. T. A. Hoffmann's *The Nutcracker* (1816), and although fantasy in general is associated with low-brow culture, in children's literature "it is a high and esteemed genre" (Nikolajeva 2006: 58), with some of the most famous and most frequently discussed masterpieces, including Lewis Carroll's *Alice in Wonderland* (1865) and *Through the Looking-Glass* (1871) and Frank L. Baum's *The Wizard of Oz* (1900). Until today, the most successful children's novels (in terms of copies sold, but also considering what kinds of books are turned into movies – realistic children's fiction enjoys much less popularity for filmic adaptations) can be ordered into the fantasy genre, most notably of course Joanne K. Rowling's *Harry Potter* (1997–2007) books, but also Michael Ende's *Neverending Story* (1979), C. S. Lewis' *The Chronicles of Narnia*, and Philip Pullman's *His Dark Materials* (1995–2000), all of which have been turned into major box office hits. Fantasy has a firm standing in children's culture, but it is not easy to pin down.

> [Fantasy] is one of the most ambiguous concepts in literary criticism, as it has been treated as a genre, style, mode, or narrative technique, and it is sometimes regarded as purely formulaic fiction. In some sources, fairy tales and fantasy are discussed together without precision, while in others fantasy is treated alongside science fiction and occasionally horror. (Nikolajeva 2006: 58)

Although around the turn of the nineteenth century, children's stories introduced more and more fantastic beings that were decidedly different from the staple fairy tale creatures, I would classify few of them, if any, as actual monsters. For example, the famous Cheshire Cat is, despite its ability to become invisible and to leave only its grin behind, a recognizable cat. Many more fantastic creatures as well as an abundance of animate objects populate Lewis Carroll's two famous novels, including the Rocking-horse-fly ("made entirely of wood, and gets about by swinging itself from branch to branch," eating sap and sawdust), the Snap-dragon-fly ("[i]ts body is made of plum-pudding, its wings of holly-leaves, and its head is a raisin burning in brandy" and it lives on "'[f]rumenty and mince pie") (Carroll 1871: ch. 3) Undoubtedly, Carroll set standards for many of the most popular children's writers to come, and the emphasis on new magical or purely fantastic creatures is one of the central elements.

In 1896, Hilaire Belloc and Lord Basil Temple Blackwood published *The Bad Child's Book of Beasts* which somewhat compares with Hoffmann's much earlier *Struwwelpeter* in that it joins into the tradition of cautionary tales. Unlike *Struwwelpeter* (despite of its rhymes), its use of nonsense rhyme establishes a connection with Carroll's by then famous nonsense poems in *Alice*, and it also elaborates a fine sense of irony with respect to the image of the child. Contrasting the dedication, "To Master Evelyn Bell of Oxford – Evelyn Bell, I love you well," with the first stanza of the introduction already gives a first impression of this humor that constantly oscillates between affection and ridicule:

> I call you bad, my little child,
> Upon the title page,
> Because a manner rude and wild,
> Is common at your age. (Belloc 1896)

Fig. 3   Left: *The Bad Child Book of Beasts* (Belloc and Blackwood 1896)
Right: *Where the Wild Things Are* (Sendak 1963), detail

The main part of the book introduces a number of realistic, often exotic or extinct, animals like the kangaroo, the yak or the dodo, and describes them in relation to the 'bad child,' including warnings and admonitions to be like or unlike such and such animal in certain respects. Only on the very last page an unexpected fantasy creature appears (fig. 3). This creature is not represented in the text. The caption underneath its image, "Oh! My!," does not even connect with the stanza on the preceding page. But its resemblance to one of Maurice Sendak's wild things is astonishing. The image of 'the child' (the boy child, of course) is clearly articulated as uncivilized, closer to wild nature than educated society; but at the same time as the narrator takes on an admonishing tone, the verses are evidently funny. By the end of the century, the tradition of nonsense was established "as the most appropriate vehicle for subversive energies" (Briggs 1995: 170). As subversive as these texts may be perceived, they also very strongly build on an adult writer's superior knowledge of language and the world.

One early fantastic creature that plays a major role and is still widely known today is the Psammead in Edith Nesbit's *Five Children and It* (1902). The Psammead, a grumpy and ugly sand-fairy, bears some resemblance to the jinn of Islamic mythology because it fulfils wishes, yet its external appearance could be considered as precursory characteristics of later monsters in children's culture. The Psammead is quite child-like in some aspects but ultimately comes across as condescending. John Stephens describes it as "a kind of super-ego which asserts the values and order of the adult world and discloses that childhood imagination is acutely limited" (Stephens 1992: 125-130). Although contemporary picturebook monsters are not usually presumptuous as the Psammead, many of them retain an educative and often well-hidden motivation, as will become clear in the course of my interpretations in part four.

Fantasy did not make such a strong appeal in the USA as it did in Britain (Hunt 1995: 227), and even afterwards "fantasy as a genre remained the great strength of British post-war publishing" (Hollindale and Sutherland 1995: 252). Winsor McCay's comic strips *Little Nemo in Slumberland*, published between 1905 and 1914 in the *New York Herald* and *New York American*, are perhaps an exceptional early example from the U.S. where fantasy is not only a central feature, but is incorporated into the emerging new genre of the comic (which, as part of the funnies, was read by children and adults (Kelleter and Stein 2009: 92). Each strip focuses on the boy Nemo and his fantastic and often bizarre dreams that include fantastic creatures, such as Queen Crystalette who shatters into pieces when Nemo touches her. Another strip shows Nemo's and his parents' house

> slowly but surely ascending skyward but by what mysterious power Nemo's Papa could not make out. Nemo suggested, that it might be some monster giant but his Papa called him a 'rattle brain' and ordered him to pacify his Mama who was making elaborate pains to faint. (McCay 26 Nov. 1905: np)

Fig. 4   *Little Nemo* (McCay 1905), detail

The picture in the middle of the page shows a gigantic Godzilla-like turkey with Nemo's house in the clutch of his beak, stomping through the cityscape. Maurice Sendak has named *Little Nemo* as an important inspiration for *In the Night Kitchen* (1971), and, indeed, visual and conceptual similarities are easily found. The emphasis in both texts lies less on imaginary beings, let alone monsters, but more on the power of dreams and the suggestion that children have a somehow purer access to this power. This assumption is different but not very far removed from the image of the child as a primeval savage. Interestingly, anthropological accounts of colonized people saw a clear connection between 'the child' and what they termed 'the savage.'

> Children were of central importance to these theorists because they provided a direct link between savagery and civilization. [...] The stance of both Tylor (*Primitive Culture: Researches into the Development of Mythology, Philosophy, Religion, Language, Art and Custom* 1871) and Lubbock (*The Origin of Civilization and the Primitive Condition of Man* 1870) was explicitly evolutionary: the highest stage of evolution was the European adult male while the savage and

the child were at the bottom of the hierarchy. (Montgomery 2009: 18)

These views were soon discredited by Franz Boas (USA) and Bronisław Malinowski (UK) who, with detailed analyses from fieldwork, acknowledged children's role in the family, kinship and political systems (ibid: 35). But although nineteenth and early twentieth century views of the colonized "to be different to [a self-styled civilized person, i.e. the early 'evolutionist' anthropologist], on a scale of advancement" (Jenks 1996: 4) today no longer possess any credibility, adults today still "recognize the child as different, less developed, and in need of explanation. Both of these positions proceed from a pre-established but tacit ontological theory, a theory of what makes up the being of the other, be it savage or child" (ibid).

> As childhood came to be seen as a state distinct from and potentially opposed to being 'grown-up', so it came to be figured as 'other,' with all the idealization, horror, and projection that such a status implies [...] the theological doctrine of original sin came to be replaced by scientific theories of evolution which represented the child as biologically, intellectually, or socially primitive. Children were 'savages,' awaiting the education that would transform them into civilized adults. (Briggs 1995: 167f.)

I think that this is a decisive turn in the way people thought about children, especially with regards to the genesis of picturebook monsters. Some of the fantasy creatures in texts produced around the turn of the century can be read as fulfilling the function of the bestial educator. Simultaneously hilarious and wild, it was assumed to create an immediate and unadulterated bridge to this 'other' that was the child.

An explosion of meanings and media – the 20th and 21st centuries

In his book *Monsters in English Literature: From the eighteenth century to the First World War*, Paul Goetsch very briefly comments on the omnipresence of monsters in contemporary children's culture: "As toys, characters in tales, television plays, and computer games, they have become companions for children and adolescents" (Goetsch 2002: 1). But children's culture is not Goetsch's focus nor is it monsters as literary figures in present times, and so I have to find my own answers to the question what monsters in children's culture today mean with regards to the construction of boys and girls. There is a big historical and conceptual gap from the fantasy creatures and beasts that appeared here and there in children's stories in the late nineteenth and early twentieth centuries and the hundreds and thousands of children's monsters in the types of media mentioned by Goetsch. One plausible reason for the quasi absence of monsters during the first half of the twentieth century is the two world wars that dominated much of that time. The very real horrors of the battle fields and the Holocaust might have been prominent reasons for creating harmonious, peaceful fictional worlds where adults, via their children, could take refuge. In America, the 1920s and 1930s were a particularly prolific time for child-rearing advice: raising children was no longer an inborn female capacity, but required professional skills that were usually disseminated by white men via women's magazines and radio shows (Spigel 1998: 113). Children were fashioned as pliable creatures in need of adult guidance. This view provided little space or right to exist for monsters.

After the end of the Second World War, a revival of the separate spheres could be observed both in the U.S. and in Britain as women were encouraged to leave their wartime jobs and to concentrate instead on purchasing modern household items, keeping the house tidy and clean and raising children. This was also the start of the baby boom that lasted roughly until 1965 (ibid: 111). A concerted effort in the cultural industry was made that expressed the hope for a better future that was placed on this new generation. The 1960s mark the birth of Maurice Sendak's *Where the Wild Things Are*, the popularization of Dr. Seuss' fantastical creatures in his Beginner's Books, and also of the educational TV show *Sesame Street* that first aired in 1969. This is the decade when monsters in fictional/educational narratives for children appeared in the shape that persists to this day. A plethora of functions and meanings are inscribed in these creatures, ranging from changing paradigms in parenting attitudes, the perceived threat of children turning into criminals, to a more inclusive and less authoritarian concept of education and learning and a new interest in 'the child' that was reflected by an exponential growth of the toy market and new emerging fields in academia dedicated to the study of children and childhood.

One of the reasons why *Where the Wild Things Are* remains a classic is that it directly or indirectly addresses all of the themes I just mentioned. Max represents the disruptor of the social order, a dormant wild thing whose powers are awakened by his mother's reprimand to be quiet instead of chasing the dog with a fork and hammering nails into the wall. Of course, Max is tame and harmless compared to actual child criminals – such as eleven-year-old Mary Bell who strangled two boys in 1968 and whose case, regardless of its extremity, sparked an enormous public debate about the criminal potential in children and a proclaimed "death of childhood," holding sociologists' fascination until today (Jenks 1996: 126). Alison James and Adrien James further contribute to this debate by making out a paradoxical public discourse of risk and protection surrounding children and adolescents. While public policies overtly create social structures "in the child's best interest," that is, to protect children (for example, through social workers who come into families and are supposed to ensure a healthy environment for socially disadvantaged children, or traffic-reducing measures, neighborhood-watch initiatives, and "no-loitering areas" that effectively eliminate skate-boarding and other urban youth sports), they might covertly work to control and to take punitive measures on children and adolescents who continue to take the risk of ignoring these legal measures (James and James 2008). As the authors conclude, behind this discourse of protecting children and childhood, real children are actually also perceived to represent the very risk from which they are meant to be shielded.

But *Where the Wild Things Are* also presents its readers with the kind of anarchical humor that Inge Wild connects with adults' encouragement of an autonomous and creative personality in their children, an embrace of a parenting style that tried to cut itself loose from the traditional constraints of society (Wild 1995: 82f.). This playful humor almost seamlessly (and treacherously) blends in with the creation of a special space for children that already started emerging in the nineteenth century and was now receiving a

new boost. It was connected to the growing interest in infant education which, in turn, withdrew most children from the public
world of the city. Further subdivisions in the private sphere – the
nursery became a standard room in middle-class houses – and in
the public sphere (playgrounds, schools, and playschools) emphasized the changed attitude towards children and childhood. These
special spaces for children are generally thought of as 'in the
child's best interest' but they can also be paralleled with conceptions of space in monster studies: the child's bedroom, the school,
the playground – these are all spaces that are separated from the
ordinary social and legal rules. The nursery is usually situated in
the calmest area of the house or the apartment – away from the
hustle and bustle of the kitchen or the living room where everyday
life happens (cooking, eating, receiving guests, watching TV). The
school or playschool can be seen as a microcosm of its own that
children have to attend: school is compulsory but not paid. While
at school, children are prevented from taking part in the social life
of employment and the family. Just as the playground is a designated outdoors area, usually fenced, that is not accessible by motor
vehicles and thus shielded from purportedly dangerous traffic, so
the monster in children's culture is a figure that designates at once
wildness and domestication. The picturebooks monster is a fictional friend who is all the things that the (male) child can never
be, simply because these things are too contradictory: domesticated
and adventurous, tame and wild, integrative and disruptive – all at
once.

Another merging of contradictions may be found in the blur-
ring of age that Lynn Spigel detects in characters of popular family
TV programs of post-war America:

> Drawing upon the fantasy figures of children's literature, puppet
> shows, the circus, movies, and radio programs, these television
> shows engaged the hearts of children (and often of adults as well) by
> presenting a topsy-turvy world where the lines between young and
> old were blurred and literally re-presented by clowns, fairies, and
> cowboys who functioned as modern-day Peter Pans. (Spigel 1998:
> 111)

The monsters of *Sesame Street* are not far removed, and neither are
Maurice Sendak's wild things which were inspired by his old aunts

and uncles (Sendak, interview by Moyers, 2014) but, at the same time, represent the boy protagonist's 'childish' aggressions and, with these strong emotions, a child's potential to question adult norms of behavior and conduct.

The monster has an economical component, too: the more it entered children's culture the more it could be exploited for its financial benefits by giving it a prominent part in the merchandising of TV shows such as *Sesame Street* and *Barney & Friends* (1992-2009) and movies, such as *Shrek!* (2001) and *Monsters Inc.* (2001), and their sequels.[4] Ever since the world conquest by the global franchise Pokémon, monsters have become staple characters in video games even for very young children. Picturebooks make up a sizable segment of this monster market: apart from the wild things which cannot only be seen in the picturebook but also in the movie adaptation *Where the Wild Things Are* by Spike Jonze (2009) and in the form of plush toys and prints on consumer goods, another bestselling monster is the Gruffalo, based on Julia Donaldson and Axel Scheffler's two picturebooks *The Gruffalo* (1999) and *The Gruffalo's Child* (2004) – marketed in similar ways as the wild things. Monsters in children's culture have become valuable and precious.

Of course, this is an intentional allusion to Vivian Zelizer's claim that "the priceless child" is valued for both its financial worth and for its emotional capital (Zelizer 1985). While, according to Zelizer, this mechanism applies to the majority of middle-class children in America, she also draws attention to the perverse discrepancies of childhood consumerism in the West and the enduring existence of child labor in other parts of the world that contributes to the persistence of this system. Lynn Spigel picks up on this perspective when she claims that, in the U.S., "the exploitation of child laborers (who came largely from black, immigrant, and working-class families) [was still widely practiced after the Second World War and] created a common cause for 'child-saving' movements [...] by proposing wide-reaching reforms for children

---

[4] The Japanese cult fim *Tonari no totoro* (*My Neighbor Totoro*) (1988) by Hayao Miyazaki has become extremely popular in the U.S. and in Britain. Its eponymous monstrous hero is visually referenced just as often as Sendak's wild things, for example in Disney's *Toy Story* (1995).

of all classes and races" (Spigel 1998: 112). TV programs were considered an appropriate and accessible form of universal family entertainment. One reason why the creators of *Sesame Street* Joan Ganz Cooney and Lloyd Morrisett included Muppets, such as Oscar the Grouch, Grover or the Cookie Monster, might have been that these furry fantasy creatures were racially undetermined and thus more likely to appeal to an ethnically diverse audience. Initially, psychologists had advised that Muppets and human actors not interact because it would confuse children, but when studies found that children were attentive during the Muppets segments, but not during street scenes (i.e. with human actors), the producers decided to make humans and Muppets interact.

In the light of the background of production, marketing and merchandising of popular TV shows like *Sesame Street* or of box office hits such as *Monsters Inc.* or *Shrek!*, it may be tempting to join many critics' judgment that childhood is governed by principles of regulation, surveillance and prescription. Thus, Chris Jenks ends his description of the image of childhood in our days on a gloomy note:

> Routinely, children find their daily lives shaped by statutes regulating the pacing and placing of their experience. Compulsory schooling, for example, restricts their access to social space and gerontocratic prohibitions limit their political involvement, sexual activity, entertainment and consumption. Children are further constrained not only by implicit socializing rules which work to set controls on behavior and limits on the expression of unique intent, but also by customary practices which, through the institution of childhood, articulate the rights and duties associated with 'being a child'. [...] In sum, a dominant modern discourse of childhood continues to mark out 'the child' as innately innocent, confirming its cultural identity as a passive and unknowing dependent, and therefore as a member of a social group utterly disempowered – but for good, altruistic reasons. (Jenks 1996: 122 f.)

Jenks' claim is convincing because the reasons he gives for children's disempowerment are undeniably in operation: compulsory schooling, age restrictions on consuming alcohol and drugs or on watching films that are judged as too explicitly violent or sexual, the prohibition of sexual activity between minors and persons of age, or simply the expected and intentional holding back of knowledge in order to protect children's innocence. Especially in contrast with *Orbis Pictus*, where all areas of knowledge are represented, the difference between now and then seems enormous. However, one might question whether children were not regulated and disciplined in other ways three or four hundred years ago, since childhood "historically has been an unstable category, one that must be regulated and controlled constantly" (Spigel 1998: 114). In some sense, monsters in children's culture could be considered as the very expression of adults' desire and simultaneous inability to control children's lives and personalities. As tame and friendly as most monsters come across in stories told to children today, they always carry within them at least a shred of rebellion and danger that threatens to collapse the concerted effort of the cultural industry (of which we are all a part) to control and contain children. But how much subversive potential do monsters as a popular figure really possess? Is subversion even a relevant concept in the discussion of monsters in picturebooks? What are picturebook monsters really like?

Picturebook child and picturebook monster

To begin with, picturebook monsters appear to be much like the ominous 'child:'

> [The] child is familiar to us and yet strange, he or she inhabits our world and yet seems to answer to another, he or she is essentially of ourselves and yet appears to display a systematically different order of being. (Jenks 1996: 3)

Chris Jenks' attempt to define 'the child' may be symptomatic for a general fluidity of definitions found in childhood studies which sometimes goes as far as refusing definitions entirely (e.g. Montgomery 2009: 7). Jenks' definition in particular also uncannily reverberates with some of the concepts of monsters sketched out above. Thus, one could easily replace "child" with "monster" and Jenks' definition would still be coherent. As has become clear in my brief historical sketch above, this proximity of children and monsters in academic but also in colloquial and media discourses is a recent phenomenon which only emerged in the second half of the twentieth century. The picturebook monster is a similarly recent occurrence and unlike early monsters in children's literature, such as Edith Nesbit's Psammead or Lord Basil Blackwood's illustrations of Hilaire Belloc's *The Bad Child's Book of Beasts*, picturebook monsters are a firmly established element within the mass market of children's publishing.

In my search for historical convergences of conceptions of 'child' and of 'monster' on the preceding pages, I worked with references to many different academic disciplines: from cultural theory and philosophy to historical accounts reaching back as far as Greek Antiquity. In this final subchapter, I am offering a general definition of the picturebook monster, based on the sixty-five titles of my corpus and with a consideration of the concepts and development of the monster motif that I have discussed above. The picturebook monster's most striking characteristic – which is also the reason for its exclusion from academic discussion about monsters so far – is arguably its difference from monsters in cultural artefacts for grown-ups. But only by putting picturebook monsters in relation with already existing discourses on monsters in adult culture is it possible to understand the functions of monsters in picturebooks and, by extension, in children's culture at large. There is virtually no scholarly literature, safe a few isolated articles, on monsters in children's culture and picturebooks in particular. My objective here is to present a set of recurring characteristics that distinguish picturebook monsters from other fantasy creatures in children's texts and that provide a basis for the analysis of individual picturebooks later on.

Hybridity
Picturebook monsters' most defining characteristic is the impossibility to order, classify or systematize them into any already established monster schemata. Despite countless attempts at describing, identifying and classifying monstrous races – from the Ancient Greek traveler Ktesias' reports about the wondrous inhabitants of the rims of the earth to recently published encyclopedias about monsters (e.g. Müller and Wunderlich 1999) – it is stated again and again that monsters, *per definition*, "resist attempts to include

65

them in any systematic structuration" (Cohen 1996:6), "offer resistance to attempts to pin them down" (Goetsch 2002:1), and represent a scandal within the order of living creatures (Brittnacher 1994:184). Monsters' relation toward order is ambivalent: on the one hand, they appear as a breakage, incommensurable with and external to any order; on the other hand, they are constituent of the very principle of order (Overthun 2009:52). Foucault's assertion that "the monster is essentially a mixture [...] of two realms, the animal and the human" (Foucault 2003:63) may not be entirely accurate[5] but it illustrates the monster's ambivalence toward classification rather well. Being both human and animal and neither nor at the same time, or else having body parts missing, redundant, or misplaced, being oversized or undersized, having a weird color, texture or simply extreme abilities, the monster brings about a moment of crisis by compelling monster theorists to ask this crucial question: What does it mean to be human?

Despite these critics' repeated emphasis on the 'unclassifiability' of monsters, most of the monstrous creatures they write about *do* have names and *are* unambiguously identifiable: the vampire, the werewolf, or the dragon, to name just three examples. Of course, what the subtitle of this section ('hybridity') means is that the vampire, for example, is neither human nor bat and that the werewolf is neither human nor wolf, and the dragon is a giant serpentine creature that breathes fire and, in its European variant, has wings. Picturebook monsters may also be 'hybrids' in the sense that they represent a 'mixture,' but this mixture cannot be deconstructed into its parts as it can in the previous examples of the vampire, the werewolf and the dragon. These fantastical creatures

---

[5] This quote is taken from Foucault's lecture (22 January 1975) about the "three figures that constitute the domain of abnormality" (2003:55) and his description of monsters as mixtures should be considered within the context of the fictitious monstrous races of the Middle Ages and Antiquity, rather than that of physical disability, like the Siamese twins and hermaphrodites whom Foucault also talks about in this lecture within his theoretical framework of the monster. Although Foucault would certainly not describe Siamese twins as human/animal mixtures it is just as inaccurate for the monstrous races to be described in these terms. Many of them had, in fact, no animal parts at all, like the Sciapodes (one leg with a very large foot) or the Blemmyae (headless, with face on the chest).

are, in fact, unidentifiable within the 'classical' canon of monsters and at the same time they seem to form their very own species – despite great individual variety. Picturebook monsters come in all shapes, sizes and colors. Some have fur, some have scales, some are naked, some are clothed, some are huge, some are tiny, some have claws, some have paws, some have feet, some have wings, some have sharp teeth, some have no teeth. The only thing that can be said about them that is reminiscent of monster discourses in adult culture is that picturebook monsters, too, are neither human nor animal. But while many of them do not display any clear references to a certain animal, rather presenting indistinct non-human features such as fur or claws, many picturebook monsters mirror a selection of external and/or character traits of the main male child protagonist in those picturebooks with both human and monster protagonists: the same hair color (*Hungry! Hungry! Hungry!* (2004) by Malachy Doyle and Paul Hess), the number three printed on t-shirt and fur respectively (*Jeremy Draws a Monster* (2009) by Peter McCarty), or a similar physical stature and body shape (*Leonardo the Terrible Monster* (2004) by Mo Willems). Thus, although picturebook monsters do not belong to legendary or mythological monster races, they can be said to make up their very own species, a hybrid of boy and uncategorized monster parts.

In some respects, the boy-monster has much in common with the most well-known and most conventional hybrid figure in children's literature: the talking animal. Very often, the talking animal is not only in possession of human speech but also carries other anthropomorphized characteristics, such as wearing clothes or walking upright. Many studies about talking animals in children's literature agree on at least one observation: that the talking animal represents a certain stage of growing up, of being (like) a child (e.g. O'Sullivan 2005: 85; Nikolajeva 2002: 96). Considering the animal's conceptual proximity to the monster and its supposed connection with masculinity, I was surprised to read that female animals by the 1990s outnumber male animals (72% vs. 28%) in Caldecott-winning picturebooks (Clark 2002: 288).

Fairy tales
Fairy tales, and more particularly the fairy tales by the Grimm brothers and Charles Perrault, have had an undeniable impact on

the development of children's literature in Europe and North America, as it is understood today. Some of the most popular fairy tales, such as *Little Red Riding Hood* and *Cinderella*, continue to be adapted and retold in picturebooks, illustrated stories, novels, and movies, not always necessarily for children. Fairy tales in the late twentieth and early twenty-first centuries have developed into a market that must be distinguished from general picturebook publishing. Fairy tales provide picturebook makers with inspiration just as other text forms and genres do, such as comics, letters, adventure novels, legends, myths, art, music and even instruction manuals. Of course there are many picturebooks with witches and wolves and possibly even more with dragon protagonists. The difference to the picturebook monsters I examine is that, through their anchorage with a historical genre such as the fairy tale or the legend, they carry a very specific baggage and history, and rarely appear in picturebooks without reference to their respective traditions of interpretation. And because of these traditions, these creatures are quite apart from the functions that 'typical' monsters in picturebooks fulfil.

The only exceptions in my corpus are two picturebooks with goblins: *Outside Over There* (Sendak 1981) and *Hungry! Hungry! Hungry!* (Doyle and Hess 2004). These two books turned out to play a crucial role in part four of this dissertation because they each highlight central issues. While the representation of the goblin in *Hungry! Hungry! Hungry!* is in many ways similar to the majority of monsters in my corpus, the goblins in *Outside Over There* are extremely atypical. However, through the interrelation of *Outside Over There* with *Where the Wild Things Are* – respectively the last and the first parts of a picturebook trilogy – the interpretation of these goblins as monsters makes sense. Furthermore, the relation of both *Outside Over There* and *Hungry! Hungry! Hungry!* with specific fairy tales as well as the very different relationships between the child protagonists and their respective monsters provide compelling material for an analysis of gender dynamics in these books.

Hungry! Hungry! Hungry! further contributes to the gender-comparative impetus of this study: from the twenty picturebooks that I have found about the fear of the monster there is only one with a female protagonist: *The Monster and the Teddy Bear* (1989) by David McKee. The configuration of characters covertly plays with narrative patterns of *Little Red Riding Hood* – just as *Hungry! Hungry! Hungry!*, which, as a consequence, practically forced itself into my first analytical chapter. At the same time as it plays with this well-known fairy tale, the goblin in *Hungry! Hungry! Hungry!* functions in exactly the same way as the less specified monsters in the other nineteen books in this group. Furthermore, *Hungry! Hungry! Hungry!* is a great example for discussing the use and significance of visual gender coding with a simultaneous lack of a verbal determination of the protagonist's gender.

Positive identity

This idea of the monster's negativity was already introduced in Canguilhem's essay on 'Monstrosity and the Monstrous' in 1952, where the "monster remains 'the living example of negative value' whose purpose is to reinforce a dynamic and polemical concept of normality" (Canguilhem 2008: 172). With reference to Canguilhem's foundational text, the monster was later alternatively described as "the perfect figure for negative identity" (Halberstam 1995: 22) or as "*via negativa*" (Toggweiler 2008). These critics ascribe the monster the fundamental function of presenting a projective space that is everything that the dominant culture is *not*. This dominant culture is usually described by the identity categories whiteness, middle-class, Christianity, masculinity and heterosexuality. These are the same attributes that mark children's literature, including picturebooks. Yet picturebook monsters, in complete opposition to their adult colleagues, mark a space for *positive* identity for that dominant culture by inhabiting, representing and endorsing its values. With the background of the aforementioned theorists it seems almost paradoxical that monsters in picturebooks fulfil what Karen Coats describes as a premise for children's texts in general: they "provide children with the cultural and visual literacies and narrative patterns that allow them to craft identities that will be functional and recognizable in their society; they are an important element in the scaffolding on which children build coherent and effective selves" (Coats 2008: 76). If the general "children's texts" is replaced with "picturebook monsters" and the general "children" are specified as "male, white and middle-class children" then Coats' claim would adequately describe the effect the majority of monsters has in picturebooks. The primary frame of these affirmative monster narratives clearly emphasizes a positive interpretation of the bond between boy and monster, along the lines that it is normal and beneficial for male children to behave like monsters.

But more than showing off classical monster qualities, such as inducing fear, being violent or in other ways dangerous or disturbing, these picturebook monsters incorporate primarily a set of values that must be acquired by white, middle-class males if they are to succeed socially and economically in the dominant culture. Thus, the male child protagonists learn through their interactions with the picturebook monsters to be polite, loyal, funny, resourceful, diplomatic, curious and bold. This list could be read as a re-animation of late nineteenth century values within boys' literature, but it is not yet complete. Some titles in my corpus feature monsters that represent 'new' values for a 'new' kind of masculinity: they are caring and dorky (*Love Monster* (2012) by Bright; *Leonardo the Terrible Monster* (2004) by Willems), or dreamy and fond of picking flowers (*YUCK! That's Not a Monster!* (2010) by McAllister and Edgson), or sad and lonely (*The Octonauts and the Only Lonely Monster* (2006) by Wong and Murphy). Further, the codification of 'new' sets of legitimate masculine behavior via monsters might not be 'new' in the sense that it softens up the boundaries to legitimate femininity for (self-identified) females: girl protagonists in my corpus are only successful with their individual characteristics when the monsters in their stories are either subordinate pets without much agency of their own (*Princess Smartypants* (1986) by Babette Cole) or terrifying magic adversaries (*Outside Over There* (1981) by Maurice Sendak). In other words, monsters are never strong girls' equal associates as they are in stories with strong boys. As much as the picturebook monster is a figure of positive identity for boys, the same cannot be said for girls.

Fear and Laughter

This set of specifically white, middle-class and male values is matched by the monsters' bodies that are only very occasionally fierce or beastly, and then only in the beginning. The emphasis on the bodily representation of the monster clearly lies on their humorousness: while they might at first sight induce fear, this 'negative' affect is almost simultaneously overpowered by laughter. Laughter as the dominating affect in picturebooks might be the decisive aspect that transforms monsters from figures of negativity into figures of affirmation. In monster theories about narratives for grown-ups, the monster is attributed the affective values of fear and disgust. Thus, the monster is a re-enactment of the "fears of contamination, impurity, and loss of [group] identity" (Cohen 1996: 15), a representation of our "fear of the monstrous Other" (Andriano 1999: xi), it "condenses as many fear-inducing traits as possible in its body" (Halberstam 1995: 21), and it lurks at the borders of danger and fear (Schade 1961: 37). In many accounts, the fear of the monster is inextricably linked to pleasure and desire. Goetsch describes the experience of reading monster fiction as a "mixture of fear and pleasure" (Goetsch 2002: 18). For Halberstam too, fear and desire occur simultaneously: "fear of and desire for the other, fear of and desire for the possibly latent perversity lurking within the reader herself" (Halberstam: 13). Cohen continues in a similar vein: "the fear of the monster is really a kind of desire" (Cohen 1996: 16) as the monster becomes a "temporary egress from constraint" (ibid: 17).

The effect of producing desire through fear is not entirely absent in picturebooks; it has its fair share in making these stories attractive to a large audience. But laughter arguably provides more fertile ground for the implied readers to embrace positively the monster's identity without any sense of ambivalence for doing so. Thus, the monsters' bodies are, with very few exceptions, designed to make the readers laugh or smile (or, at the least, acknowledge their fundamental harmlessness). Often, these monsters have rounded shapes and big eyes, clownishly red noses or brightly colored and soft-looking fur. Apart from offering a visual outlet for the tension that is inherent to fear-inducing monster narratives, humor has a number of other functions. Thus, humor is one of the 'skills' of boy and monster protagonists for resolving difficult situations. In some titles, humor is used in the form of parody: *Princess Smartypants* (Cole 1986) parodies gender stereotypes associated with fairy tales; *Shrek!* (Steig 1991) is itself a parody of chivalric romance; *Goodnight, Goon* (Rex 2008) parodies the very popular goodnight story *Goodnight, Moon*. These forms of literary humor are, of course, not characteristics of the monster characters as such, but they significantly contribute to establishing a comic framework. The use of humor reaches a high level of complexity when it infiltrates stories about the power struggles between children and adults. When monsters in picturebooks incite laughter they usually invite readers to laugh *with* them and *at* the norms they are violating. But sometimes the narrative voice ridicules the monster and compels readers to laugh *at* the monsters and/or children and *with* the norm-representing adult authorities. In those stories where laughter and power are interwoven, negotiations about the child character's physical and emotional boundaries are carried out.

Boundaries

The clearest illustration of the negotiation of boundaries is the omnipresent threat to the child character of being devoured by or of transforming into a monster. Sometimes the act of devouring is ambiguously interchangeable with the monstrous metamorphosis, for example when Bernard claims there is a monster in the garden that will eat him up, in *Not Now, Bernard* (McKee 1984). Then he does get eaten by the monster and his parents still take him/the monster for Bernard. Even when nobody is devoured or transformed, the question where the monster begins and the boy ends can often not be answered unambiguously. That monsters are given human names is only one conventional device among many others that contribute to this very ambiguity. There is a constant shift then, between the states of monster and boy, a simultaneous acknowledgement and affirmation of boys' wildness and a warning thereof.

Boundaries are also relevant for the establishment of spatial limits. Contrary to monster theorists' conceptualization between the centers of human civilization and the peripheries that are populated with monsters (Goetsch 2002: 11f.), picturebook monsters tend to dissolve this classical division. Monsters meet and become friends with the boys in their homes, often in their very bedrooms. But this appropriation of the child's home has little to do with Halberstam's interpretation of the gothic monster's invasion of the home and the bedroom as utterly uncanny:

> [The monster] will find you in the intimacy of your own home; indeed, it will make your home its home (or you its home) and alter forever the comfort of domestic privacy. The monster peeps through the window, enters through the back door, and sits beside you in the parlor; the monster is always invited in but never asked to stay (Halberstam 1995: 15).

Again, picturebook monsters act within a different semiotics: they are also often invited in but they are usually asked to stay, and thereby they actually *contribute* to the boy's private comfort and confidence (*There's a Nightmare in my Closet* (1968) by Mercer Mayer; *I Need My Monster* (2010) by Noll and McWilliam; *Mr. Underbed* (1986) by Chris Riddell). Monsters are an integral part of the picturebook world that sometimes does not even make any distinction between inside and outside. *Leonardo the Terrible Monster* (Willems 2004), for example, does without any visual indications of the protagonists' surroundings and any corresponding borders. Very often, monsters are 'interiorized' to the degree that there are no human characters at all, rather the monsters have become human, mirroring the average middle-class and heterosexual family: father, mother, and two (or three) kids – they are all visualized as monsters, but their behavior, their dialogs, their relationships, and sometimes even their lodgings, are perfectly human (*YUCK! That's Not A Monster!* (Allister and Edgson 2010); *The Worst Monster in the World* (Hutchins 1986).

Masculinity
Opposite to monster fictions for grown-ups, where monsters usually mark a marginalized alterity, the picturebook monsters represent, by and large, a type of masculinity that is tightly interlinked with notions of whiteness and contemporary middle-class values. The overwhelming majority of the sixty-five titles in my corpus features male protagonists and projects ways of reading and internalizing success for white, middle-class and male individuals in the dominant culture (I provide a detailed overview of my corpus in

chapter 3.2, as well as some relevant counts and discussion). As I have suggested above, the qualities represented by picturebook monsters are a mixture of nineteenth century and contemporary values and codes of white, middle-class masculinity. At first glance the inclusion of formerly feminine attributes (soft, loving, caring, domestic, and so on) into a 'new' code of childhood masculinity can be read as an appropriation of a culture of diversity. But even though gender-diversity has become more acceptable and more encouraged in these picturebooks, ethnically, economically and ability diverse subjectivities are still more or less absent. The few books that encourage such gender diverse types of masculinity can surely be seen as a support for (white and middle-class) boys who do not fit the grid of heterosexual dominant masculinity. Some picturebook monsters might well be understood as an expression of awareness (of picturebook makers, producers and buyers) for the ominous 'boy crisis,' as an offer for male child readers to identify with imaginary creatures that represent both traditional and modern values of successful masculinity.

Commodity Value

Monsters sell. As icons on consumer products designed for children (and the adults who buy these products), monsters are evidently lucrative: adorning (primarily boys') clothing items, featuring in animated movies, available as toys and action figures, included as ice-lolly molds in McDonald's Happy Meal, or as principal characters in picturebooks, video games, fantasy fiction for children, and movies. On the few occasions that this phenomenon is acknowledged, as in Goetsch's introduction to his study on monsters in English literature, it is bypassed as a side comment (Goetsch 2002: 1). What is it about monsters in children's culture that makes them so attractive? My historical survey as well as this account of recurrent and general features of picturebook monsters already indicate some possible explanations: as a figure that historically functioned in a strictly negative dynamic (as harbingers of category crises, as threat to social order, simply as the abhorred 'other'), monsters in children's culture have *in addition* become figures of affection and projection. It is because so many contradictory characteristics can be united in the figure of the monster that it is such a profitable creature in the culture industry. It is to some extent undefinable, and yet, everyone recognizes a monster when they see one.

Obviously, monsters are not simply sold as cute, little mascots devoid of any deeper meanings. Monsters also sell a certain idea of the nature of 'the child.' They are useful to adults for infusing child consumers with certain ideologies of 'appropriate' and 'suitable' behavior. Monsters function as ideological and pedagogical aids that are, at least in picturebooks, very distinctly oriented towards the fashioning of successful contemporary boys. While these boys may be gay or timid or artistically gifted, being white, male and middle-class is still taken for granted as a self-evident, invisible requirement.

Power and Pedagogy
The picturebook monster may be far from condensing "various racial and sexual threats to nation, capitalism, and the bourgeoisie in one body" (Halberstam 1995: 3) – quite the contrary – but what it does condense in one body is the question of who has power over whom. With this question the picturebook monster addresses one of the central questions of childrearing and pedagogy at large. For the longest part in the histories of the West, children were more or less unanimously thought of as 'naturally' inferior to adults and therefore in need of adults to put them on the right path, with violent measures if necessary. Since the movement of progressive education that started in the late nineteenth century with early theorists and practitioners such as Maria Montessori, Friedrich Fröbel, and John Dewey, adults' autocratic power over children has come under sustained criticism. The assurance that parents are the rightful owners of their children and in charge of disciplining them has given way to the conviction that children should be given the space to experience their self-efficacy and learn to be autonomous and responsible for their actions. One might ask, however, if progressive educationalists (and parents following their agenda) do not, in effect, only conceal the power hierarchy that characterizes adult-child relationships (Reiß 2012). The picturebook monster with its ambiguous incorporation of both friendliness and threat works extremely well as a signifier of contemporary childrearing practices.

Furthermore, the picturebook monster does not only represent the "precarious border between human and non-human" (Brittnacher 1994: 184; *my translation*), as monsters do in adult culture, but the mechanisms of identity formation through the picturebook monster operate primarily through assimilation of represented characteristics rather than opposition. In most picturebooks of my corpus, there is none of the traditional "Self/Other dialectic" (Andriano 1999: xi). Instead, there is a complex network of different and unstable subject positions that influence each other. The child protagonist's subjectivity is not only defined in its relation to the monster but also in relation to the adult – and the adult's subjectivity in relation to the child and/or the monster. Although the picturebook monster can always be singled out and identified as a monster, it is more human than monsters in adult monster narratives could ever be, precisely because it is used as a cultivating machine in disguise. That is to say, picturebook monsters represent (particularly male) children's perceived 'otherness,' their wildness and potential danger – all the while they are employed with clearly pedagogical purposes. These monsters contribute to establishing a double standard particularly for boys, since their monstrous attributes are normalized and disciplined at the same time (ref. Nodelman 2002: 11f.). On the one hand, many adults seem to consider it normal for boys to be attracted by monsters, and on the other hand, these same adults want to control this attraction and its effects on the construction of 'the child.' After all, it is perhaps the picturebook monster's quality to assemble all these contradictions in one body that make it attractive as a literary and visual signifier in a time when it is difficult to get 'right' or 'wrong' answers to questions concerning the raising and educating of children. Out of the many relevant topics arising from this thematic complex, negotiating gender norms for boys is the number one priority for picturebook monsters.

2.2 Gender, children and children's literature

Introduction

On the previous pages I offered a definition of the picturebook monster that already outlined its intricate and multi-dimensional connections with gender constructions in children's literature. More specifically, the picturebook monster's design and conception contribute to establish an affirmative image of the male child. But not only is this imaginary child male, he is also firmly rooted within a white and middle-class context. However, the idea of hegemonic masculinity that looms behind this construction appears to be counteracted by portraying these white, middle-class boys and their monstrous alter egos as representatives of a concept of 'new masculinity' that embraces and encourages values and characteristics formerly attributed only to the female gender. A question that arises from this observation is in how far this change in the representation of an ideal masculine behavior can be considered as transgressing gender boundaries. Or might it be more adequate to speak of a change in paradigms, a kind of necessary adaptation to contemporary demands and expectations of boys and men in the family and the workplace? While possible answers to these questions will be explored in my close readings of some picturebooks, I am intrigued by another observation that is closely connected: in my corpus, female child characters are disproportionately underrepresented. The very few girls and female monsters that do exist mostly help to further increase a gender dichotomy that by now should be outdated in literary criticisms. The underrepresentation of female characters combined with their own specific relations with *their* monsters clearly suggests that the construction of girls in picturebooks with monsters is marked as different, if not opposite, to the construction of boys.

The title of this dissertation, "Making Boys and Girls in Picturebooks with Monsters," is meant to draw attention to a number of theoretical assumptions and aspirations that are essential for the subsequent analysis of my corpus and that are worth making explicit at this point. In this study, I examine boys and girls as literary and visual constructions, not as living social individuals or groups of individuals. Nevertheless, picturebooks as part of children's literature can and often do play a role – among many other literary and non-literary texts and institutions – for the construction of gender of real living humans, which is why I consider social constructionism a relevant theoretical approach to my corpus. In the following section, I will explicate in more detail how I understand and use this concept here while also pointing to already existing research on children's literature influenced by social constructionist ideas.

Another, though related, theoretical assumption concerns the binary distinction between 'boys' and 'girls' in my title which reflects a general belief in gender difference as well as an exclusion of other genders. Both the belief in binary gender difference and the resulting exclusion of other genders are dominant features in English language picturebooks with and without monsters, despite the already mentioned tendencies of deconstructing, or rather: reconstructing, at least some of these assumptions for male-defined protagonists. In many, if not the majority, of discussions of gender in children's literature, psychoanalysis is used as a viable interpretative framework, albeit often without any of the critical reflections that I think psychoanalytical approaches to children's literature require. Notwithstanding my reservations about psychoanalysis, which I will also lay out in the following, I am aware that traditional psychoanalysts like Sigmund Freud and Jacques Lacan have sparked controversial and productive debates within the humanities. Without Freud's enormous impact on the development of cultural theories of the twentieth century neither feminist psychoanalysis nor queer theory could have emerged, and both of these fields have contributed immensely to original and diverse research on gender in children's literature. Impulses from theoretically queer minded scholars of children's literature have opened my eyes to the possibility, perhaps even the necessity, of analyzing the picturebooks in my corpus in a "queer readerly way" (Hall 2003: 148-150; Crisp and Hiller 2011; Pugh 2011). The fact that there are recent publications that still advocate an essentialist and dichotomist view of gender identity in children's books (Huck 2001; Allen 1999) certainly encourages me to pursue this approach. In the following two sections I describe how social constructionism and queer theory respectively inform the theoretical framework of this dissertation.

Who does the 'making'? – Picturebook monsters from a social constructionist perspective

By choosing the verb 'make' rather than 'construct' I intend, among other things, to emphasize the crafting side of picturebook production. In picturebooks, the visual text is very often much more complex and vibrant than the verbal text. The way in which child, monster and other protagonists – for example in relation to their genders – are drawn, painted or collaged plays an enormous part in the creation of the kind of images I examine here. But of course, the writing side of picturebook production is just as much part of this idea of 'making.' By using 'making' I distance myself somewhat from the term '(social) construction,' especially from its often vague and undefined overuse as criticized by Ian Hacking (2001), all the while maintaining the ties to its perspicuous basic tenets. I find Chris Beasley's definition of social constructionism a helpful starter for my own thoughts:

> [...] the Social Constructionist framework takes as its central 'brief' a refusal of any naturalised set account of the self. It is particularly opposed to biological essentialism but also resists any social essentialism – that is, accounts of a socially fixed singular core identity. Rather than attending to what people *are*, Social Constructionism is concerned with what *people do together*, with the generation of social relations and processes in specific historical cultural settings. Hence, the focus on the terms 'social' and 'construction' [...]. (Beasley 2005: 99)

When I postulate in my title that boys and girls are *made*, I take a social constructionist stance insofar as I want to emphasize that these two categories, 'boys' and 'girls,' are fabricated through a number of ultimately social actions and processes. Picturebook makers (writers as well as illustrators) capture on paper their ideas of what male, female and, very rarely, gender non-conforming child protagonists should represent in this medium. This includes physical attributes such as hair styles, facial expressions and

79

clothes, but also behaviors and characteristics. Picturebook publishers then accept or reject these authors' proposals, partly based on their preconceptions of what a picturebook protagonist should be like. Once the book is published, adult consumers buy or ignore it, again partly based on their preconceived notions of what picturebook protagonists should be like. Then, finally, adult and child readers will have the opportunity to evaluate the representation of gender according to their knowledge, preconceptions, tastes, and so on. While the construction of gender in picturebooks results from a series of social interactions that involves all of the instances just listed, my focus lies on the *making* of boys, girls and gender nonconforming children as protagonists, that is, as fictional texts by writers and illustrators as well as on my own reading of this making. Keeping in mind the interactive chain of picturebook production as a social process, my primary interest lies in what picturebook protagonists do together and what I (as a reader and critic) do with them. In other words, my analytical gaze is directed towards the modes of production of a fictitious narrative world and its repercussions on the receptive side of this communication model rather than towards the interactions between people and/or institutions of a social world – although both fictional and social worlds obviously influence each other and their respective participants are constructed through various discourses.

The textual perspective I assume for this research project might already anticipate some of the criticism that social constructionism has met with in the past two decades. One of its most prominent critics is philosopher of science Ian Hacking who describes this theoretical framework as a "code" which is "both obscure and overused" (Hacking 2001: vii). With his criticism, Hacking attacks one central tenet of postmodernist thought according to which individuals as historical beings are just as constructed as fictional characters, although, of course, discourses other than literary ones might shape this construction in each case. For example, for the construction of a living individual, genetics or medicine as discourses might be more significant than narrative theory or grammar. But when scholars in childhood studies, most often sociologists and anthropologists, talk about the construction of childhood (as, for instance, Alison James and Adrian James do in *Constructing Childhood – Theory, Policy and Social Practice*) they

80

also implicitly talk about constructions of 'the child,' and from their perspective it makes little sense to distinguish between 'real' children and the idea of 'the child,' because what they are interested in is how the two are shaped by the same ideas, political and religious movements and institutions. In other instances, I agree with Hacking that more clarity and precision would be beneficial for readers' understanding of an argument. For example, in an article on postmodern picturebooks, Karen Coats writes that these books "reveal their constructedness" (through self-reference but also through meta-language that aims to disrupt the readers' suspension of disbelief) and, without further qualification of her definition of 'constructed,' she also writes "that we are constructed [by cultural narratives]" and that "both modernism and postmodernism recognize [...] the construction of the self" (Coats 2008: 79, 85). While in the first instance I think that Coats refers to the constructed nature of the picturebook itself and not to the idea of the picturebook, in the second instance it might make more sense, and it would make her writing clearer, to specify that she is talking about the idea of the self and the idea of "us" (and also to specify who this "us" is supposed to be).

Although I have been unable to find any explicit positioning towards social constructionism as a theoretical perspective in children's literature theory, many writers clearly adhere to this approach, at the very least inasmuch as their aim is to expose 'the child' in children's texts as an invention that has nothing or little to do with 'real children.' One early and still very influential case in point is Jacqueline Rose's *The Case of Peter Pan – Or the Impossibility of Children's Fiction* (1984) where the author argues that 'the child' in texts written for children is the paradoxical product of adults' desire for (their own) sexual innocence.

> There is no child behind the category 'children's fiction,' other than the one which the category itself sets in place, the one which it needs to believe is there for its own purposes. These purposes are often perverse and mostly dishonest, not willfully but of necessity, given that addressing the child must touch on all of these difficulties, none of which dares speak. (Rose 1984: 10)

With this book, Rose not only helped establish children's literature criticism as a field of innovative thought, she was also among the first to question the narratives underlying texts written for children. These narratives are centered around the idea of the child as innocent and pure, and this idea is mirrored and simultaneously concealed in a highly stylized linguistic aesthetics that calls for a 'simple,' 'pure' and 'natural' language. Rose's diagnosis of the "perverse" motivations behind the writing of children's fiction broke the long treasured taboo of thinking 'child' and 'sexuality' as interdependent constituents of one and the same discourse, namely children's literature. Rose's book is one example for an extremely productive use of some of Freud's ideas.

Karín Lesnik-Oberstein hits a similar note in *Children's Literature, Criticism and the Fictional Child* (1994) when she agrees with Rose that

> the child does not exist. For the purpose of children's literature criticism, so closely involved with children's supposed emotions and states of mind [...] the 'child' is a construction, constructed and described in different, often clashing, terms. (Lesnik-Oberstein 1994: 9)

Both Lesnik-Oberstein and Rose make it reasonably clear that they speak of 'the child' in children's fiction and its criticism as a fictional one, or as an idea, to use Hacking's phrasing. This 'child' is constructed through adult discourse. Chapleau points out that children's literature critics generally make a sharp distinction between the "real child" and the "constructed child" and that these entities are "often kept wide apart for various ideological reasons" (Chapleau 2006: 45). Although Hacking may be right in deploring the overuse of the term 'social construction' in the humanities in general, I would argue that children's literature theorists base their interest in this thematic complex on their observation of 'real children's' complete lack of power in taking any self-determined part in the very process of their own construction. Or, as Tison Pugh puts it:

> As a result of these dynamics, that under most circumstances one must be no longer a child to write well enough to publish children's fiction, and that literature performs cultural work often in service of larger ideological objectives, children do not define the genre of

children's literature as much as they are defined by it. (Pugh 2011: 3)

And insofar as the awareness of a fundamental inequality in the creation of images of 'the child' is the motivator for a social constructionist perspective on children's literature, I think that this perspective is justified. Many children's literature scholars clearly articulate their wish to make a contribution towards social change – and be it only within their research community. Thus John Stephens claims in his introduction to *Language and Ideology of Children's Fiction* (1992) that "[...] all developmental paths are ideologically constructed, involving conformity to societal norms, and it is important for anyone concerned with children's fiction to develop an awareness of the processes and ends of this construction" (Stephens 1992: 3). Perry Nodelman also makes a point in clarifying his own role as critic in this process of construction: "Reading these texts as an adult places my attention exactly where I think it should be – on the constructed nature of the children involved in what we call children's literature" (Nodelman 2008: 85). Furthermore, he pronounces his responsibility for making the middle-class bias of children's literature – one of the many facets of the construction of 'the child,' both as a character and as an implied reader – explicit in his theoretical discussion:

> Since its beginning, in the eighteenth century, children's publishing has been primarily a middle-class venture, pursued by middle-class writers and intended most centrally and most often for audiences of middle-class children. For this reason more than any other, generalizations about children are dangerous – they construct as normal a middle-class vision of childhood for the vast population of children without the economic circumstances to be able to share it. Any conclusions I finally reach about children's literature will have to take that fact into account and make the middle-class bias that is so central to the literature equally central to any theories I develop about it. (Nodelman 2008: 101)

What Nodelman does not explicate in this paragraph – he does that in other parts of his research – is that children's literature not only incorporates a bias towards the middle-class but also towards whiteness, imperialism and able-bodied subjectivities in the form of naturalized modes of being in the world. That a main protagonist in a children's book is white, able-bodied and represents a stereotypical middle-class perspective of inhabiting the world is taken for granted. The very fact that any protagonist who does not fit this description arouses critics' attention just on the basis of this *deviation* is evidence enough for the perception of these aforementioned markers as 'natural.' It might appear as if masculinity literally suggests itself as the fifth bias in this list. While it is true that until today the majority of iconic characters in children's literature is male there is a sizeable number of female icons to diversify this picture of hegemonic masculinity – such as Alice in *Alice's Adventures in Wonderland* (Carroll 1865), Pippi Longstocking in the famous series of the same name (Lindren 1945-48), Dorothy from *The Wizard of Oz* (Baum 1900), Wendy from *Peter Pan* (Barrie 1902), the titular heroine from *Harriet the Spy* (Fitzhugh 1964), Hermione Granger from the *Harry Potter* series (Rowling 1997-2007), or Lyra from *His Dark Materials* (Pullman 1995-2000). Even picturebooks have their staple heroines: Princess Smartypants (Cole 1986, 2004 and 2009), Eloise (Thompson and Knight 1955-2002), Winnie the Witch (Thomas and Paul 1987-2012), Clarice Bean (Child 1999 until present) or Olivia (Falconer 2000 until present). The same cannot be said for characters representing ethnic diversity, class diversity, the subaltern, diasporic people or persons with impairments. Some critical attention has been paid to children's texts that represent minority subjectivities (e.g. a special issue on disability in *Children's Literature Association Quarterly* in 2013; McNair 2013; Chou 2009; Clark et al 1993). Nevertheless and despite the evident existence of such texts, to my knowledge none of them has as yet gained that status of a classic, comparable to the texts listed above and compared with an even longer list of children's 'classics' that feature white, middle-class boy heroes. In other words, there are virtually no protagonists that represent any of these characteristics and that are, at the same time, well-known and established enough to create substantial alternatives for readers' identity formations through children's literature.

In this respect, gender as an identity marker is different. Through the very possibility of comparing representations of male and female characters, gender appears as a factor that authors and producers pay considerably more attention to than race, class, imperialism or disability. One reason for this may be historical: during the 1970s and 1980s when Second Wave feminism was climbing its zenith, many literary critics deplored the lack of emancipated females in children's texts (e.g. Weitzman 1972; Jaggar and Rothenberg 1978; Clark, Kulkin and Clancy 1999: 71-82; Stephens 2002: x). An increasing public awareness of gender inequalities and a broader acceptance of political activism may further have stimulated the creation of more female characters with the capability of self-assertion, determination and independence. I find it fascinating that the very few female protagonists in my corpus who display such characteristics were mostly created at this time: Ida in *Outside Over There* (Sendak 1981), Princess Smartypants (Cole 1984), and Hazel in *The Very Worst Monster* (Hutchinson 1985). The other females from the more recent publications in my corpus are decidedly more timid and tend to retreat to more stereotypically feminine modes of gender performance: Jenny in *The Huge Bag of Worries* (Ironside and Rodgers 1996; Lucretzia in *Bad Habits!* (Cole 1999); Bernadette in *Mostly Monsterly* (Sauer and Magoon 2010); and Beegu (Deacon 2003).

There is another aspect that differentiates gender from other subjectivity markers: it is usually represented in a binary way. A protagonist is either male or female. Children's texts rarely leave space for interpretative liberties and hardly ever create deliberate ambiguity when the assignment of a character's gender is concerned. To the extent that they exist at all, descriptions in children's literature of class, race, imperialism and disability seem to offer more room for fluidity in the sense that they are slightly less caught up in a binary system of either/or. In my literature analysis I take into account the acute lack of diversity of the picturebook characters in terms of class, race, imperialism and disability. The domination of white, middle-class and able-bodied attributions to the protagonists in these picturebooks considerably shapes readers' notions of childhood and 'the child.' Increasing awareness in critics and readers is all the more important because these aspects often remain invisible. Although gender in children's literature has been critically discussed much more often than these other aspects of character formation, characterizations of girls and boys respectively are nevertheless often designed (by their authors) as 'natural' and 'normal' as long as they do not trespass their designated areas of gendered meaning-making. Within this meaning-making framework, boy protagonists tend to be assertive, adventurous, resourceful, courageous, honest, and individualistic, while girl protagonists have a different emphasis in their 'typical' traits: they are usually represented as empathetic, caring, community-minded, shy, passive. Interestingly, many of the iconic heroines of children's literature, such as Pippi Longstocking, Harriet Welch from *Harriet the Spy*, Jo March from *Little Women*, or Lyra from *His Dark Materials*, seem to have acquired their fame partly due to their adoption of some stereotypically 'masculine' traits. While this observation might be employed in favor of a deconstruction of this gender dichotomy, there remains an enormous quantitative imbalance between child heroes versus child heroines in children's fiction.

Children's literature research in general adheres to a social constructionist approach with respect to the idea of the child as a character in this literature, including its critical discussions, authors' conception and readers' reception of it. When it comes specifically to questions of gender in children's literature, theoretical perspectives start to diversify and to put an emphasis on different theoretical tenets. Many social constructionists' take on gender in children's literature focuses on the effects of education and socializing children through and with texts. The underlying argument here is that masculinity and femininity as ideas or abstract concepts do not necessarily have to be represented the way they are now and that their representation as it is now, may actually have detrimental effects on the unfolding of the personal potential of readers. This political motivation has produced an overwhelming number of publications in the field often originating from authors with an explicit feminist agenda, focusing on female protagonists alone. The view of gender in many of these publications is often not explicitly social constructionist in orientation but clearly motivated by its political drive. John Stephens affirms that feminism has had and continues to have a tremendous influence on the production and criticism of children's literature:

> This is hardly surprising, given the substantial impact of feminism on children's literature and culture during the past quarter century, and its reflection of a wider feminist agenda to understand and change the social and textual structures through which patriarchy

has attempted to regulate female bodies and behaviors. (Stephens 2002: x)

The long neglect of masculinity as an equally constructed phenomenon as femininity demonstrates just how naturalized masculine characters in children's literature are. Perry Nodelman makes this point particularly clear in his essay "Making Boys Appear – The Masculinity of Children's Fiction" in which he analyzes the mechanisms in picturebooks that make 'being a boy' appear natural. Once Nodelman and his students had unmasked this image as a code, they identified a number of assumptions they had about 'boys' representing normative masculinity. For example, the heroic 'boy code' dictates that male protagonists should be aggressive, violent and detached. Paradoxically, such characteristics are simultaneously desirable (in the literary hero figure) and despicable (in the real boy who might imitate these very characteristics). As a phenomenon that runs parallel to this traditional boy code, the participants of Nodelman's research project identified a type of boy they described as "bookish" and, as a result, "girly" (Nodelman 2002: 11 f.). Although Nodelman's explanation for these very different formulas for 'boys' remain speculative, the very identification of these formulas illustrates their constructedness.

One possibility of showing that the categories 'boy' and 'girl' do not necessarily have to be the way they are now is to trace their historical transformations. For example, by showing that the representation of girls and boys in children's fiction has not always been as it is today, Kimberly Reynolds draws her readers' attention to the social and economic paradigms that are necessary to produce certain images of boyhood and girlhood. In *Girls Only? Gender and Popular Children's Fiction in Britain, 1880-1910* (1990) and *Children's Literature in the 1890s and 1990s* (1994) Reynolds shows that a commercial distinction between girls' and boys' literatures did not emerge until the late nineteenth century, when boy and girl characters were written with the specific purpose of creating future men who would govern the empire effectively and women who would wholly identify with their role as mother and housekeeper (Reynolds 1994: 30-33).

Sarah Toomey makes another contribution to viewing gender in children's literature as socially constructed. In *Embodying an*

Image: Gender and Genre in a Selection of Children's Responses to Picturebooks and Illustrated Texts (2009), she demonstrates through her interactions with elementary school kids how certain images of femininity, such as the princess or the witch, and of masculinity, like the monster, are already firmly rooted in children's minds at a very young age. Her reader-response approach includes strikingly more girls than boys as participants, possibly reflecting girls' (stereotypically) more pronounced interest in books and reading.

This selection of social constructionist inspired research on gender in the field of children's literature is of course far from being exhaustive. Nonetheless I chose to provide a brief survey of these publications because each one influenced my own perception of gender in the picturebooks of my corpus. The visual codes of representing boys and girls respectively are only one of many examples. Apart from short hair and casual sportive clothing for boys, contrasted with long hair and frequently skirts or dresses for girls, the toys with which these fictional children's bedrooms are equipped belong to the more prominent elements of this code. According to this code, a boy protagonist has a combination of the following things scattered in his room: toy cars, trains and planes, toy robots, sporting equipment such as footballs or skateboards, and in one of the earliest books in my corpus toy guns and soldiers (*There's a Nightmare in My Closet* Meyer 1968), and books. Interestingly, the girl protagonists in my corpus possess very few or improbable things that are no match for the abundance of everyday objects present in boys' rooms. The most realistic and at the same time the most stereotyped may be a dolls' house and a witch mobile in *The Monster and the Teddy Bear* (McKee 1980). What I find stunning about the representation of girls' spaces is that, by and large, they do not have any. If girls are in a room by themselves, that is to say, a room that does not obviously have a communal function such as the living room, the objects that surround them are commodities that are strictly no toys: a stove (Sauer and Magoon 2010), a desk and a laptop (Cole 2004), a horn (Sendak 1981), pet monsters (if they can be at all considered 'things' – Cole 1984). There are exceptions, such as Max's bedroom in *Where the Wild Things Are* (1963): its severe scarcity has often been reason for comments (Sendak 1963). But is it not remarkable that critics comment on Max's lack of toys but not on Ida's, heroine of *Out-side Over There* (1981), also by Sendak? Whether or not the type and number of objects in a boy's room or in a girl's room (if they have one) is a reflection of reality is a question I cannot answer here – although I reckon that it is not. But why do picturebook illustrators use these codes at all? Why not aim for something more individual, more realistic perhaps? Korky Paul, illustrator of the very popular picturebook series *Winnie the Witch* (Thomas and Paul: 1987-2012), openly admits to using stereotypes to his advantage: "Whether I am drawing witches, pirates, mad professors or Middle Eastern travelers, there are certain items of clothing (clichéd as they may be) which instantly communicate who or what they are." (Paul: np 2014). So representing boys with stereotypical 'boy toys' is a way for an illustrator to communicate to his readers: "This is a boy." This is how the code works. Placing a girl character into a room with 'boy toys,' perhaps even making her play with them, would create a disturbance in this communication process that threatens the conventions of meaning-making. It would instantly cause questions that put this protagonist's gender into focus.

What I consider socially constructed in these picturebooks then is first and foremost a textual and a visual construction, but one with clearly social repercussions. Unmasking these modes of representation as 'code,' as something fabricated that does not necessarily have to be this way, exposes some of the mechanisms of constructing gendered child protagonists. Furthermore, it makes visible an inequality in the liberties, obligations and expectations that are thrust upon girl and boy characters respectively. Despite this overwhelming codification that forces these picturebook characters into an extremely normative gender 'cast', it is possible to detect in some of these texts interpretive gaps that allow for the creation of alternative views of gender expressions, as my discussion of *Hungry! Hungry! Hungry!* (Doyle and Hess 2004) in chapter 4.1 will illustrate.

Creating queer spaces – queer theory and psychoanalysis

The strongest theoretical influence on discussions of gender in literature, children's literature and picturebooks included, has to be psychoanalysis. In many articles and books within children's literature studies that I have come across during my research for this project, this psychoanalytical influence usually does not exceed a very basic usage that consists primarily of catch phrases and key words, such as the 'Oedipus complex,' 'polymorphous perversity' (I admit this does sound pretty impressive), 'desire' or 'mirror stage.' Even more frequently, psychoanalytical ideas imperceptibly and inexplicitly slip into authors' interpretations of gender. This way of employing psychoanalysis has nothing in common with the complex psychoanalytical investigations and criticisms that Judith Butler, Eve Kosofsky Sedgwick and many other queer theorists undertake in their work. My criticism of psychoanalytically tinged interpretations of literature is directed against a vague and often unqualified use of mostly Freudian terms that effectually upholds and perpetuates gender essentialism and dimorphism.

Despite the apparent lack of psychoanalytical expertise of many scholars of children's literature, their very use of psychoanalytical ideas as a kind of backup argument can have devastating effects on the perceived rules and limitations of gender representation. Of course, critics use psychoanalysis with differing degrees of attention to details or complexity. When L.M. Poole, for example, writes that "[*Outside Over There* by Maurice Sendak] is about oedipal conflict" and that "the Law of the Father is present as a ship on a raging sea" (Poole 1996: 108) the author imposes the concept of the Oedipus complex and the Law of the Father as authoritative meaning-makers upon her readers, as if these concepts were hardboiled facts that need neither further explanations nor justifications. In comparison, Michael Reed does a meticulous job in delivering a detailed Freudian interpretation of Ida in *Outside Over There*, diagnosing a female oedipal complex whose manifestation Reed sees in Ida's "desire for the father, the desire to replace the mother and have sexual relations with him, the desire for a baby from the father and the hostility and jealousy toward the mother" (Reed 1986: 177). Of course, Reed is representative for a very popular preoccupation with psychoanalysis by many literary scholars at this time. But although this research trend has produced some interesting debates, I think Reed's article is highly problematic. By making Ida a patient of Freud, Reed casts her into the same subjugated and utterly dependent position that was common to all of Freud's real female patients. Reed's psychoanalytical lens completely occludes the active heroism that Ida displays in this story: she goes on a quest and succeeds – through cunning, bravery and magic – in rescuing her baby sister who was kidnapped by nasty goblins. Not only do Reed and Poole bar the recognition of Ida's strength and courage, they also contribute to an essentialized view of 'femininity' and 'masculinity.'

Essentialism in gender discussions is still widespread in children's literature criticism, and I hold psychoanalysis, which, in this field, mostly concentrates on the most popular Freudian concepts, at least partly responsible for this problematic tendency. Children's literature scholar Maria Nikolajeva generally avoids explicit psychoanalytical terminology since her focus in picturebook studies lies on formal and structural patterns of image-text interaction. And yet, when she analyzes *Where the Wild Things Are* and *Outside Over There* with respect to their main protagonists' characterizations, she falls into the same essentializing patterns that inform Poole's and Reed's articles:

> [*Outside Over There*] demonstrates an exciting counterpart to Max's masculine aggressions [in *Where the Wild Things Are*], showing a girl's terror connected with a typical feminine theme. Ida's parents have abandoned her: the father literally, as he is "away at sea" and the mother, emotionally. (Nikolajeva 2010: 172)

Why would parental abandonment be a "typical feminine theme?" Is not Max also completely abandoned by his mother? As Nikolajeva with good cause points out elsewhere, parental absence is one of the principal prerequisites for any story written for children (Nikolajeva 2010: 22). Why then does she read this motif as typically feminine here? The only explanation I can offer is that sexual essentialism, amongst other factors via the infiltration of psychoanalysis into mass culture, is so deeply rooted into semiotic systems, into the codes that are supposed to help people understand the world, that even critically versed academics can be blind to the problems that these codes imply. Perhaps 'careless' would be a more appropriate word here because it expresses a sense of taking gender essentialism for granted – which I think is what happens in the extract I just quoted. Stephen Frosh, who explored both the critical debates in favor of and in opposition to Freud, writes that

> ... there is now a sense of banality about many of the psychoanalytic claims about gender and sexual difference. Freud's phallocentrism and misogyny, as well as his confusion over feminine development and sexuality, is so clearly documented as to require no detailed repetition. [...] The influential object relational idea that girls, because of their close ties with their mothers, struggle with issues of autonomy and separation whilst boys trip up over intimacy can now be seen both as a truism and as a tautology, describing a socially induced state of affairs without grasping hold of the complexities of the psychological mechanisms at its root. (Frosh 1997: 202 f.)

To me, Frosh's polemical summary of criticism that is directed against an unqualified use of Freudian ideas expresses the underlying, though rarely explicit, beliefs that I have occasionally come across in the field of children's literature research. Although object relations theory is often implicitly referred to in these Freud-oriented criticisms, it does not, strictly speaking, originate in Freud's writings, but first emerged with Sándor Ferenczi and Otto Rank (Ogden 2005: 27). As a framework, object relations theory is very prominent in Nancy Chodorow's work, most popularly in *The Reproduction of Mothering: Psychoanalysis and the Sociology of Gender* (1978), in which she turns the tables, as it were, and focuses on most women's urge to mother and other 'characteristics' common to women, in her view. Chodorow is an influential example for the transformation of Freudian concepts into a psychoanalytical version of difference feminism, a position that also some children's literature critics represent, yet without acknowledging the theoretical sources of their works. For example, Marjorie Allen, in *What Are Little Girls Made of? A Guide to Female Role Models in Children's Books* (1999), sets out to explore ways in which children's texts define 'female identity,' implying that girls are more in need of diverse role models than boys (since male protagonists are already brave, independent, etc.). Allen's vision of masculinity, it seems, is naturalized to the extent that she considers male protagonists with their 'typical' characteristics as an ideal of (human) 'self-expression' that should be made accessible to and desirable for female protagonists and children too. Her mission can be described as (modernist) difference feminist in the sense that she postulates an identity politics that implies women's or girls' commonality with each other and consequently women's/girls' fundamental difference from men (Beasley 2005: 47). Charlotte Huck makes this belief in essential gender difference explicit in her introduction to a book whose title does not match her argument. In *Beauty, Brains, and Brawn – The Construction of Gender in Children's Literature* (2001), Huck writes:

> It is ... important to select books that are true to the nature of both genders. We can't simply substitute girl characters for adventuring boy characters, nor do we want to produce unisex characters. We still have to capture the essence of femininity and masculinity, or children will have a difficult time identifying with the character. Boys and girls are innately different. Boys are more action oriented and do demand more excitement than girls. Girls seem to be more in touch with their feminine side, openly showing their feelings, seeking love and belonging. (Huck 2001: viii)

Any positioning towards feminist or other gender theories is absent in Huck's introduction. She seems to feel no need to put her essentialist claims into relation to forty years of ongoing debates about 'the nature' of girls and boys and, indeed, about the question whether such a 'nature' actually exists. Huck simply claims that it does and pays no attention to the effects that her call for an even more gender restrictive and gender divided children's literature might have. Although she does not mention psychoanalysis, her beliefs about femininity (implicitly reserved for individuals with female sexual organs, i.e. 'girls') being synonymous with emotionality and fragility and masculinity (reserved for individuals with male sexual organs, i.e. 'boys') with adventurousness and activity mirror precisely those truisms that Frosh criticizes in the overgeneralized and outdated use of Freudian ideas. Although Huck's contentions are exceptionally conservative and out of touch with academic discourses on gender as a whole, the general gist of her argument is likely to resonate with many adults (family members as well as professional educators) who shape children's beliefs and preconceptions about their own and other persons' genders on a daily basis.

Children's literature scholars who write about gender tend to emphasize gender difference. Gender difference here signifies the conviction that gender makes a difference and that there is no such thing as a universal, ungendered child. This might come across as a commonplace observation, but there are scholars who have contributed enormously to the field of childhood studies and children's literature studies, who write about 'the child' using exclusively masculine pronouns while they explicitly mean *all* children (Ariès 1962, Bettelheim 1976, Dreikurs 1948), and who continue to be referenced in journal articles and books. Yet others and considerably more recent authors emphatically deny that gender – at least in early infancy and up to the age of three or four – makes any difference at all (Nikolajeva and Scott 2001: 107). However, for the majority of scholars working on gender, the existence and relevance of this difference for the production of children's fiction, of which picturebooks are a part, seem evident. One of my starting points was indeed the striking asymmetry in the representation of female and male child characters in the books of my corpus. Not only are the females by far outnumbered by the males, their relationships to the monsters or their images as female monsters also differ enormously from the males. Thus, my project of examining the hypothesis that picturebooks with monsters are a means of constructing gender in childhood is a gender difference approach in so far as it matters for the characterization of the protagonists and for the development, unfolding and resolution of the story whether these protagonists are male or female.

Chris Beasley points out that gender difference approaches tend to be psychoanalytical in orientation: thinkers who write within this framework "argue that the self comes into being through gender [...] – that is, the path to becoming a person is a gendered path. Selfhood *is* gender identity." (Beasley 2005: 61) After reading and re-reading the sixty-five picturebooks of my corpus I would support this view insofar as these stories lay out a gendered path for the child character which leads them to a fuller understanding of how they are expected to look and behave as girls *or* boys. When children's literature criticism is concerned, (mostly Freudian) psychoanalysis is sometimes explicitly and often implicitly used to endorse gender essentialism. But that does not mean that psychoanalysis is, *per se* and always, used for normalizing heterosexuality and promoting gender dimorphism, as Judith Butler makes clear:

> [The] recruitment of psychoanalytical vocabularies for the purpose of preserving the paternal line, the transmission of national cultures, and heterosexual marriage is only one use of psychoanalysis, and not a particularly productive or necessary one. It is important to remember that psychoanalysis can also serve as a critique of cultural adaptation as well as a theory for understanding the ways in which sexuality fails to conform to the social norms by which it is regulated. (Butler 2004: 14)

It is Butler's queer theoretical stance towards psychoanalysis that I wish will become more frequent in children's literature criticism than the outdated and uncritical views expressed by some of the scholars cited above. "Queer Theory", according to Beasley, "offers a Postmodern critique of metanarratives of identity, a critique of universal homogeneous and fixed identity gender/sexuality categories, which are deemed essentialist" (Beasely 2005: 162). Queer theorists base their arguments on the social constructionist view that 'identity' is fragmented, fluid and incoherent. Although, as I said before, the majority of children's literature scholars interested in questions of gender write from a gender difference approach, not many seem to go into the theoretical complexities of queer theory. In the course of my research, I found that those scholars I identified who do present a queer theoretical perspective often make intriguing and challenging contributions that have shaped my own thinking about gender in picturebooks. Quite unlike the examples I cited above, these scholars use psychoanalysis in a way that resonates with Virginia Goldner's description of contemporary psychoanalytic thinking on gender and sexuality as "theories that refuse to sit still, retaining the density of the analytic perspective while digging up the ideological infrastructure of normativity, objectivism and biologism" (Goldner 2003: 114). If psychoanalysis is used from within a queer theoretical framework it can offer enriching perspectives to an otherwise largely heteronormative children's literature research. Politically, queer theory contributes to raising awareness within this research field on restrictive and sometimes disrespectful conceptions of gender in texts designed for children. Four scholars in particular had a perceivable impact on my own research: Tison Pugh, Victoria Flanagan, Thomas Crisp and Brittany Hiller. For this reason I will briefly introduce their main ideas and show how they influenced my project. Being queer theoretically oriented, they are all indebted to psychoanalysis and they make this explicit to various degrees. Although Freudian and Lacanian concepts are discussed, often via Judith Butler, this is with the express purpose of deconstructing their ideas and making them fruitful for queer readings of children's literature.

Tison Pugh's *Innocence, Heterosexuality, and the Queerness of Children's Literature* (2011) uses Rose's premise of the paradoxical relationship between innocence and sexuality in order to offer a queer-theoretical revision of some of children's literature's most celebrated classics and most widely read series fiction, such as C. S. Lewis' *The Chronicles of Narnia*, Philip Pullman's *His Dark Materials*, Frank L. Baum's *The Wizard of Oz*, J. K. Rowling's *Harry Potter*, and Stephanie Meyer's *Twilight Saga*. His contention is that the disavowal of sexuality through the celebration of innocence renders much of children's literature queer. This queerness rests on the encouragement of children's (paradoxical but 'naturally' innocent) homosocial behavior while at the same time expecting them to develop into heterosexual adults (Pugh 2011: 6). In other words, establishing a gender identity that meets with the expectations of what is *either* 'male' *or* 'female' is fundamental from early childhood on, but the telos of this insistence on gender identification – heterosexuality in adulthood – is consistently concealed. While Rose's attention concentrates on the perversity of adults, thereby highlighting the powerlessness of real and fictional children, Pugh turns the tables, trying to create some normativity-disrupting space by exposing the queer foundations on which children's literature depends. More significantly, Pugh puts into focus the (non-)sexual relationships between the fictional children themselves, thus ascribing them more (queer) agency.

I found Pugh's observations of homosocial relationships in the texts he examines to be relevant for many books in my own corpus, but only for male child characters bonding with male monsters. Perhaps needless to say, the homosocial relations Pugh examines in his book are also predominantly between boy protagonists. Pugh is right in emphasizing that homosocial behavior in children's fiction is always de-eroticized and rendered 'innocent,' but rather than reading this motif as a queer subtext, it could also be criticized for its quality of constituting an important element in hegemonic constructions of masculinity. Although heterosexuality might well be the underlying telos of this masculinity-building motif, I find it difficult – if not impossible – actually to detect this supposed vested interest. The few books with female characters present a rather different picture: however 'emancipated' or 'strong,' the child heroine is often put in direct or indirect relation to the institution of heterosexual marriage or heterosexual love. In fact, the more emancipated this girl heroine appears to be the more explicit the framework of heterosexuality becomes.

Victoria Flanagan's *Into the Closet – Cross-Dressing and the Gendered Body in Children's Litrature and Film* (2008) is similarly influenced by queer theory and, most notably, Judith Butler. Like Pugh, Flanagan departs from the contention that adults seemingly need to desexualize narratives for children – even in narratives about cross-dressing, a practice which, in adult culture, is highly sexualized. Most interesting from my perspective is the disproportionate representation of female-to-male cross-dressing narratives in relation to male-to-female ones, considering that, in adult culture, "cross-dressing is popularly perceived to be a male activity" (Flanagan 2008: xv). Flanagan's observation seems to suggest that, for girls in children's texts, it is more acceptable, even encouraged, to break gender expectations while, for boys, cross-dressing is nearly always represented as comical and degrading. From Flanagan's account one may conclude that for boys the border between what counts as socially acceptable gender performance and what does not is considerably more clear-cut than for girls. I find Flanagan's conclusion particularly fascinating when I contrast it with my observations about monster picturebooks where the paradigms for transgressive behavior appear to be arranged the other way around: boys enjoy considerably more gender performative freedom than girls. One way of looking at picturebooks with monsters, then, is to emphasize their creation of space for diverse male gender performance while simultaneously tending to restrict the diversity of female gender performance.

Thus far, I have concentrated my survey of gender theoretical discussions on the categories 'male' and 'female,' 'masculine' and 'feminine,' and similar binary labels. Judith Butler, Jack Halberstam, Kate Bornstein and other queer theorists/activists have challenged the very use of such pre-existent, identity-creating elements.

> (Butler's) framework is a very thorough-going refusal of assumptions regarding the biological underpinnings of gender groupings to the far point of conceding no 'interior' or 'essential' foundation to the self. Gender does not 'express' a self, a way of being, or a bodily difference, but rather is a performance or enactment of power. One is a woman or man as an effect of power. (Beasley 2005: 101)

Viewing gender this way opens up new possibilities of looking, as Thomas Crisp and Brittany Hiller demonstrate in their article about re-thinking sex-role representation in Caldecott medal-winning picturebooks from 1938-2011 (Crisp and Hiller 2011: 196-212). The authors build on Butler's conception of gender as a set of repeated actions that only appear 'natural' and 'real' through their very repetition. In their systematic and partly statistical study of picturebooks published over the course of seventy-three years, Crisp and Hiller destabilize the traditional perception of the categories 'masculine' and 'feminine' as contradictory and complementary by "attempt[ing] to make space for those who reject or cannot fit into these previously rigid categories" (ibid: 196). They do this not only by examining the picturebooks themselves but also the previous research on them, thus extending their focus on these (according to the authors) discursive mechanisms of reproduction and reinforcement of a binary gender system. Thus they state that "researchers often rely upon visual depictions within illustrations to determine whether or not a character is 'male' or 'female'" (ibid). Crisp and Hiller challenge these previous research findings because

> relying upon visual cues in illustrations to determine the gender of a character or figure necessarily entails relying upon normative constructions or personal understandings of what it means and looks

like to be either male or female (i.e., assuming that carrying a purse or wearing a dress identifies a character as female or that a figure wearing a suit is male). It privileges particular conceptions of the ways in which these genders may appear at the expense of others: in the "real" world, there are self-identified males who become pregnant and/or who wear dresses and there are self-identified females with beards and mustaches and/or who wear tuxedos. If a character is not explicitly gendered in the text of a book, it ultimately falls upon the reader to interpret the gender identity of the character depicted. (Crisp and Hiller 2011: 197)

The authors acknowledge that their position privileges verbal text over visual text because it ascribes the former more fixity and the latter more flexibility. Their motivation for assuming this position lies with their political purpose: to identify possibilities for more flexible gender interpretations of characters in widely read English language picturebooks. Since these possibilities occur far more often in the visual images than in the written language, their approach can be seen as a matter of pragmatism rather than theoretical conviction (they refer to Jacques Derrida's contention that "written text is ultimately as slippery as visual images" (ibid)). Whenever the verbal text of a picturebook leaves the protagonist's gender unidentified (through lack of pronouns and proper names), Crisp and Hiller read this protagonist as ungendered, even if the illustrator may rely on cultural cues (visuals) to indicate male or female gender. I find their approach extremely enriching, but also difficult in some respects as my two alternative interpretations of *Hungry! Hungry! Hungry!* (Doyle and Hess 2004) in chapter 4.1 show. Through the exclusive use of direct speech (and the absence of a third person narrative), this picturebook – following Crisp and Hiller – leaves the determination (or non-determination) of the child protagonist's gender up to the reader. With my two alternative readings of this book I want to illustrate some of the effects that such differences can have.

I want to point out one more article that has not so much influenced the practical approach towards my corpus, but instead provided me with critical material about the very question with which I set out for this section: What is psychoanalysis doing with gender and 'the child' in children's literature research? – a question that I have taken the liberty to adapt from Karín Lesnik-

Oberstein and Stephen Thomson's article "What is Queer Theory doing with the Child?" The authors examine two Queer Theorists' texts (Eve Kosofsky Sedgwick's *Tendencies* and Michael Moon's *A Small Boy and Others*) for their use of "the child" as a "random figure" which is "resistant to analysis" and a "figure deployed *as* resistance" (Lesnik-Oberstein and Thomson 2010: 35, 36). The figure of "the child" is, via this representation, implicated (by these authors) with Freudian psychoanalysis in highly problematic ways. More specifically, Lesnik-Oberstein and Thomson criticize both Sedgwick and Moon for failing to treat the figure of "the child" with more caution and rigor when they implement it into psycho-analytical rhetoric:

> Even where an effort is being made to qualify the child's role this has not been carried through to its ultimate consequences. We are not suggesting that there is a safe way to invoke the child, but rather that this can only be risked in an acceptance of its full danger. (Lesnik-Oberstein and Thomson 2010: 45)

These authors' criticism and my reservations about the uncritical use of psychoanalysis for reading children's texts ultimately converge in this point: the dangers that a psychoanalytical approach signifies for the position of 'the child' as a figuration of gendered becoming. While Lesnik-Oberstein and Thomson primarily make the point that it is important to be aware that 'the child' is inherently tied up with a psychoanalytical-theoretical problematic, I hold that the creation of possibilities of reading child protagonists' genders as fluid and flexible concepts is far more "necessary," to reuse Butler's word, than the further cementing of a gender dichotomy based on antiquated Freudian concepts. In this sense, I side with David Hall who urges critics "to undertake their own queer readings, even of those texts that are seemingly 'straight' (...) all texts have 'queer internal aspects, traces and resonances'" (Hall 2003: 148). Girls and boys are undeniably constructed in very different ways in the picturebooks of my corpus, and this verbal and visual construction reverberates with social constructions of gender outside of these texts. At the same time, I think it is important to look for and emphasize interpretive gaps that enable the destabilization of heteronormative gender categories. In some respects, a loosening of heretofore rigid frameworks for (hegemonic) masculinity is visible in quite a few picturebooks of my corpus: a truly successful (in the logic of the narrative) process of maturation requires the boy character to get in touch with a whole range of his emotions, not just the stereotypically masculine anger and rage, but also the stereotypically feminine love and empathy. But once these occurrences of seemingly dissolving gender norms for boys are paired with the ultimately regressive gender constructions available for girl protagonists, a gender divide dictates once more what is what in the world of picturebook monsters.

3   Methodological Approaches

3.1 What is a picturebook? Some formal considerations

So what exactly is a picturebook? Depending on their academic background, perspective and research focus, scholars in the past have given very different answers to this question. Some consider the textbook for children *Orbis Sensualium Pictus* (usually translated as "A visible world in pictures") written by Czech educator Comenius in 1658 as one of the earliest precursors of the modern picturebook (Whalley 2004: 318), while the sheer abundance of in-depth discussions of *Where the Wild Things Are* seems to suggest that many critics take Maurice Sendak's classic from 1963 as the actual starting point for the establishment of the picturebook as it is known today. Between those two extremes, picturebook studies have become a prolific and growing field within children's literature research. Despite the obvious differences in the two examples just cited there is some common ground in the definition of the 'modern picturebook.' If children's literature constitutes a genre, as Thorben Weinreich or Perry Nodelman argue, in the sense that "'genre' [is] a notion of a group of texts characterized by recurrent features" (Weinreich 2000: 34; also cf. Nodelman 2008), then I would argue that picturebooks are at least a sub-genre, if not a genre on their own. Although David Lewis emphatically rejects the categorization of the picturebook as a genre, preferring instead the idea that picturebooks "exploit" genres (Lewis 2001: 74), the picturebooks in my corpus do share recurrent features and components, which, in their combination, are unique descriptors of this type of print medium. These most dominant describing terms comprise the following elements: narrative content and narrative mode, dual audience, historical and geographical location, material composition, and the distinction from other print media with similar components.

Narrative content

The use of the word 'narrative' seems to place a focus on picture *story*books, as opposed to, for example, alphabet books, counting books, or other types of non-fiction. Although Lawrence Sipe claims that "the dynamics in picture storybooks are unique" (Sipe 2012: 4), I have found that, in practice, such a distinction is not always possible, nor is it absolutely necessary. For example, *Glad Monster Sad Monster* (Emberly and Miranda 1997) could be described as a mini-encyclopaedia that introduces young children to the most prevalent emotions, but this introduction is enacted by a monster figure engaged in various activities that trigger the respective emotion. The monster figure establishes a mini-narrative that the child readers are invited to translate into their own emotional worlds by removing and wearing the monster masks that the book provides. Another example is a counting book in rhyme, *One Hungry Monster* (Heyboer O'Keeffe and Munsinger 1989), that in addition to its counting theme tells a story that is both action-packed and suspenseful. My understanding of 'narrative,' then, is a relatively wide one that includes poetry and even one strictly non-fictional book that imparts knowledge on healthy eating and life-style habits (*The Monster Health Book – A Guide to Eating Healthy, Being Active & Feeling Great* by Edward Miller, 2006). That being said, my close readings in the following chapters all concentrate on the kind of picture storybooks that Lawrence Sipe had in mind.

But even those books that do not meet Sipe's criteria for 'story' share a few elements in terms of their narrated content. The first is that they usually have a main protagonist who is a child or childlike, or whose adult main protagonist interacts in crucial ways with child or childlike characters. This element applies to picture-books in general. The second element, which is only relevant for the compilation for my research corpus, concerns the presence of monsters that needs to be decisive for the development of the plot. These monsters usually display childlike qualities, but they are not always and automatically displacements of the child protagonist.

Narrative mode

The narrative mode that defines the picturebook more than any other characteristic is its multimodality. Usually, the term 'multimodality' signifies the interaction of words and images, in other words, the simultaneous and inseparable use of two different sign systems: the conventional and arbitrary (verbal language), and the iconic (pictures). In this respect, picturebooks are very similar to comics, but both genres – if I may use that term – retain distinctive features. For example, the succession of several frames per page or the use of speech balloons is characteristic for comics while picturebook images usually spread over one or even a double page, and the use of speech balloons is rare. One other difference relates to the practice of reading picturebooks and comics respectively, the first being designed to be read out loud, and the latter being notoriously unsuited to being read out loud – largely due to its dependence on speech balloons.

Much picturebook research is devoted to the analysis of the kinds of image-word relationships that exist. Lawrence Sipe provides an overview of different approaches to describing these relationships, while at the same time offering a brief survey of some critical positions within the field. Although most scholars do not make explicit connections to the study of comics, their ways of describing text-picture relationships can be equally applied to comics. Sipe makes out four distinctive approaches. He describes the first approach by its use of metaphors that are intended to elucidate the image-word relationship. Very prominent are musical metaphors, such as counterpoint, harmony, or rhythm; but metaphors inspired from the performance arts, textiles, and science are also present (for example, "interweaving," "plate tectonics," or "ecological"). The second approach is dominated by theoretical concepts such as "irony" (Nodelman 1988, Kümmerling-Meibauer 1999) or "indeterminacies" (Iser 1978; and Graham 2000). A large corpus of research develops and employs typologies and taxonomies of image-word interaction, with two main categories (congruency and deviation) and many sub-categories (e.g. Schwarcz 1981; Nikolajeva and Scott 2001). The fourth group of scholars is guided by phenomenological questions such as "what goes on inside the minds of readers/viewers as they make sense of picturebooks" (Sipe 2012: 5).

Every one of these approaches has its merits and its drawbacks. Thus, describing the image-word relationship in purely metaphorical terms is arguably restrictive since it neglects the many aspects that differentiate that relationship from its metaphor: a picturebook may be like a fugue in some respects, but both have distinctive characteristics that the other does not. Likewise, a focus on one theoretical concept such as irony risks subsuming even those texts whose image-word interaction might be more aptly described as complementary rather than ironic. Concentrating on taxonomic categories can lead to an almost compulsive ordering at the detriment of considering the ideological content of the text. Finally, the question "what does the text do with the reader?," or so it seems to me, cannot be answered at all without recourse to any/all of the other reflections. For my own readings, I use an amalgam of all of these approaches, taking whatever concept promises to be most productive for my research questions.

Dual audience

One defining characteristic of picturebooks is that their intended audience comprises to very different age groups. Although commercially advertised for children aged four to eight, picturebooks must appeal in equal measures to the adults who buy these books and then read them with their children, grand-children or pre-school and elementary school students. The means through which this effect is achieved is described as "dual audience" (Scott 1999: 99-110), "dual address" (Nikolajeva 2002: 105), or similar terms.

Historical and geographical location

As I have mentioned before, there exists no consensus about the historical date of the emergence of picturebooks. For Maurice Sendak, the first "real" picturebook was Randolph Caldecott's *Hey Diddle Diddle* and *Baby Bunting* (both 1882) (Sipe 2012: 7).

Elisabeth Wessling convincingly discusses Heinrich Hoffmann's *Der Struwwelpeter* from 1845 on the basis of its ironic interplay of words and images (Wessling 2004: 319-345). Jane Doonan makes out the First World War as a turning point in the historical development of the picturebook when "perceptions about the picturebook and the nature and structure of publishing have changed considerably" (Doonan 2012: 230), and then offers a list with picturebook authors "whose body of work rewards study" (ibid: 233), the earliest of whom have published in the late 1920s and 1930s (William Nicholson, with *Clever Bill* (1926) and *Pirate Twins* (1929), or Jean de Brunhoff with his *Babar* picturebooks from 1931 to 1937, which, on top of being commercially successful picturebooks until today have been turned into a global brand). As these few examples show, the picturebook cannot be ascribed to one geographical origin either: notable early picturebooks or picturebook precursors have appeared in Germany, France, England – and were soon followed by other innovative publications in the United States. As such, picturebooks are a Western genre that has only relatively recently started being taken up by authors and illustrators in non-Western parts of the world (cf. Chou 2009: 19-32). Thus, as with most things, there is no one original point in time or space that has given birth to the picturebook.

However, if the focus is narrowed to picturebooks with monsters I think that such an origin can, indeed, be established: Maurice Sendak's *Where the Wild Things Are*, published in the United States in 1963. Apart from making exceptional use of the possibilities of image-word dynamics, Sendak here also provoked public attention by bringing together the figures of the monster and the child in a way that had heretofore never been done. As Perry Nodelman explains:

> When Maurice Sendak's *Where the Wild Things Are* first appeared, in 1963, it created something of a controversy exactly because the depiction of monsters was perceived to be a new and unsettling idea. Sendak had, apparently, taken a position that was not actually there to be taken in the field of children's literature as it existed at that time. (Nodelman 2008: 120)

Nodelman rightly points out that the success of Sendak's picturebook was based on his continuation of a literary tradition that confronted child protagonists with evil creatures (such as the Wolf in *Little Red Riding Hood*, or the tailor in Hoffmann's "Die Geschichte vom Daumenlutscher" (The story of the Thumb-sucker) and on Sendak's simultaneous realization that this tradition was increasingly discredited in the context of then changing ideas about parenting and education. In this light, the wild things can be seen as a timely answer to the question of what role monsters could still play in children's literature when they were no longer to function as a deterrent – because a deterrent was no longer believed to be a legitimate component in child-rearing practices. The proliferation of monsters in picturebooks *after* 1963 and the many visual and conceptual similarities to *Where the Wild Things Are* institute this picturebook as a starting point for a new kind of picturebook narration.

Material parameters

Picturebooks marketed to child audiences aged four to eight are published in various, non-standardized formats ranging from 20x20 centimeters (*The Trouble with Mum* by Babette Cole) to 23x32 centimeters (*Leonardo the Terrible Monster* by Mo Willems) or 25x23 centimeters (*Where the Wild Things Are*). Commercially successful titles will be offered in many different formats and editions, including board books, hardback, and bath books. In the UK and United States, paperback picturebook editions are by far the most dominant on the shelves of book stores, while in Germany, for example, hardback editions of picturebooks seem to be more popular.

Unlike the format, the number of pages is standardized and almost always restricted to 32. As author and publisher Darcy Pattison explains, this has economic reasons:

> [...] when you fold paper, eight pages folds smoothly into what's called a signature, while any more results in a group of pages too thick to bind nicely. In addition, the 32 pages can all be printed on a single sheet of paper, making it cost-effective. In extremely rare cases, picture books may be 16, 24, 40 or 48 pages, all multiples of

eight (a signature); but 32 pages is industry standard. (Pattison 2008).

Although there is variation as alluded to by Pattinson, the picturebooks in my corpus more or less adhere to this standard. Just as the number of pages is dictated by the publishing industry, the page numbers are never printed on picturebook pages. Whenever I cite from a picturebook, I use the abbreviation 'np' (no page number).

Closely related to these parameters above is the material make-up of the picturebooks. So far, I have only covered picturebooks that rely on simple paper (or cardboard) pages and print colors. Although some scholars keep lift-the-flap books or pop-up books or other picturebooks that work with paper art apart from the category of picturebooks (cf. Smith 2001: 226), I do not make this distinction for my own corpus. Thus, I have included Henrik Drescher's *Pat the Beastie* (1993), which combines touchy-feely elements such as artificial fur, paper sculpture (Beastie's closing jaws), and lift-the-flap elements (a pink rubber shower curtain). Another book that explodes the conventional picturebook make-up is *Mommy?* (2006) by Maurice Sendak, Arthur Yorinks, and Matthew Reinhard: this book is an example of extremely sophisticated paper engineering and tells its story with only one recurring word ("Mommy?"). There are more titles that make use of the material composition of the picturebook by building it into their narratives. For example, readers of *The Monster at the End of This Book* (1971 by Jon Stone and Mike Smollin) derive much of their pleasure from being warned by the book's protagonist of turning the next page because of the lurking danger at the end of the book. Or in Ed Emberly's and Anne Miranda's *Sad Monster, Glad Monster* (2006), the readers are encouraged to remove and try out the paper monster masks that are provided on the attachment of every page opening. Extending the sensory dimension that books have by definition, these lift-the-flap books and paper art books create endless possibilities for author/reader interaction that have to be taken into account in any detailed analysis.

Distinction from other print media with similar characteristics

Despite my rather permissive selection criteria for what counts as a picturebook that is eligible for my corpus, there are types of books that I categorically exclude although they also depend on the interaction of words and images. The books I did not consider for my corpus can, to some extent, be defined by their target audience's different age – but since there can be overlaps I will make this distinction more explicit. On the one side of the spectrum there are books with great emphasis on the sensory dimension, often advertised as 'touchy-feely-books,' that are characterized by elements that invite manipulation (such as wheels, finger-puppets, flaps, mirrors, and so on), and electronic books with buttons that produce sounds. In sound books, vehicles and animals are particularly popular, but very successful original picturebooks, such as *The Gruffalo*, can also be purchased in the form of sound book and other formats. These books are generally aimed at very young children, from as young as newborn to about three to four years, and as the example of *The Gruffalo* suggests, there can be overlaps to the ideal targeted picturebook audience.

On the other side of the spectrum, there are the books written and illustrated for emergent readers. These are more easily distinguished from picturebooks because their focus lies – as one might expect – on language and words that are easy enough to read and yet that, in their combination, create a captivating narrative. Big publishing houses such as HarperCollins or Random House have created their own line for emergent readers, 'I Can Read' and 'Beginner Books' respectively. The age of the targeted audience is also four to eight, but I suspect that, in practice, child readers' average age here is slightly higher than for picturebooks. Theodore Geisel, who is more widely known under his pseudonym Dr. Seuss, played a key role for the establishment of the 'Beginner Books' imprint by creating *The Cat in the Hat* in 1957. From a list of basic vocabulary consisting of 225 words, Theodore Geisel wrote the rhyming narrative of *The Cat in the Hat* (Morgan and

Morgan 1996: 154).[6] Dr. Seuss is, of course, an icon of U.S.-American children's culture and in many respects comparable to Maurice Sendak. I mention him here because he has created many fantasy creatures that are not much unlike the picturebook monsters I examine. For example, Thing One and Thing Two in *The Cat in the Hat* are childlike in their smallness (though actually much smaller than the child protagonists), they wreak havoc in the house (just like children, supposedly) and they epitomize the notion that nonsense is a literary form that is firmly associated with children. Other fantasy creatures, such as the Yop or the Ish in *One Fish, Two Fish, Red Fish, Blue Fish* (1960), are also represented as the child characters' companions and associates. These creatures are not as clearly monstrous as the wild things, for example, but they already incorporate some characteristics common to picturebook monsters, such as cheekiness, irreverence, and a sense of threat. Arguably, Dr. Seuss' most well-known character, the Grinch, does not correspond to this characterization. Although I explicitly distinguish picturebooks from books for emergent readers, Dr. Seuss' books are noteworthy for precisely this juxtaposition of childlike figures and cheeky fantasy creatures.

3.2   Overview of the corpus

In the table underneath, I present all the picturebook titles of my corpus. The numbers in square brackets indicate the thematic group into which I have sorted each title and which I will explain in more detail on the subsequent pages – just as the icons I use here. After some methodological reflections that arise from this

---

[6] According to John Ptak (2008), *The Cat in the Hat* was composed of 236 words. It is interesting to compare the list that Ptak offers with the words in *Where the Wild Things Are* whose small number of words (350) seem simple enough to be featured in that list. But although Sendak's language – to pick out the most well-known example from my corpus – seems strikingly simple, words such as "gnashed," "rumpus," or "mischief" are not exactly standard vocabulary for beginning readers. Thus, picturebooks may be read by children, but they are primarily designed to be read by fluent readers (the implication here is 'adult').

table I will end this section with some thoughts on the implications of quantitative research and my positioning towards this methodological stance.

Year	Title	Author	
963	*Where the Wild Things Are* [d]	Maurice Sendak	♂
1968	*There's A Nightmare in My Closet* [a]	Mercer Mayer	♂/o
1971	*The Monster At the End of This Book* [a]	Jon Stone, Mike Smollin	♂
1981	*Outside Over There* [b]	Maurice Sendak	♀
1983	*The Trouble with Mum* [c]	Babette Cole	a♀
1984	*Not Now, Bernard* [d]	David McKee	♂
1984	*I'm Coming To Get You!* [a]	Tony Ross	♂
1985	*The Very Worst Monster* [b]	Pat Hutchins	♀♂
1985	*Two Monsters* [d]	David McKee	♂
1986	*Princess Smartypants* [b]	Babette Cole	♀
1986	*The Monster Bed* [a]	Jeannie Willis, Susan Varley	♂
1986	*Mr Underbed* [a]	Chris Riddell	♂
1987	*The Trouble with Gran* [c]	Babette Cole	a♀
1988	*The Trouble with Grandad* [c]	Babette Cole	a♂
1989	*The Monster and the Teddy Bear* [a]	David McKee	♀
1989	*Monsters* [c]	Russell Hoban, Quentin Blake	♂
1989	*One Hungry Monster* [a]	Susan O'Keeffe, Lynn Munsinger	♂/c
1990	*Good Night, William* [a]	Allen Baker	♂
1990	*Shrek!* [ ]	William Steig	a♂
1991	*Have You Seen Who's Just ... ?* [c]	Colin McNaughton	nmp
1992	*Go Away, Big Green Monster!* [a]	Ed Emberly	o
1993	*Pat the Beastie* [d]	Henrik Drescher	♂♀
1994	*The Boy Who Ate Around* [d]	Henrik Drescher	♂
1995	*Five Ugly Monsters* [a]	Tedd Arnold	♂/o
1996	*When Mum Turned Into A Monster* [d]	Joanna Harrison	a♀
1996	*The Huge Bag of Worries* [d]	Virginia Ironside, Frank Rodgers	♀
1997	*Sad Monster, Glad Monster* [d]	Ed Emberly, Anne Miranda	nmp
1998	*Imagine That!* [ ]	Jack Prelutsky, Kevin Hawkes	nmp
1998	*Bad Habits!* [d]	Babette Cole	♀
1999	*The Gruffalo* [a]	Julia Donaldson, Axel Scheffler	♂

1999	*My Monster Mama Loves Me So* [d]	Laura Leuck, Mark Buehner	♂/○ a♀
1999	*The Absolutely Awful Alphabet* [ ]	Mordicai Gerstein	nmp
2000	*POG, the Monster Who Was Afraid ...* [a]	Lyn Lee, Kim Gamble	♂
2000	*Hungry! Hungry! Hungry!* [a]	Malachy Doyle, Paul Hess	♂/○
2003	*Beegu* [c]	Alexis Deacon	♀
2004	*The Big Ugly Monster And the Little ...* [c]	Chris Wormell	a♂
2004	*Under the Bed* [a]	Paul Bright, Ben Cort	♂
2004	*Long Live Princess Smartypants* [b]	Babette Cole	♀
2005	*Leonardo, the Terrible Monster* [c]	Mo Willems	♂
2005	*Three Monsters* [c]	David McKee	♂
2006	*G.E.M.* [d]	Jane Clarke, Garry Parsons	♂
2006	*The Monster Health Book* [d]	Edward Miller	♂/○
2006	*Mommy?* [a]	Sendak, Yorinks, Reinhart	♂/○
2006	*The Octonauts* [c]	Vicky Wong, Michael C. Murphy	♂
2007	*Dexter Bexley and the Big Blue Beastie* [a]	Joel Stewart	♂
2008	*The Monster Who Ate Darkness* [a]	Joyce Dunbar, Jimmy Liao	♂
2008	*Night of the Veggie Monster* [d]	George McClements	♂/○
2008	*Goodnight Goon* [a]	Michael Rex	nmp
2009	*Monsters Are...* [ ]	Sarah Gibbs	nmp
2009	*Jeremy Draws A Monster* [a]	Peter McCarty	♂
2009	*I Need My Monster* [a]	Amanda Noll, Howard McWilliam	♂/○
2009	*Anh's Anger* [d]	Gail Silver, Christiane Krömer	♂
2009	*Morris the Mankiest Monster* [c]	Giles Andreae, Sarah McIntyre	♂
2009	*Princess Smartypants Breaks the Rules* [b]	Babette Cole	♀
2010	*Tickle Monster* [a]	Josie Bissett, Kevan J. Atteberry	○
2010	*Monsters – An Owner's Guide* [d]	Jonathan Emmett, Mark Oliver	♀♂/ ○○
2010	*YUCK! That's Not A Monster* [c]	Angela McAllister, Alison Edgson	♂
2010	*Mostly Monsterly* [c]	Tammi Sauer, Scott Magoon	♀
2010	*Monsters Eat Whiny Children* [d]	Bruce Eric Kaplan	♀♂

2011	*The Day Louis Got Eaten* [d]	John Fardell	♀♂
2011	*Monstersaurus* [a]	Claire Freedman, Ben Cort	♂
2011	*Bedtime For Monsters* [a]	Ed Vere	♂
2011	*Steps and Stones* [d]	Gail Silver, Christiane Krömer	♂
2012	*The Monster's Monster* [d]	Patrick McDonnell	♂
2012	*Love Monster* [c]	Rachel Bright	♂

The number coding: thematic patterns

The thematic patterns and their exemplary analysis are the core of this research project. I have designed this table for an immediate visual overview. Every title of my corpus is letter-coded according to the category into which I have sorted it.

[a] Motif "fear of the monster", Chapter 4.1 "The Monster under the Bed"

[b] Motif "strong girls", Chapter 4.2 "Monsters, Marriage, and Maidens

[c] Motif "exclusion/inclusion", Chapter 4.3 "Outsiders: Sissies, Freaks and Foreigners"

[d] Motif "parenting styles", Chapter 4.4 "On Raising Monsters. Errhm: Children."

[ ] Titles that cannot be categorized into any of these four groups.

For preliminary clarification, I will outline the unifying traits of each of these four categories now, although each category constitutes its own chapter in which I discuss some exemplary picture-book texts in detail and in which the characteristics that I consider important will be fleshed out more fully.

The Monster under the Bed. The motif 'fear of monsters' is at the center of these stories. Except for one, all books feature single male child protagonists. Although the initially fearsome monster is not always located under the child protagonist's bed, the story is almost always set in the child's room and often takes place in the evening or at night. In all books, the parents are absent and the male child characters have to deal with their fear on their own, a process through which they mature, lose their fear and learn a set of soft skills that I interpret as useful assets for success in a white male dominated world. Thus the overt pedagogical intention of alleviating (male) children's fear of monsters is interwoven with a hidden agenda of teaching boys the values and behaviors that are necessary to thrive in the dominant culture. The only example for this motif that I was able to dig up that features a female child protagonist transmits the exact opposite message: the parents are present at least at the beginning, only to be replaced by an adult babysitter later on, the female child is shown to be unable to solve the difficult situation on her own, needing the help of a superhero teddy bear who saves her. My analysis of *The Monster and the Teddy Bear* is contrasted with *Hungry! Hungry! Hungry!*, a book that I use as a complex example both to illustrate the pattern for this type of story for male characters – by reading the child protagonist as a boy – and to make visible the effects of reading this same character as an ungendered child in an alternative interpretation. I read both picturebooks in parallel with historical and contemporary receptions of the tale of Little Red Riding Hood whose intertextual presence is particularly explicit in *Hungry! Hungry! Hungry!*. In relation to the very widespread interpretations of *Little Red Riding Hood* as a tale of sexual violence and rape (of a female) my alternative readings of gender of the main protagonist in the picturebook *Hungry!* bear significantly different implications.

Monsters, Marriage and Maidens. In this chapter I focus on Babette Cole's *Princess Smartypants* and Maurice Sendak's *Outside Over There*. Both of these books are the only ones in my corpus whose heroines are unambiguously self-confident and successful in their quests. Two other books, *The Very Worst Monster* or *The Day Louis Got Eaten*, also feature strong girl protagonists. But while Princess Smartypants and Ida in *Outside Over There* are solely accountable for solving their dilemmas, the heroines of these latter examples have to share their success with their younger brothers. Despite Princess Smartypants' and Ida's strong-mindedness and striving for independence, they are both entangled in a net of romantic heterosexuality: both stories interweave the motif 'marriage' into their plots in different yet decisive ways. I treat these two picturebooks as atypical texts within my corpus because of the singular characteristics and social relations of their

116

heroines. In addition, both books rely very strongly on intertextual references to the fairy tale as a genre and to some fairy tales in particular. A closer look at this type of intertextuality is especially productive with regards to the first chapter in which I read the two books in focus with regards to historical and contemporary receptions of the tale of *Little Red Riding Hood*.

Outsiders: Sissies, Freaks and Foreigners. Another prominent motif group focusses on social mechanisms of excluding difference. Here I identified three main types of difference that mark the main characters as outsiders: an appearance perceived by others as ugly, deformed or even disabled; a cultural, ethnical or national background that differs from that of the dominant group; a gender performance that is judged as deviant by the dominant group. Because I wanted to examine if and how these markers correlated with gender I decided to analyze a larger sample of books than in the preceding two chapters and eventually produced thematic clusters that produced numerous links particularly to the first group (fear and social skills for boys) with regards to the connections between the figure of the monster and the construction of masculinity and femininity. In the first cluster (ugliness as monstrosity) all main protagonists whose ugliness prevents their interaction with others are male. Despite the obstacles they encounter on their way, their aesthetical difference is portrayed by the narrative voice as special and ultimately valuable. In the cluster 'foreigners,' the gender bias is perceptible in so far as the only female protagonist, an alien, is also the only one who needs others' (her parents') help to escape the ostracizing and abuse she is confronted with on earth. Leaving gender aspects aside, the picturebooks in this cluster were the least optimistic about the possibility of harmonious cultural/national/ethnic diversity. The third cluster, which I named somewhat incorrectly but nevertheless in reference to Michael Kimmel's four rules of masculinity 'sissies,' at first glance appears to provide the most unexpected outcome in this chapter because gender-disruptive performance is actually encouraged. The male protagonists all succeed because they *adopt* stereotypically feminine behaviors and not because they repel them (as Kimmel's rules would dictate). At a second glance and with a look back at the first group (fear), this outcome is not quite so surprising. It rather contributes to a consolidation of the picturebook monster as a pedagogical aid to construct an ideal of a 'new,' softer kind of masculinity – one which is, however, reserved for boys.

Raising Monsters, errhm: Children. In this last chapter, I look at picturebooks that explicitly focus on the relationships between adult figures – parents in most cases – and child figures. My methodological proceedings here are similar to the previous chapter with respect to the thematic clusters I form around three different concepts of child-rearing and related images of 'the child:' the evil child, the competent child and the child as king. Especially the first and the third image of 'the child' are accompanied by types of humor that make pinning down of the seriousness of these texts somewhat problematic. But even accounting for the irony, sarcasm and carnivalesque humor, I find it striking how much in accordance the portrayal of boys and girls respectively and their relation to monsters are with those of the preceding chapters. Thus Lucretzia in *Bad Habits!* is scared out of her monstrous behaviors by her parents, thus emphasizing the utter incompatibility of girls and monsters. In contrast, Max in *Where the Wild Things Are* can count on monsters for helping him deal with his rage. A yet more pronounced affinity to monsters is displayed by Mo in *The Boy Who Ate Around*, who, in order to avoid eating the dinner provided by his parents, transforms into a series of ever bigger monsters and devours his parents and then the rest of the world.

Of the four books that I did not categorize, three have no unified storyline (one poetry book, one alphabet book, one very simplified, minimalistic version of a compendium/encyclopedia). That does not mean, however, that some of their narrative elements at least allude to the four themes I suggest here. The fourth title that I did not categorize (*Shrek!*) is a witty picturebook parody of chivalric romance that does not easily fit any of my other four groups: *Shrek!* does not portray any child characters nor does it recognizably speak to an implied child audience – quite unlike the extremely successful movie (and its sequels) that is roughly based on this picturebook original. Nevertheless, I use *Shrek!* as well as most other titles in my corpus for cross-references, in order to highlight differences or similarities, and to make overarching patterns more visible.

Icons and abbreviations

♂   The main protagonist is a male child or childlike character. His gender is verbally and visually assigned. This includes books with two or three male main child protagonists.

♀   The main protagonist is a female child or childlike character. Her gender is verbally and visually assigned. There are no books with more than one female main protagonist.

♂♀   There are two main child protagonists, one male and one female. Their genders are verbally and visually assigned.

♂/○   The main child protagonist is visually coded as male, but the verbal narrative does not specify the protagonist's gender which could hence be read as linguistically "ungendered" (ref. Crips and Hiller 2011).

♂♀/   The two main child protagonists are each visually coded as
○○   male and female respectively, but the verbal narrative does not specify their genders, which could hence be read as linguistically "ungendered" (ref. Crips and Hiller 2011).

a   The main protagonist is an adult.

nmp   There are **no** **m**ain **p**rotagonists, the narrative is instead built around various different characters that change from page to page.

Some counting

There are 36[7] books in my corpus in which the main child protagonists are coded as male. The majority of these books have a male human child and a male monster counterpart both of whom have the status of main protagonist, so the exact number of protagonists exceeds the number of book titles. Of these 36, there are ten books in which the main child protagonists are coded as male only visually but not verbally, which leaves 29 books in which the main child protagonists are coded as male both verbally and visually.

---

[7] Due to this subchapter's topic and for better legibility, I use numerals for all numbers greater than twelve.

There are nine books in which the main child protagonists are coded as female both verbally and visually, three of these nine are one and the same protagonist (Princess Smartypants). In contrast to the 36 books with male-coded protagonists many of whom have same gender monster partners or alter egos with equal agency, the female-coded main protagonists only ever appear single.

There are five books with two child protagonists, one coded male, the other female. Both are of similar importance for the development of the story. Although most of these narratives do not explicitly verbalize the type of relationship between these two child characters, I would argue that they are implicitly suggested to be siblings. In four cases, the protagonist pairs are human, in one case it is a monster sibling pair. There are no mixed-gender human/monster pairs.

There are 6 books with main adult protagonists that are explicitly coded as either male or female. If these protagonists are human they are presented as family members that stand in a direct relationship to the child figure which then often acts as the first person narrator and simultaneously as a minor character within the story. If the protagonists are monsters (two books: *Shrek!* and *The Big Ugly Monster and the Little Stone Rabbit*), there are no human child protagonists or narrators in the story. However, one could argue that the implicit reader is constructed as a child reader – although this is difficult for *Shrek!* as I have already suggested. There are more than only these two books in my corpus that have a main monster protagonist who could be read as adult (e.g. *The Monster at the End of this Book* or *Love Monster*). But these last two examples do not exclude the possibility that the monsters be children or childlike characters. For example, the Sesame Street character Grover, hero of *The Monster at the End of this Book*, displays both adult and child characteristics.

The authors' biographical background

Although my focus for this study was clearly not on the authors' personal markers such as gender, race, or nationality, I did undertake some biographical research because I wanted to find out if it was possible to detect correspondences between the biographical information of the authors and the themes of their picturebooks. Before I sketch out my observations underneath I have to put a disclaimer here: my research was based on information published online that boiled down to authors' profiles on the websites of their publishing houses, to their professional homepages if they had one and, in some cases, entries on Wikipedia. I was unable to find biographical information on every single author and illustrator in my corpus so the following observations are to some extent speculative and necessarily incomplete.

There is a noticeable imbalance of male versus female authors and illustrators (48 versus 27). These numbers are not absolute but they seem to express a tendency. I read the authors' and illustrators' first names as an indication of their self-identified gender and referred to publisher's notes whenever their first names were ambiguous (e.g. Mo Willems and Kim Gamble). This is not to suggest that a first name that is considered female automatically makes the person carrying it also a female – or vice versa. I did not find any authors who self-define or are defined by third parties as transsexual, transgender or intersexual. There are more male illustrators than female ones and more male single authors (writer and illustrator in one person) than female ones. This distribution differs somewhat from Crisp and Hiller's statistical counts of 74 Caldecott medal-winning picturebooks between 1938 and 2011 (Crips and Hiller 2011: 201f.), however, it might not be statistically significant. Out of a total of 77 authors and illustrators, Crisp and Hiller found 35 (44%) to be female and 42 (56%) to be male. In my corpus, males constitute 64% versus 36% of females. Further, male writers tend to create male child protagonists while more female writers also create male protagonists. For example, there are only three male authors who have created single heroines (*Outside Over There*, *The Monster and the Teddy Bear*, and *Beegu*), but 14 female authors who have created single heroes. As a consequence, the gender disparity that is already noticeable on the level of the authors themselves grows considerably when transferred to the picturebook characters. I read this as an indication of a (Western) cultural bias towards an association of boys and monsters that is largely independent from the authors' gender.

Considering the whiteness of all except one human main protagonist (Anh in *Anh's Anger* and in *Steps and Stones*) in my corpus, I was interested to what extent this dominant whiteness on the story level is reflected by the authors' and illustrators' racial backgrounds. As far as I could see, there is only one person of color[8] among the 75 authors and illustrators (Vicky Wong – *The Octonauts and the Only Lonely Monster*). Although my observations may well be inaccurate – particularly considering the complex theoretical implications of 'race' as socially constructed and the problematic stance I take when I assign these authors and illustrators a certain 'race' based on their looks (cf. Eggers, Kilomba, et al. 2005; Hill 1997; Delgado and Stefancic 1997) – despite these misgivings from my part, I think that the appearance of whiteness of the large majority of authors and illustrators in my corpus intersects with and influences the overwhelming representation of white and middle-class characters in the picturebook stories.

One last biographical aspect I researched was the authors' nationality or current home country. Most authors live or lived in the USA or in the UK, but some are located in Australia (e.g. Lynn Lee, Kim Gamble) or Canada (Vicky Wong, Michael C. Murphy). Some have biographies of migration, either themselves or their parents having moved continents once or several times in their lives (For example, Maurice Sendak was born to Jewish-Polish immigrants in New York, while many of his extended family members stayed "in the old country" – a phrase often used by Sendak in interviews (e.g. with Bill Moyers) – died during the Holocaust. Henrik Drescher lived in Denmark before his family immigrated to the United States. Russell Hoban was an American expatriate writer based in London). My initial motivation was the question whether there are any noticeable differences or thematic preferences for original U.S. publications and UK publications respectively, but I was unable to find any obvious connections. Whether this is because there are no differences (perhaps due to a culturally unified international English language children's publishing indus-

---

[8] "The term 'People of Color' emerged in reaction to the terms 'non-White' and 'minority.' [...] The term 'People of Color' attempts to counter the condescension implied in the other two." (C. Clark 1999: 17)

try) or because my sample is too limited or for other reasons will have to be left open to speculation.

Editions, publication dates and publishing houses

Throughout this study, I have only provided the original publication dates of the picturebooks and their original publishing houses, although in many cases I have not been able to get hold of these original editions. In the picturebook publishing industry it seems common that subsequent editions – in the relatively rare cases that there are any – are published by other publishers than the original ones. Occasionally the change of publisher implies changes of the title image. Often different editions of the same book are issued in the U.S. and British markets respectively and sometimes the outer appearance of these books can diverge quite drastically. Apart from national idiosyncrasies, the types of divergence between different editions of the same book can lie within format changes or material changes. The more commercially successful a picturebook is the more likely it becomes for it to be published in miniature versions or cardboard versions. Although I believe that all of these material and aesthetic aspects influence a reader's experience and evaluation of a book, for the purpose of this research project I found these differences to be negligible. I based my decision for only referring to the original publication date and publisher on my intention to locate these books both geographically and, more importantly, historically.

Verbal coding and visual coding regarding protagonists' gender

The intricate connections between verbal and visual signs are one of the specific characteristics of picturebooks. But words and images are generally used for conveying different types of information. For example, Scott and Nikolajeva state that "[t]he function of pictures [...] is to describe or represent. The function of words [is] [...] primarily to narrate" (Scott and Nikolajeva 2001: 1). Nevertheless, some aspects are usually over-determined, that is to say they are described both verbally and depicted visually. Gender appears to be one of those aspects. The verbal gender-coding concerns primarily personal pronouns and the use of gender-indicating first names. When the first name is gender-ambiguous, such as Jo-Jo in *The Monster Who Ate Darkness* or Beegu in the book of the same name, this ambiguity is usually dissolved by the unambiguous use of personal pronouns. Many sociologically oriented scholars study the occurrence and frequency of words associated with stereotypically feminine and masculine emotions or other descriptors (e.g. Tepper and Wright Cassidy 1999: 265-280; Turner-Bowker 1996: 461-488), or of occupational role attributes (Trepanier-Street and Romatowski 1999: 155-159), or simply of the number of male and female picturebook characters (Weitzman et al. 1971: 1125-1150; Brugeilles, Cromer, et al. 2002: 237-268). Often, these scholars do not differentiate between verbal and visual signs (somehow assuming that both complement each other), but some explicitly focus on verbal codes, for example by counting certain words. In such an approach, a male personal pronoun is the unambiguous sign for a character's maleness – regardless of this character's possibly ambiguous visual representation.

Visual coding seems more complex because it relies on various stereotypes and conventions of cultural representation and appears more flexible than standardly used pronouns and names. As I have already described in more in chapter 2.2.3, one way of evaluating the visual encoding of gender in more detail is represented by Crisp and Hiller who support the idea that the lack of a verbal gender assignment to a picturebook character should be used to read this character as ungendered, encouraging the use of gender-nonconforming pronouns when talking about this character. The other view is expressed by Samuel Delany's then three-year-old daughter who refuses to accept her dad's insistence upon reading the denim overall-wearing teddy bear Corduroy as a girl bear (Delany 1999: 6f.). Despite her father's previous blotting out of all the male pronouns and his replacing them with the female pronouns, the girl did not buy into his well-meaning attempt at an equal opportunities picturebook reading. Not even his pointing out that she was "wearing the *same* kind of Oshkosh overalls that Corduroy is wearing" and that *she* was, after all, a girl – not even this weighty reference to 'reality' could change his daughter's mind. She insisted: "But Daddy [...] that's a *book*." At the age of three, Delany concludes, his daughter had learnt the meaning of discourse. According to this discourse of children's literature, "pants (in books) meant male" (ibid). Of course, this was 1977 and one might argue that things have changed since then.

One aspect that clearly influences my own take on these two opposing views is that wherever protagonists' genders are assigned verbally (which is the case in most books), their visual representation almost always corresponds with rather stereotypical modes of visual representation. Thus almost *all* the verbally assigned girls have long hair, many wear skirts or dresses or color-coded clothes (predominantly pink and violet) or a combination of these. All the verbally assigned boys have short hair, most wear casual pants, shirts and sneakers (also following color-codes signifying 'boy,' notably any dark colors that are not pink) and many are surrounded by toys or other commodities that emphasize stereotypically masculine characteristics, such as an affinity to technology or sports. Having read a relatively large number of picturebooks in which gender is encoded in this way (as well as simply living in this world at this time and being permanently surrounded by these discursive parameters) obviously also influences my reading of those picturebook characters whose gender is not assigned verbally.

The modes of this visual discourse influence me to such an extent that, until I came across Crisp and Hiller's article, it did not occur to me that the child character in *There's A Nightmare in my Closet* (1968), to name just one example for a character whose gender is not verbally fixed, could be read as anything other than a boy. The story is told by a first person narrative voice representing the child's view. This child figure is seen in a room with a toy soldier, a toy gun and a toy canon. The child has short hair and furthermore wears a soldier's helmet – and romper suit that stands in a disturbing contrast to the belligerent paraphernalia that are a stand-in for adult male (and white) aggression. What the words do not say, the images seem to express two- and threefold: this child is a boy. Or is it? One way of looking at this child is on the grounds of habituated socialization that has taught me to associate weapons, including toy weapons, with soldiers and soldiers with boys and men. This association seems to gain even more impact when the historical context of this picturebook is taken into account: at the time of the book's publication the Vietnam War was escalating and while women have always constituted a large part of the U.S. military workforce (predominantly in medical and clerical roles), the U.S. military's ban on women serving in combat units was only lifted in 2013 and remains controversial (Votava 2013: np). Another way of looking encourages me to discard the hegemony of habituated gender codes for a different kind of knowledge, one that acknowledges, for example, the historical evidence of cross-dressing women in combat throughout world history, and that gives credit to the many possibilities of expressing and experiencing gender in childhood as well as in adulthood, including the play with toy weapons by children of all genders.

There are a few other titles in my corpus whose protagonists' genders are not verbally prescribed (cf. chart above). For example, in *Monsters – An Owner's Guide*, two child figures with absent parents or other adults are alone in a family house when a huge delivery arrives, containing a large monster-robot. One of the children has short blond hair and wears jeans, a green shirt, and sneakers. The other child has long dark hair and a fringe and wears a violet mini skirt with tights and a violet jumper. In addition to these gender-coded representations of appearance, the child with the short hair and jeans recklessly and joyfully engages with the monster-robot, while the child with the long hair and mini-skirt cautiously and skeptically observes the other child and the monster wreaking havoc in the house. In other words, the children's gender is not only encoded through their appearance but also through their behavior and engagement with their environment. It is likely that someone who knows these codes and signs will, like Samuel Delany's daughter, read the active jeans-wearing child with the short hair as a boy and the cautious skirt-wearing child with the long hair as a girl. As Dorothea Löbbermann, who lent me Delany's book, drily commented in an email to me: "Clearly, you can't change the discourse."

I guess that is true. I cannot change the discourse on my own. But on the other hand, the discourses on gender practices and representations have undergone tremendous changes in the past decades, thanks, in part, to queer theorists and activists like Judith Butler, Jack Halberstam, or Kate Bornstein, or thanks to linguistic in(ter)ventions, like epicene pronouns, and their popularization in (some) social spaces. Alternative uses of language or the implementation of a radical refusal of identity politics in everyday life might count as marginal practices and they are perhaps largely futile in terms of "changing the discourse" in any concrete, measurable terms. They might very likely never make it to the center of mainstream culture. Nevertheless, I believe that it is worthwhile, even necessary, to keep playing with these ideas and inventions, for example by suggesting, as Crisp and Hiller do, gendernonconforming ways of reading picturebook protagonists. Their contribution is, in my opinion, extremely important and productive for discussions of reading practices within children's literature criticism, for all the reasons I have outlined in chapter 2.2.3. At the same time, their article can be used to indicate that there is a difference between reading practices and analyzing discourse. While the former cannot take place without knowledge of the latter, proposed reading practices may very well be in opposition to dominant discourses. The challenge of this dissertation is to find a balance between the two, because one of my main concerns for this dissertation is to analyze the mechanisms and grammar of picturebook monsters that, by and large, undeniably function as signifiers for child masculinity. But since these discursive rules work to create such disparities with regard to gender – as well as race, class and ability – I think it is worth undertaking the effort to interpret these texts in a queer readerly way wherever this promises to be productive. I attempt one such alternative interpretation in chapter 4.1, where I discuss *Hungry! Hungry! Hungry!* (Doyle and Hess 2004) and *The Monster and the Teddy Bear* (McKee 1989) as picturebook continuations (not adaptations) of the *Little Red Riding Hood* tale. My intention is to make visible the disparate effects that these two different readings of *Hungry! Hungry! Hungry!* can have.

What is a main protagonist in a picturebook?

The icons I used in the table in order to indicate the main protagonists' assigned gender require a short explanation of how I determined these protagonists to begin with. When picturebooks follow the conventions of a classical narrative, this question is easy to answer: the main protagonist is the figure around whom the story unfolds. Despite the great originality and creativity of picturebook making, most books in my corpus actually meet this criterion of having one single hero or heroine, or, as a variant of this type, having a single hero with a monster alter ego (for example in *Not Now, Bernard* (McKee 1984) and *Jeremy Draws a Monster* (McCarty)). In some books, the number of characters is so drastically reduced that all two or three characters carry equal weight in the story (*Two Monsters* (McKee 2009) and *Three Monsters* (McKee 2005)), usually in an antagonistic way. Because in these cases the characters are all gendered male, only one icon was used for indication. In another group of books there are numerous characters none of whom can be considered a main protagonist. The most obvious cases for this type are books with no story, such as the poetry picturebook *Imagine That!* or Sarah Gibbs' *Monsters Are...* (2009), an enumeration of monstrous characteristics. A more complex example for this type of protagonist-conception is Colin McNaughton's *Have You Seen Who's Just Moved In Next Door to Us?* where a story is told that involves numerous characters and creatures but no main protagonist.

Finally, I want to mention a type of character-creation that is used with remarkable frequency in picturebooks: the narrator's direct address to a 'you.' This 'you,' the implied and the actual reader, can incorporate any gender. There are no occurrences of direct address in which the 'you' is gendered. Usually, the 'you' is not the main protagonist but a slightly antagonistic side character (*Bedtime for Monsters*, *Tickle Monster*) or simply an observer (*The Big Ugly Monster and the Little Stone Rabbit*). In one book, *Go Away, Big Green Monster!*, which are discussed more fully later on, the ungendered monster in this book is consistently addressed as 'you' by a first person narrator who turns out to be the main antagonist *and* implied reader at the same time. The multiple possibilities of interaction between verbal and visual texts enable the conception of various protagonist formations that contribute to the diversity of relations between gender constructions.

Dividing lines between categories

Perhaps needless to say, sorting the picturebooks of my corpus into five distinct categories was a somewhat artificial undertaking; just as categories themselves are, by definition, artificial constructs. In many cases, the dividing lines between those categories are not nearly as distinct as the table I offered above suggests. One could argue, for example, that *Where the Wild Things Are* is a story in which a boy learns to control his fear of his own destructive tendencies. Indeed, the initial encounter between Max and the wild things is visibly fraught with elements of fear (on both sides). However, I based my decision to analyze this book from a perspective of child rearing attitudes on my comparison of *Where the Wild Things Are* with those books I had sorted into the group 'fear of the monster.' Having a relatively large amount of picturebooks to compare enabled me to identify certain patterns, and the pattern of the 'fear of the monster'-books is one of the most distinct: at the beginning, a male child is explicitly afraid of a monster or monsters (the beginning in *Where the Wild Things Are* is already quite different), then this child develops a strategy to deal with the monster on his own (obvious parallels to *Where the Wild Things Are*), and in the end, he has either realized the harmlessness of the monsters (I would argue that this is also different in *Wild Things*) or, in many cases, boy and monster have become friends (this does not apply to *Wild Things* either).

One could also argue that all picturebooks for children are inherently about education and therefore, at least indirectly, about parenting styles. While this is certainly a convincing perspective, some picturebooks build parental figures into their stories as active agents whose action or inaction triggers the narrative, thereby making parenting a dominant and visible theme of the book. For every book, I have based my decision on the degree of their adhering to one of the patterns I have identified as productive for this study.

Selection process

The books I selected into my corpus had to meet three require-ments. Firstly, they had to define as a picturebook as it is defined in chapter 2.1.7. Secondly, the monster figures in them had to be prominent within the narrative. And thirdly, the language of the original publication had to be English. If a picturebook met these criteria, it was entered into my corpus, which now covers a time-span from 1963 to 2012 and comprises sixty-five picturebooks. Although my literature research stretched over several years and despite my inclusive approach I am sure that quite a few publica-tions that would also have met these criteria have escaped my no-tice. Not every picturebook containing monsters declares this con-tent in their title. But the absence of the word 'monster' in the title obviously makes the search so much harder.

Historical patterns

One of my initial intentions for this dissertation was to detect his-torical patterns in the use of monsters in picturebooks. Surely, there had to be some. But whether this was due to the (relatively small) size of the corpus, the (relatively) restricted timespan or the specialized focus on picturebook monsters, I did not detect histori-cal patterns that entertained an obvious tie to representations of monsters and children. One pattern, or rather correspondence, I noticed was that the very few monster picturebooks with inde-pendent-minded, affirmative and resourceful female protagonists are most frequently represented in the 1980s. This may be an effect of growing feminist activism in the book publishing industry as well as in education that declined again in the 1990s and following decades. Furthermore, I noticed an accumulation of inclusion-themed picturebooks about child characters in the last two decades and a virtual absence thereof before the year 2000. (The *Trouble with*... picturebook series by Babette Cole, all published in the 1980s, only features adult family members who are shown to be 'weird' and 'troublesome' for the child narrator.)

Quantification as a research method

My choice of presenting the picturebook titles of my corpus in a table and my counting of certain features of these titles, as discussed on the previous pages, obviously lends some importance to quantification. Although my research focus lies on exemplary and in-depth readings of individual picturebooks, I do think that the numbers I present here are significant insofar as they establish some useful background information. There are two problems about this methodological approach that I want to address here. The first is that quantification appears to be somewhat unusual in literary criticism. The second problem concerns the often inherent claim within quantitative research that it establishes some kind of 'objective' insight into a question.

In defining my own methodological approach, I found Roger Clark's article on the question why there is so much counting in feminist social science research particularly helpful (Clark 2002: 285-295). When Lenore Weitzman and her co-authors published a study in 1972 in which they admonished the extreme imbalance in the representation of male and female picturebook characters, both in numbers and in their attributed roles, this marked the beginning of an avalanche of studies to follow in their footprints. Most of these studies, including Weitzman's, have a liberal feminist impetus, in the sense that they strive for gender equality and equal opportunities for girls and boys. Some adhere more closely to radical difference feminist claims (e.g. boys/men and girls/women are essentially different and, in addition, typically 'feminine' traits can help to overthrow the oppressing system). A third group is identified as "multicultural feminist" by Clark (2002: 287) – a term I find somewhat inept with its focus on 'culture' – and characterized by a strong concern for intersectionality and more emphasis on qualitative research. Quantitative research is conducted both on the basis of content analysis of texts and with experiments. What interested me most in Clark's account were the benefits of this research methodology. Here, Clark contends that quantitative research – in spite of its shortcomings – had a perceivable impact on the children's books publishing industry, as well as on authors, educators and parents by raising awareness to these issues. Clark cites a number of studies that show that "[by] the 1990s [...] prize-winning children's picture books had become much more gender-balanced by Weitzman's standards" (Clark 2002: 290). A slightly self-deprecating passing comment on one of Clark's "obsessions," namely pictures of animals, surprised me: from the late 1960s to the late 1990s, the representation of female animal characters in Caldecott-winning picturebooks went from 1% to 72% (ibid: 288). It surprised me because I had assumed that 'the animal' in picturebooks has many significant overlaps with 'the monster' – for example, both images are associated with ideas of 'wildness,' and a lack of 'civilization' – and that for this reason this image similarly connected to the representation of male childhood as the image of the monster. Apparently, this is not the case (anymore).

One of the benefits of counting, then, is to make changes over time visible as well as to make comparisons between different motifs or themes possible on a larger scale. That possibility of comparing was particularly relevant for my decision to use this approach. Even without a formal training in social science research methods, quantification seems plausible to me in my endeavor to get a feeling for existing thematic patterns in picturebooks with monsters. I use the word 'feeling' here because I did not strive for detailed and accurate statistics, but rather aimed for an impression of general tendencies. It is perhaps needless to say that I consider my description of these tendencies – based on counts as they are – as part of my interpretative agency and not as an indication of some objective 'truth.' As such, my observations are meant to constitute a basic context in which I can situate individual texts and from which I can allow myself to formulate more general hypotheses.

3.3 Analytical concepts for reading picturebooks

Finding focus

Rather than elaborating on the countless concepts that exist for analyzing picturebooks – some of which I have referred to in the first section of this chapter – I am going to use this subchapter to think about these concepts in relation to their relevance for this project. I am here primarily concerned with the methodological (narratological, visual-semiotic) perspective from which I will examine the picturebooks in the following four chapters. Which analytical frameworks promise to be most productive for exploring my principal research questions? For the sake of simplicity I phrase these research questions, for the moment, as follows: How is the child protagonist constructed in relation to the monster protagonist? And what does this say about contemporary Western images of 'the child'?

The first, rather obvious, realization that I have to keep in mind with these questions is that the picturebook stories do not exist on their own. As obvious as this statement might be, it directs my attention towards the two sides that endow the story with meaning in the first place: the authors (illustrators and writers) and the readers. Needless to say, the meanings that authors and readers invest in these stories can diverge substantially from one another. In addition, while the authors of a picturebook usually consist of only one or two persons, the readers must be multiplied by thousands, and sometimes millions. Furthermore, the readership of picturebooks is extremely diverse in terms of age: as part of its aesthetic, conceptual and consumer-oriented make-up, the picturebook narrative addresses a dual audience that consists of child and adult receivers. Even within these two generalizing terms, 'child' and 'adult,' individuals' ages differ enormously, as well as other individual markers that social reality is composed of, including gender, educational biography, economic resources, race, class, and geographical location. All of these factors allow for almost infinite ways of meaning-making so that, theoretically, there could be as many differing views on the nature of represented child-monster relationships and related images of 'the child' as there are readers.

Initially I considered conducting reading sessions with primary school children to find out what sense actual children make of some of the monster picturebooks. There are many recent studies that focus on children's understanding of picturebooks – although none are limited to picturebooks with monsters, of course. Thus, Lawrence Sipe conducted several studies with young children to investigate, among many other things, to what extent they had a concept of 'narrative' (Sipe 2007). Coosje van der Pol pursues a similar direction when she asks what constitutes 'literary competence' for children in kindergarten and elementary school (van der Pol 2012: 93-106). Visual, rather than verbal, reading competences are also frequently, if not more so, the focus of studies with young children (e.g. Arzipe and Styles 2003; Sipe 2008b: 381-392). Other scholars focus on abstract concepts that are imbued with ideological weight, such as gender or race, in their reading/interview sessions with children, and sometimes parents, too (e.g. Toomey 2009; McNair 2013: 191-207). What these studies appear to have in common is that they are first and foremost motivated by questions concerning the practices of education: How can teachers make literature for children more accessible? How can educators sensitively approach racial and gender content in stories? What cognitive requirements are necessary for making sense of picturebook stories? What can be expected from children at different stages of their cognitive and emotional development?

Although there are some overlaps, my own research concern is much less situated in the fields of education or social science. Nevertheless, one of the questions that seem to be vital and that I share with the studies above is of course, how do children understand these stories? For, in order to keep an image of 'the child' alive, it seems, actual children must to some extent respond to or enact this vision. This might well be the case, but I think that, ultimately, adults that play a central part in children's lives can and do impart the often concealed messages all the time, in their everyday interactions with children, and not only when they read picturebooks with them. In this respect, picturebooks are only one (fictitious) location where these dynamics that pervade adult-child relationships can be made visible. And while they would not exist without actual children, these dynamics can be critically and productively examined without consulting actual children.

One way of doing this that explicitly acknowledges the importance of children in the construction of childhood images without, however, collecting empirical 'data,' is a more theoretical reader-response criticism as it was established by Wolfgang Iser (e.g. Iser 1974 and 1980). The invention of the category of the 'implied reader,' who is constructed by and resides within the text, puts the researcher's focus on this very text, rather than on readers' responses. I pursued this theoretical reader-response approach for quite some time, convinced that it was possible to distinguish clearly between implied adult and implied child readers, by taking cues from specific drawing styles, particular types of humor that depended on different amounts of knowledge or levels of cognition, or different styles of address within the same book. I tried to reveal that "mystery" that surrounds the question, "who is the implied child reader inscribed in the text?" (Benton 2005: 86). But I was dissatisfied with my answers because they were based on my assumptions on what children know and what intellectual capacities they have. Furthermore, implying that 'children' are a general, homogeneous group, of course, directly contradicts my conviction that meaning is made by individuals and that, consequently, there can never be one single valid way of reading and understanding a text. Even instituting the theoretical category of the implied child reader and basing a reader-response approach on the text alone is ultimately always speculative.

Because of these and other, more pragmatic, considerations, I eventually focused on my own subjective meaning-making of picturebooks with monsters. I consider this a reader-response criticism insofar as I am that reader who responds to the ways that writers and illustrators 'make' boys, girls and monsters in these stories. Whenever I speak of 'the child' it is either as a concept, indicated by the inverted commas, or as the protagonist of a picturebook story. Because I do not want to make assumptions about implied readers, let alone real ones, I have decided to present my interpretations clearly as what they are: my own readings that work in an intimate dialogue with the picturebook texts. This dialog is fuelled by questions such as: Who, in the story, sees or perceives the fictional world? Who is represented as having any agency in the construction of the story or the establishment and designing of contact with other protagonists? And does the narrative incorporate any devices that establish a direct contact with me, the reader, or that explicitly refer to the authors? I consider my task here in suggesting plausible ways that make sense of the figure of the monster in picturebooks. By situating my individual discussions in the broader context of other, similar picturebooks, by presenting thematic patterns, and by reading these stories in a consistent analytical framework, I hope that my interpretations become compelling arguments that are not only relevant for the image of 'boys' and 'girls' in picturebooks with monsters, but provide helpful starting points for discussing constructions of gender and 'the child' in children's culture at large.

In the remaining part of this subchapter, I will present two analytical concepts with regards to their importance for attributing sense – in the two-directional manner that I have discussed above – of the picturebooks in the following chapters. The first concept I will discuss is focalization. Broadly speaking, focalization gives insight about the narrative situation. It also puts attention to the fact that stories are always fabricated by someone (cf. Baker 1981: 156) or, as is often the case in picturebooks, by several people. The second concept is actually an amalgam of two concepts, but both create similar effects: the direct address of the reader through the personal pronoun 'you' and the so-called demand-picture that consists of a represented figure whose gaze meets the reader's eyes (Kress and van Leeuwen 2010: 118).

Focalization

The term 'focalization' was coined by French narratologist Gérard Genette and as such it is firmly rooted within verbal language/literature. Focalization is primarily defined by the extent to which the information given by the narrator is limited. Initially, Genette defined the term by the question 'what does the narrator perceive?' but in a later recapitulation he changed this question into 'what can the reader know?' (Jesch and Stein 2009: 60). Genette identified three basic ways in which this limitation of knowledge can take place: internal, external and zero focalization. Internal focalization is achieved through the presentation of information through the perception of a character, usually with a heterodiegetic narrator, who talks about the protagonists in the third person and may or may not refer to him- or herself in the first person, or a homodiegetic narrator, who writes from a first person perspective – in picturebooks almost always the perspective of the child protagonist. This is by far the most common type of focalization in picturebooks, including those in my corpus. External focalization is achieved through a narrator who knows (or pretends to know) nothing about any of the characters' thoughts, feelings and perceptions. In my corpus, only one author uses external focalization (*Not Now, Bernard* 1984, McKee). Finally, a narrative with zero focalization provides information of all characters' perceptions. This type of focalization seems to be equally rare as external focalization. To the extent that *Sad Monster, Glad Monster* can be considered a continuous story, featuring six different protagonists who each represent one emotion, its narrative would be zero focalized. The categorization of narrative models harbors many practical and theoretical differentiations, problems, contradictions, questions, and insufficiencies (cf. Strasen 2004: 111–140), and there are better places to discuss them than this dissertation.

What I find interesting about focalization in picturebooks is, firstly, that the narrative situation is usually much less straightforward than one might expect from these stories for young children, and secondly, that this concept calls attention to the fact that there is always a narrator even if this narrator is not made verbally explicit. Although the latter observation is true for a large part of fiction for grown-ups, it bears particular repercussions on the intentional or conventional concealment of adults in children's literature in general. One of Nodelman's (and others') central claims is that children's literature is defined like no other literature by its target audience, children, and at the same time produced by people who try to make their role in this process invisible (Nodelman 2008).

But what makes focalization really intriguing as an analytical concept for picturebooks is that the information is not only given through words but through images, too. One reason why Genette introduced the term was because he wanted to depart from the visual connotations of the concept 'perspective' that Stanzel had made popular in narratology (Jesch and Stein 2009: 60). I think Genette's attempt is counteracted by the connections of the word 'focalization' with optical concepts, but of course this does not automatically make focalization an apt analytical concept for interpreting images. The most essential requirement for using focalization in visual semiotics is to attribute images a narrative function. While picturebook scholars Carol Scott and Maria Nikolajeva explicitly deny pictures this function (Scott and Nikolajeva 2001: 1), visual semioticians Gunther Kress and Theo van Leeuwen argue that images are narrative whenever they represent participants that are connected by a vector because this connection represents action, or, in their words, "the participants are doing something together" (Kress and van Leeuwen 2010: 59). A participant is any visual representation of an object, person, or idea – and "vectors are formed by depicted elements that form an oblique line, often a quite strong, diagonal line [...] The vectors may be formed by bodies or limbs or tools 'in action,' but there are many other ways to turn represented elements into diagonal lines of action." (ibid). The important idea here is that, according to these two authors, images with vectors connecting participants always constitute a narrative.

There used to be a nightmare in my closet.

Fig. 5   *There's A Nightmare In My Closet* (Mayer 1969)

To make this idea more concrete, here is an example: the first page opening of Mercer Mayer's *There's A Nightmare in My Closet* (1969) shows the reader a – presumably male – child in his bed (fig. 5). His room spreads over the entire two pages and contains so many "participants," to use the term I have just introduced, that their description alone could fill the pages of a book. Here, I want to concentrate on one particularly dominant vector that connects the closet door, which is slightly ajar, with the boy's gaze, his toy armory that is also pointing towards the closet door, and the curtains which are blown towards that same door by a night wind through the open window that is right next to the boy's bed where he has set up camp. Thus, even without the words, the central narrative is already established through the tension between the boy and whoever or whatever is lurking in that closet. The verbal narrative consists of a single, short sentence: "There used to be a nightmare in my closet." There are two important things that these words tell the reader that the picture cannot. The first is that the story happened in the past. The reader can assume that the nightmare is no longer in the closet. The second aspect concerns the internal focalization through the child character with the first person pronoun. While the knowledge that the nightmare is over might bring a sense of relief, the internal focalization achieves the opposite: it compels the reader to re-experience the story through the boy's senses.

This example illustrates how pictures and words complete each other, but also how the pictures can enhance the type of focalization used for the verbal narrative. There are, however, many other examples that are more complicated and complex. Here, information is not only given via two different sign systems, but in addition that information is often contradictory, especially with respect to the stricter definition of 'focalization' as an exclusively verbal concept. Thus, if internal focalization, which is, as I have stated above, by far the most frequently used in picturebook stories, was translated into the visual semiotic system, the represented world would have to show only what the focalized protagonist sees, but not the protagonist eirself. While this device is occasionally used in film and in comics I have never seen it in a picturebook. Nevertheless, I do not think that this means that the visual narrative is always externally focalized, but rather that focalization works differently on the visual level and can, perhaps, not usefully be divided into the three categories proposed by Genette. Obviously, the visual information in a picturebook is limited in some respects just as the verbal information of the story. The images are an imitation of reality just as the words. And just as the verbal narrative provides information within very specific limits, so does the visual narrative represent only partial information that is further formed by stylistic and intertextual components.

An example where words and pictures provide contradictory information is Henrik Drescher's *The Boy Who Ate Around* (1993). The first opening shows a figure that the verbal narrative designates as "a boy named Mo" (Drescher 1993: np). The picture shows a clownish child figure sitting at a table, bent over a plate with a frog's head and something that looks like long, stripy worms. The verbal narrative informs the reader that these are "actually, string beans and cheese soufflé" (ibid). As a reader I might ask: who is right? Words or pictures? Nikolajeva and Scott condense the potential contradictions and tensions that arise from the coexistence and co-dependence of words and images into the question: "Whose picturebook is it?" (Nikolajeva and Scott 2006: 21)

140

And of course the answer could be "both the words' and the images', because one cannot fully be understood without the other." On the other hand, one could argue as Elizabeth Parsons does, claiming that "narratological focalization is deconstructed in picturebooks" (Parsons 2004: 9) precisely because images have a different narratological setup.

Although internal focalization, especially from a first person narrator, is never realistically mirrored through the images, I would argue that many picturebooks nevertheless achieve a similar effect – namely by making monsters appear only in the presence of the child character from whose point of view the story is told. Almost all of the titles of the first group about the fear of monsters correspond to this pattern. If the monsters can only be seen in conjunction with the represented child figure, but not when others (grown-ups) are present, this clearly suggests a form of internal focalization. In sum, I consider focalization a vital concept that reminds me of the fact that there is a maker behind the words *and* behind the images and that this maker decided to represent the characters and the story in a certain way that is never just neutral information, but rather an extract that includes some elements and puts its emphasis on even fewer of these elements. The "interactive participants" (Kress and van Leeuwen 2010: 114) who sit on both ends of the communication process, i.e. the writer and illustrator on the one side and the reader/viewer on the other side, have many possibilities of making sense of the story. And these possibilities are to a large extent guided by principles of focalization that make some interpretations more relevant or plausible than others.

Direct address and demand pictures

Both words and images can address a receiver more directly than focalization. If the verbal narrator uses a second person pronoun, this 'you' has a deictic quality that explicitly acknowledges and thereby includes the reader/listener into the story. Images can achieve a very similar effect through the representation of a participant who looks directly into the viewer's eyes. Both the verbal and the visual 'you' are strikingly frequent devices in the picturebooks of my corpus. Despite their basic similarity they can have quite different effects. In order to illustrate what the difference of verbal and visual direct address can be, I will first turn toward the concept of the demand picture and then discuss the use of the direct personal address through words. Kress and van Leeuwen, who have established the visual concept, explain the mechanisms of 'demand pictures' as follows.

> This visual configuration has two related functions. In the first place it creates a visual form of direct address. It acknowledges the viewers explicitly, addressing them with a visual 'you'. In the second place it constitutes an 'image act'. The producer uses the image to do something to the viewer. It is for this reason that we have called this kind of image a 'demand', following Halliday (1985): the participant's gaze (and the gesture, if present) demands something from the viewer, demands that the viewer enter into some kind of imaginary relation with him or her. (Kress and van Leeuwen 1996: 118)

In some sense, demand pictures represent a special case because the by far more frequent mode is the offer picture where "the viewer's role is that of an invisible onlooker" (ibid) and the represented participants are "the object of the viewer's dispassionate scrutiny" (ibid). Demand-pictures have their roots in devotional images from the thirteenth century (Belting 1990: 57, qt. in Kress and van Leeuwen 1996: 118) and in self-portraiture from the fifteenth-century (Panofsky 1953: 198, qt. in ibid.). However, when images are primarily narrative, as in comics, films or picturebooks, demand-pictures are very rare and, at least in comics and films, actually break with the conventions of the genre. When an actor, who plays a character in the story, suddenly looks and talks into the camera, most viewers will notice this as something unusual or even disruptive. One example for this is Woody Allen's *Whatever Works* (2009), where the lead character Boris Yelnikoff repeatedly breaks the conventional cinematic narrative mode by looking directly into the camera and explaining details of the story to the audience. In contrast to film and even comics or graphic novels, picturebooks use demand poses much more frequently. But as in film, these poses are used as a kind of special effect, an extra effort at capturing the viewer's attention. The most frequent places in the picturebook story where demand pictures occur are the title page, the first page opening and the final page opening, i.e. either the beginning or the end of the story. As Kress and van Leeuwen claim, a demand picture at the beginning visually invites me to make contact with the participant from whom the gaze originates and to follow them through the story, while a demand pose at the end of a story tends to request from viewers to position themselves in relation to the story that has just been told.

But in addition to Kress and van Leeuwen, an analysis of and a comparison between several picturebooks reveal some astounding commonalities, especially when I compare books written by the same person. For example, David McKee's *The Monster and the Teddy Bear* (1989) and *Not Now, Bernard* (1984) both feature a monster character in a demand pose: in *The Monster and the Teddy Bear* this pose occurs on the half-title page, that is, before the story has even started. Significantly, the girl character's gaze is always averted from the viewers. At the end of this story, the monster is defeated and gone. In *Not Now, Bernard*, the monster – who has devoured and incorporated Bernard – looks sadly into the viewers' eyes on the very last page opening, while sitting in Bernard's bed with a mug of milk in his paws, apparently unable to believe that Bernard's parents have still not realized that a monster has taken his place. Although the monster is shown to be helpless, he engages the viewers' opinion and their sense of justice. The monster is visibly aghast, but his imaginary demand nevertheless turns him into an active agent. Another example is Princess Smartypants who, on the last page, triumphantly grins at the readers who have just witnessed how she has put even her most ardent suitor to flight so that now she can remain unwed as was her wish in the first place. In contrast, *Bad Habits!* (2004), also by Babette Cole, begins with the female main character, Lucretzia Crum, angrily staring out of the first page. Here, a girl is established as active and in control at the beginning. The end of this book creates an extreme contrast with Lucretzia's face in profile and with her eyes closed: in combination with the knowledge of Lucretzia's 'civilization process,' her offer pose at the end suggests that she is now entirely dominated by others. Many other picturebook titles exhibit a comparable pattern. Thus, although a demand picture *generally* implies an active agency of the represented participant, in picturebooks this tends to apply to demand pictures at the end (and sometimes in the middle) more than it does at the beginning of the story.

Now, the visual 'you' almost always originates from the main character – most often a child. In contrast, the verbal 'you' is most often used by a heterodiegetic narrator who represents the voice of an adult. Whereas in fiction for grown-ups the direct address of the reader is extremely rare, in picturebooks this is a widespread feature. The implication of the 'you' in picturebooks is that it addresses a child reader/listener. In contrast to the demand picture, the verbal 'you' builds on to a power hierarchy that consists primarily in different levels of knowledge and experience. More explicitly than images, the verbal 'you' is often accompanied by commands and questions, as in the following example:

> This is the cave. And in this picture the monster is just about to come out. So be careful when you turn the page. [Page turn.] There he is. Pretty ugly, eh? (Just look at those nostril hairs!) Of course this is only a picture, so you're not getting the whole effect. You're not getting the ugliness at full strength. It was pretty powerful. (Wormell 2004: np)

Addressing child readers in this way is a widely accepted and conventional practice in children's literature. The reader who follows the narrator's guidance in turning the page is confronted with a staring, glaring, and indeed ugly, monster whose face seems to burst out of the boundaries of the double spread. In this example, the "you" addressed by the narrator is aimed at stirring up recognition and even identification in the child who reads or is being read to. Interestingly, in this example the visually represented monster could also be said to constitute a demand picture since at least one of his eyes establishes a vector with the viewer's gaze – the other eye goes in a slightly different direction. At the same time as I acknowledge that a direct address, both visual and verbal, potentially achieves identification or at least a connection with the originator of that address, I realize that the narrator here is not identical with the monster. In fact, the monster's demand gaze does not evoke the viewer's recognition or identification at all but rather shock, horror and perhaps disgust. As with verbal language, the meaning of a certain sign is always contextual. And here, the monster's bulging eyes are set in a warty, gristly and angry face with

144

giant hairy nostrils, crooked teeth and one protruding fang. Despite the monster's repellent appearance his gaze is equally engaging as the narrator's "you." But both suggest very different subject positions and affect the reader/viewer in a different way. While the verbal narrator urges the reader to agree that this monster is incredibly ugly, thereby objectifying and ridiculing the monster at the same time, the monster also actively expresses his agency and potentially causes a moral dilemma that questions the justification of the narrator's patronizing and discriminating attitude.

Conclusion

Focalization as well as the direct address through a visual or verbal 'you' are only two out of many possible concepts that can help to understand the interaction between words and images in picturebooks. I have chosen these two because they make explicit that the text is never there on its own. It needs a creator and it needs a receiver. In addition, the text must present an overlap of shared cultural knowledge of the two sides of this communication model. In this model, the creators as persons are entirely negligible; their interpretational relevance is limited to the text, as it were. And so my approach to analyzing picturebooks can perhaps be most aptly described as a position that Rosenblatt developed. According to her, reading occurs as "a transaction, a two way process involving a reader and a text at a particular time, under particular circumstances" (Rosenblatt 1982: 268; qt. in Brooks and Browne 2012: 77). Although this position allows the reader to pursue many different strategies of meaning-making, these strategies must refer to the text which works with a set of rules and systems. One of my concerns here was to suggest that images, as part of the picturebook text, work with a certain grammar just like sentences. Images are not, as Roland Barthes claimed in an essay in 1964 a "floating chain of signifieds" and too "polysemous" (Barthes 1977: 32-51; qt. in Kress and van Leeuwen 2010: 18) to make definite sense without words. Although a picturebook page is only complete when image and words are read and understood together, my exemplary discussions have shown that images not only have a distinct narrative quality that often privilege one character's point of view, but also that they can directly evoke a viewer and compel this viewer to take on a certain position toward the represented participant.

4   Picturebook Analyses

4.1   The monster under the bed

What 'Little Red Riding Hood' has to do with soft skills for boys and some effects of ungendering 'the child' in this narrative

Introduction

Roughly one third of the picturebooks in my corpus tell the story of a child who is afraid of monsters. Because of this motif's dominance and because of its enmeshment with the construction of gender in picturebooks, I start the analytical part of this dissertation with this theme. The fear of monsters in most of these books bears strong relations to and many similarities with other, monster-less picturebooks about bedtime. Children's literature scholars so far have approached bedtime narratives in picturebooks from the perspectives of attachment theory (Galbraith 1999: 172–180), of power-theoretical frameworks (Stallcup 2002: 125–158), or of transnational and cross-cultural considerations (Chou 2009: 19–32). Despite their different foci, all three authors have drawn my attention to two aspects that are also relevant for the books I examine in this chapter. The first is that the overt pedagogical motivation of these books is to relieve children's fear of sleeping alone, as opposed to sleeping in the same room or same bed as the parent(s). All authors seem to agree more or less explicitly that picturebooks about bedtime, and particularly those that address children's fears, are actually counterproductive to their pedagogical intentions. The second aspect concerns the cultural, ethnical and class specificity of these bedtime narratives: they transport Western, predominantly white and middle-class ideas about how and where a child should sleep (alone, in her own bed) and, implicitly, about the need of bedtime rituals (such as parents reading a picturebook about bedtime to their child). However, one observation that is missing from these accounts is that the child protagonist's gender always influences the development of the story and, even more distinctly, the nature of the feared object. Nowhere can this be seen more impressively than in picturebooks about the fear of monster.

When I began looking at the picturebooks within this thematic group I was struck by an enormous gender imbalance: out of twenty-two books with this motif, eighteen feature male main protagonists, three have ungendered or no main protagonists, and only

148

one tells the story of a girl's fear of a monster. Supported with these statistical data, I formed the idea that picturebooks about the fear of monsters contribute more significantly to images of child masculinity than perhaps the books in my other thematic groups. This idea further consolidated when I noticed that despite occasionally great individual differences the stories about boys' fear of monsters by and large follow a distinct pattern: a male human child protagonist is by himself and afraid of monsters, once alone he encounters an actual monster and works out – by himself – that either the monster is no threat or/and makes a good friend of that monster. Sometimes, this dynamic is reverted so that a male monster child is scared of humans, but the mechanisms of resolution are essentially the same. Although the overt pedagogical motivation of these books is to alleviate child readers' fear of monsters, another lesson can be found underneath: boys who acquire a set of values and soft skills, such as generosity, wit, and empathy, are better equipped to integrate themselves successfully into unknown and perhaps initially threatening social situations.

This story pattern appeared to me even more gender-specific when I included the only story with a female main protagonist into my analysis because it presents such an extreme contrast to the texts with male protagonists in this group. In David McKee's *The Monster and the Teddy Bear* (1989), Angela, although initially bold enough to demand a monster as toy and playmate, learns not only that she had better be afraid of monsters but also that she is utterly dependent on the help of a male rescuer, namely Teddy Bear, for defeating the vile monster. As outdated and appalling as the gender representations in this story may seem, the character constellation of male perpetrator, female victim and male savior is a well-established one in the history of Western literature and beyond. One particularly well-known story in the West that helps keep this narrative alive is *Little Red Riding Hood*, especially the Grimms' text and all subsequent versions that are based on it. The connection between picturebooks about the fear of monsters and this popular fairy tale became all the more imposing when I considered *Hungry! Hungry! Hungry!* (Doyle and Hess 2004) which playfully uses and adapts the famous dialogue between the Wolf, disguised as Grandmother, and Little Red. My first impulse was to read the child in *Hungry! Hungry! Hungry!* as a boy and the story as a whole as representative for picturebook stories about boys who master their fears through the acquisition of useful social skills and habits. In this reading, the circumstance that the child is male would explain why the authors have opted for a peaceful reconciliation between boy and monster rather than for a contemporary version of the violent, scary ending of Grimms' fairy tale, as it can be seen in *The Monster and the Teddy Bear*. The authors simply followed the rules of children's books discourse in which male children learn to be independent, resourceful and active, while female children learn to be dependent, fearful and helpless.

However, after a few months' consideration, further research, and the completion of several drafts for this chapter that examined the mechanisms of this gender discourse, I recognized the possibility of reading the protagonists in *Hungry! Hungry! Hungry!* as ungendered: through the exclusive use of dialogue and the omission of a third person narrative, the protagonists' genders are not verbally fixed. In other words, the verbal text provides a gap that I decided to use for a queer reading of the same text. But rather than erasing one interpretation in favor of the other (thereby keeping up the established pretense of having written the truest and most valid of all interpretations), I here offer two alternative readings of this picturebook: one which makes visible cultural ideals of boyhood as opposed to girlhood, both seen as narrative constructs, and another one which not only draws attention to the workings of hegemonic masculinity but which actively seeks to disrupt it.

In order to illustrate the deep impact that *Little Red Riding Hood* continues to have on the production of literature, including children's picturebooks generally and the two picturebooks I discuss here specifically, I proceed chronologically, beginning this chapter with a cursory overview of the history and reception of this fairy tale before discussing in detail *The Monster and the Teddy Bear* (1989) and then offering my two readings of *Hungry! Hungry! Hungry!* (2004).

"Oh! grandmother," she said, "what big ears you have!"
"The better to hear you with, my child," was the reply.
"But, grandmother, what big eyes you have!" she said.
"The better to see you with, my dear."
"But, grandmother, what large hands you have!"
"The better to hug you with."
"Oh! but, grandmother, what a terrible big mouth you have!"
"The better to eat you with!"
(Grimm, *Little Red Riding Hood*)

In English speaking countries, popular receptions of this tale go back to the Grimm brothers' versions (the first being published in 1812) and, to a lesser extent, to Charles Perrault's version from 1698 in his *Histoires ou contes du temps passé, avec des moralités*. Both texts were announced, by their authors, as recordings of 'the essence' of various circulating oral versions of a folktale that was widely known under the name "The Story of Grandmother," but in fact, neither of these texts fulfilled its pretended truthfulness to the oral 'originals.' Perrault had censored his version a great deal in order to make it suitable to the late seventeenth century morality of the French Court. He applied his censorship specifically to excretory parts and most of the violence, more particularly the cannibalism, which recorded oral versions of the tale retained. Most significantly, however, Perrault erased the girl's agency. Folklorist Alan Dundes goes as far as to describe the two most well-known versions by the Grimms and Perrault as "atypical […] in comparison with the original folktale from which they surely derive" (Dundes 1989: 13). He refers to folktale specialist Paul Delarue's amassing thirty-five oral versions of the tale from which an "idea of what the original tale was like" (ibid) may be derived. In this "original", the Wolf kills the Grandmother, puts some of her flesh in the pantry, some of her blood in a bottle on a shelf, and prompts the girl to eat and drink of both before asking her to undress and lie beside him in the bed. The girl, however, after critically examining the Wolf in disguise, cunningly claims she needs to relieve herself outside (Delarue, qt. in Dundes 1989: 15 f.). The Wolf ties a rope around her leg, but the girl is smart, ties this rope around a tree and goes home. Although Perrault did preserve the sexual content of the tale, he wrote out the girl's autonomy and independence. Perhaps needless to say, in contemporary versions for children, little or nothing of the sexual aspects has survived. Already the Grimms had disguised and blotted out all sexual allusions to such an extent – and continued to "[eliminate] those passages which they thought would be harmful to children's eyes" (Zipes 1993: 48) – that I suppose it is easy for most readers (particularly for those with children as listening embodiments of innocence in mind) to ignore them. Nevertheless, the abundant history of critical receptions of *Little Red Riding Hood* testifies to the topic of sexuality as a continuing field of relevance.

Psychoanalytical and feminist readings respectively may have shaped academic ideas of the tale most lastingly, albeit in very different ways. Psychoanalysts Bruno Bettelheim and Géza Róheim, for example, read all three main figures of the tale (Little Red, the Grandmother, and the Wolf) as stages of one individual's psychosexual development, focusing on infantile oral fixation (Róheim 1989: 159-167), or on adolescent genital fixation (Bettelheim 1989: 168-191). Questions of gender do not occur in these influential psychoanalytical readings. In fact, Bettelheim blatantly ignores questions of gender difference by consistently referring to "the child" with male pronouns as well as ascribing to fairy tales the capacity "to state an existential dilemma briefly and pointedly. This permits *the child* to come to grips with the problem in its most essential form" (Bettelheim 1976: 8; my emphasis).

Feminist readings, in contrast, derive all their potency from attributing gender a decisive influence in the formation of fairy tale types, characters and plots. Simply reading these tales as stories about sexual initiations or rites of passage, as psychoanalysts Bettelheim and Róheim do, ignores the tales' reflection of these experiences in a sexually stereotyped manner (Stone 1985: 127), "where boys are shown as active, clever, resourceful, and courageous, and girls as passive, pretty, dependent, long-suffering, and self-sacrificing" (Stephens and McCallum 1998: 204). Stephens and McCallum, alongside many other scholars, describe and unmask the persistent pattern of female passivity in the written tradi-

152

tion of fairy tales. In the case of *Little Red Riding Hood*, this tradition clearly overrules the courage and cunning of the girl in the original tale, as recorded by Paul Delarue, as well as in its Chinese variant *Grandaunt Tiger*, as documented by Wolfram Eberhard (1989: 21-63). Jack Zipes affirms that

> [i]t is impossible to exaggerate the impact and importance of the Little Red Riding Hood syndrome as a dominant cultural pattern in Western societies. In this regard, I want to stress that in her two most popular literary forms, which have fully captured the mass-mediated common imagination of our own day, Little Red Riding Hood is a male creation and projection. Not women but men – Perrault and the brothers Grimm – gave birth to our common image of Little Red Riding Hood. (Zipes 1989: 126).

In Perrault's version, which ends with Little Red being swallowed by the Wolf and a conclusive moral, this image dictates that order, discipline and chasteness will keep young girls, "especially attractive, well-bred young ladies" (Perrault) safe from "strangers" (ibid), particularly from "the gentle wolves who are the most dangerous of all" (ibid). In addition to creating an image of the female as a sexual victim, Perrault contributed enormously to the idea of (pretty) women as being helpless and naïve, and ultimately stupid. In the Grimms' version, the authority of the state, represented by the policeman figure of the huntsman, ensures the girl's repentance for her pleasure-driven individualism (Zipes 1989: 125). In both versions, Little Red's femininity is ensured by her lacking agency which is framed by active and powerful males. Feminist interpretations of the tale unanimously see the Wolf's devouring of the girl as rape (Zipes: ibid; Brownmiller 1985: 309 f.; Orenstein 2003). It is a commonplace that images of consumption often serve as metaphors for sexual intercourse, and in relation to the *hungry* monsters in the picturebooks this notion is important to keep in mind.

Before moving on to the two picturebooks, I want to emphasize two points that the preceding discussion has brought forward. The first is that Little Red's selfhood is defined against and dependent on the male protagonists. The second point derives from the first and concerns the tale's need for the girl to be saved by a man, rather than allowing her to save herself, as it was the case in the oral versions recorded by Delarue. If the tale describes a rite of

Fig. 6   *Little Red Riding Hood* (Schart Hyman 1986)

passage, it teaches Little Red the following: in order to be a (good) girl she must keep away from (bad) male (hetero-) sexuality as well as from her own sexuality until marriage and if she is ever in trouble she must perform her femininity according to sexual stereotypes and hope for a (good) male to come and save her.

'The Monster and the Teddy Bear'

Fairy tales are an inspiration for many picturebook authors, some of whose works have been critically acclaimed for their uncanny take on one specific tale (Anthony Browne's *Hansel and Gretel* 1981), or for their post-modern nonsense humor (Jon Scieszka and

Lane Smith's *The Stinky Cheeseman and Other Fairly Stupid Tales* 1992), or for their ingenious mix of genres (Janet and Allen Ahlberg *The Jolly Postman and Other People's Letters* 1986), or for their irreverent reversal of gender roles (Babette Cole *Princess Smartypants* 1986, *Prince Cinders* 1987). Children's literature scholar Elizabeth Marshall observes that "[t]he Anglo-American fairy tale canon often appears in elementary reading curricula in the form of children's picture books and represents one set of materials in a larger pedagogical tradition aimed at reproducing and reinventing gendered identities" (Marshall 2004: 262). Out of all the popular fairy tales in English speaking countries, *Little Red Riding Hood* must belong to those most often adapted as picturebooks. Although some very few picturebooks take up the smartness and courage of the heroine of the oral versions or of the Chinese variant, such as Ed Young's *Lon Po Po* (Caldecott winner from 1990), the overwhelming majority of adaptations perpetuate the image of the pretty girl who is incapable of saving herself and evidently too stupid to notice the difference between Grandmother and the Wolf. Many of these adaptations are of poor literary and artistic quality, but in terms of content even award-winning books such as *Little Red Riding Hood* by Trina Schart Hyman (1983, fig. 6) help cement Perrault and the Grimms' view of women as physically and morally weak and needful of male protection. *The Monster and the Teddy Bear* is not as such a picturebook adaptation of *Little Red Riding Hood*, and yet it bears a number of striking resemblances to this tale, in its dominant Western reception.

"Aunt Jane has sent you a teddy bear," said Angela's mother.
"I don't like teddy bears," said Angela. "I want a monster."

Fig. 7 *The Monster and the Teddy Bear* (McKee 1989)

A third person narrator begins the story about ginger-haired (instead of red-hooded) Angela who is unhappy about a present by her aunt, just unwrapped by her mother: a letter and a teddy bear (fig. 7). Like *Little Red Riding Hood*, the story starts with an exchange of gifts between the girl and her mother and an admonition about their appropriate handling. Thus, Angela's mother, upon Angela's first dismissive remarks about her aunt's present, lectures that "[e]veryone likes teddy bears [...]. They're warm and cuddly." Angela is visibly discontented and sulky when she retorts: "And monsters are big and strong and exciting", repeating that "[she] want[s] a monster." Right at the beginning of the story, there is a "path" set out for Angela that separates right from wrong for her. If she was behaving within the path's demarcations she would *appreciate* and *like* the teddy bear. On these first two pages, Angela is wearing white sneakers, a yellow t-shirt with a colorful print on the front and green pants. Her clothes are intriguing for a number of reasons. First, for picturebook representations of girls, they are strikingly boyish. Second, from the third page until the end Angela wears a pink night gown and slippers with red pompoms. And third, her clothing style corresponds with her degree of deviating from normative femininity: on the first two pages, Angela's wish for a monster is strongest. After her wish has become a reality, her initial desire for a "big and strong and exciting" playmate/toy quickly diminishes and is soon replaced by her insight that a protective "warm and cuddly" teddy bear is a far more appropriate companion for her. It is this interplay of gender performance (predominantly through acts and speech) and gender representation (through clothes, gestures, facial expressions, positioning on the page, and other factors) that describes femininity and monstrosity as incommensurable.

When her parents are out and a babysitter has taken her place in front of the TV, Angela's wish comes true and a monster climbs in through the window and into her pink-walled room. Compared to *all* the other monsters in my corpus, I find this to be the only genuinely horrible and fearsome one: the monster has blood-shot, bulging eyes, brown hair sprouting out of ears, nose and armpits – an extremely rare sight of sexual maturity in picturebooks! – and unlike any other picturebook monsters that I have seen, razor-sharp teeth, yellow bristly toe- and fingernails, warty green skin, and yellow slime drooping out of his mouth. It is perhaps interesting to consider that David McKee seems to have a knack for monsters: I have found three other books by him that feature monsters. Two of these present an all-male world, *Two Monsters* (1985) and *Three Monsters* (2005), and one, *Not Now, Bernard* (1984), has an equally domestic setting as *The Monster and the Teddy Bear*, only with a boy protagonist. In all three publications, but particularly *Not Now, Bernard*, the monsters are depicted in a decidedly more affable, congenial manner. Considering these three publications, it seems unlikely that the visual horror of Angela's personal monster is simply an effect of the artist's style of drawing monsters.

The presence of adults in this picturebook story could also be paralleled to the fairy tale, although again with qualifications. Angela's parents, oblivious to her feelings and wishes, set a babysitter in place when they go out for the evening. Although this babysitter is equally oblivious I find it remarkable – especially in contrast to the picturebooks with male protagonists where adults are usually altogether absent, at least when the real action unfolds – that this adult caregiver appears on three separate pages as the only figure, each time to reprimand Angela to "be quiet!" so the babysitter can undisturbedly continue watching TV. As an incompetent parental substitute, though no more incompetent than the actual parents, the babysitter might be seen as a reflection of Little Red mother's failure to protect her daughter from harm. At the same time the babysitter's very presence emphasizes a kind of formal necessity that girls be guarded by adults at all times – a necessity that boy protagonists in my corpus are rarely objected to. As a rule, parents in children's literature have to be absent before the action can unfold. And although *Hungry! Hungry! Hungry!* does not comply with it, almost all picturebooks in my corpus do, in fact, work with this premise. In *The Monster and the Teddy Bear*, the adult's presence with her simultaneous and utter ignorance of the horror going on in the house is a device that increases the dramatic tension of the story considerably.

Not only is Angela's monster physically repulsive, it is also portrayed as an aggressive intruder and housebreaker, introducing himself as "[Angela's] monster" who wants to "do monstrous things." The first of these things is using Angela's bed as a bouncing castle, ruffling the linen and shaking the lamp shade. The monster's tongue is protruding from his gaping mouth with drops of spit squirting out. Angela is demure, but consents in taking part – though rather passively – in doing those monstrous things. The monster's request to eat something is followed by Angela's "shudder[ing] when she [feels] the monster's slimy hand". Here again, the verbal text is paired with an image that showcases the monster's thick, glistening tongue with yellowy white saliva oozing out of his mouth. On the facing page, the babysitter shouts into the direction of Angela's room to be quiet, without leaving her comfortable armchair in front of the television and munching away on her cookies and chocolates.

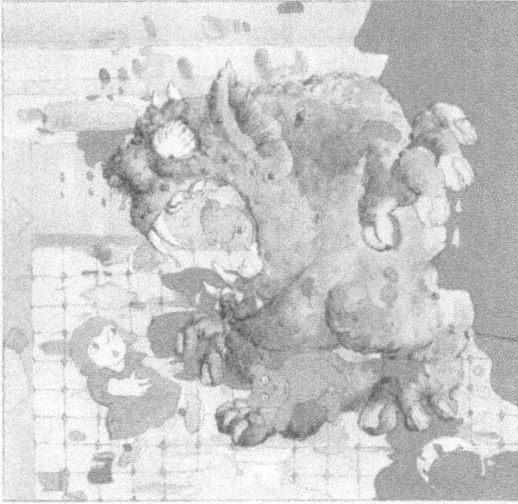

"Nothing!" roared the monster. "Or I'll eat them, and if you start moaning I'll eat you as well. Monsters can do anything."

Fig. 8   *The Monster and the Teddy Bear* (McKee 1989)

Particularly with the background of *Little Red Riding Hood* as a tale "about the regulation of sex roles and sexuality" (Zipes 1983: 124), the interactions between Angela and her monster are extremely sexualized (fig. 8). The monster's insatiable appetite may be transferred to the food that the kitchen has in store, but the excess with which the monster devours everything edible in his vicinity is, in fact, only a continuation of the first scene in the bed. The narrator makes a note that the monster "even [eats] the flowers": three red roses. The bleakness of this side-comment somewhat conceals the rich symbolism of both language and imagery. Both a symbol for love (the flower was associated with Aphrodite in Greek mythology and is, today, probably the most frequently sold flower on Valentine's Day) and a symbol for sexual purity (in Christian mythology, the rose became associated with the Virgin Mary), the rose is here profanely devoured, ground to pulp in the

159

monster's stinking mouth. Angela's symbolic deflowering is followed by the monster's "redecorating" of the kitchen by splashing the walls and furniture with paint. The blue and yellow are soon joined and mostly covered by the color red which reaches its most disturbing quality when the monster is already halfway out of the house but still has one arm and one foot inside the kitchen, now completely drowned in red, with some red paint dripping from the open door behind which Angela, engulfed in red, cowers fearfully. The portrayal of Angela's 'defilement' corresponds uncannily with the image of the female body as Ann Cahill analyzes it by building on the Foucauldian idea of the production of the subject through disciplinary measures and punishment:

> In acquiring the bodily habits which render the subject "feminine," habits which are inculcated at a young age and then constantly redefined and maintained, the woman learns to accept her body as dangerous, willful, fragile, and hostile. It constantly poses the possibility of threat, and only persistent vigilance can limit the risk at which it places the woman. (Cahill 2000: 56; qt. in Marshall 2004: 266 f.)

The "habits" Cahill describes are exactly what Zipes calls the Little Red Riding Hood syndrome: the female/feminine subject is constituted through the permanent threat that it be raped or otherwise sexually violated. These mechanisms are naturalized to the degree that the continuing publication of adaptations of this fairy tale and of picturebook narratives such as *The Monster and the Teddy Bear* appear unproblematic, even unremarkable, to the majority of adults in the picturebook industry. Sometimes, picturebook scholars, too, can be blind to the structures at work here, such as Maria Nikolajeva and Carol Scott who discuss *The Monster and the Teddy Bear* with respect to the narrative mode of the text, finding the only thing that is "remarkable" (Nikolajeva and Scott 2001: 197) about this picturebook is "that, unlike *Not Now, Bernard*, the book allows the good [Teddy Bear] to win without any further complications" (ibid).

The very moment when Angela is symbolically bleeding, Teddy Bear, whom Angela has been dragging along, becomes alive and steps in, countering the monster's claim that "monsters can do anything" (ibid) by objecting that "they can't be warm and

Outside in the garden Teddy spun the monster round and round above his head.

Fig. 9   *The Monster and the Teddy Bear* (McKee 1989)

cuddly" (ibid). Their dispute escalates with Teddy growing into a giant super hero bear who hurls the monster, finally intimidated, into space "so far [he]'ll never come back" (ibid, fig. 9). As soon as Angela drops her pretense of liking the monster and admits to herself that she is really quite scared, she loses her agency. Just like Little Red, Angela is metaphorically swallowed – visually depicted as a little speck on the threshold in the lower left-hand corner of the page – and rendered incapable of action. Just like Little Red she must rely on the prowess of a male hero to save her. Once she is free and the monster is gone she says admiringly: "Oh Teddy, you were wonderful" (ibid). Even without the context of *Little Red Riding Hood* it is difficult not to read her utterance as a sexual innuendo, even more so in light of the final page where

161

Angela cuddles Teddy who invites her to go back to bed with him, thus comparing the monstrous romping in the bed from the beginning with a harmonious and affectionate relationship that consists of a protective and strong (yet cuddly) male and a subdued and admiring female.

Although *The Monster and the Teddy Bear* is not a fairy tale adaptation in a strict sense, the parallels, especially regarding the (sexual) education of girls, between both stories are more than suggestive. Just as the Wolf, the monster is cast in the light of sexual predator and housebreaker whom the girl is unable to fend off on her own. Angela's initial trust in the monster's suitability for her desires is thwarted by her realization of his destructive violence and his ultimate threat to devour Angela's parents and even herself if she dares tell anyone about the "monstrous things" (McKee 1989: np) they have been doing together. Doing "monstrous things" is evidently not an option for Angela if she wants to get back on the path of female righteousness. Embracing Teddy Bear as her benevolent savior is her only way out of looming catastrophe – just as Little Red is only too happy about the noble huntsman's interaction. As extreme as the depiction of gender roles may seem in *The Monster and the Teddy Bear*, it is a case in point that the sexism of the early nineteenth century tale of *Little Red Riding Hood* has not only survived, but thrived well into the late twentieth century (and beyond).

In *The Monster and the Teddy Bear*, the female protagonist is a perfect instance of the Little Red Riding Hood Syndrome. Just as this and many other fairy tales, Angela's representation reinforces a gendered pattern of the "Western civilization process" (Smith Chalou 2002: 37) in which sexuality is seen as a male threat to women who are at the same time essentialized as naturally helpless, passive, and seductive. Despite the pervasiveness of this narrative in contemporary culture the blunt display of such reactionary gendered behavior in *The Monster and the Teddy Bear* stands out in my corpus. Feminism is said to have had a great impact on the production and (academic) reception of children's literature (Nodelman 2002: 5; Stephens 2002: x), but none of that can be perceived in *The Monster and the Teddy Bear*.

In anticipation of my discussion of *Hungry! Hungry! Hungry!* and other picturebooks about fear that feature male main protagonists, I want to say a few words about the role violence plays in *The Monster and the Teddy Bear*. The most obvious violent actor is of course the monster, with his rampage in the house as well as his existential threat to eat up Angela and her parents. While this extent of material destruction seems rare – the only other book where the house is shredded to pieces is *Monsters – An Owner's Guide* (2010) by Jonathan Emmett and Mark Oliver – the threat to eat the child is an extremely common characteristic for picture-book monsters across all my four categories, occasionally already announced or alluded to in the title, as in *One Hungry Monster* (O'Keeffe and Munsinger 1989), *Monsters Eat Whiny Children* (Kaplan 2010) or, indeed, *Hungry! Hungry! Hungry!*. There are even some books where this threat is actually carried out: *The Day Louis Got Eaten* (Fardell 2011) where a boy is gobbled up), *Not Now Bernard* (a boy is eaten), *G.E.M.* (Clark and Parsons 2006) where, again, a boy is devoured, and *Pat the Beastie* (Drescher 1993) where a boy and a girl are swallowed. Against the backdrop of these books, the monster's violence in *The Monster and the Teddy Bear* does not appear all that extreme, after all – and certainly not tied to Angela's gender. But there is one aspect of violence that is unique in my corpus. It is the violent struggle between Teddy and the Monster during which Teddy reveals sharp, pointed teeth and grows in size to dominate even the already huge monster. Teddy and Monster fight each other for the girl as trophy and Teddy is evidently much stronger since he hurls Monster into space without any visible effort. But Teddy's violence is sanctioned, of course, because it saves the little girl and is directed against the evil perpetrator, just as the huntsman's extreme violence in cutting open the Wolf's stomach is presented as an act of justice. In no other book in my corpus is the bad monster disposed of – cast out to some place that might well be synonymous with death – with such punishing finality. I suggest that this is because in no other book is the monster presented as unambiguously evil as here. The horror of Angela's Monster cannot even be entirely explained with his kinship to Little Red's Wolf. As Debra Mitts-Smith shows in her study *Picturing the Wolf in Children's Literature* (2010), the Wolf has been largely rehabilitated, only rarely still cast as predator, and much more often as a hunted, endangered, and even tame creature. The Monster in McKee's picture-book, in contrast, is purely bad and corrupting.

For Angela herself, there are no ambiguities in character either. Her initial boldness to want to have a monster is implicitly reprimanded when Teddy takes over her agency, signaling to her that she stands no chance in fighting the monster alone. And fight it she must, for there is no doubt that the monster's thorough badness represents a serious threat to the girl's very existence. There is even an anticipated repentance built into the end of the narrative when Angela fearfully wonders what her parents will say about the bloody red battle field that the kitchen has become. While sexuality in the books with boy characters can only be discerned as one of many configurations, in *The Monster and the Teddy Bear* the sexual theme is a lot more explicit. Angela is made to reject her 'bad drives,' represented by the monster's repulsiveness, and to recognize Teddy, the strong protector, as her true love object. The rite of passage for her is a step back to being passive and helpless, while all the boy characters learn to internalize the double-standard required for a successful contemporary masculinity. As I will discuss in the following, the narrative instance in *Hungry! Hungry! Hungry!* offers a fluid positioning for the implied reader, whereas the third person narrator as well as the clear separation of words and images in *The Monster and the Teddy Bear* suggest little space for maneuvering outside the essentialist and restrictive image of femininity propagated by this book. The motif of a monstrous, male predator who threatens to devour a child is inextricably intertwined with ideological messages about sex morals, implying a depiction of gender difference that is heterosexist in the worst possible sense: the Wolf/Monster *has got to* be male and the child *has got to be* female. As Marshall points out, "the reading of the girl's body as innocent exposes the white, middle class girl lodged at the center of most educational and popular discourses" (Marshall 2004: 268). Moreover,

> discourses around sexuality and gender offer different subject positions in relationship to how race, class, nationality, or sexuality are inscribed on the body of the girl. [...] Black and Latina girls, for instance, are even less likely to be protected by the law in cases of sexual violation than their white, middle class counterparts" (ibid).

Teddy's protective behavior towards Angela then should also be read as an indication of Angela's racial and class status. What I find interesting is that their hetero-erotic relationship is much more explicit than that between Little Red and the Huntsman in versions intended for child readers/listeners. As Orenstein (2003) remarks, Little Red remains one of the very few popular folktale heroines to stay unwed. As if to shield off any suspicions readers might harbor about Angela's possibly still lingering striving for independence, McKee makes sure to end his story with Angela and Teddy's romantic union.

Little Red Riding Hood has contributed considerably to popular images of the Wolf as male the Little Red as female. Some postmodern versions play with these gendered images. In a 1990s commercial for Pepsi One, for instance, Kim Cattrell from the TV series *Sex and the City* plays an extremely sexualized Little Red with unmistakably wolfish eyes. There exist other versions of this tale that cast the Wolf as female,[9] but the picturebook *Hungry! Hungry! Hungry!* is so far the only one I have come across in which the child passes as male. What happens to all the sex in this fairy tale when the child is a boy? Can the story possibly retain the same message about immoral desire, rape, and redemption? In other words, how gender-essentialist is the narrative around Little Red Riding Hood really?

---

[9] In fact, the Wolf's gendering as female can be traced back to medieval sources, such as a bestiary from the thirteenth century in which the Latin *lupa* means both "female wolf" and "whore" because both "plunder a man's goods" (Greenleaf 1992: 50).

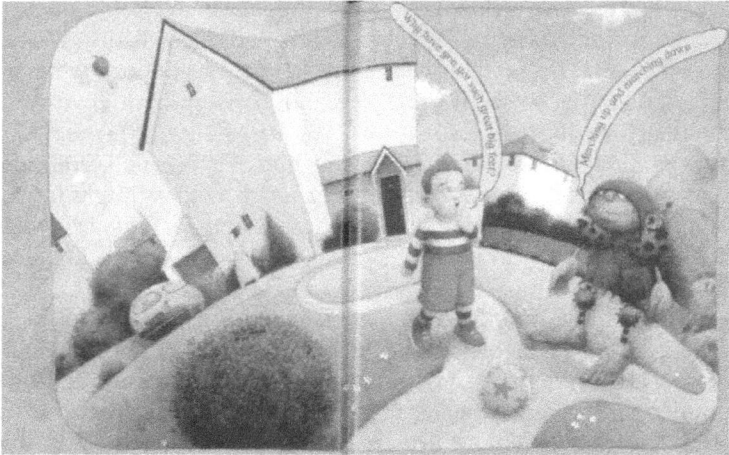

Fig. 10   *Hungry! Hungry! Hungry!* (Doyle and Hess 2004)

'Hungry! Hungry! Hungry!'

In this first reading of *Hungry! Hungry! Hungry!* I let myself be directed by my own indoctrination with current gender discourse in picturebooks which initially led me to read the child figure in this text as a boy – automatically and without thinking twice. This boy has short ginger hair – just like Angela – but it is dressed into a miniature punk, he has jug ears and freckles, wears a jumper with white-blue stripes, red shorts and red sneakers (fig. 10). On the half-title page he watches in surprise and with round, open mouth a yellow ball with red stars fall from the sky. I found my first impression of this child as male further supported on the ultimate and penultimate page openings that depict a stereotypical boy's room, fully equipped with stereotypical boy toys such as rails, fire engine with firemen, a knight, an astronaut, a sailboat, a baseball bat, a car, a stuffed dinosaur, and quite a few balls (cf. Miller 1987: 473-487; Seiter 1995). All of these verbal signs encode ideas about how adults (in this context, professionals of the picturebook industry and adult picturebook readers) think about boyhood – and also how these adults want others, mainly children, to learn to think about

166

boyhood: boys wear practical clothes and practical, ideally "cool", haircuts, their rooms are stuffed with toys that are predominantly vehicles, action figures or sports equipment. Boys can be jug eared and still be a picturebook hero. Oh, and boys have balls – actually and figuratively speaking.

Although the verbal narrative is limited to the dialogue between child and monster, *Hungry! Hungry! Hungry!* immediately and despite its evidently male child hero calls for a comparison with *Little Red Riding Hood* – simply because this dialogue is so well-known and so emblematic. The end of the dialogue in this particular and very loose picturebook adaptation runs like this:

> [...]
> "Why have you got such powerful hands?"
> "Grabbing things and squeezing things..."
> "Why have you got such a scrag of a neck?"
> "Hungry! Hungry! Hungry!"
> "Why have you got such a horrible head?"
> "I'm a grisly, ghastly goblin..."
> "What have you come for?"
> "YOU!" (Doyle and Hess 2004: np)

Aesthetically, this dialogue is contained within speech bubbles, following the stylistic convention of comics. Another unusual trait of the verbal text is its formulaic structure, mirroring that particular part of the folktale, and the lack of a narrator. Instead, the action of the story is exclusively told on the level of images. On every double spread the boy asks the monster a question, such as "Why have you got such great big feet?" (Doyle and Hess 2004: np) or "Why have you got such spidery legs?" (ibid), and the monster's respective answers alternately describe his actions, which are loosely connected to his bodily characteristics in question ("Marching up and marching down..." (ibid)), or simply exclaim his physical distress ("Hungry! Hungry! Hungry!" (ibid)). The game of question and answer makes the reference to *Little Red Riding Hood* very explicit, mirroring the dialogue between the girl and the Wolf in a loose yet unambiguous way. However, it is not just the linguistic formula that is reminiscent of the literary predecessor, but also the theme of food and hunger that is most often read in terms of sexual appetite and desire. I will come back to the monster's apparent insatiability later.

There are more aspects that support the intertextual reference to the fairy tale. The story is told in luminous, saturated, and sensual colors – perhaps a graphic realization of the wood's manifold temptations in the form of colorful flowers, luscious grass, and warm sunrays. Unlike the fairy tale, however, this picturebook story contains no warning to stay on the path, the mere concept of "path" being entirely absent. Boy and monster chase each other in and around the house and garden, without any apparent moral value attached to either of these places – but there is a lot of running in and out of doors and windows. The images are laid out over the entire double spreads and display a panorama-like view of a suburban house, both from the outside and inside: this white, middle-class setting that is so typical for the picturebooks in my corpus.

Another visual allusion to Little Red Riding Hood is the protagonist's ginger hair, supplemented by his red short pants and red sneakers that I have already mentioned at the beginning. The monster, a "ghastly goblin" (ibid), green and barefoot, displays the same color of hair as the boy. The sharing of an external trait between boy and monster is a fairly common device in picturebook stories about the fear of monsters.[10] One of its effects is a diminishment of otherness between human child and monster. While in the world of picturebooks it will be difficult to find a portrayal of the wild, hungry Wolf and the little, innocent Little Red Riding Hood as associates that are not so different after all, the suggestion of similarity between boy and monster is in almost all books about the fear of monsters one of the first indications that the boy's initial fear has no solid foundation. Right from the start, the readers are

---

[10] Other picturebooks in my corpus that work with this stylistic device in order to create a doppelganger motif include David McKee's *Not Now, Bernard* (1984), in which the monster eats up the boy and is then seen dragging the boy's teddy bear along; Henrik Drescher's *The Boy Who Ate Around* (1993) where one of the boy's many monstrous incarnations wears glasses just like him; and Peter McCarty's *Jeremy Draws a Monster* (2009) whose boy protagonist wears a t-shirt with the number three on the front and back, and whose monster also features a prominent three on his belly.

led to believe that Little Red Riding Boy and The Big Bad Monster are not much more than reflections of one another. The most obvious reason for this constellation seems to me, indeed, that the child is not female but male.

The fact that the picturebook protagonist passes as male but is nevertheless embedded in the complex literary matrix of *Little Red Riding Hood* leads to significant changes in terms of approved and required gender behavior vis-à-vis the popular fairy tale text. Despite the fact that *Hungry! Hungry! Hungry!* was published nearly 200 years after the Grimms' version of the fairy tale, it would be challenging to imagine a male child being objected to the forces of male monstrosity and male authority in the same way Little Red and Angela are. In other words, *Little Red Riding Hood* has claimed its status as a tale about rape only because the main character is female. It is difficult to imagine Little Red as a boy and yet, if I follow my suggestion of *Hungry! Hungry! Hungry!* being a modern version of the tale, this is what happens here: the child character who is chased and threatened by a monster is no longer a girl, but a boy. How does this gender difference change the story's morale?

Fig. 11 *Hungry! Hungry! Hungry!* (Doyle and Hess 2004)

Just as in the fairy tale, the child character is on a quest of identifying, or rather: defining the monster and handling the threat it represents. The accomplishment of this task is a prerequisite for the hero's own definition of (gendered) selfhood. But unlike the fairy tale heroine, at least as she is popularly known today, the picturebook hero solves the problem on his own. He is relentless and persevering in asking the monster questions about his identity. He asks thirteen questions, to be precise, and does not let go until this game of question and answer reaches its climax. On the ultimate double spread, the boy is fearfully looking up to the monster from under his bed, asking "What have you come for?" (ibid: np, fig. 11) The monster, in an assaulting pose, with his huge black mouth gaping in the center of the page, answers in upper case: "YOU!" (ibid: np) This key scene mirrors of course Little Red's exclamation "Grandmother, what big teeth you have!" and the Wolf's reply "The better to eat you with!" To further support the readers' anticipation of the expected ending of the story, the boy is placed on the right hand side of a folded-in page with a regretful expression on his face and a thought bubble over his head in which he sees himself in a large kettle above a fire and the monster next

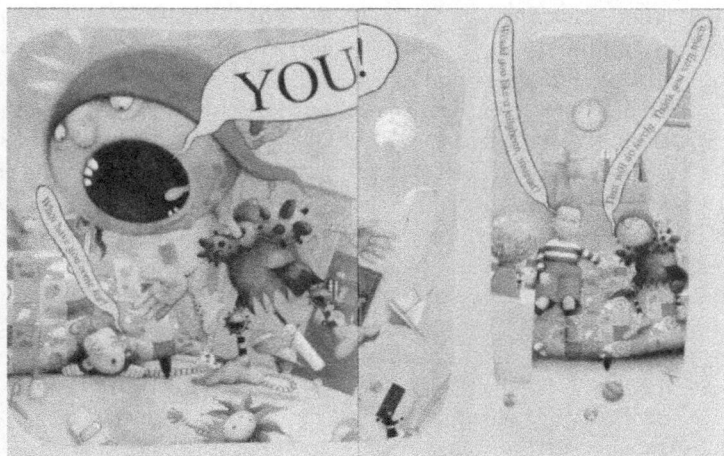

Fig. 12   *Hungry! Hungry! Hungry!* (Doyle and Hess 2004)

to it in a chef's costume. Once the folded-in page is opened, the resolution of the story is revealed: boy and monster sit smilingly on the boy's bed (fig. 12). The boy asks: "Would you like a jelly-bean, instead?" (ibid: np) And the monster answers even more gallantly: "That will do nicely, thank you very much." (ibid: np)

The crucial divergence of the plot's ending from the fairy tale lies both within the omission of the violence and the boy charac-ter's granted autonomy and power in overcoming the monster's threat. The boy does *not* allow the monster to devour him. The cunningness of his reaction is reminiscent of the girl's in the non-canonical versions of the fairy tale where she pretends she needs to relieve herself outside. The difference is that she needs to get away from the wolf, no matter what, whereas the boy's invitation of the monster to share sweets transforms his role from hunted to host, thereby reforming the power hierarchies. Monster and boy are depicted in an act of homosocial complicity over the sharing of colorful jellybeans and because homosociality is such a common-place in children's literature (Pugh 2011: 6 f.) any potential sexual undertones that this invitation might imply can be easily brushed aside. The sweets replace both violence and sex, exemplifying

Peter Hunt's succinct comment in an article about food in children's literature: "No sex, no violence: what are you left with? Food" (Hunt 1996: 9).

I find Hunt's comment particularly interesting when I compare the obvious violence and the sexual metaphors and imagery in *The Monster and the Teddy Bear* with the quasi absence of both in *Hungry! Hungry! Hungry!* Is McKee's book only an unfortunate gaffe? Or did Hunt only speak about children's literature with male child heroes, the default of children's literature? Or do I (and perhaps Peter Hunt if he were to comment on it) not see the sex and the violence in *Hungry! Hungry! Hungry!* simply because I am/we are so accustomed to not seeing them in boy-boy-interactions in picturebooks?

There is – of course – violence in *Hungry! Hungry! Hungry!* The difference to *The Monster and the Teddy Bear* is its potentiality: the immanent devouring of the boy is never realized. This impending threat of being swallowed is equally explicit and also never actualized in *I'm Coming to Get You!* (Ross 1984), *The Gruffalo* (Donaldson and Scheffler 1999), *Dexter Bexley and the Big Blue Beastie* (Stewart 2007), and *The Monster Who Ate Darkness* (Dunbar and Liao 2008). In the other books about the fear of monsters, this threat may not be explicitly formulated but it is nevertheless alluded to through the depiction of the monsters' large mouths, sharp teeth and claws. But despite the allusion to potential aggression, all monsters in picturebooks with boy protagonists are fundamentally harmless: even those boys who do get devoured will eventually, as a rule with very few exceptions, [11] be spat out again. Nevertheless, violence is clearly an important theme; it is implied in the very configuration of the monster and yet is never acted upon. An avoidance of violence in books about boys is intriguing precisely because violence is such a frequently debated concept in the definitions of what constitutes boys and men. "No single subject, save for work and economics, receives so much attention in masculinity literature as violence. For gender theorists and criminologists, the concepts of masculinity and violence are practically intertwined" (Atkinson 2011: 51). The avoidance of violence in the

---

[11] *Not Now, Bernard* (McKee 1984), *Pat the Beastie* (Drescher 1993).

picturebooks I discuss here is part of a set of values that promotes a softer, kinder masculinity than the one described by Atkinson.

The means by which the boy characters succeed in solving the problem can be summarized as follows: wit, courage – and politeness. These are all not only educated middle-class values, they are also highly gendered. The other titles of this story type present comparable values and illustrate the persistence of the principal plot pattern: the male child character (alternatively male monster child or male animal) succeeds in overcoming his fear on his own. Apart from initiative and politeness (*Hungry! Hungry! Hungry!*), other encouraged values include loyalty and negotiation (*I Need My Monster* (Noll and McWilliam 2009), care and the provision of comfort (*The Monster Who Ate Darkness* (Dunbar and Liao (2008); *POG – The Monster Who Was Afraid of Children* (Lee and Gamble 2000); *There's A Nightmare in my Closet* (Mayer 1968); *The Monster Bed* (Willis and Varley 1986)), innovation, resourcefulness and creativity (*Dexter Bexley and the Big Blue Beastie* (Stewart 2007); *Go Away, Big Green Monster!* (Emberly 1992); *The Gruffalo* (Donaldson and Scheffler 1999)), and humor (*The Monster At the End of This Book* (Stone and Smollin 1971)). The underlying message of all of these books is that boys need to learn how to use non-violent strategies in solving conflicts with threatening situations, other (male) individuals or aggressive parts within themselves. These strategies could also be labelled 'soft skills' or 'social skills,' comprised in a cluster of learned personality traits, habits, attitude and communication that makes social relations and interaction successful. The threat is represented by the monsters that contain two closely related issues. The first issue is synonymous with the monsters' potential to obstruct or reverse the acquisition of these social skills. The root of this potential, the second issue, lies within traditional definitions of boys, according to which such 'soft skill behavior' would be inappropriate.

These picturebooks with boy characters who negotiate their fear of monsters create a vision of the contemporary boy who is clearly marked off from notions of traditional boyhood, both in terms of boys' supposed penchant for violent behavior and the value of their acquisition of 'soft' skills. In the 19th century, violent demeanor as a valuable character trait of "real boys" was cultivated in what Glenn Hendler calls "bad boy books," such as Mark

Twain's *The Adventures of Tom Sawyer* or William Dean Howells' *A Boy's Town*. As Hendler states:

> A "real boy," Howells says in *A Boy's Town*, has no love for flowers, never appears in the parlor when his mother has company, **nor, most important, does he feel or express sympathy**. These are all traits of girls, or worse, what he calls "girl-boys". [...] **Lacking the capacity for friendship**, incessantly disavowing any desire to sympathize with others, boys appear to be **atavistically presocial** in these books. Indeed, judging by his statements in *A Boy's Town*, Howells's concept of "boy-nature" is equivalent to "**savagery**," and the "world" boys inhabit resembles nothing more than a state of precivilization. "Everywhere and always the world of boys is **outside of the laws** that govern grown-up communities," Howells says; a boy obeys his world's unwritten laws "instinctively," like "the **far-off savages** from whom his customs seem mostly to have come." Charles Dudley Warner seems to have agreed, stating that "[e]very boy who is good for anything is **a natural savage**." (Hendler 190) [my emphasis]

The "bad boy books" clearly glorify boys' "savagery" and display a distinctly favorable attitude towards a disposition for physical aggression, combined with a lack of sympathy towards others and an emphasis on solitary independence.

Another literary genre which was increasingly directed at (male) children was the adventure story which was economically very successful at the end of the 19th century (Yarbrough 2011: 17). In its portrayal of masculinity it may well have laid the foundation against which boy characters of the twentieth and twenty-first centuries are inevitably read. Wynn Yarbrough makes an explicit connection between the adventure novel of the late 19th century and children's literature of the early twentieth century.

> Defoe, Stevenson, Haggard and other writers constructed English heroes in exotic settings where manliness was proven by resilience, courage, individualism, and physical prowess. [...] Various characteristics of this "adventurer" exist in characters as diverse as Mowgli, Toad, Peter Rabbit, and Pooh. [...] In many ways, the boy character has always been on his own, at least in how we are to recognize the characters of bildungsromans [sic] and epics. The Western idea of masculinity as a force that individually makes its way to reveal heroism and nobility appears in English literature, especially

as inherited from the adventure story tradition, in plots where the individual boy makes his way through a series of tests that mold character [and] reinforce values deemed manly by society [...]. (Yarbrough 2011: 111)

The narrative pattern in picturebooks in which male children pass the 'test' of defeating their monster is likely to have evolved, at least partly, from the adventure story tradition. The focus of values such as "resilience, courage, individualism, and physical prowess," which enforce manliness in the literature examined by Yarbrough, has greatly shifted in the picturebooks of my corpus to complex verbal skills, good manners and, most prominently, mutual care and empathy. The values emphasized in the picturebooks create a strong contrast to those portrayed in books for boys a century ago. In this historical light, the picturebook monsters can be seen as symbolizing a threat to which contemporary boys are exposed, namely the threat of incorporating a gender identity stuck in the 19th century ideology of the adventure story that fits Howell's 'job description for the bad boy' above – but not contemporary demands on boys.

Evidently, many of these ideological stances pervade hegemonic discourses concerning gender. Within these discourses, there is still a heavily gendered divide between socially required behavior for boys (active, strong, violent, transgressive, independent, protective, rational, etc.) as opposed to girls (passive, peaceful, caring, emotional, compliant, dependent, intuitive, etc.) (cf. Grauerholz and Pescosolido 1989: 113-125; Turner-Bowker 1996: 463). With these schemata in mind, the degree of border-crossing of the male child heroes in the picturebooks might seem surprising. In order to be successful boys they must adopt traditionally feminine characteristics, engaging in non-violent problem-solving by being soft, emotional, sharing, caring, dependent, and intuitive. To specify, the 'problem-solving' here only refers to conflicts enacted between male child and male monster, where the monster represents those characteristics conceived of as traditionally male/uncivilized/pre-social: strong, violent, aggressive, transgressive, rapacious, being a 'hunter,' active, thinking quantitatively. Thus, the boy genre 'picturebooks with monsters' puts on display an intense debate between concepts of traditional masculinity and new demands made on socially successful boys. In fact, the narrative pattern of these books carves out the double-standard which 'the new boy' has to fulfil in order to fit into his role. The monsters as the boys' mirror images enable the boy characters to enact their stereotypical male 'savageness' while at the same time setting them up as their own domesticators. Read in this way, the boy protagonist in *Hungry! Hungry! Hungry!* tames the hungry goblin by inviting him to sit on the bed and eat jelly beans. Transforming Little Red Riding Hood into a boy turns out to be a successful narrative strategy, but only as long as contemporary gender codes are respected. This means that boys must remain distinguishable from girls. They cannot, for example, be the passive spectators of their own salvation. In order to be desirable, Nodelman argues, boys must at once be wild and counter the public and paradoxical sanctioning of "the boy code" (Nodelman 2002: 5 and 11). Picturebooks about the fear of monsters, then, seem to belong to those

> books about boys that purport to transcend the formulas of popular fiction [which] are about boys seeing through conventional constructions of masculinity, learning to be more sensitive or more loving or more openly imaginative or literate, or less caught up in the pleasures of aggressive bullying. [...] As a result, children's literature often tends to be a maternal sort of literature, even when produced by men following the conventions of the genre. It often admires the kinds of boys that mothers might most easily love – good, safe, nonrowdy boys who do not break rules and cause maternal anxiety. Whatever the reason, books for children written by both men and women tend to admire boys who share the author's interests in reading and writing and in valuing imagination. (ibid)

Considering the 'masculinity crisis' as a phenomenon with a palpable impact on the public perception and evaluation of boys (Atkinson 2011: 79 f.), it is reasonable to extend the source for the transformation of boy characters in picturebooks from the sphere of literary production to a wider public arena, encompassing pedagogic, medical and media discourses. While traditionally feminine qualities are encouraged and necessary character traits for the boys in picturebooks with monsters, here the traditional side of masculinity is not erased, but rather embraced in the form of the monster who becomes a friend and companion. Thus the boy, by identifying with the monster, gets to be both: aggressive and soft, savage and well-behaved, pre-verbal and eloquent. The persistence of old conceptions of 'proper' behavior can also be traced on the story level: although the goblin is surrounded by the most colorful and plentiful fruit on every page, what finally appeases his monstrous appetite is one tiny jellybean. Thus, although the boy protagonist is encouraged to behave according to contemporary requirements, adopting the aforementioned values, or eating fruit and vegetables instead of sweets, he is granted a space in which to negotiate his supposedly masculine needs.

Hungry! Hungry! Hungry! may ostensibly allude to *Little Red Riding Hood* in its playful reference to the fairy tale's dialogue, but in its representation of the protagonists, the text completely conflates the old divide between good and evil as traditionally transported by the tale's morale: rather than being punished and made to repent for 'hooking up' with the monster, the boy is rewarded for being a generous host and companion. The uncivilized, evil 'other' that the Monster is for Angela is made self *for* and *by* the ginger-haired boy protagonist. What I mean by this is that the authors construct that narrative in a way that enables the male child to become an agent active in his own salvation by unifying two seemingly disparate sets of masculine values: savagery with civility, rapaciousness with modesty, destruction with order, and solipsistic egocentricity with mutual and caring friendship. The boy does not deny or negate his more 'feminine' traits. In light of Annette Wannamaker's observation that the adolescent heroes in Louis Sachar's YA novel *Holes* have to negate their femininity in order to gain access to the kingdom of publicly recognized and acclaimed masculinity (Wannamaker 2006: 18) – as is the case in YA fiction generally, it seems plausible to me that boy characters in picturebooks are granted more 'gender freedom' than adolescent boy characters in YA fiction because of their tender age and their ideological status as 'pure' and 'innocent' children, as yet 'untainted' by sexual drives and under the loving female wings of mother and other female caregivers.

There seems to be a strong investment in the establishment and upholding of this image of the boy as both 'mother's darling' and 'wild rapscallion' because so many books in this thematic group repeat this same pattern that I have just laid out in *Hungry!*

Hungry! Hungry!. If a heterosexualized identity politics is the default position for reading texts – one of the starting points Judith Butler uses in *Gender Trouble* – the underlying narrative of these picturebooks can be understood to lay the foundation for male children to grow into such men that women will be bound to love them, in other words, they build the groundwork in early childhood for a functional and stable heterosexual adult life style. Further, the endless repetition of this narrative creates the illusion that these male characters (or, rather, their artistic creators) all imitate an original masculinity. Butler, of course, claims that "there is no original" (Butler 1991: 722), and that the repeated imitation of gender produces "the very notion of gender as an *effect*" (ibid). This abstract idea becomes very palpable in the face of all these picturebooks reproducing the same story of gender imitation, over and over again:

> That there is a need for a repetition at all is a sign that identity is not self-identical. It requires to be instituted again and again, which is to say that it runs the risk of becoming de-instituted at every interval. (Butler 1991: 725)

Butler precedes her remark on the motivation behind that repetition by stating that "[...] heterosexuality is always in the process of imitating and approximating its own phantasmatic idealization of itself – *and failing*" (Butler 1991: 722). One way of getting to the ground of this, in my eyes, slightly cryptic but at the same time alluring contention is to read *Hungry! Hungry! Hungry!* as a failure to establish (heterosexual) child masculinity as an original, as one instance where readers can "de-institute" the heterosexualized identity of the child protagonist.

Queering 'Little Red Riding Hood' via 'Hungry! Hungry! Hungry!'

It would be easier for me to conclude this chapter without Butler's inconvenient theories: there exists a group of picturebooks that are, on the surface, about combatting boys' fear of monsters, but that are actually little tales about negotiating old, but not quite overcome ideas about boyhood with more recent images of childhood masculinity that would help foster successful (and, by definition, heterosexual) adult men. Because of its neatness and perhaps also because of its unexpectedness – consider all the parallels of motifs and plotlines within this group of books, not to forget the extreme contrast between these stories and their gender-specific evolution from the prototype of *Little Red Riding Hood* – this argument is appealing and convincing even to myself, being aware first-hand of its constructedness according to principles of academic persuasion, intertextuality and discourse; so convincing, in fact, that for a long time, finishing this chapter like this appeared to me the only reasonable thing to do. It is only a few years into my research – and only three months before my personal submission deadline – that I open up to reading these narratives in other ways; readings with different discursive agendas but with an equally firm grounding in the text itself. I am going to offer one of those possibilities as my second reading of *Hungry! Hungry! Hungry!* This is not to suggest that my two different interpretations are arbitrary – far from it. My motivation for this rather unusual procedure in academic writing can be summed up like this: I want to draw attention to the multiple meanings that picturebooks can harbor – picturebooks that are often mistaken for the most simple stories in printed form –, as well as to the radical idea that a narrative pattern that describes codes of masculinity might, under certain circumstances, be used to deconstruct these very codes.

In this second reading, I use the verbal gap created by the specificities of the speech-bubble narrative that contains nothing but the question-and-answer dialogue between the child protagonist and the monster. There are no words that dictate to the reader the protagonists' gender. Rather than referring to my knowledge of gender discursive theory and visual semiotics, I choose to refer to my acquaintances, friendships and love relationships with cis males who occasionally wear skirts and dresses, with transgendered people who may or may not be transitioning from their birth-assigned gender to their self-claimed gender, with people who refuse gender categories altogether and with people who are as yet unfamiliar with the socially inscribed meanings of these categories – and with all tomboys, including the tomboy I once was myself. I will use the net that all these real people create as part of a queer discourse that has established and continues to establish alternative rules and methods for reading visual codes. One queer readerly approach to this enterprise is the use of gender-neutral third person pronouns when writing about the picturebook characters. Out of many different sets of invented pronouns, I am using Michael Spivak's pronouns, subsumed under the Wikipedia entry of 'Spivak pronoun,' which stands in relation to other epicene pronouns, such as 'ze,' 'hir,' and 'hirs,' as employed by Crisp and Hiller and also by Kate Bornstein. These pronouns are 'ey' (subject), 'em' (object), 'eir' (possessive adjective), 'eirs' (possessive), and 'emself' (reflexive). According to the Wikipedia entry, they were popularized in the online community LambdaMOO (an online space in which multiple players participate in a real-time virtual world, that is usually text-based) in the 1990s. There exist several variants of 'Spivak pronouns,' and the advantage of those I have chosen is that they are more easily distinguishable phonetically in comparison with 'hir'/ 'her' and 'hirs'/ 'hers' and, unlike the singular 'they' that is more commonly used to describe gender-nonconforming people, the Spivak pronouns allow the same grammatical flexibility as standard pronouns. Thus, when I write of one person I can use a singular pronoun without having to resort to phonetic ambiguities. In practice, I concentrate the use of these pronouns on my alternative reading of *Hungry! Hungry! Hungry!* in chapter 4.1.5, because I am interested in the effects of this linguistic and grammatical disruption. In most other cases – for instance, whenever I write of 'the child' outside of the binary gender system – pronouns are not necessary and their omission or replacement with a noun contributes to a smoother reading which, I hope, still makes place for non-conforming genders.

With the realization that neither the child nor the monster in this book are gender-fixed comes the possibility of undoing the gender of every other character in this picturebook. Before I focus on the child and the monster I am taking a moment to savor the effects of doing this. In the background of the first page opening, a human figure in a yellow summer dress and long brown hair, waving in the wind, is watering the lawn with a hose. The figure is holding the hose at hip height and the water splashing out of the hose is painted as white sprayed dots. I read this as a figure that combines feminine attire with a masculine sexual gesture. Eir facial features are blurry on this first opening. This figure is visible on two more page openings, each time far in the background and each time positioned in a way that hides the interactions between, indeed the very presence of, the child and the monster. On another page there is a figure that is almost entirely concealed by a big newspaper behind which only a pair of legs in yellow pants and stripy slippers, two hands and a spiky shock of hair are visible. Again, the action in the room between child and monster remains unseen by any of the other inhabitants of the house. Eir not noticing is also evident on the last page opening that shows an adult: a figure in a tender violet bath robe, pink dotted slippers, and a striped towel on eir head, walks along the base of the staircase, completely absorbed in a book. Rather than creating an atmosphere of emotional distance, obtuseness and aversion, as in *The Monster and the Teddy Bear*, the adult figures here are merely immersed in eir own worlds (reading or doing housework), but eir physical presence and closeness to the child in many instances suggests that the child always has the option to call an adult for help. The fact that ey chooses not to already alleviates some of the danger and fear.

Just as the human figures the monster can be ungendered, too. Ey describes eirself as a "grisly, ghastly goblin" (Doyle and Hess 2004: np), and that ascription can include all genders. Eir ginger hair hangs down almost like plaits on both sides of the face, eir armor and pantyhose are black and violet, ey wears a vibrant green handbag and a garment that looks somewhat like a hippie dress. For the longest part of the dialogue, the goblin refuses to give an answer to the child's questions about eir identity, or rather the reasons for the goblin's bodily appearance: "Why have you got such powerful hands?" or "Why have you got such spidery legs?" The goblin does not say who ey *is* but instead gives descriptions of eir actions and sensations: "Grabbing things and squeezing things…" or "Creeping here and crawling there" (ibid). Each description of an action is alternated with the goblin's exclamation "Hungry! Hungry! Hungry!" Although the child asks consistently about the reasons or functions of the goblin's body parts, the goblin's refuses to provide an intelligible, logical answer – much unlike the Wolf in the classical tale. Another important difference to the Wolf's answers is that the goblin does not put eir physical attributes in relation to the child. Ey does not say, for example, 'The better to grab you with!' but instead describes what ey is doing with eir "powerful hands." I think this semiotic shift in the well-known dialogue is important: rather than using the monster's bodily particularities in order to establish an interpersonal relationship that is based on a glaring power imbalance between an active, aggressive doer (the Wolf) and a passive, unprotected victim (Little Red), this picturebook narrative establishes these physical attributes as largely self-sufficient. Although the picturebook dialogue maintains enough elements to make the intertextual connection with the fairy tale clear, it diverges in that most essential characteristic which consists of the perpetrator-victim dynamic. If the power dynamic between the Wolf and Little Red are understood as characteristic for a specifically heterosexual interaction, then the dialog between the goblin and the ginger haired child can be read as breaking up this dynamic, as undoing a part of the 'gender-script' of the fairy tale. In this sense, the goblin's self-description presents me with a challenge to heteronormative gender performativity.

> [...] performativity is not a singular act, but a repetition and a ritual, which achieves its effects through its naturalization and the context of a body, understood, in part, as a culturally sustained temporal duration. [...] The view that gender is performative sought to show that what we take to be an internal essence of gender is manufactured through a sustained set of acts, posited through the gendered stylization of the body. In this way, it showed that what we take to be an "internal" feature of ourselves is one that we anticipate and produce through certain bodily acts [...]. (Butler 1999: xv f.)

Evidently, the goblin in *Hungry! Hungry! Hungry!* cannot do away with a hundredfold repetition of Wolf and Little Red interacting in ever the same ways. But what the goblin can do is establish a different kind of stylized body, a different set of acts. Although the dialogue in this picturebook thrives on a sense of anticipation, based of course on the intertextual reference to *Little Red Riding Hood* and readers' knowledge about Little Red's fate, the themes of food and eating are given more space and more importance than fear.

On the cover page, the goblin sits at the table, visibly disheartened at the sight of one single green pea on eir gold plate.

Fruit and vegetables continue to accompany the narrative like a colorful thread on every page. Often the fruits appear in unexpected places, for example a red bell pepper in the shape of a hot-air balloon high up in the sky. Large items of food, such as an apple hovering in front of a cloudy sky, or a huge pumpkin, are decorating the walls inside the house as big, framed paintings reminiscent of some of René Magritte's artworks. Fruits, and particularly certain kinds of fruits, have an interesting history of sexual symbolism. There are bananas on several pages, flying through the air or standing upright in their fruit basket, defying gravity. One very erect carrot is displayed on a poster on the cellar door. The apple, the infamous forbidden fruit and symbol of sexual seduction, enjoys several appearances throughout this book. Other round fruits that look like a pineapple, plums, oranges or peaches are also implemented into almost every image. Taking the sexual symbolism of these picturesque fruits even farther, I could now suggest that the 'hunger' is really an expression of awakening sexual drives that embrace masculinity as much as femininity and that cannot be identified as either heterosexuality or homosexuality, simply because the desiring agent escapes normative gender.

My associations with sexuality are not only triggered by the representations of fruits but also by other visual motifs that can be read as sexual imagery, such as the long red garden hose or the goblin's squirting bout with bottles of shampoo and body lotion or simply the chasing of each other around the house and garden. The playfulness of these scenes is not aggressive nor is it always clear who chases whom. Instead the changes of the goblin's and the child's body positions relative to one another as well as on the page itself create a topsy-turvy world in which gravity seems an equally odd phantasm as gender categories and hierarchies. This playfulness that saturates colors, principles of gravity and gender discourse is epitomized on the very last picture of child and goblin. The child's question whether the goblin "would [...] like a jelly-bean instead [of the child]" (Doyle and Hess 2004: np) makes the drama of the previous scene of the child hiding under eir bed and the goblin hovering over eir with huge gaping mouth tumble all over and crumble. The single tiny red jellybean that travels from the child's to the monster's hand is, quite literally, an adequate substitute for the child. The monster is satisfied: "That will do nicely. Thank you very much." (ibid)

Just before this anticlimactic resolution the ginger-haired child has asked in an unmistakable homage to *Little Red Riding Hood*: "What have you come for?" It is the goblin's completely unexpected and understated acceptance of the child's modest gift that transforms the goblin's calamitous answer to the child's question, "YOU!", into a radical reform of thinking gender. The "YOU" can now be expanded to: "I have come for you as my friend with whom I want to share the pleasures in life. I will not perpetuate the cliché of the big, bad wolf getting turned on by the little, helpless girl, nor am I here to create some kind of masculinity-enforcing secret bond with you. I like you and I *am* like you and we can be boys or girls or "something else entirely" (Bornstein 1997: title page). I have come for you and together we will get past that "evil cult" that is gender (Carrellas 2014). And we will start by eating jelly beans."

Ann Alston claims that

> [i]t is boys in children's literature who are greediest, who can eat the most and are most concerned about food. In turn it is boys who fall easily into temptation and who succumb to their desires most readily. [...] the provision of exotic food and drink [...] both arouses and temporarily sates masculine appetite. (Alston 2008: 116)

Another way of reading at least *Hungry! Hungry! Hungry!* is to underscore the child protagonists' (both human and monster) desire, their hunger, for overcoming this binary thinking that divides the world into greedy, lusty males and frugal, frigid females, into domination and submission, active and passive, powerful and powerless – the list could continue endlessly. The monster does *not* fall into temptation to eat the human child, precisely because the object of eir desire was not annihilation of some 'other,' but rather the forming of a beautiful friendship based on countless similarities and differences. Just as the clock in the child's bedroom has moved four minutes past twelve the spook of *Little Red Riding Hood* has lifted. The stuffed jester no longer pokes eir worried face into the middle of the page opening to point out to the reader the troublesome performance going on in this room. The jester, that "embodiment of speaking truth to power [...] taking on the ultimate

184

authority of a medieval monarch" (Carlyon 2002: 14), is done away with: the jester has nothing left to say because there *is* no "truth" and the ultimate authority lies with every person who does gender consciously, ironically and actively. Everything is peaceful and quiet now. Having broken down the gender binaries of an age-old fairy tale, child and monster sit amicably on the bed. The monster is in plain sight but there is nothing "monstrous [or] frightening" (Butler 1999: viii) about the breakdown of these binaries. In her preface of the 1999 edition of *Gender Trouble*, Judith Butler asks if "the breakdown of gender binaries [...] must be held to be definitionally impossible and heuristically precluded from any effort to think gender" (ibid). I am taking the liberty here of re-writing Butler's rhetorical question and transforming it into an affirmative claim, so that the breakdown of gender binaries, such as in this queer picturebook reading I have just offered, must not only be held to be possible, but positively to *enforce* any effort to think gender. This breakdown of gender binaries is never a complete collapse, but rather the emergence of alternative options or, at the least, the struggle for their cultural articulation.

In *Bodies that Matter*, Butler says that "[the] construction of gender operates through exclusionary means" (Butler 1993: 8), that it is, in other words, enabled through differentiation between what is "human," i.e. male or female, masculine or feminine, conforming to intelligible gender norms; and what is "inhuman" or even "humanly unthinkable" (ibid). Eve Kosofsky Sedgwick employs this meaning of 'human' with regard to boys, claiming that in order to be accepted as human, boys need to erase any trace of effeminateness and fully submerge themselves in whatever counts as 'masculine' in contemporary American society (Sedgwick 1998: 231–240). As a consequence, this logic posits girls and women as 'inhuman' or 'monstrous,' as many earlier feminists have argued (ibid). None of this association between monstrosity and femininity can be perceived in *Hungry! Hungry! Hungry!* – nor in any other picturebook in my corpus. In this queer reading of the picturebook, I read the interaction between the child and the goblin as an integration of the 'monstrous', the 'non-human' into the 'human.' Gender here operates through the means of mutual affection and hospitality towards the 'unknowable.' An individual without a gender is unthinkable, but at the same time gender nonconformity does not have to be unintelligible or threatening.

Conclusion

My queer readerly approach to *Hungry! Hungry! Hungry!* was an experiment that, in my eyes, led to a slightly paradoxical outcome. On the one hand, this reading made visible the existence of many signs, both verbal and visual, that had remained invisible in my first interpretation of this text. For example, building an argument around the absence of certain words, such as (gendered) pronouns, opens up the possibility of using alternative pronouns that have the potential of destabilizing the supposed fixity of visual codes in terms of gender ascription. On the other hand, the very use of these gender-neutral pronouns presented a kind of stumbling block to me. On several occasions, whilst in the flow of writing, my fingers hammered into the keyboard the masculine pronouns 'he', 'his', and 'him', instead of the 'ey', 'eir' and 'eirs' that I had planned to use. In other words, the employment of the gender-neutral pronouns required my premeditation and my conscious effort every single time. One reason for this is arguably my unfamiliarity with these pronouns, my lacking habit of using them. But I see another reason: my willful reading against the gender discourse in picturebooks is only one single act against countless repetitions of writing, drawing and reading gender in a normative way. This realization to some extent supports Butler's skepticism about the very possibility that an individual might at all be able to create an alternative gender identity that escapes a compulsory binary classification (Butler 2004). But even if the child and the monster in *Hungry! Hungry! Hungry!* are fixed as males, through their visualized bodily attributes but also through this narrative's similarity with more than a dozen other picturebooks with this motif, the allusions to and the gender-specific divergence from *Little Red Riding Hood* make clear to what extent the discursive rules for femininity and masculinity are made up by stories written for children.

4.2   Marriage, monsters and maidens

Why picturebook monsters interacting with strong girls are different and what fairy tales have to do with it

Introduction

In a discussion of an early draft of the previous chapter in a colloquium at my department, someone asked me what would make a strong girl in a monster picturebook. The person who asked this question was evidently appalled by the hyper-sexist image of Angela in *The Monster and the Teddy Bear* – a picturebook that is, by all means of comparison, admittedly extreme in this respect. But however extreme Angela's representation may seem, most other girl protagonists in my corpus tend to be constructed around similar ideas about childhood femininity as characterized by dependency on males/masculinity or adults, a connected belittled naiveté, and a pronounced aversion against everything monstrous. Not even my active search for admirable heroines in monster picturebooks produced much worthy of mentioning. The only two truly independent-minded, powerful heroines (who do not have to share their triumph over adversity with younger brothers)[12] are the girl protagonists in Babette Cole's *Princess Smartypants* (1986) and Maurice Sendak's *Outside Over There* (1981). Their activity and agency can, in every respect, be paralleled to the representation of the large number of male child heroes; but their relationships to the monsters cannot. So if I built the preceding chapter on the observation of the frequency and dominance of the motif of fear, the two books that I will discuss in the following stand out because of their

---

[12] In *The Day Louis Got Eaten* (John Fardell 2011), Louis' sister saves her brother with wit and courage, only to be then saved by her brother who mimics a monster's threatening behavior (again, there is an alignment of boy and monster and a deplorable 'need' for the boy to have the last word as savior). In Pat Hutchin's *The Very Worst Monster* (1985) a girl who, after the birth of her brother, feels neglected and ignored by her family, fights for the status of 'worst monster' which she ultimately has to share with her baby brother.

singularity. Their common ground comprises three aspects: they both have a powerful female agent, they are firmly tied to a narrative framework of fairy tales, and in both stories marriage is a constitutive motif.

In the preceding chapter, I discussed the perseverance of *Little Red Riding Hood* as a cultural narrative about gender norms. In this chapter, fairy tales again play a major role. What is it with fairy tales and girls? Or, perhaps the question should rather be: What is it with fairy tales and feminism? – A short answer may be that because of the patriarchal values that are embedded in the canonical fairy tales and because of their high degree of popularity, these texts lend themselves for feminist retellings and revisions aimed at creating 'emancipated' females. A more complex answer will have to address the question whether this strategy actually produces the desired effects. To complicate matters, not all fairy tale inspired picturebook stories are feminist in orientation and yet, some of those still have a strong female protagonist, as Ida showcases in *Outside Over There*. In addition to the historical connection between feminism and fairy tales, I will provide a basic introduction to some formal theory of fairy tales that is relevant for this discussion. I consider both the feminist history and the formal parameters as contextual information that is necessary for understanding how femininity is constructed in both picturebooks. *Princess Smartypants* transports a clearly feminist message through the very subversion of the gender patterns in traditional fairy tales. In *Outside Over There*, in contrast, a feminist bias is less than obvious, while fairy tales have an equally high impact on the story as a whole. Despite *Princess Smartypants*' feminist mission, I will argue that the female protagonist in Sendak's book carries more potential to transcend gender boundaries than Princess Smartypants who simply acts in opposition to the expectations imposed on her.

Marriage, fairy tales and feminism

In *Princess Smartypants*, the plot centers on the heroine's quest to evade marriage with the help of her monstrous pets. In *Outside Over There* the heroine's quest is triggered by the horrifying idea that goblins have abducted her sister in order to wed her to one of them. While Princess Smartypants' refusal to marry is an unmistakable feminist comment on the classical happy ending of almost all canonical fairy tales, the treatment of marriage in *Outside Over There* resembles a dreamlike and puzzling reflection of its importance for the logic of fairy tales rather than feminist concerns. Regardless of their ideological differences, both picturebook stories heavily draw on two formal characteristics of fairy tales: the imitation of the typical narrative pattern, also called morphology, of the magic tale and the use of staple characters, namely that of princess/prince and that of (supernatural) adversary. Moreover, both stories are built upon multiple allusions to specific fairy tales. In the following paragraphs, I will sketch out these formal aspects and their interplay with the two picturebooks and then consider some theoretical implications for feminist retellings of fairy tales, of which *Princess Smartypants* is one example.

Although neither is an adaptation of a specific fairy tale, *Princess Smartypants* and *Outside Over There* both make use of the morphological markers of the fairy tale, as distinct from other tale types according to the Aarne-Thompson-Uther classification system (Dundes 1997: 195). Unlike the animal tale or the realistic tale, the fairy tale, occasionally also referred to as "tale of magic" (Uther 2004), is characterized by elements of the supernatural. Russian formalist Vladimir Propp's influential view can be summarized as a thesis according to which

> there are a limited number of functions in the magic folktale with an identical succession of events. The hero lacks something and goes in search of aid (intermediaries) to achieve happiness, most often marriage. The structure of every magic folktale conforms to this quest (Zipes 2012: 5).

This view is complemented by Swiss folklorist Max Lüthi, "who sees the hero of a magic folktale as a wanderer charged with carrying out a task. Because the answer or solution to this task is known in advance, there is no such thing as chance or coincidence in folktales" (ibid). Both Propp and Lüthi suggest that the action consists of a search, a journey, or a quest. I wonder whether these two structuralists' formulae for the 'hero' also apply to the 'heroine,' because most fairy tale heroines that come to my mind (Rapunzel, Sleeping Beauty, Little Red Riding Hood, Snow White, the miller's daughter in *Rumpelstiltskin*) are rather inactive about "achiev[ing] happiness" (ibid). Instead, they simply sit out the ordeal through which they are dragged by an omniscient, but surely male, narrator, and wait for their prince to come and marry them. Another question that tickles me: why is it that, even though male characters are evidently so much more active about finding a wife, tales with female main characters seem to enjoy so much more popularity in contemporary fairy tale collections for children?

Regardless of the protagonist's gender, however, they all have to pass a trial which usually ends in marriage, fairy tale sign for happiness. Both Ida in *Outside Over There* and Princess Smartypants have to pass a trial, neither of which, however, ends in marriage. Rather, marriage becomes the trial itself.

As already mentioned, the staple characters of the magic folktale are present in both picturebooks. Princess Smartypants is obviously cast in the role of universal 'princess' and her adversaries are all her unwanted male suitors. Ida, I will argue, corresponds in many respects with the figure of the 'prince' and her supernatural adversaries are the goblins who kidnap her baby sister. *Princess Smartypants* overtly relates to the popular image of *the* princess in contemporary children's culture, influenced by a small number of fairy tales that have made it into the popular canon. The tales most frequently found in American editions include the following twelve, all featuring female protagonists which have contributed to shaping the Grimms' heroines into stereotypes of all princesses: 1. *Sleeping Beauty*, 2. *Snow White*, 3. *Cinderella*, 4. *Rumpelstiltskin*, 5. *Hansel and Gretel*, 6. *The Frog King*, 7. *The Goose Girl*, 8. *King Thrushbeard*, 9. *Rapunzel*, 10. *Little Red Riding Hood*, 11. *Mother Hulda*, 12. *The Six Swans* (Dégh 1983: 123). A closer look at this selection will reveal that not all of the female protagonists are or become princesses and that the tale of *Hansel and Gretel* could even be used as an example for female initiative. But the girls and young women in these tales are all characterized by a strong willingness to suffer, to be subservient and passive and to wait for their male rescuers or 'fate' to redress the balance between good and evil. Any attempt to argue for the agency of the princesses, such as

Elke Feustel's chapter on the female youth in the Grimms' tales (Feustel 2012: 252-298), is bound to end up in emphasizing minute details and imposing interpretations that I find problematic for many reasons.[13] Most details that Feustel uses for her analysis of the Grimms' original texts have not survived the heavy editing and smoothing out that is most impressive and certainly most influential in the Disney versions. Folklorist Linda Dégh could only identify four or five authentic and complete translations of the Grimms' tales in the USA, and those are generally addressed to academic readers (Dégh 1983: 118). What has instead shaped the image of the fairy tale princess are countless incomplete editions, picture-books and children's book, which often only contain one or few tales. Disney's impact on the popular cultural reception of the princess can indeed not be overestimated. It is this merged princess figure that cannot be traced to any one particular tale, that Babette Cole uses as a contrast to create the headstrong Princess Smartypants.

Ida in *Outside Over There*, despite her being a girl and going through a fairy tale adventure, does not display any of the typical princess characteristics – other than, perhaps, having long blond hair and wearing a long dress – but neither is she a feminist construction of a counter-narrative to an antiquated gender stereotype like Princess Smartypants. Instead, her behavior during her fantasy journey is somewhat reminiscent of Propp and Lüthi's summaries of the fairy tale *hero* as "a wanderer charged with carrying out a task" (Zipes 1983: 5), namely to save her sister from marrying "a

---

[13] Despite Feustel's efforts to illustrate the princesses' autonomy, the only type of princess who can be said to have any agency, however limited, is the "riddle princess" (Rätselprinzessin) who refuses to marry anyone unable to solve her riddles (ibid: 283). Her initial unruliness unfailingly ends, of course, with marriage. What is more, the riddle princesses' affinity to intellectual or physical challenges might be the very reason why none of them have made it into the popular canon of princesses. On the other hand, only two of the six tales which Feustel cites as examples of the riddle princess actually feature a princess who sets the riddles (KHM* 114 and KHM 191), the others have the princess' mother or father set the riddles, thus making the princess a more or less lifeless, will-less trophy (KHM 17; 71; 133; 134) for the suitor to carry home.
*KHM = *Kinder- und Hausmärchen*

nasty goblin" (Sendak 1981: np). She overcomes a series of obstacles, aided by magical assets: a flying cloak, a magic song, and her wonder horn. She returns home with the goblins vanquished and her sister retrieved. However, this – perhaps inadvertent (by the author) – gender subversion is complicated by the fact that Ida, once returned, has to reconcile her princely achievements with her parents' expecting her to be babysitter, mother's protector and father's confidante all at once.

The other staple character of interest for my analysis of the two picturebooks is that of the adversary. Only in *Outside Over There* can the adversaries be labelled 'monsters.' It is noteworthy, however, that 'monster' as a term does not occur in the Grimms' corpus and that there are "only a few tales of dragon and giant slayers among hundreds of tales" (Tatar 1999: 282). Nevertheless, the 'princess and dragon' story is a tremendously popular one which only serves to cement further the image of the princess as helpless and of the prince as her brave savior. In the context of the enormous influence of psychoanalytical interpretations of fairy tales in the twentieth century, Lüthi notes that the fight with the dragon is a translation of the prince's rival who, in the guise of the dragon, may be unobjectionably slayed (Lüthi 2004: 106). The 'monsters' in *Outside Over There* are not dragons or giants but goblins. In *Princess Smartypants*, the adversaries come in the role of suitors whereas the monsters are the princess' friends and helpers, thereby complying with the book's general theme of reverting traditional fairy tale roles.

The third fairy tale element that both picturebooks share is the reference to specific tales, rather than just a general employment of morphological patterns and typical characters. In *Princess Smartypants*, these intertextual references are made in passing by incorporating single plot elements, such as the princess' setting her suitors tasks (in the tradition of the riddle princess, cf. footnote 10), the specific nature of some tasks (the prince rescuing her from the tower can be read as an allusion to *Rapunzel* and *Sleeping Beauty*), and the reversal of what must be one of the most famous fairy tale metamorphoses of frog into prince (*The Frog Prince, or Iron Henry*). In other words, Babette Cole gaily assembles a collage of the most well-known fairy tale motifs that can be connected to the tales just mentioned. *Outside Over There*, in contrast, is inspired by one specific tale and a very obscure one at that: *Die Wich-telmänner* (KHM (= Kinder- und Hausmärchen) 39) (Sendak 2011: interview). Unlike *Princess Smartypants*, which does not harbor any significant comprehension difficulties to anyone even superficially familiar with the Western canon of fairy tales, understanding some of the more cryptic elements of *Outside Over There* becomes easier with the knowledge of this particular tale.

The theoretical background of these formal characteristics informs both picturebooks to a considerable extent as will become clearer in the close readings that follow. Equally important, particularly for my discussion of *Princess Smartypants*, is the gender bias that is particularly glaring in the canonized tales and in the Disney movies and that has prompted many feminist scholars in the 1970s and 1980s to publish academic works that draw attention to and criticized the cultural reverberations of these tales (e.g. Lieberman 1972: 383-395; Stone 1975: 42-45; Bottigheimer 1987); Tatar 1987). These critical voices gained momentum in these years and were probably partly accountable for the prolific production of feminist retellings or recoveries of lost tales, for adults and children alike (e.g. Janet Yolen *Sleeping Ugly* 1981; Babette Cole *Prince Cinders* 1987; Martin Waddell and Patrick Benson *The Tough Princess* 1986). Both the recoveries of lost tales with strong heroines and the feminist retelling of folk tales are motivated by the desire to reset the gender balance, as it were. At the same time, these authors, editors and collectors implicitly express the belief that fairy tales are an apt means for spreading feminist ideas and educating the young. With the example of Janet Yolen's *Sleeping Ugly*, Vanessa Joosen examines the tension between the overt didactic intentions behind such texts and their status of literary works in their own aesthetic right (Joosen 2005: 129-139).

> The irony, the exaggerations, the humor and the ambiguities in *Sleeping Ugly* offer the reader a way out of a programmatic feminist-didactic reading of the text. This book makes possible multiple readings, and invites discussions and re-readings. By teaching how to read against a text, Yolen's story at the same time asserts and undermines its feminist didactic message. (Joosen 2005: 137)

Because of its shared feminist motivation, *Princess Smartypants* could be discussed from a similar perspective, one that investigates this picturebook as a multidimensional work of art in dialogue with literary feminist theories. My own approach, however, diverges somewhat from Joosen's. It is fuelled by the question how Babette Cole's specific reworking of the fairy tale forms sketched out above impacts the shaping of the book's heroine in contrast to Ida in *Outside Over There*, a picturebook that also heavily relies on fairy tale forms but has no feminist agenda – and yet a strong heroine. Another way of putting this question: what are the effects for the construction of gender of a more or less avowedly feminist-didactic picturebook compared to one whose moral is less fixed and perhaps not even existent?

'Princess Smartypants'

Princess Smartypants is fond of her pets. On nearly every page, including the cover, she is seen with at least one of them. The verbal text, however, does not reveal what the pictures show: most of her 'pets' are monsters. A little dragon is riding with her on her motorbike; a slightly bigger dragon is walking and puffing on a leash; giant slugs, snails and dragons populate the royal gardens and successfully challenge Princess Smartypants' bothersome suitors; together with two small dragons, two dogs and a fully grown horse sprawling on the sofa the princess is watching television. As in *The Monster and the Teddy Bear*, a female protagonist defies the gendered behavior that is expected of girls by associating herself with monsters and, very prominently here, by opposing marriage. Princess Smartypants' monsters are the visualization of her contrary behavior. While for princesses in traditional fairy tales marriage, at the exclusion of everything else, holds all the promises for happiness, in *Princess Smartypants* it is an object of disdain which the princess does everything to keep at bay. Similarly, while dragons – the nearest approximation to monsters available – in fairy tales are always evil, keeping the princess prisoner until some prince comes to her rescue and slays the dragon, Babette Cole's picturebook shows dragons and a range of other monsters as the

194

princess' most loyal friends whose company is the only thing she needs to live happily ever after.

In the FAQ section on Babette Cole's homepage she answers the following question: "Are your characters based on yourself or anyone else you know?" Her answer, "[...] Princess Smartypants is my autobiography," (Cole 2013: np) is of course primarily funny. But her choice of a princess as her alter ego (instead of a witch, for example) might be indicative of her awareness of the role princesses play in many girls' (and women's) lives, including her own. In a field study of children's responses to genre and gender in picturebooks, Sarah Toomey notes that "[p]rincesses proved to be a particularly popular choice for a number of Year One[14] girls in both schools [where she conducted her research]" (Toomey 2009: 51). For one girl, discussing *Barbie as the Princess and the Pauper*, being a "real princess" is synonymous with having "blond hair, a pink dress on and a white cat" (ibid: 53). The external traits of fairy tale princesses (long, often "golden" hair, fair skin) in actual fairy tale texts are neither numerous nor very detailed, but they translate directly into a moral code of goodness and purity (Lüthi 2004: 30) which is embedded within popular culture (Warner 1994: 364). Toomey sums up her conversations about princesses with school girls saying that the

> ideological construction of beauty as a finite category [...] offers young girls a culturally overdetermined, perpetual representation of [...] the myth of woman and, by doing so, exposes certain cultural assumptions about femininity which serve to reaffirm the tradition of Western iconography which equates 'woman' with a type of generic, manufactured, white, westernised, flawless beauty. [...] The romantic construction of femininity is intrinsically connected to the heroine's quest for love, a quest that is epitomised in so many "definitive" versions of well-known fairy tales in which marriage is the ultimate goal. [...] Although gender ideologies are not passively internalised, they do become part of a repertoire of ways of thinking about what it means to be female. (Toomey 2009: 61 f.)

---

[14] In schools in England where Toomey conducted her research, Year One is currently the first full year of compulsory education, with children being aged five to six years old.

Fig. 13   *Princess Smartypants* (Cole 1986)

These apparently defining characteristics of the princess, i.e. her beauty and her will to marry, also form the basic ingredients for Cole's picturebook. Thus, Princess Smartypants "was very pretty and rich", which is the reason why "all the princes wanted to marry her" (Cole 1986: np). Like a "real princess", Princess Smartypants has long, blond hair. She paints her nails, wears earrings and a crown – but also red slippers and a t-shirt with a very colorful puzzle/flower pattern underneath a pair of dungarees. Thus, Cole ironically mixes iconic princess attire with clichés of a feminist appearance of the 1970s and 1980s. This ironic tension has been described as "ironic counterpoint" (Nikolajeva and Scott 2000: 225-239), but I would argue that at least in this instance it is created through the complementation of verbal and visual level. For example, the attribute "pretty" in the verbal text corresponds to the pictures of Princess Smartypants uniting signifiers both for feminine prettiness (long blond hair, nail varnish, jewelry, etc.) and for the emancipation from this beauty regime (dungarees, dirty boots, and unkempt hair). In other words, the verbal text does not send a message that opposes that of the images. Rather, the text offers a reliable, however brief, description of the princess' activities.

While watching television, painting nails and sunbathing in a red bikini could be said to conform to readers' expectations of a contemporary princess' idling and beauty care, the tension of fairy tale setting filled with contemporary pastimes is also humoristic. This tension is further heightened by the portrayal of Princess

196

He rescued her from her tower.

Fig. 14   *Princess Smartypants* (Cole 1986)

Smartypants' other activities: grooming her monstrous pets (fig. 13), cleaning the stables, involving a lot of animal feces on her boots, cross-country motor biking and dressage. The princess' perfect mastering of these activities is even more evident in contrast to her suitors' failing at these same tasks. Rather than fulfilling the genre and gender expectations of the helpless, suffering and enduring princess, this picturebook's heroine does the exact opposite: she is active, cunning, and driven by her own sense of pleasure – and that excludes marriage.

As Princess Smartypants prematurely considers herself safe from the horrid fate of getting married, Prince Swashbuckle enters the scene and, much to the princess' dismay, passes all her tasks with flying colors (fig 14). He is kempt and mustached and smiles a little too confidently, all the while displaying his large and even white teeth. Princess Smartypants, in contrast, looks increasingly annoyed, with furrowed brows and drooping corners of her mouth. The verbal text confirms the prince's arrogance: "Prince Swashbuckle didn't think Princess Smartypants was so smart" (Cole 1986: np). In response to his over-confident demeanor, "[Princess Smartypants] gave him a magic kiss" which turns him

197

"into a gigantic warty toad" (ibid: np). The toad's fate, who, visibly miffed, leaves in his red cabriolet, becomes a warning to every prince near and far never to woo Princess Smartypants again, "… so she lived happily ever after" (Cole 1986: np).

Princess Smartypants can be read as a feminist attack against a widespread development after the Second World War in the USA and in Great Britain of "sending women, who were already in the work force, back home into isolated and frustrated circumstances. […] And, despite some changes in the work force, this policy of keeping the woman at home has been maintained to the present" (Zipes 1989: 30). By letting her picturebook heroine refuse the very foundation of this development, i.e. marriage, Cole propagates feminist claims which were, at the time, no longer a novelty. What I find intriguing – because it almost completely slipped my notice – is that Princess Smartypants is not a woman but a girl. Of course many picturebook adaptations of fairy tales make children out of the heroines, but these tend to be adaptations in which explicit romantic or sexual themes are erased or covered.

Princess Smartypants is not an ageless female. Although some of her actions, such as riding a motor-bike or drinking possibly alcoholic cocktails, suggest that she is of age, her statue and clothing style could be considered as very childlike. For instance, on most pages she wears overalls with a colorfully patterned t-shirt underneath her pants, and she is barefooted. Her physical frame betrays no signs of sexual maturity, such as wider hips or breasts, which are usually employed in picturebook or comic illustration to ensure that a character's age can be appropriately estimated. (Needless to say, these illustrated and often exaggerated physical features do obviously not reflect the infinite shapes and sizes of actual humans' gendered physique.) Some of Princess Smartypants' suitors have mustaches (Prince Boneshaker, Prince Swashbuckle, two unnamed princes on the second page), or they appear in royal uniform (the three unnamed suitors on the second page, Prince Compost, Prince Grovel and, again, Prince Swashbuckle) – a style of dress generally associated with adulthood. Admittedly, some princes look as young and childlike as Princess Smartypants (such as Prince Pelvis or Prince Bashthumb), lacking Prince Swashbuckle and some other princes' broad shoulders, facial hair, and potent armory. Despite these ambiguities, I

198

So Prince Cinders married Princess Lovelypenny and lived in luxury, happily ever after . . .

Fig. 15   *Prince Cinders* (Cole 1987)

want to pursue this point a little further by comparing the depiction of Princess Smartypants with that of the eponymous hero of *Prince Cinders* (Cole 1987) and his female counterpart.

In *Prince Cinders* (fig. 15), a specific fairy tale retelling of *Cinderella* with a male protagonist, the romantic relationship unfolds between two protagonists of approximately the same age: Prince Cinders is depicted as an adolescent or young adult with a stubble and his princess shows the contours of breasts, and on some pictures she wears red lipstick and a skin-tight, leopard-patterned suit; so she is visually characterized as a beast of prey, that is, in an active and possibly destructive role. The male hero, Prince Cinders, is on a similar physical developmental stage as his wife-to-be while Princess Smartypants, in comparison and despite her feminist ado, appears to me almost too much like a child for having to ward off the sexual advances of adult males.

This seems like a harsh statement about a picturebook which has been heralded as a subversive and empowering fairy tale adaptation for girls ever since its publication in 1986. And, of course, it is not as simple as that. As I have pointed out above, reading Princess Smartypants as a child is not mandatory. On the other hand, there are visual signs that might lead to such a perspective. In support of these visual clues, there is the conventional practice of making the picturebook heroine or hero a child or childlike character, presumably so that they appeal more to child readers. However, this convention becomes problematic when the child or childlike character is involved in a romantic set-up with other seemingly adult characters. This perspective is further complicated if the protagonist's childlikeness is not even perceived, and possibly not even intended. One plausible reason for this lack of perception is that female characters, in picturebooks and other narratives of fiction, regularly deal with issues of heterosexual (romantic) relations, even though they are depicted as children. The princess narrative, of which *Princess Smartypants* is one – however feminist – example, is likely to be the most popular type of story that represents a female character of a very young age in search for ultimate fulfilment through love.[15] The naturalization of a sexually desired female child becomes all the more obvious to me when I try to imagine Prince Cinders as a prepubescent boy being wooed by an adult woman, or even just a pubescent girl. The relation between Princess Smartypants and her male suitors is – despite the princess' success in driving them all away – set in the conventional codes of a romantic framework. *Princess Smartypants* stands out not only because of its female protagonist, but also because her trial, as it were, consists in standing her ground regarding marriage and romance – themes which are virtually absent in the titles with male protagonists of my corpus.

When it comes to Princess Smartypants' relation to the monsters, this book seems to fit well into the roughly two thirds of my corpus in which a boy protagonist entertains a relationship with a

---

[15] The Disney Princesses, for example, are all based on their versions in the movies, in which they are young adults. But the princess narrative by far exceeds the borders of the movies, growing and flourishing in the shape of countless items of merchandize that portray the Disney Princesses in more and more childlike features. There is even an actual child princess, Sofia the First, who, in her television series, gets to meet the older Princesses and learns how to behave and dress in order to become a 'real' princess, including how to entice her future prince charming.

monster or monsters. This relationship is marked by solidarity and friendliness. But in fact, the monsters in *Princess Smartypants* only play a subordinate role. Sixteen out of twenty-nine frames, excluding the pictures on the title and half-title pages, portray one or several of her monsters as images, but only six of these frames refer to these creatures verbally as "pets" (three times), "slugs" (twice), or "animals" (once) – not once as 'monster.' Not only is the ratio between the two modes of representation extremely unbalanced, but the words which are used to represent the images are an ironic understatement of the monsters' enormous size. When the Princess is standing on the back of one of her "pets" to dust it with a broom she is no bigger than the saurian creature's front leg. A giant snail and a huge dragon tower to the left and to the right. The "slugs" are similarly gigantic, fully equipped with razor-sharp teeth and many pairs of little claws. Although these monsters visibly play a decisive role in securing the princess' freedom, their lacking verbal acknowledgment partly denies them this role.

Evidently, the discrepancy between images and words is the main cause for the humor in this book (here I fully subscribe to Nikolajeva and Scott's terminology of "ironic counterpoint"). It is also a technique which Cole uses in some of her other books. For example, *The Trouble with Mum* (1983) adopts a seemingly unassuming tone on the verbal level, not once betraying the fact that the trouble with mum is her being a witch complete with magic powers, while the visual narrative delves into fantastic detail. The "pets" to which the first person narrator introduces his school friends look very similar to those in *Princess Smartypants* and they are just as big, but their role is peripheral and thus their attribution as "pets" justified in terms of their function (if not their size). In *The Trouble with Gran* (1987) and *The Trouble with Grandad* (1988), Cole uses this technique with much less vigor, Gran being an alien not only in the images but also verbally, and Grandad creating a giant caterpillar also both in word and image.

While the discrepancy between the two levels of representation is a safe source for humor, the lack of words for Princess Smartypants' monstrous friends also yields the possibility for readers to misrecognize their agency, at least on the verbal representational level. When I read *Princess Smartypants* for the first time, I focused on the verbal narrative, fully focusing on the subverted fairy tale pattern. I only marginally noticed the princess' pets. They are supporting cast rather than equal partners. In line with this observation, the final sentence of the book – "When the other princes heard what had happened to Prince Swashbuckle, none of them wanted to marry Smartypants… so she lived happily ever after." (Cole 1986: np) – only acknowledges the princess' happiness although the four monsters surrounding her look just as content. They have fought as much as, if not more, than the princess herself to ward off her suitors. As emancipated as Princess Smartypants may be from patriarchal demands, her monstrous associates and friends are not.

Although the relationship between Smartypants and her monstrous pets is an intimate and empowering one, her monsters' lacking personality and agency sets them apart from boy protagonists' monsters. In fact, they are nothing but the humoristic continuation of another popular fairy tale motif that requires the heroine to be surrounded and supported by a company of animals (Joosen 2005: 137). The impact of Disney movies is of course enormous for the popularization and perpetuation of this motif. Consider, for example, *Snow White and the Seven Dwarfs* (1937) with Snow White's furred and feathered friends from the forest, *Cinderella* (1950) with the trusty mice, *The Little Mermaid* (1989) with Flounder the fish and Sebastian the crab, or *Mulan* (1998) with the small dragon Mushu. In these cinematic adaptations of fairy and folk tales, animal companions are not restricted to female main characters – heroes, too, have their support and friendship: Jiminy Cricket (*Pinocchio* 1940), Baloo (*The Jungle Book* 1967), and the kleptomaniac pet monkey Abu (*Aladdin* 1992) are comparable in many respects to the animal friends of Disney's princesses cited above. However, with the notable exception of *Princess Smartypants*, monsters in picturebooks are more than just supporting cast that are installed for comic relief and sometimes as the hero or heroine's externalized conscience. The function of the monsters in *Princess Smartypants*, then, corresponds with the fairy tale framework that provides this motif and that Cole uses for a kind of counter-narrative. In contrast, picturebooks with both human and monster characters are based on an initial or lasting antagonistic relationship between the two species. For this very reason, the monsters in these books are much more prominent, important and

202

decisive for the development of the story. The monsters in *Princess Smartypants*, on the other hand, just as the animal companions in so many fairy tale narratives with female protagonists, are denied any semblance of *human* agency, and thus largely support "the absence of female collaboration in [...] fairy tales" (Mendelson: 1997: 111).

Princess Smartypants is situated at the periphery of my corpus because the monsters are ultimately cast as supporting acts only. Princess Smartypants is doubtlessly a strong, emancipated female character in a picturebook that features monsters, but these monsters share very few functions and characteristics of the picturebook monsters in other titles. Consequently, my answer to my colleague's question how a strong girl protagonist might be constructed in a monster picturebook has to take into account that Smartypants' monsters are atypical compared to most monsters in my corpus. As I have argued above, their atypicality must be attributed to the fairy tale framework of the book as a whole which situates itself as a feminist retelling. As such, it is integrated into the tradition of viewing fairy tales and children's literature as a means of "socializing children to meet definitive normative expectations at home and in the public sphere" (Zipes 2012 [1983]: 9). Babette Cole as the creator of *Princess Smartypants* has "entered into a dialogue on values and manners with the [classical] folktale" (ibid: 10), as part of a discourse that she seeks to disrupt. Her attack is aimed at the portrayal of the princess as demure and eternally waiting for her prince to come. Smartypants' entire personality draws its power from opposition – which is, in a sense, simply another way of relating to an already existing discourse. By opposing the gender norms of fairy tale princesses, Smartypants comments on their existence and expresses a felt need for resistance among members of the educated middle-class who want to teach their daughters that heterosexual romance is not or no longer a requirement for women's individual happiness and fulfilment. In this respect, *Princess Smartypants* participates as a didactic vehicle in a shift of values in feminist-minded parts of middle-class society. While presenting an alternative example of constructing femininity that is based on opposition, other values traditionally associated with fairy tales and children's literature are left intact. Thus, material wealth (Smartypants' activities include cross-country motor biking, dressage, sunbathing and drinking cocktails) and a Western ideal of beauty (light skin, long blond hair, red nail varnish) and fashion (for each of her hobbies, Smartypants is dressed in appropriate attire, such as black leather motorbike armor, or horse riding clothes and helmet, or a red bikini for sunbathing), all contribute to stabilizing and idealizing upper middle-class whiteness as the norm. As subversive as *Princess Smartypants* may come across with regard to gender stereotypes, it is nevertheless a story that endorses values and social codes rooted in the bourgeoisie (ref. Zipes 2012 [1983]: 193). Because of its oppositional attitude, this endorsement of a bourgeois *habitus* seems to me more blatant than, for example, in *Outside Over There*. I find this interesting because Sendak's book builds on the cultural capital of the educated Westerner even more than *Princess Smartypants*.

'Outside Over There'

Outside Over There is the story of a girl named Ida, who has to watch her baby sister and, in a moment of inattention, loses her to monstrous goblin kidnappers. Ida is furious. She ventures out to save her sister and returns home successfully. Meanwhile her absent-minded mother has not budged from her bench "in the arbor" (Sendak 1981: np), looking out to the sea from where Ida's father is expected to come "home one day" (ibid). Maurice Sendak already proved a keen interest and fascination with the Grimms' fairy tales through his complex and dense illustrations of twenty-seven selected tales in *The Juniper Tree* (1974). Here in this picturebook, he emphasizes the symbolism that has drawn many folklorists and literary scholars to analyze fairy tales in terms of psychoanalysis. In my own reading of *Outside Over There*, in contrast, I am focusing on the pattern of home-away-home that that is constitutive of countless texts for children, but that Maurice Sendak has explored, in my eyes, particularly artfully. *Outside Over There* is often named as the third book of a trilogy that starts with *Where the Wild Things Are* (1963) and continues with *In the Night Kitchen* (1970). All three tell the story of a child compelled to leave his or her home and whose journey can easily be read – and

204

most often is – as a fantasy or a dream. Each book is stylistically distinct, but Sendak's style in *Outside Over There* is more reminiscent of his drawings for *The Juniper Tree* and for *Dear Mili* (1988) – another reworking of a very little known text by the Grimm brothers – while *Where the Wild Things Are* and *In the Night Kitchen* are stylistically more related to one another, possibly because they have no intertextual relations with fairy tales. Sendak is often praised for 'knowing the child' and rendering 'universal' problems that all children encounter into stunning artwork and poetic language that appeals to adults and children alike. But of course, such a view does not withstand a closer reading of any of his texts. What sets Ida apart from Max and Mickey[16] – in addition to the artistic style of the book – is that she is a girl. While Max and Mickey revel in their pleasurable fantasies, Ida has to watch and then save her sister. Right from the start of the story, Ida is described in terms of the responsibility she has for her younger sibling. Max and Mickey have no responsibilities at all. What I find intriguing about *Outside Over There* is that the story is inspired by a Grimms' fairy tale, but its heroine does not at all fit into the description of the classical fairy tale heroine; not even by a feminist opposition or subversion like Princess Smartypants. Rather, Ida integrates the character of prince into her own personality. Although Sendak relies on classical fairy tale motifs and story lines, he creates a female character whose strength and determination derives from the crossing back and forth of the very gender boundaries that are often cited as endemic to this genre.

Throughout this book, Sendak's uses idiosyncratic, compressed, poetic language that evades clear definitions in favor of ambiguity, complexity, and fracture. It is this language which makes any summary I have read of this book inadequate and already heavily influenced by the critics' own interpretations. For example, many critics summarize the story as one about sibling rivalry (Clemons 1981: 102; Griswold 1981: 674). However often I have read this description of the relationship between the two sisters, none of the authors specified the textual or visual basis for

---

[16] Max and Mickey are the heroes of *Where the Wild Things Are* (1963) and *In the Night Kitchen* (1970) respectively. Both books are part of a trilogy, of which *Outside Over There* is the last one.

their judgment – and this despite the allusive richness and symbolic density of both visuals and text that would surely enable such a reading, just as many others. Sendak's language is complemented by a visual aesthetics of the nineteenth century full with art historical references, including Philipp Otto Runge, Claude Lorrain, J.M.W. Turner and Caravaggio, and references to popular culture, such as Eddie Cantor dressed as a baby in the 1930s, the Dionne quintuplets mirrored in the five naked babies/goblins, Baby Snooks, and the Lindbergh kidnapping (Poole 1996: 108). In addition to the literary, popular cultural and art historic references, Sendak also includes allusions to and representations of music. Thus, Ida's "wonder horn" alludes to the collection of German folk songs *Des Knaben Wunderhorn* by Achim von Arnim and Clemens Brentano (Doonan 1997: 59), songs of which were set to music by several Romantic composers, most notably Gustav Mahler. (Interestingly, all the twelve songs of Mahler's collection focus on issues of gender relations.) Another allusion to music, Mozart's summer cottage just outside Vienna, where he finished his *Magic Flute*, is part of one of the tableaux of Ida's return (Poole 1996: 79). I agree with Poole when she says, "no amount of explanation will account for the haunting quality" of *Outside Over There* (Poole 1996: 115). My focus here will be, as I have said, a reading of Ida as merging the figure of prince and of fairy tale female, and on the representation of the goblins as monsters and hosts of a wedding – as well as their relationship with Ida.

Despite the many differences between the individual titles of Sendak's trilogy, Max, Mickey and Ida all encounter fantasy creatures that can be read as symbols of their emotional turmoil. Max meets the wild things, Mickey has to shake off three giant bakers that look like Charlie Chaplin incorporating Hitler, and Ida has to outsmart the goblins who stole her sister. But where Max's journey is framed by only one human person, his mother, and Mickey's parents only make "a racket" (Sendak 1970: np) and remain invisible just as Max's mother, Ida is tied into a network of family relations right from the start of the story, and remains so until the end. While Max's journey "to where the wild things are" (Sendak 1963: np) is triggered by his quarrel with his mother, Ida's initial problem is more complex. Having to cope with her father's physical absence, since he is "away at sea" (Sendak 1981: np), and her

Fig 16   *Outside Over There* (Sendak 1981)

mother's emotional absence (she sits on a bench "in the arbor" (ibid), staring straight ahead, empty-eyed, at two goblins carrying a ladder; she has turned her back to her daughters), Ida additionally has to babysit her little sister. At the outset, the story is about the burden of (possibly unwanted) responsibility, care and a sense of parental abandonment from Ida's perspective.

Child care with its accompanying responsibilities and worries is a central concern in the story. Maria Nikolajeva reads this "typical feminine theme" in connection with "anxiety" as the principal emotion in this picturebook (Nikolajeva 2010: 171). Child care is undeniably a prominent theme in many feminist debates and also the trigger of Ida's adventurous quest. But rather than causing mainly "anxiety," Ida's reaction to her discovery of her sister's abduction unfolds over several pages in the form of a nuanced study of multi-layered and contradictory emotions. Thus, Ida intends to "rock the baby still" (Sendak 1981: np) by playing her wonder horn, which implies her caring mind, but simultaneously plays on the ambiguous formulation of "[rocking] the baby *still*," inciting images of infanticide. Her already contradictory emotions of love and anger are deflected by her turning away from the baby, toward the window. Thus she does not see how goblins come inside the other window to steal her sister (fig. 16). The impending danger, the loss of the child, Ida's subsequent realization and following rage, are visualized by the sunflowers which, in a sequence of six frames menacingly creep further and further into the room, as well as the surreal view of the other window, where a sailing ship, symbol for the absent father, is first depicted taking its course and then lost to a violent thunder storm. Unlike Nikolajeva, I cannot make out any "vague and diffuse feelings of anxiety that have no particular target" (Nikolajeva 2010: 171). Quite the contrary, Ida is "mad" (Sendak 1981: np) when she realizes that "goblins had been there" (ibid) to steal her sister and replace her with a changeling, "all made of ice" (ibid). She shakes her fist in anger; in the background the raging sea transforms the landscape behind Ida's windows. In the following frame, Ida's figure fills the whole picture, with her outstretched arms and clenched fists touching the top, and her right foot pointing energetically into the opposite direction, nearly touching the bottom (fig. 17). Her pose is one of resolve and fierce determination. In the next frame, Ida's expression has changed yet again: she looks pensive and focused, wrapped in "her Mama's yellow rain cloak" and "her horn safe in her pocket" (ibid). Ida's emotions are infinitely more vivid and varied than Max's, on the visual as well as the verbal level. Both language and images make these six consecutive frames into a key scene of the book by visualizing the protagonist's emotions in a complexity which is extraordinary for a picturebook. These six frames are also the starting point for Ida's fantasy journey during which she slips into the role of the prince.

"They stole my sister away!" she cried.
"To be a nasty goblin's bride!"
Now Ida in a hurry

snatched her Mama's yellow rain cloak,
tucked her horn safe in a pocket,
and made a serious mistake.

Fig. 17   *Outside Over There* (Sendak 1981)

With the goblins kidnapping the baby, the starting point of action for the fairy tale hero, according to Lüthi, is established: a situation of lack (Lüthi 2004: 25). This lack is on one level Ida's loss of her sister. On the level of Ida's fantasy, however, it is the loss of her bride as Ida cries out: "They stole my sister away! [...] To be a nasty goblin's bride!" (ibid). In one fell swoop, Ida becomes the prince, and the goblins are the evil adversaries who must be vanquished. The wedding is mentioned three times in a verbal narrative with only 350 words: first, in Ida's anticipated fear that her sister will be "a nasty goblin's bride"; second, in her "Papa sailor's song" in which "she'd spoil their kidnap honeymoon"; and third, when she finds herself "smack in the middle of a wedding" (ibid). Despite these three occurrences, the wedding itself has never to my knowledge been commented upon in scholarly criticism. However, the story in general has been described as "sexually really overt" and as a psychological process by Ida (Chang-Kredl 2013: 184). Perhaps adults' feeling of discomfort and inappropriateness created by the combination of an infant in the sexual context of marriage in a picturebook is one reason for this. On the other hand, the wedding seems to be robbed of its meaning when the kidnappers are revealed as babies. Contrary to weddings in fairy tales, the wedding (or, rather, its prevention) in *Outside Over There* does not mark a happy ending nor is it the endpoint of the story. In fact, it becomes irrelevant as soon as Ida has rescued her sister. Rather, as part of Ida's fantasy journey and her prince persona, the wedding is a narrative requirement. In other words, Ida adopts the fairy tale morphology in which marriage is a necessary element and creatively uses this pattern in order to solve her own moral conflict of having neglected the task of looking after her sister. The figure of Ida is an example for crossing the gender boundaries that are usually imposed on picturebook characters and fairy tale characters alike.

Proper to the fairy tale hero, Ida is equipped with two magic assets: her wonder horn, with which she tames the goblins, and her mother's cloak, which serves her as a flying vehicle, followed by a third magical aid: her father's song which guides her to the goblins' cave. Her mistake to climb out of the window backwards could be interpreted as one element in a series of obstacles she has to overcome, or of riddles she has to solve, before she can find "the robber caves" (ibid). Thus she has to "[tumble] right side round" in her flying cloak in order to *really* see (and this is why "climbing backwards out the window" is "a serious mistake") (ibid); and she has to play the right tunes on her wonder horn in order to single out the real baby, her sister, from all the pretend-babies, the goblins. While the mother's cloak and the father's song are clearly external aids, the wonder horn is a symbol of Ida's very own resourcefulness and giftedness. In its reference to the Romantic collection of folk songs, the wonder horn is also a masculine attribute ("Des *Knaben* Wunderhorn", i.e. "The *Boy's* Magic Horn") – just as the musical instrument itself is arguably played more often by men, and certainly was in the nineteenth century when this story is set. During this fantasy part of the story, Ida's gender performance reflects some of the genre rules for masculine characters. With the aid of her magical assets, Prince Ida is able to annihilate the monsters, rescue her sister-princess and take her home again, safe and sound.

Ida's relation towards the goblins is another element of the story that shapes Ida's characterization. The goblins' representation as both hooded creatures of doom and as dancing, naked babies visualize in some sense Ida's contradictory feelings towards her sister: she wants to get rid of her so she can do what she likes and not what she is told and at the same time, Ida is fond of her sister and sees her as the baby she is, including a baby's dependence on someone to take care of them. The goblins' heinous part in the story is already hinted at through their looming presence even before the story starts: on the page before the half-title page, the half-title page and the dedication page. But since at this stage they are not named yet, their tie to fairy tales is not obvious; all they do is cause a feeling of unease. The wording, unlike that of *Princess Smartypants*, bears no reference to fairy tales either. It is thanks to another scholar's comment that I was able to trace this picturebooks intertextual relation with the third tale of the Grimms' *Die Wichtelmänner* (KHM 39). In this tale, goblins steal a mother's child to replace it with a changeling, also a goblin, with a big head and staring eyes. Taking her neighbor's advice, the mother puts the changeling onto the stove and cooks water in two eggshells which makes him laugh and exclaim (and thereby betraying his real nature): "Now I am as old as the Wester Wood, but have never seen anyone cooking in shells" (ibid). The goblin's laughter breaks the charm and the real baby is returned to his mother.

In *Outside Over There*, Sendak chooses to represent the goblins as little hooded and faceless creatures, departing from the image of the typical picturebook monster as cute and cuddly. They lack the repelling appearance of the monster in *The Monster and the Teddy Bear*, which is the only other properly *evil* monster in my corpus. Indeed, the goblins resemble the Nazgûl in J.R.R. Tolkien's *The Lord of the Rings*, cloaked wraiths of former men whose physical appearance has faded away and who cause unconsciousness, nightmares and eventual death. Considering Sendak's sketches for Tolkien's *The Hobbit*, which can be seen at the Rosenberg Museum in Philadelphia, it is not unlikely that Tolkien inspired Sendak's idea of the goblins. They are, in short, utterly terrifying. These nightmarish figures in a picturebook, which in so many respects diverge from 'normal' picturebook monsters, might raise the question in how far they even classify as picturebook monsters. I base my 'classification' primarily on these goblins' similarity, in some important respects, to the wild things. The most striking link between the wild things and the goblins – apart from their psychological function of translating the child protagonist's emotions into images – is the baffling similarity between the procession of the wild things on one of the three wordless dou-

"What a hubbub," said Ida sly,
and she charmed them with a captivating tune.

The goblins, all against their will, danced slowly first,
then faster until they couldn't breathe.

Fig. 18   *Outside Over There* (Sendak 1981)

blespreads and the dancing goblins on a doublespread in *Outside Over There* (fig. 18). In fact, these two scenes practically mirror each other: five wild things dance to the reader's left, with Max royally directing them (fig. 30, p. 279). Five goblins dance to the reader's right, with Ida conducting their pace with her horn. What crown and scepter are for Max, the wonder horn and the magic cloak are for Ida. In these two respective scenes, each child is in control of the monsters, symbols of the child's powerful emotions. Despite the initial horror that emanates from the faceless hooded creatures and that is very unlike the open and friendly appearance of the wild things, the goblins turn out to be controllable once they are turned into babies and ultimately, at least in this respect, come to resemble the wild things.

The appearance of these stark naked babies is another unusual sight in picturebooks, especially surprising in connection with their previous monstrosity and utterly evil nature. The reference to the fairy tale *Die Wichtelmänner* makes this representation more intelligible: the goblins are simply impostors. It is perhaps this fairy tale relationship which makes the fatal end of the goblins/babies more easily acceptable. When Ida plays a "frenzied jig," (Sendak 1981: np) the goblins cannot help but dance an "ecstatic death dance" (McNulty 1981: 220). The compulsive dancing is certainly a reminiscence of the goblin in the fairy tale who is thrown into a laughing fit at the sight of a woman cooking in egg shells. The egg

212

shells themselves, as they are lying around in the goblins' cave, seem random unless they are connected to the Grimms' tale. The goblins' fatal end is somewhat concealed by a dense, metaphorical language: "Those goblins pranced so fierce, so fast, they quick churned into a dancing stream" (Sendak 1981: np). The image above this caption-style text shows the five goblins as babies in wild water up to their chests, stretching out their arms, losing their balance, but not really looking alarmed. In the background, water-falls cause the water to rise up in clouds of mist, spray and foam. The danger of the situation, as McNulty describes it, can be in-ferred from the visual clues in the background, but it is not directly and unambiguously imposed on the reader. However, even in its allusion, the violent end of the goblins as Ida's adversaries is a drastic solution – albeit within the narrative logic of fairy tales. Contrary to *The Monster and the Teddy Bear*, in which the monster is done away with, though not killed, by big strong Teddy, here it is the female protagonist Ida who alone is responsible for the gob-lins' defeat.

Because of its ambiguities, shifting meanings and abundant cross-references in *Outside Over There*, the figure of Ida cannot easily be classified within the usual binaries of femi-nine/masculine. I see this refusal to be categorized as the key to Ida's resolve and cleverness in steering through the crisis. In other words, I read *Outside Over There* as a story of gender confusions and gender ambiguities. In an interview, Sendak said that another inspiration for this book was that his elder sister sometimes had to watch him as a baby – and was never very pleased with that task. I can think of many reasons why the baby in *Outside Over There* is a girl. It could be the author's desire to detach this story from his biography, or to make it a more 'universal' story, or perhaps to enact upon a fantasy to be a girl. In any way, I take this biographi-cal anecdote as a first instance of gender crossing. Similarly, Ida inhabits many different personae and genders at the same time: she is the baby's elder sister, the princess' prince, her mother's care-giver, and her father's loved one (or lover?), as the story's conclu-sion shows. Her father, in a letter, says: "[…] my brave, bright little Ida must watch the baby and her Mama for her Papa, who loves her always."

The father's address to Ida is another ambiguity in this picturebook. Quite a few critics interpret the father's cryptic role in this text as part of an Oedipal triangle (Gardner 1981: 64; Reed 1986: 177; Poole 1996: 108; Nikolajeva and Scott 2001: 201; Chang-Kredl 2013: 184). As I have explained in detail in chapter 2.2.3, I find psychoanalytical interpretations of literature questionable, but particularly problematic when it is applied to children's texts as here. Reading Ida's journey as a tale of "the displacement of the mother in the sexual embrace of the father and the desire to have the father's baby" (Reed 1986: 178), naturalizes passivity and helplessness as female characteristics that are 'healthy' and 'normal' points in the psychosexual development of girls. In spite of Ida's problematic relationship with her parents, including possibly romantic components, she is a resolute and resourceful female character who cannot easily be straight-jacketed by the female Oedipus complex.

Bypassing psychoanalysis altogether in my interpretation of *Outside Over There* seems impossible since this would require me to ignore the majority of already existing interpretations of this text. And although I refuse to buy into or perpetuate the misogynist gender system that Freud set into place, I also acknowledge the aesthetic and intellectual appeal his theories have for literary analysis, including this picturebook. But rather than applying the Oedipus complex, female or not, to Sendak's text I look at Virginia Goldner's recapitulations of feminist psychoanalysis. By seeing gender and sexuality as compromise formations (and not as fixed entities), "[g]ender would be construed as a fixed social identity *and* a fluid psychic state, constituted in the tension between objectification (however that is defined in a particular cultural and family context) and agency (the individual subject's continuous project of self-creation" (Goldner 2003: 131).

> None of gender's attributes are inherent to gender; […] in the process of genderizing human capacity, we get more than we bargained for. For example, if "agency" codes as masculine, it will be infested with the defensive splitting off of dependency. Gender's multiple meanings are ultimately normative conveniences whose every deployment reinscribes the very polarities that have been so injurious. Ultimately, gender formations succeed "so well" as compromise formations *because they lean on the paradoxes inherent in gender*

categories themselves, paradoxes that [...] simultaneously potentialize and foreclose. [...] The issue ... is not gender per se, but how rigidly and concretely it is being used in an individual mind or family context, and what psychic and intersubjective work it is being deployed to do. [...] the question becomes the extent to which the subject experiences herself as personally investing gender with meaning, or whether gender is a "meaning happening to her". (Ibid: 134 f.)

Ida is a powerful figure precisely because she does not allow gendered attributes to "happen to her." Although she is firmly tied in her family network and has to bear a responsibility which is both beyond her actual age and clearly coded as feminine, Ida is not subdued by this role. She recovers and asserts her agency all the while she complies with her familial duties. In this sense, *Outside Over There* is, to quote Goldner again, an artful portrayal of "gender [...] as a fixed social identity *and* a fluid psychic state." Ida is shown as well aware of her role as sister and daughter by assuming responsibility for her temporary negligence of the task to look after the baby. She does so by effortlessly slipping into a performance of masculinity, displaying bravery and putting up a ruthless fight against her monstrous adversaries.

Conclusion

I started out this chapter with the question what makes a strong girl in a picturebook with monsters. Although there are a small handful of independent-minded, resourceful and resolute heroines in my corpus, these attributions come with a certain trade-off: the protagonists might have to share their monstrous success with their younger brothers (*The Day Louis Got Eaten* and *The Very Worst Monster*), or they have to do their favorite hobbies in secret for fear of losing their monster friends' recognition (*Mostly Monsterly*). The two girl protagonists whose agency and individuality appear to me as the least compromised are Ida and Princess Smartypants. But as much as they compare with the majority of self-confident, smart and courageous boys in my corpus, their monsters are very different. Where Smartypants' monstrous pets act as her loyal and good humored servants with no will of their own, Ida's adversaries are nightmarish goblins that need to be transformed into babies and then got rid of by torrential masses of water. In neither book do the monster characters provide a set of additional skills and characteristics that the girl protagonist would be able to integrate into their self-image – as it is the pattern for the books with male protagonists that I discussed in the previous chapter.

Although many of the stories with male characters describe rites of passage of some sort, very few of them are even remotely concerned with marriage or other initiations into romantic, sexual relationships. One of two exceptions, *Shrek!* (1990) by William Steig is a parody of chivalry romance and, as such, tells the story of the ugly and utterly despicable anti-hero Shrek (who has none of the amiability of his cinematic rendition) on a quest away from home and in search of his bride, "the most stunningly ugly princess on the surface of the planet" (Steig 1990: np). They marry and "[live] horribly ever after" (ibid). The two protagonists in *The Big Ugly Monster and the Little Stone Rabbit* (2004) by Chris Wormell could be argued to entertain a romantic friendship or relationship in that they spend the monster's entire life together, the rabbit being unfailingly loyal, albeit made of stone (i.e. inanimate) and of neutral gender, and the monster being unfailingly happy about the rabbit's companionship. Both books, however different, feature a monstrous protagonist who is either coming of age (Shrek) or already grown-up, growing older and eventually dying of old age, throughout the story. In other words, neither of them is a childlike character as it is the case in all the other picturebooks in my corpus in which a monster is the main protagonist (e.g. *POG – The Monster Who Was Afraid of Children*; *The Monster At the End of This Book*; *Leonardo, the Terrible Monster*; *Not Now, Bernard*; *Beegu*; *The Boy Who Ate Around*). Due to the lack of a childlike character, neither *Shrek!* nor *The Big Ugly Monster and the Little Stone Rabbit* negotiate images of childhood or 'the child.'

What struck me in *Princess Smartypants*, in comparison with Steig's and Wormell's picturebooks, was the ambiguity of Smartypants' age. When I take into account that the representation of romance in picturebooks is usually played out between characters of a similar age (they are either grown-ups or children), Smartypants' involuntary involvement in marital preparations with adult

216

men could be interpreted as undermining the book's feminist message seems almost perverse – supposing, of course, that she is still a child. Smartypants' bodily representation could be interpreted in Jacqueline Rose's sense as the author's hidden desire to render her heroine innocent. On the other hand, as I have pointed out, some visual details do suggest that Smartypants is of age, so that, ultimately, readers are left with a sense of ambiguity concerning this question. And of course, historically, children and sometimes infants from the aristocracy were often married well before they reached adulthood. The difficulty of determining Smartypants' age, as well as numerous other contradicting visual elements, might also be understood as a reference to the fairy tale genre as indeterminable with respect to historical dates or facts.

Remarkably, Ida is also forced to position herself towards the institution of marriage, albeit in a more open and ambiguous way: she sets out to prevent the goblins from marrying her sister and she saves her from experiencing an awful honeymoon. In both books, the heroines are shaped by their opposition to (a) marriage. But while in *Princess Smartypants* this opposition rests on a feminist conception of marriage as a patriarchal trap, in *Outside Over There* it functions as one of many dreamlike and sometimes disturbing elements that are interlocked with fairy tale motifs, morphology and specific texts. The fact that Ida's opposition to (her sister's) marriage is motivated by the necessity to retrieve her from captivity, rather than embedded into a feminist retelling, enables reading her character as a gender collage. The caring role that falls to Ida is a stereotypically female one but her quest narrative shows how her task of looking after her baby sister is tough and heroic in a way usually associated with masculinity. In this respect, Sendak's narrative also destabilizes the gender stereotypes surrounding caring roles with a greater appreciation for the challenges and importance of such tasks.

4.3 Outsiders: sissies, freaks and foreigners

How ideas about masculinity and femininity impact the construction of bodily, cultural and sexual difference

Introduction

In fictional narratives for grown-ups, cultural and/or racialized otherness counts among the most frequent themes for which monsters are used. This symbolical or metaphorical use can be traced back to Ancient Greek travellers' reports, such as Ktesias of Knidos and Megasthenes, who have purportedly witnessed such wild imaginings as the Blemmyae (headless creatures with one big eye on their chests), the Sciapods (creatures with one big leg and foot, alternately used for hopping and for sun-shielding) and the Kynokephaloi (dog-headed people) (Cohen 1996: 6). In early modern Europe, these monstrous races still enjoyed a strong foothold "not as pure fantasies but rather as distorted and stereotyped perceptions of people [...] from other regions and other cultures (Asians, Africans, and later Americans)" (Burke 2004: 25). The figure of the African-American and that of the Jew, to name but two examples, were rendered monstrous in fiction and in political discourse in Europe and the U.S. well into the 20th century (Halberstam 1995: 14; Nussbaum 2010: 23). The point of view from which these ascriptions take place is invariably that of the white Westerner.

Despite its ubiquity in monster narratives for adults, this motif is surprisingly sparse in picturebooks with monsters. My entire research corpus contains only two titles in which the dichotomy human versus nonhuman/monstrous is played out with the purpose of dismantling cultural and/or racial stereotypes. These are Colin McNaughton's *Have You Seen Who's Just Moved in Next Door to Us?* (1993) and Alexis Deacon's *Beegu* (2003). A third book, David McKee's *Three Monsters* (2005), deals with xenophobia in an exclusive monster world. Apart from these three titles, racial exclusion is not a theme in my corpus.

Despite the paucity of racially diverse characters, tolerance and acceptance of other forms of 'difference' are, in fact, a sizeable

218

motif: fourteen books of my corpus can be argued to be motivated by questions of 'otherness' and inclusion. In its most simple form, the pattern for all of these books posits a principal character that is excluded or ostracized by one or several representatives of the dominant culture on the grounds of his or her difference from this culture. Her or his exclusion results in the principal character's desire for acceptance and support from the 'in-group' and in a fictional negotiation, i.e. the story, of how this character's inclusion might become possible. 'Difference' in these picturebooks is described in terms of race, 'ugliness,' and gender norms. Evidently, these three markers intersect and they are further complemented by characters that stand out due to special or supernatural abilities. The pedagogical thrust behind these books could be pinned down as 'inclusive education,' but one that goes beyond the focus on disabled students with which this term is traditionally associated (cf. Baglieri and Shapiro 2012; Biklen 2000). The approach to inclusion that these books embrace here corresponds somewhat to current debates about rethinking the concept of inclusion in education. According to some educationalists, inclusion should not only be aimed at students with special educational needs, but should be equally concerned with marginalized groups, such as sexual/gender, religious or ethnical minorities, or economically disadvantaged people (Thomas 2013: 473-490). As one might expect, the overt message in the picturebooks is that someone who appears different from what is constructed as normal actually has a lot in common with 'normal' people. The most important commonality in these picturebook stories is their characters' striving for love and acceptance. Interestingly, this desire for acknowledgment, confirmation or simply security has been described by neuroscientists as a fundamental *human* need for emotional and intellectual development (Hüther 2013: 72-75). How can the supposedly human quality of this need be read in concordance with the monstrosity of the characters expressing that need in the picturebooks? Do the monsters in this group of books serve any other purpose than signifying otherness?

Leslie Fiedler suggests that the key to understanding monsters or "Freaks," as he calls them, in children's books is to be found in the psychology of childhood: "children's ever changing size, their uncertainty about their status as human or animal, adolescents' worry and uncertainty about their freakishly developing sexual organs. [...] What children's books tell us, finally, is that maturity involves the ability to believe the self normal, only the other a monster or Freak." (Fiedler 1978: 30f.) Quite contrary to Fiedler's claim, the overwhelming evidence in the picturebooks I examine here points towards an affirmation of (monstrous) difference, a request to interrogate existing norms about what is considered normal. However, this general observation needs further qualification: the questioning of existing constructions of normalcy and the concomitant striving for acceptance is not always crowned with success or even just a satisfying ending. And Fiedler has a point, of course, when he connects the phenomenon of monstrous figures in children's literature with the question of who or what is considered normal.

The picturebooks that I discuss in this chapter could be summed up as asking precisely these questions: What is 'normal'? And how 'normal' does one have to be in order to find acceptance by representatives of the culturally dominant group (or any group at all)? In the first section, I will look at one particular book, Chris Wormell's *The Big Ugly Monster and the Little Stone Rabbit* (2004), as the basis for discussing how notions of beauty impact constructions of disability. The second section focusses on Colin McNaughton's *Have You Seen Who's Just Moved in Next Door To Us?* (1993), while also referring to McKee's (2006) and Deacon's (2003) books (see above). Here I will be concerned with picture-book politics of negotiating racial and ethnical inclusion. Finally, the last section will deal with three picturebooks that I read as comments on masculine and feminine gender norms via a main character that deviates from these norms: *YUCK! That's Not a Monster!* (McAllister and Edgson 2010), *Mostly Monsterly* (Sauer and Magoon 2010), and *Leonardo the Terrible Monster* (Willems 2007). What strikes me as disconcerting, if perhaps unsurprising, is that in the majority of these books, a character's 'difference' causes feelings and reactions of disgust; disconcerting, because showing disgust to be a 'normal' reaction towards the perception of someone else's difference is surely not on any educational agenda; and unsurprising, because disgust has been theorized as a central factor for the creation of an insider/outsider dichotomy in all social contexts.

For example, Martha Nussbaum writes that

[Disgust] appears to be an especially visceral emotion. We readily
grant that emotions such as compassion, grief, and anger are affected by social learning. What are significant losses? Which people
should we care about? What damages is it right to be upset about?
All these questions form part of children's upbringing in their social
environment, and the social norms they learn in the process of investigating these questions powerfully shape the child's emotions.
(Nussbaum 2010: 13)

Winfried Menninghaus describes disgust as equally "visceral"
when he calls it "a vomitive judgment: *away* with it, from the
belly" (Menninghaus 2003: 92). As Nussbaum continues, however,
disgust is shown to contain considerable cognitive components
since it is possible to distinguish *primary objects of disgust* and
projected disgust. Primary objects of disgust supposedly remind
(adult) humans of their own animality and mortality (all kinds of
excrements, corpses, and animals that have related properties, i.e.
that are smelly, oozy, slimy etc.). This does not mean, however,
that this form of disgust is innate. Rather, infants learn from their
adult carers to identify these primary objects of disgust.

Some picturebooks are dedicated to young children's toilet
humor that may be read as an indication of the tension surrounding
adults' desire to "civilize" their young. One example is *Morris the
Mankiest Monster* (Andreae and McIntyre 2009) that seems to
assemble all possible primary objects of disgust in one story: Morris lives in a house made of animal feces, he likes to lick the walls
so that the house is always smelly, he snacks on the yellow wax
oozing from his ears, takes a bath in the sewage canal – and so on.
Nussbaum's suggestion that a "high level of disgust-anxiety"
(Nussbaum 2010: 26) is particularly characteristic for U.S. Americans might find support in my observation that those picturebooks
that take the most explicit pleasure in disgusting matter tend to
originate from British authors. In addition to *Morris*, I have found
The Disgusting Sandwich (Edwards and Shaw 2013) and Roald
Dahl and Quentin Blake's successful series of *Revolting Recipes*
(1996, 2002 and 2009) that, according to reviews on Amazon UK,
enjoy much popularity. Even though none of these titles is concerned with questions of normalcy, difference and inclusion, their

focus on disgust illustrates one particular mechanism that is very relevant for the picturebooks I will discuss here: it is that most immediate association of disgust with food, something that has to be ingested, taken in by the body in order to survive. According to Paul Rozin, the psychologist whose findings Nussbaum employs,

> [d]isgust [...] concerns the borders of the body. Its central idea is that of contamination: the disgusted person feels defiled by the object, thinking that it has somehow entered the self. Further experiments show that behind this idea of personal contamination lies the idea that "you are what you eat": if you take in something base or vile, you become like that yourself. (Nussbaum 2010: 14)

Although Nussbaum seems to endorse a differentiation between primary objects of disgust and projected disgust, her comment also implies a metaphysical component of the phenomenon of disgust. If I *am* what I eat then there is always already a transportation of the disgusting object into a cultural dimension. In her book *The Cultural Politics of Emotion*, Sara Ahmed illustrates this view with the help of an anecdote that Charles Darwin uses to explain the evolution of disgust. In this episode, a native of Tierra del Fuego is utterly disgusted at the touch of a slice of cold preserved meat that Darwin is about to eat. Darwin, in turn, is disgusted by that native's touching of his food although, as Darwin admits, the native's hands "did not appear dirty" (qt. in Ahmed 2004: 82). As Ahmed postulates, despite the evident cleanliness of the native's hands (dirt, in contrast, would constitute a primary object of disgust), Darwin feels disgusted because "the other is already seen as dirt, as the carrier of dirt, which contaminates the food that has been touched" (ibid). Ahmed further argues that disgust is

> mediated by ideas that are already implicated in the very impressions we make of others and the way those impressions surface as bodies. [...] So feeling 'disgusted' is not simply an inner or psychic state; it works on bodies, by transforming or 'working on' the surfaces of bodies. (ibid: 83, 85)

What many of the picturebooks I discuss here have in common is what Ahmed describes as a bodily effect of disgust. The bodies of the ostracized protagonists are often read as revolting, sometimes to the extent of inducing fear in the members of the in-group.

While there are many instances in which objects of disgust could be argued to function as an outlet for comic relief – for example, when monster Bernadette's classmates are nauseated by her delicious-looking homemade cupcakes (*Mostly Monsterly*) – the attribution of disgust-related notions to bodies occasionally leads to gross violations of personhood, as in a scene where Mr Monster suggests that throwing his pink fluffy monster son in the rubbish bin would be best for everyone (*YUCK! That's Not a Monster!*). Disgust in these and other instances "is shaped by social norms, as societies teach their members to identify alleged contaminants in their midst. All societies, it appears, identify at least some humans as disgusting." (Nussbaum 2010: 16). One of the questions that I will explore in this chapter is in how far the portrayal of disgust as a 'natural' reaction to somebody's difference can actually contribute towards an affirmative stance towards inclusion.

Ugliness as disability: 'The Big Ugly Monster and the Little Stone Rabbit'

Both fear and disgust are central in Chris Wormell's *The Big Ugly Monster and the Little Stone Rabbit* (2004). This book is in many obvious respects different from the others in this category and in my corpus as a whole. Two things strike at once. First, the main protagonist, the monster, is decidedly adult, and not child. Second, the monster dies in the end – this fact alone seems synonymous with an unhappy ending. There are neither child nor adult human protagonists who would interact with the monster, as is usually the case when the monster is the main protagonist. Nor is the setting an explicitly fantastic one in which monsters implicitly mirror the social world of humans. Indeed, the Big Ugly Monster's plight lies in the very fact that no one and nothing wants anything to do with him. In this respect, his situation reflects the utmost extremity of the mechanism of exclusion underlying all the picturebook narratives in this chapter. One reason why I begin this chapter with *The Big Ugly Monster and the Little Stone Rabbit* is to analyze and reconstruct this very mechanism. The other reason lies in the representation of the monster's ugliness. Unlike the other picturebooks that construct gender, racial or other types of difference indirectly, *The Big Ugly Monster and the Little Stone Rabbit* is very explicit about the reason for the monster's exclusion: it is his indescribable ugliness. It is for the sake of ugliness itself that the monster is shut out from all kinds of community. It is perhaps because straightforwardly identifying a person's physical appearance as the reason for their exclusion from a group is unthinkable in contemporary social situations that this motif, here in this fictitious picturebook setting, is at all acceptable: it is too far removed from any obvious connection to the 'real,' contemporary world of humans. But the political incorrectness of shunning someone by judging them 'ugly' seems to be a relatively recent development: around the turn of the nineteenth into the twentieth century the so-called 'ugly-laws' were legally enforced in some parts of the U.S. I will use Rosemarie Garland Thomson's theorization of these laws in the context of contemporary disability studies as I proceed with my interpretation. In terms of *literary* history, ugliness gained some prominence in some European fairy tales of the nineteenth century insofar as it challenged the literary tradition of using ugliness as a signifier for moral baseness. I will argue that both the social and the literary history of this motif play into the construction of the Big Ugly Monster's difference.

Fig. 19   *The Big Ugly Monster and the Little Stone Rabbit* (Wormell 2004)

The first doublespread already introduces the reader to the Monster's apparently most defining characteristic: his extreme ugliness (fig. 19). The effect of his ugliness is rhetorically increased by the order of enumeration of beings and things that flee from him: animals (run/fly away), plants (wither and die), the sun (disappears and it starts snowing), a lake (dries up "with a hiss of steam" (Wormell 2004: np). While there are no human or humanized characters (other than the monster himself) in the story, animate and inanimate nature transports the same reactions to the monster's ugliness that humans would display: they recoil in horror and disgust, they want nothing to do with this freak with bulging eyes, wrinkly and warty skin, four-fingered claws, giant nostrils, hairy ears and protruding tooth. In this setting without human inhabitants it is noteworthy that the monster is the most human-looking. Rather than looking like a misshapen animal (which might be a more comprehensible reason for the other animals to run away) he looks like a misshapen human, standing upright on two legs and with a very diverse array of facial expressions, ranging from sadness, attentiveness, and surprise to boundless joy. The other protagonists (animals, plants, sun, and water) are strikingly lacking of anthropomorphized features. Nevertheless, the narrative positions them as agents acting according to *human* social rules. And these rules are partly shaped by the mechanisms of disgust as

I have described them earlier: for fear of being contaminated with the disgusting object, for fear of *becoming* that disgusting object, one must establish a noticeable barrier between oneself and the disgusting 'other.' One of the least physically aggressive ways to achieve this distance is to turn one's back, to look away. Homeless people trying to establish any form of contact with visibly wealthier people regularly incite this reaction. So Garland Thomson's thoughts about the 'ugly laws,' also known as 'beggar ordinances,' are, in fact, highly relevant to contemporary Western societies as well. Not only the Americans of the late nineteenth and early twentieth centuries, but Westerners in general and *today* could be characterized through their

> refusal to see the disabled, a kind of bowdlerizing of the body that enacted widespread consequences for people with disabilities. Among them were the slow and conflicted demise of publicly displaying disabled people as freaks, as well as institutionalizing, segregating, and medicalizing people with disabilities... even though disabled people have always been a large and significant segment of any social order, those among us whose impairments could be enlisted to symbolize disability were often hidden from public view... modernity deemed disability an improper object to be looked at. (Garland Thomson 1997: 338)

The 'ugly' people who were affected by these laws were very often visibly, that is physically, impaired as a consequence of battlefield injuries from the Civil War. In many cases, missing limbs were responsible for the individuals' inability to find employment and social security. While permanent war wounds in Western societies today are far from being a daily sight and do not directly and necessarily result in the wounded individual's social/economic decline, today's homeless people are faced with a very similar kind of exclusion that marks them as effectively disabled from interacting with and integrating themselves into society at large. A similar kind of disability is at work in Wormell's book, where the protagonist is virtually disabled from entertaining any form of contact – not only with living creatures, but with inanimate nature as well. Although the story may not explicitly be one about disability it can and perhaps should be read in this context. Thus, the monster's physical impairment 'interacts' – to use the phrasing of the World

Health Organization – with his social environment to the monster's detriment (WHO, "Disabilities"). Because the monster's appearance does not correspond with universalized aesthetic norms, his participation in social life is not only severely restricted but virtually disabled. From a historical perspective, the monster's desperate situation can be read as building on the logic of the 'ugly laws' that dictated visibly impaired individuals to hide their "incurable and incorrigible ugliness" (Schweik 2009: 87) and to become "permanent[ly] invisible" (Ferguson, qt. in Schweik 2009: ibid).

It is interesting that ugliness entered literature as a serious literary motif (as opposed to comic and carnivalesque genres) only in the nineteenth century. This development is particularly evident in the genre of fairy tales, especially *Kunstmärchen*. Starting in the early nineteenth century, the transgression of aesthetic borders signaled the transition from the literary classicism of the Enlightenment period to Romanticism. Thus Menninghaus describes the ideal of the classicist body as a reflection of Antique ideas: the beautiful body must possess a pure skin without wrinkles, warts and gristles, and conversely, it must not display any digestive, respiratory or sexual openings (Menninghaus 2003: 82). The ubiquity of this classicist ideal of beauty was increasingly contested by a new generation of writers who transported images of ugly bodies from the periphery to the center of literary production. Two examples of texts that were also intended for children are Wilhelm Hauff's "Zwerg Nase" (Dwarf Long-Nose) (1826) and Oscar Wilde's "Birthday of the Infanta" (1891). Both texts are fairy tales; and despite some important differences, both depict an ugly and socially despised, utterly dehumanized individual who is craving for love and recognition. What makes these narratives interesting with regard to their representation of ugliness is that they attack its traditional equation in literary texts with depravity and other 'evil' character traits. While the ugly laws legally enforced the shunning of ugly/disabled individuals in the history of the U.S. by implicitly "[accusing] them of moral and mental failure" (Ferguson, qt. in Schweik 2009: ibid), the literary texts challenged this very equation of ugliness and moral/mental corruption.

A time came when the monster was so old he could no longer sing or dance or do tricks. He could still play draughts, however, and though the stone rabbit was a poor player – even when the monster suggested some very clever moves – he was happy nonetheless.

Fig. 20   *The Big Ugly Monster and the Little Stone Rabbit* (Wormell 2004)

In many respects, Wormell takes up this motif of ugly innocence, as it were, but his conclusion neither mirrors the Romantic
ending of "Dwarf Long-Nose," in which Jakob regains his hand-
some human shape, nor Wilde's fin-de-siècle mentality with the
dwarf dying of a broken heart after the painful realization of his
own ugliness. Neither is the big ugly monster liberated into sudden, magical beauty nor does he perish miserably from his grief.
Instead, he is portrayed as possessing the very resources to turn his
suffering into happiness. This ability to transform misery into comfort creates a sense of *deus ex machina* and is, at the same time, a
strikingly common turning point in many of the narratives I examined for this chapter. The ostracized hero and, in one case, heroine
suddenly and out of the blue has a realization. In *The Big Ugly
Monster and the Little Stone Rabbit* this realization is formulated
like this: "Then one day he had an idea." The focus of the narrative
on ugliness is no longer morality, but rather the infinite potential of

individual inspiration. The monster's idea is to make stone animals that he can talk to. But they all burst into pieces at his smile after their completion, except for a little stone rabbit who becomes his lifelong companion. As the narrator recounts all the activities the monster does for the rest of his life, with the stone rabbit always sitting close by, the monster's happiness about his companion is emphasized with five repetitions on five consecutive page openings. The repeated affirmation of the monster's happiness stands in stark contrast to the narrator's acknowledgment of the stone rabbit's actual non-involvement. Thus, when the monster sings, "the rabbit never joined in, not even for the chorus, still the monster was happy" (Wormell 2004: np). When the monster dances, "the rabbit never joined in, not even to tap its foot, the monster was happy nonetheless" (Wormell 2004: np). When the monster is old all he can do is play draughts, "and though the stone rabbit was a poor player – even when the monster suggested some very clever moves – he was happy nonetheless" (Wormell 2004: np, fig. 20). The narrator's understatements describing the rabbit's non-involvement serve at once as a humorous concealment of the rabbit's ultimate inanimateness and as an ironic and deeply saddening reminder that the monster is still, in fact, utterly alone.

Karen Coats reads this story as a critique of the modernist narrative "that suggests that love and acceptance in the right community can change ugly people into beautiful people" (Coats 2008: 84). Indeed, the Monster stays ugly until his death. The narrative's refusal of granting the Monster a sense of redemption through the acquisition of beauty (as in "Dwarf Long-Nose") is further complicated by the ambiguity of the Stone Rabbit as both the Monster's loyal friend and an inanimate thing. How much is the loyalty of a statue of stone worth? Does the Monster's acting as if the Rabbit was alive negate the sense of ambiguity that readers might gain through their tragicomic and unilateral 'interaction'? At the same time as the Monster's judgment and visible contentment with his stony friend might be considered as the most significant factor in evaluating the Monster's happiness, the narrator implicitly solicits the readers' judgment as well, by directly addressing them with the pronoun 'you' (cf. chapter 3.3.3).

> This is the cave. And in this picture the monster is just about to come out. So be careful when you turn the page. [Page turn.] There he is. Pretty ugly, eh? (Just look at those nostril hairs!) Of course this is only a picture, so you're not getting the whole effect. You're not getting the ugliness at full strength. It was pretty powerful. (Wormell 2004: np)

The rhetorical effects of this 'you' are complex, comprising the establishing of a direct relationship, resembling a dialogue, between the reader and the narrator, the illusion of the narrated events as happening in the present. What I find most interesting about this "you" is its specific and relatively common use in picturebooks and children's books generally, which stands in sharp contrast to the frequency of its use in fiction for grown-ups. The only genre in adult culture where the direct address of the reader is a constitutive element is advice literature. This comparison of advice literature for grown-ups and children's fiction, here: picturebooks, makes one thing very visible: the 'I' that is behind the narrative voice posits itself as superior in terms of knowledge and experience. The reader is, as a consequence, less knowledgeable and less experienced. In children's literature, such an implication almost automatically creates an image of the *child* reader. It is perhaps a matter of personal taste whether the narrator's use of the 'you' in this instance is perceived as a familiar rhetorical device to create an intimate storytelling time or as an underlying assumption of the child reader as needful of patronizing. But as a rhetorical convention in children's literature, the pronoun 'you' in a direct address of the reader undoubtedly carries with it the notion that stories for children must have an educative value. One of the more obvious educational intentions that I would presume *The Big Ugly Monster and the Little Stone Rabbit* pursues is to incite in its readers sympathy for an ostracized, isolated individual. But this sympathy is not driven toward any proactive moves that would break the Monster's isolation because the readers are told that the Monster was happy.

The ambiguity of this resolution that, strictly speaking, is no resolution at all, is to me the most challenging part of this story: although the Monster remains ultimately alone he dies happy. And the Monster's happiness is constituted by his feelings of friendship towards the Stone Rabbit. Strikingly, Coats reads the Rabbit as female (Coats 2008: 84), although several instances indicate the rabbit as ungendered through the pronoun "it" (see quotes above). By reading the Monster's relationship with the Rabbit as heterosexual love, Coats weakens in my opinion her claim that the book represents a critique of modernist metanarratives that postulate the possibility of individual happiness only under the condition of fulfilled love. With her article she seems to give voice to readers' need to grant the Monster as least some kind of meaningful solace, namely the fulfilment of the Monster's supposed request for love. But romantic love is nowhere mentioned in the story. All the Monster is asking for is a companion. By reading the relationship between the Rabbit and the Monster as an enactment of a heterosexual and lifelong romantic commitment, Coats risks surrendering to that same modernist logic that the picturebook purportedly dismantles: she presumes that heterosexual love is the only effective solution to an individual's suffering from social exclusion. The question in *The Big Ugly Monster and the Little Stone Rabbit*, in my view, is not only whether the Monster's relationship with the Rabbit should be described as love or rather as friendship but, more to the point, whether it can be described in terms of interpersonal exchange at all. After all, the Rabbit is made of stone.

Of course, the narrative responds to readers' need to see the character that incites their sympathy and pity redeemed. But by leaving open to debate just how satisfying the Monster's relationship with the Rabbit can possibly be, this picturebook proposes a much bleaker view of – ultimately human – society than most picturebooks do. This becomes clearer when I contrast its ambiguity with two other picturebooks in my corpus that do actually support the modernist assumption that lasting individual happiness is only possible through romantic love. In Rachel Bright's *Love Monster* (2012), the lonely and ugly monster protagonist eventually finds an equally ugly monster female and they both live happily ever after. In *Octonauts – The Only Lonely Monster* (2006) by design duo Meomi, consisting of Vicky Wong and Michael Murphy, the monster of the title eventually finds acceptance and friendship among other creatures that are just as unique as himself. None of the protagonists in these two examples can be described as 'ugly' – not even according to picturebook norms. And perhaps even more importantly, the relationships that the initially shunned protagonist establishes are unequivocally mutual.

In contrast to these two examples, Wormell's story does indeed seem extreme. The very fact that the rabbit remains ungendered, silent and unchangeable throughout the story renders the picturebook more radical than Coats' reading of it. The book's fundamental message appears to be that the social invisibility, isolation and, indeed, social disability of ugly people is part of contemporary reality. The possibility of inclusion is here pictured as an illusion whose reality most picturebooks tend to alleviate with a happy ending. In *The Big Ugly Monster and the Little Stone Rabbit*, the decision whether it offers a happy ending or not is largely left to the readers. Unambiguous, in contrast, is the Monster's male gender and it is worth looking at a little more closely with regard to the question of his disabling ugliness. Not coincidentally, I believe, the main characters of *Love Monster* and *The Octonauts and the Only Lonely Monster* are also male. Would these stories work in the same way if their main protagonists were female? I find this question difficult to answer and I suppose that this is at least partly due to the lack of ugly female characters that are at the same time profoundly endearing. This is true for picturebooks and children's literature more generally. If monsters, as Stephen Asma claims, "represent the most extreme personified point of unfamiliarity [and if] they push our sense of abnormality beyond the usual anthropological xenophobia" (Asma 2009: 26), then the prerequisite for these monsters' ability to question and dismantle our norms seems to be their masculinity.

The ending of *The Big Ugly Monster and the Little Stone Rabbit* further suggests that the Monster's lifelong isolation from any contact with other sentient beings is somehow acceptable or even necessary, following some sordid narrative logic:

> But one day the monster never came out of his cave and the stone rabbit sat alone. [Page turn.] That very day the sun came out and green grass began to grow. Soon the flowers bloomed and vines scrambled over rocks and hung down over the mouth of the cave. Trees grew up straight and tall and all the animals and birds came back. It was a beautiful place now, perhaps the most beautiful place in the whole world. (Wormell 2004: np)

The terms of lushness and abundance with which the Monster's former habitat is being described here creates an uncomfortable friction with the knowledge how this place became so beautiful: the Monster had to die first. Only when the Monster's excruciating ugliness has disappeared from the face of the earth is it possible for plants and animals to repopulate the landscape. The landscape's dazzling beauty can hardly be of any comfort to the Monster now, although it is a narrative device for romanticizing both the Monster's suffering and his noble character. In some respect, the fact that it is Nature that behaves in this way makes the Monster's pitiful life appear 'normal' and somehow 'natural.' Even without reading the Monster's ugliness as disability such a moral seems to be at odds with the principles of an inclusive education.

"Funny foreigner types" – racialized otherness

A second group of picturebooks which deals with questions of otherness in terms of racial and cultural heritage poses a similar challenge. In these narratives, the attribute 'ugly' or similar derogative terms are applied not so much to refer to a certain degree of deviance from a physical norm but rather to point to something lying beyond that appearance that is judged as 'ugly' by the other characters or the narrator. Although the disgust expressed by members of the 'in-group' is just as much directed against visual signs of otherness as in the books discussed above, the outsider's characteristic that is really meant here is that they are perceived as different because they come from somewhere else. In other words, abuse is directed against these protagonists in order to negotiate the in-/stability of and, even more pertinently, the belonging to the categories of a racialized 'center' and a racialized 'periphery.'

The fact that this question is negotiated through the figure of the monster is unexpected in recently published fiction for young children because of its obvious political incorrectness that appears to me irreconcilable with the general educative impetus of picturebooks. Of course, having a monster character represent disability is no less problematic, as I have argued above, and probably only permissible – partly because less intelligible as a representation of disability – by avoiding a comparison between human and monster characters. I think it is important to keep in mind that (Western) sensitivities about racial discrimination and nationalism have only emerged relatively recently on a larger demographic scale. This development can be retraced by comparing today's picturebooks with some early twentieth century British ABCs and picturebooks that represent foreign nations. As Emer O'Sullivan concludes in her article the "unadulterated celebration of imperial Englishness is, of course, a thing of the past" (O'Sullivan 2009: 345). O'Sullivan refers to Morag Styles: "[O]vert nationalism has become not just unfashionable but unfeasible because of the inescapable consciousness of the legacy of British colonialism" (Styles, 2001: 67; qt. in O'Sullivan: ibid). But racism and nationalism have not entirely disappeared from picturebook narration, as O'Sullivan's claim might suggest, but they have become more subtle, less blatant, and harder to detect.

However, considering the three picturebooks *Have You Seen Who's Just Moved in Next Door to Us?* (McNaughton 1993), *Three Monsters* (McKee 2005), and *Beegu* (Deacon 2003), the millennia-old narrative of xenophobia expressed through representatives of the monstrous races appears far from extinct. However, there is an important difference between the use of monsters as signifiers of racialized 'otherness' in these contemporary picturebooks and that in Gothic novels such as *Dracula* (1897), that Halberstam reads as a vilification of the Jew: in both types of text the monster stands for racialized difference but the picturebooks use this visual simile with the obvious intention of dismantling prejudice and stereotypes. In that sense, Styles may be right to announce contemporary authors' "consciousness of the legacy of British colonialism." However, a closer look at any of these three books reveals an ambiguous if not pessimistic stance towards the possibility of inclusion.

Apart from the fact that all three authors are British, only McNaughton's book contains explicit references to nationality rather than more general distinctions between 'own' culture and 'other' culture. It is this national specificity that makes the complex mechanisms of watching/judging and being watched/judged explicit in a very witty, humorous and self-conscious manner. The

234

book's implicit focus on the question 'who sees and judges whom?' makes it an ideal point of departure for this chapter section. O'Sullivan points out the enormous influence picturebooks can exert with respect to creating what she calls "auto- and hetero-stereotypes."

> Presenting to young readers their earliest images of a world into which they are gradually venturing, [children's literature] provides them with the vocabularies they need to read that world and the maps they need to negotiate the specific culture(s) of which they are a part. [...] As a site for tradition of information, beliefs, and customs, children's literature overtly or latently reflects dominant social and cultural norms, including self-images and images of others. In this respect it has a key function in establishing selfhood for its target audience of children. (O'Sullivan 2009:334)

In this sense, *Have You Seen Who's Just Moved in Next Door to Us?* can be examined as a prime example of a picturebook that incorporates a vast array of 'signposts' that may help readers navigate through a complex world in which cultural and racial ascriptions to minority groups can take on comic proportions. The setting is an outwardly typical English residential street. Its residents, however, represent the entire range of diversity of fictional, historical and pop-cultural figures: Mister Thing (a giant slimy green worm occupying two floors) is the Queen's neighbor who lives next to the Humpty Dumpty's. A witch, King Kong, Tarzan, Goldilocks and Siamese twins – they are all introduced as "friends [and] perfect neighbours" (McNaughton 1993: np) by the narrator, whose identity is not revealed until the very end. The residents' only commonality, it seems, is that they originate from somewhere that is decidedly *not* an English middle-class residential street. Indeed, they come from myths, legends, fairytales, from nursery rhymes, horror fiction, and the tabloids. While most characters' origin is not geographically located, their foreignness to this realistic setting that is their neighborhood is nevertheless implicit for any experienced reader. In the logic of "topsy turvy" (Lewis 2001: 53), the rhyming narrative presents all these individuals as ordinary and at the same time builds up the readers' anticipation as to

who, or what, has just moved in

Fig. 21   *Have You Seen Who's Just Moved In Next Door To Us?*
(McNaughton 1993), detail

Next Door to us. (McNaughton 1993: np)

A panorama the size of two double spreads finally reveals an entirely average English middle-class family, consisting of father, mother, two children and a cat (fig. 21). Standing intimidated in the cone of light of a street lamp, they are surrounded by the entire neighborhood, being stared at with disgusted and shocked facial expressions, with fingers pointing at them. A Hell's Angel says in dismay: "There go the property values!," Quasimodo judges them "ugly!" and Tyrannosaurus Rex "monstrous." Frankenstein's creature rigidly points his finger at them, saying, in a speech bubble: "They're unnatural" and King Kong, in that same gesture, exclaims: "There goes the neighbourhood!" (McNaughton 1993: np) All these judgments and exclamations are a consistent continuation of the topsy-turvy form, a frequent narrative device in the picturebooks of my corpus. They function to invert the usual distribution of agency between the viewers and the viewed, demonstrating the absurdity of this mechanism – at least from the perspective of those who usually occupy the position of the viewers, namely (in this case: English) middle-class, white people. The humor derives

236

not only from the reversal of this usual mechanism of who sees and judges whom, but from the simultaneous knowledge that white, educated middle-class people also constitute the majority of purchasers of picturebooks (like this one) and thus likely constitute a majority of the readership. So white, educated readers see a representation of themselves on this penultimate page, but in this representation of themselves they are, for once, not in a position to see and judge others, but rather they are seen and judged *by* others. As in Wormell's book, the narrator here addresses the readers with a direct "you" by simple repetition of the title line after every introduction of another resident. But where Wormell's narrator drew attention only to the interactive watching between implied readers and protagonist, McNaughton's narrator is homodiegetic. However, this narrator only really reveals him- or herself on the very last page with the only instance of an "I" in the whole narrative. The parent of a vampire family (it could be either father or mother, but the father is the central figure in the picture) concludes:

I think we'll leave this miscellanea
And return to Transylvania –
'Cause have you seen who's just moved in
Next door to us? (McNaughton 1993: np)

Part of the humor created by this final page lies in the horrified, disgusted glances that the three vampires cast back over their shoulders into the direction of the family of humans that has just been bashed by the vampires' loyal monstrous neighbors on the previous page. David Lewis offers very detailed close reading of the book's formal intricacies, paying particular attention to the word-image-interaction, and examines the book's semiotic and intertextual complexities (Lewis 2001: 53 f.). He does not, however, spend any time interrogating the cultural narrative that informs the book. Despite its obvious humor, I think the book's ending deserves some scrutinizing. As Lewis observes, "[s]trictly speaking, it is not a story, for nothing happens in it that could be considered narrative" (Lewis 2001: 53), nor are there any main protagonists, but there is one figure that carries the readers through the street, as it were, and that is the narrator. Although the narrator includes him- or herself in the "[nice] crowd" he or she is about to describe ("We've a lovely bunch of people in our street") through

Beegu was not supposed to be here.

She was lost.

Fig. 22   *Beegu* (Deacon 2006)

the pronoun "we," the fact that the narrator is also a resident is soon pushed into the background and replaced by the focus on the neighbors. The narrator's identity is concealed for the largest part of the book. While the panorama spread that consists of a fold-out double page already ironically subverts the prospect of success-fully including the new residents, the narrator's decision that this situation is too much to bear and to return to their home country can be seen to reflect a dominant attitude that considers racial in-clusion as an ultimately futile endeavor.

While McNaughton's book presents a sharp and witty criti-cism of the mechanisms of racial discrimination and exclusion that are at work in the English suburbs (and elsewhere), it does not offer any vision how inclusion might become possible. This obser-vation is by no means intended as an evaluative judgment, it is rather meant to examine the effects of reading this and similar books as educative tools. While I am convinced that there are many other productive ways of reading picturebooks, I have here chosen this focus because it reveals so much about what adults want young children to learn about themselves and others. And I think it is significant that the picturebooks in my corpus that are concerned with criticizing xenophobia do not offer a more optimistic or productive perspective on multiculturalism. In *Beegu*, the eponymous heroine, a cute little alien with two long ears and three eyes, has accidentally landed on earth and tries to be included into any kind of human or animal community – but to no avail (fig. 22). All her efforts are in vain, as she is excluded again and again by adult humans whose disgust at Beegu's otherness is visualized through their facial expressions and gestures. Unlike most of her male counterparts in the other books that I have categorized into this group, Beegu does not 'have an idea' that saves her from her unfortunate situation. When she is exhausted and disheartened from her search for community, she lies down alone in a desolate, bleak landscape, apparently resigned. In contrast to the ostracized male protagonists (e.g. in *Love Monster*; *The Big Ugly Monster and the Little Stone Rabbit* or *Three Monsters*), Beegu is pictured as an ultimately passive and helpless female who needs to be saved by her parents. The narrative ends with Beegu and her parents in their spaceship looking down on planet Earth and debating whether humanity as a whole or only adult humans are altogether hopeless. Besides an implicit parallel between the concepts of 'the noble savage' (Beegu) and 'the innocent child' (the friendly and welcoming human children Beegu meets), the narrative proposes that the idea of ethnic/cultural inclusion proves yet again unsuccessful.

Fig. 23   *Three Monster* (McKee 2005)

David McKee's *Three Monsters* (2005) offers an equally dis-illusioned view on inclusion, although the ending seems, at a first glance, a happier one. The portrayal of two lazy monsters (red and blue) and of a third, yellow monster, with almond shaped eyes, long black hair in a ponytail and earrings, concludes by making the "funny foreigner type" (McKee 2005: np), i.e. the yellow monster, also called "custard-coloured, cringing creep" (ibid) amongst many other similar insults, build his own island – presumably so he can be at peace from the other two monsters' unrelenting abuse (fig. 23). The yellow monster solves his existential dilemma (the loss of his land through an earthquake) with hard labor (building an is-land) and psychological cunning (consistently addressing the other two monsters in venerating and flattering terms), while the red and the blue monsters are portrayed as obtuse, lethargic and xenopho-bic. After all the aggression that the yellow monster has endured, his inviting the red and the blue monster to come visit him on his new island can only serve the purpose of consolidating the image of the patient, goodhearted and forgiving foreigner.

As in *Beegu*, the outsider here is romanticized while the 'in-siders' are rendered unlikeable through their verbal and/or visual characterizations. Compared to O'Sullivan's analysis of the por-trayal of English nationhood in *Babies of All Nations* (Byron and

Petherick 1909) that "presents an image of a self-confident, rich, white, beautiful, and privileged English child" (O'Sullivan 2009: 334), the representation of English or mainstream culture versus foreign culture in all three books discussed here, published a century later, is completely reversed. This reversal is especially obvious in *Beegu* and *Three Monsters*, but McNaughton's book, too, strives on the idea of reversing the (from a Western perspective) traditional attribution of auto- and heterostereotypes. Although *Have You Seen Who's Just Moved in Next Door to Us?* is set in a recognizably English street and could therefore be argued to address specifically English notions of national and cultural identity, the other two books have less specific settings. Beegu lands on the outskirts of a metropolis that − apart from a red phone booth − reminds me more of North American architecture than British; and McKee's three monsters live in a candy-colored fantasy land − but the yellow monster is, interestingly, reminiscent of stereotyped representations of Native Americans (yellow skin, long and narrow eyes, long black hair and earrings). What all three titles have in common is their critical presentation of xenophobic prejudice that is based on essentialized notions of what is 'same,' often automatically equated with notions of 'normalcy' and 'naturalness,' and what is 'other,' equated with opposite attributes. For example, Frankenstein's Monster in *Have You Seen Who's Just Moved in Next Door to Us?* points at the human family, saying "They're unnatural" and a couple of Siamese twins poke their heads out of the window affirming this view: "They're so normal!" (McNaughton 1993: np).

Edward Said popularly analyzed the foundation of the 'tradition' of essentializing the foreigner in *Orientalism* (1978). Although his research focus is very specific, since it is directed at European Orientalists' conception of the Orient during the nineteenth century, many of his claims can be generalized to account for Western stereotyping of non-Western cultures and nations. When Said traces "one of the important developments in nineteenth-century Orientalism" as "the distillation of essential ideas about the Orient − its sensuality, its tendency to despotism, its aberrant mentality, its habits of inaccuracy, its backwardness − into a separate and unchallenged coherence" (Said 2003 [1978]: 205), related or, in fact, similar attributes can be found within discourses about the Jew (who was one 'type' of the Oriental) or the Black American, to refer to my two examples from the beginning of this chapter. This pattern of stereotyping is congruent with O'Sullivan's analysis of early twentieth century picturebooks about different nations: British culture, from which these books originate, is portrayed in antithesis to all other cultures, including other Western cultures such as Germany and the Netherlands. To be British, in these books, means to be wealthy, upper-class, well nourished, clean, blonde, educated; just as the European Orientalists could be said to have created their image of the Oriental in antithesis to their perception of themselves as rational, loyal, accurate, and so on.

With this background, the images of 'self' and 'other' represented in the three picturebooks by McNaughton, McKee and Deacon are noticeably reverted. That is to say, those characters marked as other and foreign are consistently portrayed in a favorable light. This is particularly striking in *Beegu* and *Three Monsters* where the outsider is, in the first case, helpless, cute and naïve, and, in the second one, hard-working, smart and good-natured – as opposed to the insiders who are mean, selfish, intolerant, and aggressive. And even though McNaughton's book can be aptly described as a project of exposing the absurdity of such essentializing attributions, all three books do, in fact, build upon the very idea of essential difference between what is considered 'self' and 'other.' In addition, all three books conclude by suggesting that multiculturalism and racial diversity are ultimately illusory.

This message is further complicated by the gender implications of racialized difference in both *Beegu* and *Three Monsters*. Although the yellow monster is shown to be crafty and resourceful and therefore ultimately an active, self-determined agent, his eavesdropping and submissive reference of the other two monsters plays into the hands of an effeminized image of the perfidious and spineless 'Oriental.' Beegu, on the other hand, is the epitome of female naivety and helplessness that I have already criticized in *The Monster and the Teddy Bear*. Compared to the male protagonists in the books in this chapter, Beegu is incapable of finding a solution for her troublesome situation by herself and has to wait for her grown-up rescuers. Gender norms themselves can and do become the target for discrimination in the books I will discuss in the following.

Sissy stuff – gender norms and deviances

In most of the books I have discussed so far, the main character's deviation from a physical, racial or cultural norm caused expressions of disgust in the minor characters or the antagonists. For example, the first thing the red and the blue monsters say upon meeting the yellow monster is "Yuk!" (McKee 2005: np) while holding their nose. Both Beegu and the Love Monster are exposed to humans' pointing with their fingers at them and looking revolted and horrified. And various verbal expressions of disgust are spread over the four penultimate pages of *Have You Seen Who's Just Moved in Next Door to Us?*, such as "Yeuch!" or "Slimy!" (McNaughton 1993: np).

In this section, I look at three books where constructions of femininity are the object of disgust and repulsion. *YUCK! That's Not a Monster* (McAllister and Edgson 2010) already carries this common reaction to difference in its title. Upon their pink and fluffy baby brother's birth, his siblings exclaim: "UGH! HE'S SWEET!!" said the little monsters. "LET'S SQUASH HIM!" (ibid). This little dialogue between the sweet monster's brother Frightful and sister Horrid already contains the most salient themes that are relevant for the discussion of "gender outlaws" (Bornstein 1992) in picturebooks with monsters. First of all, the protagonist displays a quality that, in the eyes of the in-group, disqualifies him or her from belonging to that in-group. More specifically, these qualities can all be subsumed under the term gender performance although they are literally veiled by the discussion around qualities of *monster* performance. Although it consists of only twelve words, the dialogue quoted above serves as a rich illustration for this apparently twofold directionality of meaning: the attribution of the quality "sweet" to "him" represents an irreconcilable tension to the two little monsters. In their eyes, "him" and "sweet" do not belong together. The deictic "him" refers to their newly born monster brother Little Shock. The question now is whether to them "sweet" is irreconcilable with "monster" or with "male." The

243

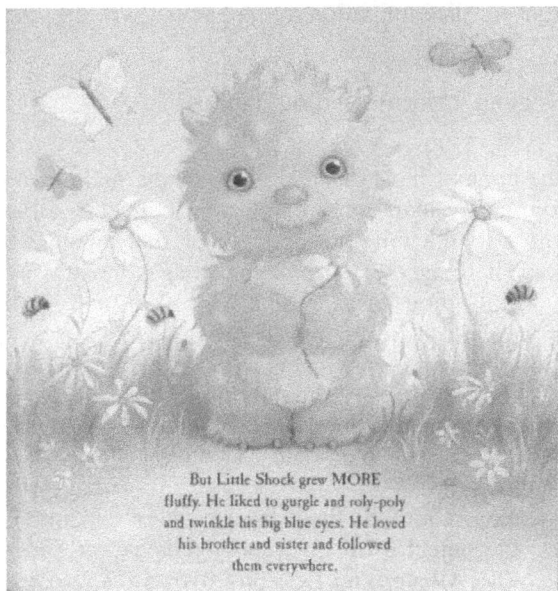

But Little Shock grew MORE fluffy. He liked to gurgle and roly-poly and twinkle his big blue eyes. He loved his brother and sister and followed them everywhere.

Fig. 24 *YUCK! That's Not a Monster!* (McAllister and Edgson 2010)

book's title certainly indicates the former, but at the same time it is impossible to ignore the heavily gendered attributes of Little Shock that make him different in the first place. In other words, if the book was really just about being or not being a monster, Little Shock would have had to climb out of his egg as a human child, because the binary goes 'monster' – 'human' (or 'monster' – 'animal'), and *not* 'monster' – 'effeminate monster boy.' The fact that 'monster' here acts as a code for gender conformity opens up a different category for discrimination and exclusion; one that is less tangible and certainly less concrete than, say, the decisively different looks of Beegu or the big ugly monster.

While the confrontation of human and monster characters as in McNaughton's book or in *Beegu* creates the greatest possible contrast, books like *YUCK!* that have only monster characters also rely on physical attributes to mark difference. Sara Ahmed's claim that disgust "is working on the surfaces of bodies" (Ahmed 2004:

85) becomes visible in this example. Little Shock's difference is visualized through his appearance and, in this respect, comparable to the yellow monster of *Three Monsters*, and as such relatively subtle in contrast to the different appearance of a human and a monster. The external marker that is arguably most gendered is his pink color (Garber 1992: 3 f.). Little Shock is furthermore described as "fluffy" (McAllister and Edgson 2010, fig. 24). While his siblings and parents are not, their visual representations nevertheless show them covered in what looks like soft, fluffy fur. The subtlety of Little Shock's difference is further emphasized by his sharing of some distinctive features: he has two horns, spiky teeth and paws just like his siblings and parents. Thus, what effectively makes him different in the eyes of his family is not only written on his body but must also be attributed to his performance: "He liked to gurgle and roly-poly and twinkle his big blue eyes. He loved his brother and sister and followed them everywhere" (Allister and Edgson 2010: np). The page on which he is thus described shows him in a friendly demand posture (cf. chapter 3.3.3), as if inviting the reader to join him on the lush meadow with the bees, flowers and butterflies – or at least to acknowledge his extreme cuteness. While Little Shock's performance is ostensibly contrasted with his siblings' 'real' and 'authentic' monster the markers of his performance are strikingly gendered: he is depicted and described as caring, affectionate, soft, harmless and sweet, a stereotypical characterization of girls (cf. Stephens 2002: x). With his entire being, Little Shock questions and threatens essentialist notions of what it means to be a monster and, ultimately, what it means to be a boy.

Michael Kimmel succinctly remarked in his essay "Masculinity as Homophobia" that "being a man means 'not being like women'" (Kimmel 2003: 58). In my discussion of picturebooks with monsters, which are, like the various texts in Kimmel's essay, sites for negotiating especially masculinity, but in picturebooks for children, this statement needs to be transformed into: being a *monster* means not being like *girls*. In my chapter "The Monster Under the Bed," this observation was already beginning to emerge. Except for *The Monster and the Teddy Bear* where the human protagonist was a girl, all titles featured a male human child and a male monster, both of whom were by various means likened to one another. I concluded that chapter by saying that picturebooks about the fear of monsters do not primarily talk about fear but about learning soft, social skills that turn fearful boys into successful boys and, eventually, men.

The titles in this chapter section make this association of monsterhood and boyhood even more visible by their questioning of the above premise. 'Being a monster means not being like girls' is the starting point of *YUCK! That's Not a Monster!* In some sense, this book can be seen as the quintessential picturebook positing a 'new' paradigm for child masculinity because not only does the main protagonist start out questioning conventional notions of monstrous selfhood but he is also allowed to maintain and thrive on his preferred mode of gender performance: The turning point of the narrative is set in the woods with Horrid and Frightful approaching another monster with the intention to scare him off – since the desire to scare others lies in their monstrous natures. When they realize that this monster is about ten times bigger than they are it is already too late for escape. The giant monster is about to devour them when Little Shock's ingenious idea to give the monster a kiss saves all their lives: the big monster runs away, crying for his mum. This heroic deed could be said to originate from Little Shock's creativity, but it is also entirely compatible with his characterization. It ultimately secures him a place at the heart of his family, his monster community: "Maybe being cute could be useful after all" is Horrid's evaluation and Frightful is described as "proud" of his cute, pink little brother. In the end, both brother and sister acknowledge and cherish Little Shock's difference. This is a happy ending, one where inclusion is made possible and desirable – but I do wonder whether a more explicit labelling of Little Shock's gendered characterization might have made this ending even more powerful or radical. It is perhaps the very inexplicitness that makes the affirmation of a deviating (gender) performance possible in the first place. A study about cross-dressing in children's literature seems to support this suggestion:

> Although cross-dressing is popularly perceived to be a male activity, the predominant type of cross-dressing behaviour in children's literature is female-to-male. [...] Paradoxically, male-to-female cross-dressers in children's literature and film are much less successful at interrogating gender stereotypes. [...] Male cross-dressers are usually prepubescent and their cross-dressing is unwillingly forced upon

them. [...] This performative failure is presented in carnivalesque terms, as the conventional gender hierarchy is comically inverted when a masculine subject suddenly finds himself forced to inhabit a feminine subjectivity. [...] male-to-female cross-dressing narratives are rarely able to construct cross-dressing as anything other than a short-lived, comic gesture which is used to reinforce the superiority of patriarchal masculinity. (Flanagan 2008: xv f.)

Conveniently enough, the monsters in McAllister and Edgson's book do not wear clothes, but the color of fur and its texture could definitely be seen as a code for clothing. Thus, the sister's fur is violet and the brother and father's furs are green (and the mother's is yellow). While not as strongly associated with male or female as blue and pink, a brief visit to a children's clothing store is likely to reveal considerably more violet items of clothing in the girls' section and more green in the boys' section (Steinberg et al. 2010: 31). Eyelashes are also often used as visual markers for gender: male monsters almost always simply have no eyelashes. While illustrator Edgson does not make exaggerate use of this device for signifying gender difference, the final page does show Horrid (the sister) and Little Shock with tender eyelashes, whereas brother Frightful has none. All these signs are very subtle and easily slip a reader's notice. The title picture offers perhaps the clearest illustration of this difference: Little Shock's eyelashes are almost as pronounced as that of the mother, while the father and the brother have no eyelashes. For all the subtleness, this is the most explicit account of gender deviance in my corpus.

Mo Willems' *Leonardo the Terrible Monster* (2005) could also be argued to feature two gender deviant protagonists: the title hero deviates in terms of appropriate monster performance (just like Little Shock) but is ultimately mirrored in the human boy Sam whom he first tries to intimidate to prove that he is, in fact, a monster – and then befriends. Leonardo realizes that Sam is a lot like him: he has no friends, is often bullied by his big brother, he is awkward, clumsy and generally unlucky. While these characteristics are not strikingly effeminate they do describe both Leonardo and Sam as weaklings and underdogs, in other words, in a position from which it is difficult to convince others of their boyhood/monsterhood. The story's turning point is, as in most other titles I have already discussed in this chapter, the main pro-

Fig. 25   *Leonardo the Terrible Monster* (Willems 2005)

tagonist's sudden inspiration: "Then Leonardo made a very big decision. [Page turn] Instead of being a terrible monster, he would become a wonderful friend." (Willems 2005: np) Leonardo explicitly renounces his pretense to 'be' a monster and, as a reward for acknowledging his heartfelt desire, gets a true friend in Sam. Both are allowed to stay just as they are (harmless, friendly, timid), as they walk hand in hand and smiling at each other, toward the end of the book (fig. 25).

In a third book that focuses on questions of gender performance, *Mostly Monsterly* (Sauer and Magoon 2010) the protagonist is a monster girl who is ostracized by her classmates at monster school because she is considered "unmonsterly" as she performs her favorite activities: picking flowers, petting kittens, baking, and being generally lovable and caring. Her behavior is much like Little Shock's in *YUCK! That's Not a Monster!* – except that here the constellation of ascribed gender and respective performance is gender conform. That is to say, her characterization corresponds with the stereotypically feminine attributes that I have mentioned earlier. To the monster children this seems irrelevant however: what matters is a "monsterly" performance. And thus, Bernadette is excluded from the community until she has an idea. She crafts particularly gross and disgusting gift cards for her class mates and consequently gains acceptance and even leadership within her group. Three separate pictures on the penultimate page illustrate her affirmed monster status as she "[lurches, growls and causes mayhem]" (Sauer and Magoon 2010: np), always at the head of the entire monster gang. Happy ending? Well, on the last page the reader is informed that "[s]ometimes... She was just Bernadette. And that was okay too" (ibid). Bernadette is pictured kneeling on the ground, watering a flower and smiling, with a faintly guilty facial expression. She is all by herself. The interaction of verbal and visual text seems to suggest that watering flowers, an activity she already enjoyed at the beginning of the story, translates most aptly who Bernadette 'really is.' Leaving aside for a moment the essentializing implications of the meaning of 'core identity', being "just Bernadette" is synonymous with enacting the aforementioned feminized attributes, whereas being "monsterly" could be translated as being "masculine."

Unlike Little Shock, Leonardo and Sam, Bernadette is torn between self-expression and isolation on the one hand, and imitation of a "monsterly" identity and social acceptance on the other. Apart from the underlying essentializing of gender inherent in the portrayal of Bernadette, the fact that it is once more a *female* protagonist whose means of self-expression is regulated and restricted from external impulses is significant and can be directly linked with Angela, in David McKee's *The Monster and the Teddy Bear* (1989). Her initial audacity in wishing for a monster as a play mate is shown as inappropriate for a girl, both through the adult protagonists' reactions to that wish and through the monster's veritable cruelty. She needs to be saved by big, strong Teddy. – In many respects, Beegu is depicted in a similar position of passivity that none of the male protagonists is subjected to: when she has no one but herself to escape from her sorrowful situation (which requires things like ingenuity, courage, and wit – all things consistently granted her male counterparts in the other books) she is literally lost. She can only be her 'true self' again once she is rescued by her parents. Now, on the surface *Mostly Monsterly* comes across as a feminist call for emancipating girls from the playground law that forbids them to behave like boys. The idea that Bernadette does not have to give up being "just Bernadette," while simultaneously being admitted into the feisty group of monster kids, can be read as an inclusive approach to tolerance and diversity. But how tolerant and diverse is that community of 'friends' really if every member has to conform to a masculine-gendered set of values and behaviors – or else be verbally abused and socially excluded? It is a community that basically rests on the repudiation of the 'feminine' within groups coded as 'masculine,' as it is described by Michael Kimmel in his article "Masculinity as Homophobia". Although Kimmel writes specifically about the mechanisms that establish certain images of boys and men, I find that his article has peculiar reverberations in the representation of Bernadette. In this picture-book, the concept of 'femininity' is clearly opposed to the idea of 'monstrosity,' which in turn encompasses the four rules of 'manhood' that Kimmel sums up as follows:

(1) "No Sissy Stuff!" One may never do anything that even remotely suggests femininity. Masculinity is the relentless repudiation of the feminine.
(2) "Be a Big Wheel." Masculinity is measured by power, success, wealth, and status. As the current saying goes, "He who has the most toys when he dies wins."
(3) "Be a Sturdy Oak." Masculinity depends on remaining calm and reliable in a crisis, holding emotions in check. In fact, proving you're a man depends on never showing your emotions at all. Boys don't cry.
(4) "Give 'em hell." Exude an aura of manly daring and aggression. Go for it. Take risks. (Kimmel 2004: 58)

Only when Bernadette has learned that asking everybody for a "group hug" (Sauer and Magoon 2010: np), while she is still engaging in "gross" things (ibid) such as singing love songs or baking "cupcakes with sprinkles" for everyone (ibid), is not going to win her peers' acceptance, and only when she has replaced these repudiating, feminine activities with lurching, growling and "[causing] mayhem of all kinds", only then is she established as a respected and admired member of her monster group. The path to her successful inclusion bears remarkable parallels to some prominent feminist voices challenging women who want to be successful professionals to be more like successful business men in some respects, such as negotiating the offer "like a man," cultivating confidence and self-esteem, or pursuing the drive to get to the top positions. Sheryl Sandberg's *Lean In* (2013) is certainly the most popular work that advocates such a stance.

The 'repudiation of the feminine' also plays a central role in *YUCK! That's Not a Monster!* and *Leonardo the Terrible Monster*. As in *Mostly Monsterly*, femininity is an object of disgust or, at least, a reason for exclusion from the male/monstrous dominant group. All three male protagonists Little Shock, Leonardo and Sam experience the isolating effects of other monsters' reaction towards their non-conforming behavior. But unlike Bernadette, the narrative does *not* require them to adopt a gender-conforming performance. In contrast, they can be described as presenting the very antithesis to Kimmel's codes of masculinity. To the extent that the rules number two to four are ramifications of rule number one, Leonardo and Sam are sissies just as Little Shock. The emphasis of *Leonardo the Terrible Monster* lies more on Leonardo's (and Sam's) failure to "be a big wheel, a sturdy oak, and to giv 'em hell." One difference from the other two books lies in this story's ending: Leonardo finds acceptance and inclusion in a likeminded soul, discarding the importance of everyone else. *Mostly Monsterly* and *YUCK! That's Not a Monster!*, in contrast, put emphasis on the importance of being accepted and included by everyone else. However, this difference is minor compared to the difference in the suggested solutions to the characters' isolation: Bernadette, a female monster, has to become more 'masculine'/'monsterly' in order to find that inclusion, Little Shock and Leonardo/Sam do not have to change anything.

Leonardo the Terrible Monster and *YUCK! That's Not a Monster!* offer a solution for the main protagonist's initial struggle and isolation that endorses the tenets of an inclusive education much more clearly than *Mostly Monsterly*. The encouragement of 'feminine' traits in boys might be surprising insofar as it could be seen to contradict the claims of masculinity researchers such as Michael Kimmel and others. Eve Kosofsky Sedgwick, to refer to another example, ironically writes that there are no parenting manuals that teach parents "[h]ow to bring [their] kids up gay" or to appreciate and cultivate 'feminine' traits in boys (Sedgwick 1998: 231-240). On the contrary, child rearing advice for parents of boys, according to Sedgwick, is geared towards erasing all traces of the 'feminine.' One way of evaluating the two picture-books about non-conforming masculinity, then, is to acknowledge their motivation to break up some of the codes criticized by Kimmel and Sedgwick.

Conclusion

All the books I have discussed in this chapter address more or less explicitly questions of normality: 'Are you a normal boy?;' 'Are you a normal girl?;' 'Are you a normal monster?;' 'Are you a normal human?' Normality, in a statistical sense, may seem an absurd concept in relation to physical appearance, race or gender. But as Marcus Reiß points out, 'the normal' plays a crucial role in the history and presence of education:

> Die Einführung von Normalschulen mit definierten Strukturen und Raumordnungen in Österreich um 1774 und die Entstehung der Écoles Normales 1790-91 in Frankreich verschafften der Normalität schon früh einen Stammplatz in den zeitgenössischen pädagogischen Diskursen (vgl. Sohn 1999, 12). [...] Ein Jahrhundert später wurde es im Zuge von Empirisierungs- und Medikalisierungsschüben zusehends üblich, Kinder statistisch zu erfassen und ihre Eigenschaften anhand von Normalitätsgraden zu skalieren. (Reiß 2012: 233 f.)

Following these trends, (children's) bodies and behaviors become comparable: they are either normal or abnormal (ibid). Furthermore, the discourse of normalization is tightly bound up with a therapeutic gaze that distinguishes between what is normal, healthy and dominant, from what is abnormal, deviant, pathological, sick or simply extraordinary (Metens 1999: 49; qt. in Reiß 2012: 234). The majority of the picturebooks in this chapter portray expressions of disgust about different kinds of 'deviance' as a widespread, automatic and therefore perhaps 'normal' reaction. Although in two books (*YUCK! That's Not a Monster* and *The Octonauts and the Only Lonely Monster*), the protagonists that are initially engaged in disgust-motivated behavior, such as aggression or fear, learn to appreciate and support a certain deviance from a 'monster' norm, the majority of picturebooks envision acceptance of the 'deviant' individual only in the form of a couple consisting of two like-minded or similar looking individuals. In some sense, many of these picturebooks may overtly come across as diversity training for young picturebook readers, but some fail to achieve this effect, because they instead contribute to normalizing dominant cultural mechanisms of identifying (and thereby constructing) difference as problematic in the first place.

Although I have categorized the bulk of books that focus on issues of inclusion and exclusion into three subordinate groups – namely, disability, race and gender – most of them work with a gendered subtext whose premise is an approximation of the concepts 'monster' and 'boy.' For example, all three monsters that are socially isolated because of their disabling physical appearance are male. I suggested that the reason why there are no ugly female monsters might lie behind an implicit necessity to make female protagonists that are to incite readers' sympathy 'beautiful' or at least physically unobtrusive. Girls may be allowed to be main-protagonist-monsters in rare cases, such as Beegu and Bernadette, but only if they incorporate certain stereotyped images of femininity: sweetness, a caring and loving attitude towards others, and a penchant for baking and petting kittens. In addition, both female characters are restricted in their potential range of self-expression. It is a restriction that none of the male monster or child characters are subjected to, regardless of the primary reason for which they are excluded from the community. All male characters are endowed with inner resources to create happy and satisfying lives for themselves by cultivating their individualism.

The stock of resourceful male characters that I have already introduced and discussed in some detail could be complemented with Jeremy from *Jeremy Draws a Monster* (Peter McCarty 2009) and John from *Monsters* (Russell Hoban and Quentin Blake 1989). In both books, the boy protagonist shows an exceptional creative artistic talent which he uses to assert himself in a social environment that presents itself as intolerant of his exceptional personality. In addition, there is a small number of books by Babette Cole that were published within a series, starting with *The Trouble with Mum* (1983), that could be said to fit loosely into the overall theme of this chapter. In every one of these books, an adult family member is presented as weird and slightly embarrassing for the child narrator and in some books of this series the respective family member is associated with monstrous qualities. In all cases, it is the adult characters' (supernatural) distinctiveness that turns them into eventually cool and envied-by-everyone parents, grandparents and uncles. Interestingly, in Cole's books with adult main protagonists, monstrosity is not as obviously linked to questions of gender as in the picturebooks with child or childlike protagonists. Finally, the very recent publication dates of most books discussed in this chapter might be indicative of the present focus on inclusion in educational discourses and mirror the pedagogic tenor that accompanies the vast majority of picturebook narratives. While the inclusion of so-called minority identities into the dominant culture plays a considerable role in these discourses and is mirrored to some extent in the picturebooks here discussed, notions of normality also encroach on images of the white and middle-class (and usually male) child. In the following and final chapter, I will focus on three popular images of 'the child' that I have encountered in a number of picturebooks that directly address issues of child rearing practices.

4.4 On raising monsters. Erhm: children.

What monstrous parenting attitudes reveal about images of boys and some girls

Introduction

Summarizing my discussions in the previous three chapters, I have suggested that monsters in picturebooks come in thematic clusters: some awaken social skills that are required for and by the paradigmatic contemporary boy, some others are figurations of minority identities whose inclusion into the dominant culture may be a politically called for educational prerequisite but is at the same time frequently constructed as impossible, and a very few monsters helped me to demonstrate to what extent picturebook creations of strong girls diverge from those of strong boys with respect to their relationships with the monsters. In the picturebooks in all three clusters an underlying didactic impetus was noticeable. Although the pedagogical messages that these picturebooks could be said to transport are manifold, I concentrated on their impact on the construction of gender norms. In this last chapter, I have assembled fifteen books where parenting and related images of 'the child' are a clear theme on the story level, and not just subliminally encoded into the text and images. In other words, the books that I will discuss now are not only overtly or covertly didactic, as picturebooks generally are; they tell stories about actual child rearing practices.

Despite their considerable variety, all of these stories implicitly ask one simple question: What should a child be like? Of course, this question can be dissected into its parts, such as: What makes a good child? – What makes a bad child? – What are the implications and effects of making such a distinction? – Is this distinction even legitimate? – Does a 'good boy' correspond to the same ideas as a 'good girl'? – What role do parents play and what responsibility do they have for the raising of these future adults? – And what am I as a reader and researcher to make of the symbolical equation of 'the child' and 'the monster,' that underlies all of the child-rearing narratives present in this chapter?

255

Because interactions and – often failed - communication between child and adult characters are so central to all of these stories, I place particular emphasis on investigating the power hierarchies inherent in these narratives. Another striking commonality of many of these books is their prominent and highly complex use of humor, irony and satire. Although they seem very different at first glance, theoretical concepts of power and humor have many overlaps, as my selective use of some humor theories will illustrate. Generally, it can be said that humor strongly correlates with an extreme image of 'the child' as either fundamentally evil or as blissfully royal. Those picturebooks that represent neither of these two extremes tend to put less weight on humor and more on the representation of the child characters' strong and troubling emotions and mental states, such as anger, envy and worries, and on their resolution.

In an attempt to pull these strands together and to find answers to some of the questions above, I draw from diverse disciplines and theories, including a Foucauldian stance on educational concepts that focusses on mechanisms of normalization and deviation, psychological studies on the interconnections of gender, class, and emotions, and humor theories, most notably Bakhtin's theory of the carnivalesque. But theories of humor that are not specifically carnivalesque can be equally productive for an account of power mechanisms in picturebook narratives. For example, Gaby Pailer points out that "[in] social interaction, laughter often works as an instrument of power: superiors only rarely make fun of themselves, whereas employees tend to make themselves a target of laughter" (Pailer 2009: 9). This observation becomes really intriguing when I try to apply it to the picturebooks I discuss here. If I transpose the suggested power hierarchy and consider the adults as the superiors and the children as the employees – both the picturebook characters and the real humans involved in the picturebook production and reception – if I do this, one thing becomes clear immediately: children never construct child characters as laughable because children do not write or illustrate published picturebooks. In other words, whenever a child character is ridiculed it is an adult's doing. If the adult picturebook artist succeeds in making child readers laugh about the comic image of a child character, that is, a representation of the child readers themselves, does this mean that these

256

child readers become complicit in the adult's ideology of a good childhood? Is humor in these picturebooks perhaps only a sneaky technique to infuse children with the means to control and discipline their own wildness?

Indeed, what is the role of 'the child' in these picturebooks? From a literary historical perspective, children's literature emerged as the result of a new conception of 'the child' as needful of suitable literature that was geared towards his or her tastes and intellectual capacities (thought of as inferior to those of adults). Certain key concepts surrounding popular images of 'the child,' such as 'nature,' 'child-centeredness' and 'healthy development,' also became central to one of the most influential pedagogical movements until today: progressive education. As Marcus Reiß suggests, these usually positively viewed terms could easily be replaced by other ideas, such as domestication ("Zähmung") and pacification ("Befriedung"), that are just as central to Maria Montessori and Ellen Key's writings (Reiß 2012: 15) – both were central figures in this movement. By doing this, Reiß asks the fundamental question whether the central business of pedagogy can actually be conceived *without* implications of power relations between adults and children (ibid), implying that it may be illegitimate to pretend that it can. I suggest that the picturebooks in this chapter, in contrast to the other books of my corpus, make these power relations explicit through the very use of monsters. While children's literature generally conceals the role adults play in defining the rules of the genre and hence the power implications that are inherent to this system (Nodelman 2008), the picturebooks here represent parental and other adult figures as (more or less) openly involved in 'the making of the child.' The use of monsters, as archetypal signifiers for the struggle over control versus chaos, spells out what this process is ultimately about: the negotiation of who gets to decide about behavioral norms and who has the authority to enforce them. Depending on the kind of relation between the monster/s, the child and the adult characters, three fundamentally different images of 'the child' emerge: the evil child, the competent child and the child as king.

In the books representing the evil child, the child characters are portrayed as ill-behaved, malicious and/or violent. The monsters function as threatening and punitive antagonists that are ultimately endorsed by an adult agenda which, at the end of the story, invariably gains the upper hand. The disciplining of the child characters consists of erasing or restricting their physical or emotional boundaries through threats, coercion and corporal punishment. This representation of 'the child' as evil as well as the process of correction they undergo is drenched in irony and other forms of humor that undermine or question the seriousness of that representation. In my analysis, I concentrate on Babette Cole's *Bad Habits!* (1998), but will occasionally refer to the other three titles I have put in this group: *Pat the Beastie* (Drescher 1993), *Night of the Veggie Monster* (Clement 2007) and *Monsters Eat Whiny Children* (Kaplan 2010). By indicating some striking parallels to Heinrich Hoffmann's popular and bestselling *Der Struwwelpeter* (1844), I will look at the interaction of humor and a vision of Black Pedagogy that these picturebooks can be said to invoke to differing degrees.

The common ground of the picturebooks representing 'the competent child' is their representation of a child character that is shown to be capable of solving a conflict by him- or herself, albeit with a certain amount of adult intervention. These stories can be seen as illustrating a progressive educative approach of child-centeredness by focusing on a difficult emotional or mental state that the child character experiences. But just as Marcus Reiß has critically examined the normalizing and disciplining ideology behind Montessori's and Key's texts, the picturebook stories, too, can be seen in a very critical light: the monsters as externalized materializations of the child character's wild emotions must always be tamed, controlled and exiled in order for the child character to be admitted back into the family, the nucleus of human society. In this section, I will concentrate on Maurice Sendak's *Where the Wild Things Are* (1963), with cross-references to the other books in this group: *Not Now Bernard* (McKee 1984), *The Huge Bag of Worries* (Ironside and Rodgers 1996), *When Mum Turned Into a Monster* (1996), *Sad Monster, Glad Monster* (Emberly and Miranda), *G.E.M.* (Clark and Parsons 2006), *Anh's Anger* (Silver and Krömer 2009) and *Steps and Stones* (Silver and Krömer 2011).

In the third section, I will examine the image of the child as king. Specifically, I look at Henrik Drescher's *The Boy Who Ate Around* (1993) which I interpret in Bakhtin's sense of the carnivalesque: in complete opposition to the books in the first group, the child protagonist here reverses the usual power hierarchy by claiming the position of the sovereign. Drescher's picturebook story contains many other elements that are crucial to carnival, such as death and renewal through acts of eating, digesting and giving birth. Although these elements are mostly absent in *Monsters – An Owner's Guide* (Emmett and Oliver 2010), the principle of a child character in absolute power is active here, too – here in the form of a monster robot toy/pet. What I find remarkable (and probably indicative of deep seated fears in adults) is that despite the pervasiveness of this image of the child as an emperor in the mass media I have only spotted two picturebooks with monsters that play with this image.

As I have already made clear elsewhere in this dissertation, with these suggested categorizations I do not want to impose rigid patterns on the picturebooks I discuss here. Indeed, some of my classifications might be subject to scrutiny and objections. For example, one may legitimately question whether the boy protagonist in *Not Now Bernard* is shown as competent in dealing with his frustration about his parents' neglect. In the same context, one might point out that the relationship between Bernard and the monster is very different from the one I described as typical for this group because here, the monster eats Bernard and permanently replaces him, without his parents ever noticing a difference. There are other picturebooks in this chapter that do not feature every characteristic I propose as typical for the group into which I have put them. And although I generally agree with David Lewis when he says that "[...] picturebooks do not take kindly to being corralled into six, eight or even ten determinate categories" (Lewis 2001: 44), picturebooks clearly do represent and perpetuate dominant cultural narratives, and by grouping them together these narratives and underlying ideologies can be made more visible. In my view, such an approach does not necessarily obliterate a picturebook's idiosyncrasies and individuality; rather it can help to provide readers with a deeper understanding of these narratives. Then again, Lewis is specifically writing about formalized modes of image-text-interaction, so he might perhaps even side with me when it comes to ideological patterns surrounding parenting attitudes, childhood and 'the child.'

The evil child: 'Bad Habits!'

The most well-known literary precursor of the picturebooks in this group must be Heinrich Hoffmann's *Der Struwwelpeter* or, in English, *Shockheaded Peter*. Despite its once immense popularity, *Der Struwwelpeter*, written by Heinrich Hoffmann for his then three-year-old son in 1845, is unofficially banned from most children's nurseries today because of the repressive and punitive pedagogy that many people perceive in the text (Maier 1993: 45) and the psychological damage it is feared to cause in its young readers (Jatzek 2012: np). The proponents of reading the *Struwwelpeter* as bearing witness to and promoting Black Pedagogy are countered by voices proclaiming the text's ironic undertones that were apparently obvious to Hoffmann's contemporaries and that a careful analysis of the book's image-text-dynamics can still reveal to readers today (Wessling 2004: 319–345). The stories in *Der Struwwelpeter* and in the picturebooks compare insofar as they present child characters as misbehaved, indulging in bodily drives and impulses, and then 'correcting' and 'reforming' these children with threats or actual punishments. But with respect to the ongoing debates about the ambiguities of *Der Struwwelpeter* (Wessling actually calls it "the *Struwwelpeter* research industry" (ibid: 321)), another commonality with the monster picturebooks might be a use of humor that makes it difficult, if not impossible, to pin down their pedagogical message.

Disregarding for the moment the complications that humor brings about, the underlying assumption in these picturebook stories seems to be that children must be corrected and reformed in order to grow into morally sustained citizens. On a historical scale, this thesis was examined by Michel Foucault in a part of a lecture series in 1974–1975, titled *Les Anormaux*. In these lectures, Foucault presents the child masturbator of the late nineteenth century as the third figure of the abnormal individual, following the human monster – abnormal because of physical irregularities – of the Middle Ages and the dangerous individual, or criminal, or the "incorrigible" of the nineteenth century. In his lectures, Foucault formulated the hypothesis that gradually the child's potentially devi-

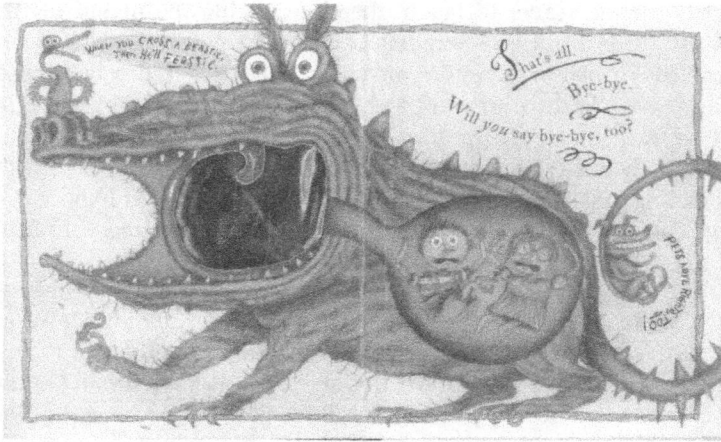

Fig. 26   *Pat the Beastie* (Drescher 1993)

ous behavior became the center of adult attention in combination with institutional measurements of correcting this behavior, ultimately giving rise to the birth of psychiatry. Although sexual acts traditionally play no overt role in children's literature, much of Foucault's claim can help to understand the underlying image of 'the child' as driven by basic and destructive impulses and therefore needful of discipline in the present group of picturebooks.

The story that most resembles the pattern of the *Struwwelpeter*-episodes is Henrik Drescher's *Pat the Beastie* (1993): Paul and Judy terrorize a monstrous animal just for fun and are punished for their misbehavior by eventually being eaten up by the beast (fig. 26). The beast's devouring of the children is final, it is the last page. The verbal narrative is an assemblage of admonitory comments made by two animals, a duck and a dog, and a final statement by the narrator. While the duck's rhyming remark is vested in a humorous neologism, "When you cross a beastie, then he'll feastie" (ibid: np), the dog spells out the story's moral: "Pets have rights, too!" (ibid: np). The narrator emphasizes that this is really the end: "That's all. Bye-bye. Will *you* say bye-bye, too?" (ibid: np) There really is no hope for Paul and Judy ever to see the light of day again. One possibility to digest the harshness of this

261

end is for the reader to laugh, thereby denying the reality of the children's death. Many parallels can be discovered to the second story of *Struwwelpeter*, in which Bad Frederick ("der bitterböse Friederich") beats a girl, tortures a dog, is then bitten by the dog and is consequently bedridden while the dog gets to eat his sausage. At the center, however, and according to Wessling and others (Wessling 2004) seems to be the assumption – wrapped in humor – that children are naturally cruel and need to be corrected with brutal force.

One aspect for understanding these stories, that is both essential and the most difficult to pin down, is that very humor. On what grounds can I claim that a certain portrayal of children in a picturebook is funny? And is it then only funny to me? It is a truism that humor is a deeply personal affair. A possible approach to humor is via an essay written by Umberto Eco where he offers a definition of the comic. He contrasts the comic frame with reference to Aristotle's definition of tragedy. While the breaking of (moral or normative) rules by the hero is common to both, only in comedy these rules are presupposed and must not be spelled out (Eco 1984: 4). Further, through his [sic] animalization, the comic hero is markedly inferior to "us" (Eco 1984: 2). These three cornerstones – (i) the breach of rules which must (ii) not be spelled out and (iii) be committed by an animal-like or otherwise inferior character – provide a helpful access to the analysis of humor in the picturebooks about the evil child. The basis of this analysis consists in acknowledging that even to talk of the child as evil is a breach of implicit rules in our times. The reason why I laugh about Paul and Judy's end in Beastie's belly is, partly, because I read it in a comic framework that corresponds to Eco's definition. Drescher subverts the usual hierarchy that attributes humans a naturalized and usually unquestioned power over animals. But in order to find this reversal funny, a reader must be aware of this 'rule.' The pinnacle of rule breaching is perhaps that in Drescher's book, the animal-like character, Beastie, devours the children and yet retains a sense of moral superiority: after all that he had to suffer at Paul and Judy's hands his resolute action comes across as perfectly justified. But animal-likeness or monstrosity do not always guarantee the comic hero or heroine gratification, as Babette Cole's *Bad Habits!* shows.

262

Fig. 27   *Bad Habits!* (Cole 1998)

The first sentence in *Bad Habits!* introduces the comic heroine as incorporating base, bestial behaviors: "Lucretzia Crum was an uncivilized little monster!" (Cole 1998: np, fig. 27) Through the book's title, these behaviors are already marked as 'habits.' It might not surprise that habits are an important key word in theories about an effective and enduring education. John Locke in *Some Thoughts concerning Education* (1693) already commented on the importance of this concept: "The great Thing to be minded in Education is, what Habits you settle" (qt. in Reiß 2012: 205). As Reiß observes, habits are an integral part of the human body (ibid) and as such, Lucretzia's description as a monster and the visualization of her body are significant for an understanding of the underlying assumptions on education. The first page shows Lucretzia's upper body filling out the entire page. She seems to be walking right out of the page, directly at the viewer. Her gaze supports this impression: with an angry and provoking smile, tongue and upper front teeth sticking out, Lucretzia stares the viewer directly in the eyes. Her face and her sweater, which reveals part of her belly, are smeared with chocolate: evidently traces from the ice-lolly she is holding in her left hand. Already on this first page, even before the narrator verbally enumerates her "bad habits," Lucretzia's pose in conjunction with the text, suggests some reasons for her monstrosity: she is grubby, inattentive to proper dress codes, the picture further suggests that she can eat all the sweets she wants, and she is, worst of all, completely irreverent in the face of adult authority.

The unambiguously negative verbal attribution of Lucretzia as a monster is related by a heterodiegetic narrative voice with zero focalization. The narrator's evaluative judgment of Lucretzia's habits as "disgustingly bad" (Cole 2006: np) is authoritative in the sense that no alternative view is embedded, as would be possible via the images. But here the visuals are complementary, that is to say that they provide complementary information to the verbal text, further strengthening its message. The description of Lucretzia as an "uncivilized little monster" remains metaphorical. At no point in the story is Lucretzia depicted in a literally monstrous appearance. Although Lucretzia's behavior and, later that of her friends who start to imitate her, is described as monstrous she nevertheless retains her human shape throughout the book.

Because of the narrator's power to determine the child as 'monstrous' and because of the complementary image/text interaction, Lucretzia's visual and verbal characterization must be read as 'monstrous' even though she retains her human form throughout the story. Apart from the complementary pictures that show her as the perpetrator that she is said to be, her very first appearance, particularly her gaze, is noteworthy. In a demand pose (cf. chapter 3.3.3), Lucretzia stares the reader directly in the eyes. Her facial expression invokes provocation: her mouth mimics a smile that weirdly contradicts her angrily furrowed brows. This impression is further underlined by her body pose – clenched fists and squared shoulders – and her unkempt and smudged outfit. To some extent, this picture creates the first comment on what being "an uncivilized little monster" means from the point of view of the narrator.

Already readers are confronted with a violation of certain rules, more specifically, with a girl's blatant disrespect for a code of conduct that children – particularly female ones – are expected to follow. In this sense, Lucretzia's breach of rules corresponds to some extent to Foucault's conceptualization of the human monster of the Middle Ages:

> The frame of reference of the human monster is, of course, law. The notion of the monster is essentially a legal notion, in a broad sense, of course, since what defines the monster is the fact that its existence

and form is not only a violation of the laws of society but also a violation of the laws of nature. [...] It could be said that the monster's power and its capacity to create anxiety are due to the fact that it violates the law while leaving it with nothing to say. (Foucault 2003: 55)

The laws Lucretzia breaks are not strictly legal, but could be more adequately described as social norms, including how a girl is expected to look like (clean and decorous) and to behave (obedient, eating moderately and healthily). By contradicting all these social laws, Lucretzia's appearance is geared towards inciting anxiety, disgust and contempt – but also laughter. Lucretzia's behavior is presented as so terrifying, so much in contradiction to these rules, that she leaves her parents and her teacher speechless. On the third and fourth pages, Lucretzia's parents are pictured with their eyes wide open in horror, but their mouths shut tight and additionally sealed with their hands. Here, in this picturebook, the laws the child character breaks predominantly impact the social domain:

> She had disgustingly bad habits like... burping... farting... and spitting! [page turn] She swore at her parents and kicked and screamed if she could not get her own way. She refused to eat at mealtimes, saying she preferred to starve rather than eat anything her parents cooked. Then she'd stuff herself with chocolates until she felt sick! [page turn] She stole from babies! She pulled little girls' pigtails. (Cole 1998: np)

The long list of Lucretzia's outrageous wrongdoings suggests that there is something fundamentally wrong with this girl. This wrongness immediately and implicitly calls for correction. This narrative point of departure weaves in different kinds of humor that can be conceptualized as rule violations: bodily transgressions and scatology, the behavioral codes for children, and finally the representation of a child character as a quasi-criminal monster. I believe that the fact that the child protagonist in this book is female considerably amplifies the effects of these rule breaches. This becomes clearer when I look at *Bad Habits!* in a broader context, by comparing the relationship between child character and monster with other books in my corpus, but also by reflecting on the gender specificity of disgust-related behavior.

'Monster' as a persona that a child character can inhabit comes with connotations that are not only very different but *opposite* to those present in the overwhelming majority of the books I have examined so far. In *Bad Habits!*, children that act like monsters carry purely negative connotations. Although in some books of my corpus, the identification of a child character with a monster can be said to be ambiguous – for example in Sendak's *Outside Over There* or in McKee's *Not Now, Bernard* – a child that incorporates a monster is, as a rule and even in these ambiguous cases, connected with affirmative qualities such as being powerful and independent. At the least, the child-monster is never characterized in detrimental, derogative terms. Of course, *Bad Habits!* also implicitly equips Lucretzia with a sense of power and independence, but here these qualities are shown in a negative light. They are undesirable and unwanted.

According to this impression and following the logic of the narration, all the details I have just listed belong to the category 'monstrous.' The narrator's introductory sentence leaves no room for interpreting the girl's appearance as positively assertive, unconventional or freedom-loving. Lucretzia comes across as an annoying and aggressive little brat. Showing up in dirty clothes without shame or remorse, revealing naked skin, throwing with food and especially reveling in excretory activities – these forms of rule-breaking behavior are more easily forgiven, and frequently even cherished, in picturebooks when performed by a male character (cf. Nodelman 2002: 1-13).

A classical picturebook that is often referred to for illustrating to what extent boy character's wildness and disrespect for parental authority is naturalized and taken for granted is Beatrix Potter's *Peter Rabbit* (1902) (e.g. Nikolajeva and Scott (2001: 108); Nodelman (2002: 3). Another 'character trait' that is represented as typical for boys, but not for girls, concerns a supposedly deep-seated (and hence 'natural') pleasure in toilet humor, filth and grime: *Morris, the Mankiest Monster*; *Smelly Peter, the Great Pea Eater* (Steve Smallman, Joelle Dreidemy 2009); *Dirty Bertie* (David Roberts 2003); *Boris's Bogey* (Paul Bright and Hannah George 2011). It is really difficult to find picturebooks with female protagonists who, first of all, indulge in a fascination with bodily excretions and who, second of all, are granted the narrator's benevolence for doing so – as is the case for all the picturebooks with male protagonists just named here. I have found one recently published book with this theme with a girl character on the cover: *Pigeon Poo* (Elizabeth Baguley and Mark Chambers 2012). The girl is pictured with an umbrella anxiously shielding herself from the pigeon's droppings falling from the sky. Interestingly, several reviewers on Amazon UK praise this book for its "boyish sense of humor" or because it appeals to boys' "typical interest in such matters." Not a single reviewer mentions a girl reading or even enjoying this story, despite its female protagonist. Considering the codification of 'disgusting' behavior as innately masculine, I suggest that the horror that Lucretzia conveys in *Bad Habits!* largely results from the degree of her deviance from established gender norms.

The attribute "uncivilized" explicitly points both at the negative associations with the image of 'monster' (children as savages) and at a narrative instance that does not try to conceal its disapproval of a child's unsocial behavior. Because of this overdetermination of the girl protagonist as "an uncivilized little monster," the narrative could be read as ironic. By literally dissimulating or feigning ignorance about the social rule that children, particularly female children, are not to be talked about as 'monsters' and as 'disgusting,' the narrator transforms this description into an exaggeration that is perhaps intended as ironic. In other words, speaking about children as monsters in picturebooks seems only possible in humoristic forms.

Of course, there are examples in the mass media that have gained much popularity and sparked a lot of controversy by presenting the equation of 'child' and 'monster' as a serious problem. For example, German psychiatrist and psychotherapist Michael Winterhoff's bestseller *Warum unsere Kinder Tyrannen werden* (2010) presented the idea of children as tyrants, carrying the same connotations (uncontrollable, destructive, autocratic) as the ubiquitous use of 'monster' in this context. Winterhoff sees the responsibility for this power reversal in parents' increasing incompetence in child rearing skills and in their desire for assimilation with their child. As a consequence, according to the author, more and more children are treated as if they were adults. Winterhoff's publication caused a lot of public uproar, from parents but also professionals, mainly on the grounds of the author's proposed pedagogical solutions: setting firm boundaries between adults and children and clear rules and punishments if these rules were breached. Thus Winterhoff's theses were condemned as promoting a cold and disciplinary atmosphere ("Erziehungskultur") between parents and children (Bergmann 2009) and favoring a mechanistic image of the child. In English speaking countries, the extremely popular reality TV show *Supernanny* (2004–2012) is based on a comparable parenting ideal that is based on discipline, order and a clear power hierarchy that designates the parents as the rulers.

Complementing these self-proclaimed professionals in parenting advice literature or TV formats, there are autobiographical accounts of parenting that, self-ironically or not, advocate a child rearing attitude that is based on respect for and fear of the mother. Amy Chua's *Battle Hymn of a Tiger Mother* (2011) is one very popular example. On the blog *Scarymommy*, the authors give vent to their occasional feelings of resentment or helplessness in a humorous and openly politically incorrect manner. Post titles such as "What if he is an asshole forever?" (Morrison-Fortunato 2013), "When the little shit is yours" (Tuttle-Singer 2013) or "10 gross things that you hope your kids will never do (but probably will)" (Jacobs Thomas 2013) mirror the humorous and politically incorrect attitude that is also displayed by the narrator of *Bad Habits!*

In many respects, *Bad Habits!* feeds into this discourse on the need of disciplining and punishing children for doing what the narrator construes as 'misbehavior.' Some of these formats, such as Winterhoff's book, *Supernanny* as well as Chua's *Battle Hymn*, propose their claims as serious and sound, while others, such as the blogs, are openly satirical. Babette Cole's contribution to this discourse obviously resembles the blogs more with regard to the use of humor. The largest portion of the laughter that the narrative seeks to generate is directed at Lucretzia. Her ridicule continues when her parents finally take action to eradicate her "inacceptable" behavior, to quote one of Jo Frost's (the Supernanny) most frequently used adjectives for describing her fosterlings. Once Lucretzia's parents assume responsibility for their disastrous family situation their tactics reverberate with the parenting blog *Scarymommy* insofar as they become so scary that this can only be read as a humoristic exaggeration: they physically restrain and torture their daughter. Of course, the extremity of these measurements indicates another breach of rule, this time an actual law that marks the exercise of torture against children (as well as adults) as a crime. The exaggeration that was already palpable in Lucretzia's description as a monster here reaches a new climax.

The narrator presents the fact that Lucretzia's father "[is] a mad scientist" as "[lucky]" because this allows him to invent and build all sorts of contraptions that are aimed at containing Lucretzia's destructive tendencies. The narrator openly sides with the adults of this story, remarking that "[the] worst thing was that her school friends began to copy her. They thought it was dead cool to be a little monster like Lucretzia Crum!" When the other parents urge Lucretzia's parents to "keep [their] daughter under control," Lucretzia's father, the inventor, gets to work. Thus, she is put into the "Blowfart Inhaler Suit" that not only contains her farts within the suit but also makes her inhale them. Then she is stuck in the "No Scream/Kick Tube", a human sized pipe that is long enough to only allow her eyes and nose and her feet to show. Considerable space is given to demonstrate the quantity and quality of these inventions, further supporting a narrative instance that is full of malicious joy at seeing the destructive child bound and incapacitated. These instruments of torture and constraint contain obvious elements of 'schadenfreude' that are reminiscent of the narrator's final sentences in *Pat the Beastie*. They are physical, grotesque, and some openly address the scatological, such as the "Blowfart Inhaler Suit" or the "Burp-bung" that consists of a rubber bung, normally used to ease the congestion in waste pipes, being put on Lucretzia's mouth – presumably to clean her mouth of the unbecoming burps that prevent her from using polite language. These contraptions openly allude to Lucretzia's faulty behavior. Not only that, the father's gleeful face while building the "Blowfart Inhaler Suit" and the teacher's contented smile while Lucretzia is captured behind the bars of the "Classroom Pacifier," a cage that is chained to and dangling from the window, both suggest that the adults in this book feel just as much satisfaction at reversing Lucretzia's insulting behavior at her expense as Lucretzia does at the beginning of the book. What I find interesting is that the extreme cruelty that Lucretzia is subjected to only further heightens the sense of this story being comic.

Part of the humor might result from the narrator's observation that torture and other physical punishment have no effect: "[Lucretzia] became wilder than ever." Speaking in Foucault's terms, Lucretzia is a child who has not yet been successfully inculcated with self-regulating mechanisms (cf. Mills 2003: 44). Not just that, she is also presented as entirely resistant to any form of disciplining. Foucault's rhetorical question seems effectuated here: "[…] if power was never anything but repressive, if it never did anything but say no, do you really believe that we should manage to obey it?" (Foucault 1995: 36). If we follow this argument, the reason why the measures thus far employed for correcting Lucretzia's behavior were unsuccessful is that they were exclusively repressive. The method that ultimately signifies the big turn is not as easily labelled as repressive as are the previous contraptions that actively constrict Lucretzia's movements. Resembling a conspiracy, all the parents band together and come to "[wreck Lucretzia's birthday] party" (Cole 2004: np) disguised as "really big monsters" (ibid).

The ingenious 'trick' that Lucretzia's parents resort to resembles somewhat the mechanism of a paradoxical intervention that is sometimes used in psychotherapy when certain behavioral patterns and power dynamics are deadlocked. In this picturebook story, Lucretzia is confronted with a behavior by her parents that is completely opposed to what she has become accustomed to. In order to civilize their daughter, her parents un-civilize themselves. The verb "to civilize" relates to the Latin *civis*, meaning "citizen", and *civitas*, meaning "city" or "city-state". In some sense, then, Lucretzia is transformed into an obedient citizen, a docile part of society. But the conclusion of *Bad Habits!* does not stop there. If I take into consideration the parents' monster party, the conclusion becomes much more complex, even paradoxical. It seems paradoxical that the monstrous qualities that Lucretzia displayed only have to be corrected in children, but obviously not in adults. Contrary to those readers' expectations which are conform with parenting guides, namely that parents should be role models, the parents in this book reverse the roles of the monster and the civilized. On a certain level, this could be interpreted as an effect of power's productivity. According to Foucault, power is never unidirectional, but multidirectional, creating different uses and effects of power. In the context of *Bad Habits!*, the parents' monster party can be read as an ironic dismantling of the power mechanisms that they used in order to transform Lucretzia into an overly adapted girly girl. But even more, the parents' monstrous rumpus completely strips down their pedagogical pretense. They revel in the very actions and expressions that they have successfully suppressed in the girl.

The monster-parents in the picturebook "[scream, kick, fart, vomit and smell] far worse than the little monsters!" (ibid). Lucretzia and the other children seem horrified as they desperately look for an escape route. The big monsters' aggressive indulgence in excretory activities is an overt imitation of Lucretzia's behavior. This is what finally makes Lucretzia come to her senses, at least from her parents' point of view: Lucretzia looks positively scared. Any reader looking at this double-page with scrutiny will discover the heads of the adults that are mostly hidden by the giant and convincingly realistic looking monster costumes. Lucretzia voices her and her guests' fear by asking her parents about the monsters' identity. Her parents pretend to be concerned when they say that "they were children once, but they turned into monsters because they grew up doing what you do!" After the next page turn, however, we see the parents looking out of the window laughing with their mouths wide open while Lucretzia and the other children look sad and disappointed at the realization that the big monsters "had eaten all the party food [...] taking all Lucretzia's presents with them" (ibid). Lucretzia's friends denounce their alliance to her because they do not want to become such horrible creatures. And, more importantly, even Lucretzia repents.

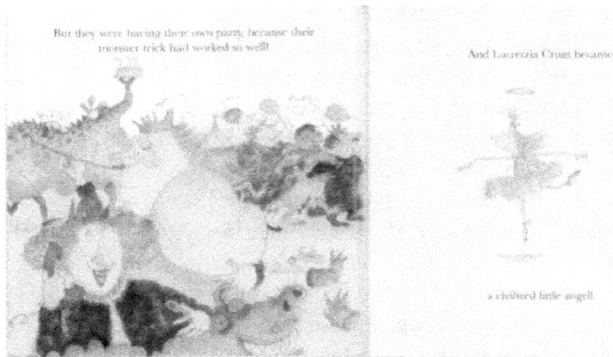

Fig. 28   *Bad Habits!* (Cole 1998)

The parents' trick has worked wonders, on the final page we see that "Lucretzia Crum [has become] a civilized little angel!" In between this final sentence that is split in two halves the girl is depicted as a prima ballerina with a halo. From a calligraphic perspective, the text as part of the visual design of this last page resembles sandwich halves and the girl inside the filling (fig. 28). She is now a likeable, well-behaved girl who comes easily digestible, in the form of a sandwich, and does what girls should do: she wears frilly pink dresses, is delicate, smiles with her eyes closed and dances ballet.

The ending of *Bad Habits!* is particularly revealing of the irony involved in the portrayal of this parenting style but it also highlights the productive potential of power. As Foucault argues particularly in *The History of Sexuality* (first published in 1978), oppressive measures, even at their most constraining, are in fact productive, giving rise to new forms of behavior rather than simply closing down or censoring forbidden ones. The monster that was characterized as so universally despicable while it was incorporated by Lucretzia is now the chosen form of joyful expression for all the adults in the story. Interestingly, the narrator does not verbalize the parents' monster status. The narrator does *not* say, for example: "All the parents had become uncivilized big monsters!" But this is exactly what the image expresses: the parents in their monster costumes celebrate their success in conga line, while in the foreground a mother is holding a red telephone receiver against her ear, in a demand-pose, appearing to talk to us, the viewers, and caressing her red-eyed monster's ear (whose red eyes also seem to be directed at the viewer). Just behind her, a father is embracing his buttocks-costume with integrated whoopee cushion, while blowing his noisemaker. This penultimate picture, then, inversely mirrors in some important aspects the opening picture. First there is the demand pose that both the mother with the telephone and her monster engage in. She is smiling with an open mouth; perhaps she is inviting other adult readers to join the party? Secondly, there are many references to Lucretzia's earlier misbehavior: excretory noises, spilled drink and food on the carpet and general disrespect for proper conduct. So although the narrator only acknowledges that the parents "were having their own party," merely implying the fun and satisfaction they feel, there is no mention of them being monsters now or of this subversive role reversal. This information is only transmitted through the image.

At a conference where I presented a paper on this picturebook, the audience voiced very different reactions, reaching from chuckling and laughter to concern and even mild shock. In our discussion, I found out that the laughter was primarily caused by the representation of the parents' infantile monster party and the concern mostly directed at Lucretzia's angelic transformation. I agree with the laughing members of the conference audience that there would be something inherently 'mad' about these parents' behavior if they were to be imagined as real, living people. This madness reverberates with Foucault's claim that "adult conduct is scrutinized for any possible trace of infantilism" and that "childhood has been the principle of the generalization of psychiatry" (Foucault 2003: 304). But rather than pathologizing the parents' behavior, the narrative enables a critical examination of their parenting strategy with Lucretzia. Because the parents have lowered themselves in moral terms they are no longer an irrevocable parenting authority. They are now Eco's animal-like comic heroes.

What does this make of Lucretzia? She was never a heroine at all, but rather a horrible, unbearable, nerve-wrecking girl. At the end, she becomes a "civilized little angel." *Bad Habits!* is extremely radical in the effected change of its female child protagonist: from monster to angel – what could possibly be more dramatic? I suggest that the author's intention to maximize the comic effect is at least partly responsible for creating a female character rather than a male one, because boys already carry with them an array of monster connotations. In addition to the picturebooks that I have mentioned above to illustrate these stereotypical ascriptions, Emily Kane states in her introduction to a study of parental beliefs about the gender of their children that slogans written on gendered clothing items include "Little Angel," "Pretty Girl," "Daddy's Princess," "Beach Beauty" for girls versus "Little Toughie," "Rebel," "The Boss," and "Wild One" for boys (Kane 2013: 1). This is only one more of many illustrations of how characteristics associated with 'monster' are almost synonymously associated with 'boy' in everyday language.

Although Cole's depiction of Lucretzia is unmistakably humorous, it is also problematic. What I find difficult about *Bad Habits!* is its underlying assumption that in order to be socially accepted, Lucretzia needs to shed off her monstrous (stereotypically male) "habits" and transform them into more becoming (stereotypically female) qualities. Just because Lucretzia's depiction might make me laugh that does not make it any less sexist – although possibly more easily accepted. In an introduction to a book on the interconnections between humor and gender, Stefan Horlacher cites several researchers who have come to similar conclusions. Humor definitely causes an audience to

> 'perceive a situation [...] [as] less discriminatory, and more acceptable' (Bill and Naus 659). But if sexism 'disguised by and delivered through humor' is potentially interpreted 'as being harmless and innocent' (646), and thus tends to escape criticism altogether, if '[p]erceiving and labelling an incident as humorous appears to diminish its sexist content' (660), this only increases the necessity for a critical analysis of the 'comic mode' (Lodge 170) with special attention to its ability to hide patriarchal, sexist, and even misogynist tendencies in literature, plays, films, and other media. (Horlacher 2009: 18)

In my view, it would be too easy to dismiss the picturebooks' sexist moral because of its obvious irony or exaggeration, or because Babette Cole is known as a humorist picturebook author with a strong interest in feminist themes. A brief look at the humor in the other three books in this group will put my evaluation into perspective. In both *Pat the Beastie* and *Monsters Eat Whiny Children* the protagonists are pairs of boy and girl. And in neither of these books are the individuals differentiated from each other. This circumstance makes sexist humor more or less impossible. Nevertheless, both books use humor in order to disguise or make acceptable a vision of parenting style that is based on threats and moralizing. In *Night of the Veggie Monster*, there is a single boy character who claims he will transform into a monster if he eats even just one pea. The threat is thus originating from the boy himself and indicative of at least some sense of autonomy. Ultimately, however, he does have to eat his greens while his parents watch him, disapproving of his showy behavior.

All four books work with intertextual allusions to Hoffmann's *Struwwelpeter*. Considering that the pedagogical message, taken at face value, of this nineteenth century children's classic is more than just controversial in today's pedagogical discourses, it can only be incorporated into children's fiction with a huge portion of humor and irony. (This is because the pedagogical and corrective measures employed appear outrageous and exaggerated while they might have been more acceptable or realistic in the nineteenth century.) In the original *Struwwelpeter*, the gist of every story is the reform or the lethal punishment of the initially misbehaved child. Out of ten stories, nine have child protagonists. Out of these nine, only one is a girl, the others are all boys. This circumstance alone might be considered as an indication of a prevailing belief that boys are more easily prone to socially disruptive or even criminal behavior and that they therefore need some kind of correction – but that they are also more easily accepted as 'naturally wild.'

In the contemporary picturebooks of my corpus, a persisting belief that children need correction and reform is played out most clearly in *Bad Habits!*. In contrast to the *Struwwelpeter* stories, where the children's 'misbehavior' invariably causes 'natural' consequences (Harriet, or Paulinchen in the original German, burns to death because she plays with matches, Bad Frederick gets bitten by the dog he has tortured, and so on), the picturebooks I examined here – except *Pat the Beastie* that is more similar to *Struwwelpeter* in this respect – could be argued to expose the power mechanisms inherent in the raising of children directly and more honestly. *Bad Habits!* does this most strikingly. Through the paradoxical exaggeration of the power mechanism between the parents, who only gain power over Lucretzia once they become monsters themselves, and Lucretzia, who needs her parents to be uncivilized in order to become civilized herself, *Bad Habits!* exposes what progressive educationalists, according to Marcus Reiß, usually conceal: education has the social function of replacing a 'wild body,' that constantly seeks immediate gratification and pleasure, with a 'habituated' and chronologically structured body (Reiß 2012: 204).

The humor that is so prominent in all of the four picturebooks I have introduced in this section to some extent facilitates the criticism. But Eco points out that humor nevertheless always also contains critical potential.

> In comedy we laugh at the character. In humor we smile because of the contradiction between the character and the frame the character cannot comply with. But we are no longer sure that it is the character who is at fault. Maybe the frame is wrong. (Eco 1984: 8)

Although humor sometimes has the effect of diminishing the criticizing power of the narrative, as I have discussed with the example of sexism in *Bad Habits!*, it can nevertheless serve as a productive tool for dismantling an ideology that marks a child as 'good' only when it is completely contained and subdued to her parents' monstrous tyranny. If the epitome of 'the good child' is presented as a girl in a pink tutu, who is subjecting her body to the excruciating postures of ballet and who has replaced her angry stare at adult authority by closing her eyes – and if I acknowledge the comic thrust of this representation, then one way of making this 'comedy' intelligible is to question the underlying sexist assumptions of this frame, a frame Lucretzia complies with all too diligently. At the same time, Lucretzia only illustrates one half of the frame. The other half is constituted by the parents' monstrous fun at having defeated the wild beast that Lucretzia once was. More than any other picturebook in my corpus or in this section, *Bad Habits!* focuses its attention on adult hypocrisy that often characterizes the power dynamics in parent-child relationships. It ends with an implicit question: is it not, perhaps, the parents who are the real monsters? Is it not the parents who are monstrous beyond moral reform and might that be the case because parenting in Western societies hinges on the image of the child as needful of correction, indoctrination and coercion?

The competent child: 'Where the Wild Things Are'

The majority of monster picturebooks that deal with questions of child-rearing do so much less explicitly and/or with less explicit criticism than the books of the previous section. In the following, I want to concentrate on Maurice Sendak's *Where the Wild Things Are* (1963) because I think that the ongoing academic debates around this picturebook illustrate particularly well an ideological divide that is based on opposed views on parenting, but that paradoxically proposes a similar image of 'the child' as competent and 'good.' In the first ideological camp, the boy only becomes competent through socialization, whereas in the latter, the boy's inherent competence is eradicated and replaced by obedience. On the one side of that divide, Max's progression from wild to tame is considered as a process of maturation and necessary 'civilization' where a boy learns how to handle his emotions; on the other side, this very process is evaluated in terms of "detachment parenting" (Zornado 2006: 171-195), where Max's taming is based on his assimilation of the belief that emotional needs must be denied and that obedience is a necessary survival tactics.

I take the attribute 'competent' from Jesper Juul's internationally successful parenting guide *Your Competent Child – Towards New Basic Values for the Family* (first published in Danish in 1995). One of Juul's most prominent claims is that all children are endowed with an acute sense for their emotional and physical needs and with an inborn ability to express these needs. Only if parents take these needs seriously and enter into a mutual dialogue with their children, Juul continues, only then can children learn to respect themselves and others. Due to traditional parenting values, however, parents often mute their children's competence by imposing 'external' rules (for example, social etiquette or fixed times for eating and sleeping) that are dissociated from the difficulties the child and/or the parent are actually experiences at a given time, such as a temper tantrum, excessive whining or any other expressions of emotions that disturb the smooth running of an adult-centred everyday life. Juul calls on parents to take their children more seriously, to respect their emotional and physical boundaries and to find a personal language that reflects the parents' own boundaries in an authentic way. He introduces the term of "equal dignity," rather than the more democratically inspired "equal rights," to describe that adults and children have an equal desire and an equal entitlement to protect and cultivate their sense of self, although they usually have different amounts of responsibility and knowledge of the world. Juul insists that children are competent in communicating their needs, but that their well-being depends on their parents' perception of this competence. The reason why Juul's ideas are productive as a pedagogical perspective on the books in this section is that they all pose a child protagonist's difficult, disturbing emotions as the starting point for the narrative.

Among the many critics of Maurice Sendak's *Where the Wild Things Are*, some attribute the story empowering potential for child readers while others criticize it for propagating a dysfunctional mother-child-relationship. Interestingly, those who read the end of this picturebook as a victory (e.g. Nikolajeva and Scott 2001: 197; Moebius 1986: 147) tend to put their critical focus more on the intricate image-text interrelation, while those who write about it in terms of dysfunctional parenting closely engage with the cultural underpinning of the narrative (e.g. Zornado 2006: 171-195; Keeling and Pollard 1999: 127-143). In the following, I want to consider both sides of the argument: (i) Max is confident and competent in solving his emotional dilemma on his own, returning more mature and victorious; and (ii) Max's homecoming must be read as a victory of adult power that the mother has forced on her son through her own detachment. I am starting my reflections with the first interpretation that Max is an archetype of the competent child and that *Where the Wild Things Are* illustrates a parenting style that provides children with the space they need in order to come to grips with their wild feelings.

This basic thrust is evident in all of the books in this chapter: the narrative instance that sometimes extends to the parental characters centers on the emotional and mental processes of the child characters. Conflicts between child and adult are thus not explained as the result of the child's misbehavior, as in the first group, but as the result of the child's feelings. In all books, difficult situations at home are explained as having literally monstrous emotions at their bottom. The emotions and mental states that the monsters represent are experienced by the characters – reflecting of course general cultural tendencies – as unpleasant or painful: anger, worry and envy. Using monsters in picturebooks in order to make these emotions more accessible makes fully visible adults' ambivalence towards monsters in the context of children's culture. In these books, monsters are simultaneously used with the assumption that children 'naturally' bond with monsters and with the more traditional representation of monsters as disturbing and threatening, here in the form of emotions that threaten the social fabric.

Structurally, the seven books in this group tend to combine the appearance of the monster/s with a home-away-home pattern. This pattern is most fully carried out in *Where the Wild Things Are*. In fact, this is the only book in which the character actually travels to a place seemingly far away from home. In all other books, the child characters are firmly situated at home. But I interpret the fact that the monster/s only appear in the middle, sometimes through transformation (*When Mum Turned into a Monster*) or through devouring the child (*G.E.M.*, *Not Now Bernard*), and are often only perceived by the child character as an adaptation of this very pattern. In the fantasy genre within children's literature, the 'away'-element is always imbued with magic. The picturebooks here – as well as those about the fear of monsters – seem to allude to this aspect of fantasy of the 'away'-phase by installing a monster that is often only visible to the child character or a monster that returns to its normal, non-threatening state at the end of the story. But unlike in stories about the fear of monsters that I discussed earlier, the monsters in the books here usually disappear at the end. Another characteristic for the books in this section is that the parental figures are involved to various degrees in the problem-solving of their child's difficult situation. In this respect, the books I discuss here contrast most strikingly with the stories about the fear of monsters where the child protagonists are always left to their own devices.

Generally in picturebook criticism, the wild things are read as Max's aggression, his anger and his frustration. By visualizing anger in the shape of monsters, Sendak emphasizes the danger of disrupting the social order that anger always implies. Anger is indeed the emotion that is most often presented in this group. This comparatively strong presence of anger can be seen as reflecting a common concern among parents that is oriented towards understanding and dealing with their young child's anger that finds its most disturbing expression in temper tantrums. Indeed, one topic that no parenting guide omits is temper tantrums, with a growing number of guide books actually focusing on this topic alone (e.g. Dobson 2014; Sears and Sears 1995 – and there are many more).

Usually, anger in the context of parent-child relationships is conceptualized as a struggle for power from both sides, as the recurring words "discipline," or "managing" in the titles of the temper tantrum advice literature indicate. Anger as one of the cornerstones of philosophy and classical literature from Homer and Aristotle to our present (Ngai 2005: 6; Lehmann 2012), is also tightly intertwined with notions of (in-)justice. Among psychologists, too, it is "quite a broad agreement that typical triggers of anger include frustration; threats to autonomy, authority, or reputation; disrespect and insult; norm or rule violation; and a sense of injustice" (Potegal and Stemmler 2010: 3). With their historically established status as signifiers for questioning norms and threatening power hierarchies, monsters provide perfect visualizations for addressing issues of dominance between parents and children in the home. However, such an approach to teaching children about their anger also implies an adult assumption that children have a 'natural' inclination to liking monsters so that the pedagogical mission, which rests on the idea that the male child understands and befriends his 'monster,' can succeed in the first place. Thus, while referring to the monsters' dangerous qualities that they possess in fictional narratives for grown-ups, picturebook makers simultaneously bet on the likeability of monsters by predominantly male child consumers, thus making the picturebook monster a creature whose ambiguity is much more complex than in grown-up culture.

In literary and cultural criticism, anger is viewed as an "affective support of oppositional consciousness with the capacity to become a legitimate weapon in social reform" (Ngai 2005: 128). While the angry monsters in the picturebooks are all born out of this very feeling of injustice, none of them do so much as hint at

Fig. 29   *Where the Wild Things Are* (Sendak 1963)

the possibility of "social reform" within the family. The power struggle is displaced from the confrontation between boy and adult to the confrontation between child and monster. Considering the identification of the child character with his monster/s, the power struggle is ultimately one in which the 'good' boy fights against and gains control over his 'bad' inner self.

In a perfect adaptation of Foucault's analysis in *Discipline and Punish*, Max internalizes his mother's appellation of him as a "WILD THING!": his immediate identification with this ascription is expressed in his part of this crisp verbal exchange: "I'LL EAT YOU UP!" (Sendak 1963: np). In only seven words, the complexity of this dramatic exposition is unfolded. Max may well have upset his mother with his "mischief of one kind and another" (ibid), for example stomping down the stairs and chasing the dog with a fork, but ultimately it is the mother who *makes* Max a wild thing by calling him this name. As other critics have pointed out, right from the beginning, Max wears a wolf suit that an adult person, perhaps his mother, must have bought or made for him (Keeling and Pollard 1999: 130). Thus, the attribution of Max as a monster actually already starts *before* the beginning of the story. Whether he wants it or not, Max is already a wild thing in his home and so, as the progress towards the climax suggests, the only way for him to retain some sense of authority is to go to a place where he is the one who makes the rules: his imagination. This 'time out' is clearly demarcated from the 'real' world of home whose social rules are never seriously challenged. The site of the power struggle is carried out within the child character himself who is both a wild thing and "the wildest thing of all [wild things]" (ibid). While the mother's status as human being is nowhere questioned, Max incorporates his 'other' nature literally as a second skin in the form of his wolf costume (fig. 29).

Except for one title (*When Mum Turned into a Monster*), apparently uncontrollable emotions, most prominently anger, are presented as a particular property of children or at least as an experience that children are more likely to have than their parents. Indeed, as Stearns and Stearns observe in their history of anger in the U.S. in the last three hundred years, the public and respected display of anger (by men) in the seventeenth century has transformed into a "complicated ambivalence [of Americans] that has focused on the need for control" (Stearns and Stearns 1986: 3). In the contemporary Western world, adults – particularly parents, and, even more specifically, mothers – are expected to control their anger. On the other hand, the term 'temper tantrum' has muted into a concept that, today, is only connected with child behavior.[17] Stearns and Stearns' suggestion that "modern anger standards [...] involve increasing separation between child and adult emotional

---

[17] Stearns and Stearns establish an "emotionology" of anger by studying advice literature (primarily marriage manuals and popular magazines). Thus, they trace the history of the word 'tantrum': "The word was initially used, always in the plural, to criticize adult outbursts and then in the nineteenth century evolved toward its present usage, marking a troubling phenomenon of childhood, one that had not needed a name before, and by extension an unacceptably childish display of emotion in later life." (Stearns and Stearns 1986: 25)

worlds" can be transported one to one to *Where the Wild Things Are* and *Anh's Anger*. Both Max and Anh are grounded: their custodians order them to have a 'time out' during which they are expected to 'cool off.' Max responds to this procedure with an elaborate fantasy journey and Anh follows his grandfather's instructions of "sit[ting] with [his] anger," using Buddhist meditation techniques (Silver and Krömer 2009: np). Neither Max's mother nor Anh's grandfather are visibly or explicitly affected by the boys' anger. Max's mother is only represented through this one incident of direct speech ("WILD THING!") and through her pedagogical interventions of first depriving her son of his dinner and then granting it to him in the end. Anh's grandfather recalls having met his anger as a boy himself, suggesting that he is now always serene and calm.

The focus of these books lies on the confrontation between the child character and his monstrous emotions. These emotions are visualized as external creatures that despite their externalization are tightly bound with the child but not with their adult guardians, thus contributing to the "separation between child and adult emotional worlds" that Stearns and Stearns have observed primarily in marriage manuals and popular magazines, such as *The Ladies Home Journal*. My own observations somewhat reverberate with Stearns and Stearns' analysis: the picturebooks I discuss here but also the parenting advice literature I have browsed almost exclusively focus on the child's problematic emotions, be it anger or envy or worries, to the extent that the parents or parental protagonists appear to be entirely unaffected by emotional disturbances. In contrast, psychological or anthropological studies on anger, to name just one example, show that children are among the prime reasons for mothers and fathers to feel angry (Reiser 1999: 68).

Anger as the most frequently represented emotion in the picturebooks in this section not only poses questions about the power distribution between child and adult but also addresses gender stereotypes about emotions. Only two characters, Max and Anh, experience anger explicitly. But the other boys' emotions are also deeply tangled up with aggression and violence. Thus, Garp's envy matches Max and Anh's anger insofar as his G.E.M. (Green Eyed Monster) becomes the more aggressive the more envious Garp becomes, eventually "gobbling him up" (Clarke and Parsons 2007:

np). Bernard's frustration about being neglected by his parents also finds expression in the form of a violent and destructive monster (*Not Now Bernard* 1984). In comparison, Jenny's worry-monsters may grow bigger but they are firmly shut in the big bag she drags around with her, very literally not daring to let them out. Although the number of these books is far from representative, I think that the manner in which these child characters express their feelings clearly corresponds with popular conceptions about gender and emotions, and gender and anger in particular, as will become clear in the following.

According to these popular conceptions, males generally display a greater emotional control or restraint – with the one exception of anger. Thus, a man who openly gives vent to his anger by acting aggressively is more likely to be perceived as performing his gender according to role expectations than a man who openly cries. If I used a woman in this example, her gender performance would be perceived as being at odds with her role expectations. The traditional stereotypes of the overly emotional female versus the rational male are, according to many researchers, culturally evident and endorsed and already perceived and perpetuated by American pre-schoolers (Locke 2011: 187). "[S]tereotypic representations of the emotional female/unemotional male are so prominent in North American culture that these stereotypes reinforce the notion that the starting point for any gender-based analysis of emotion should be gender *differences* in emotion.'" (Shields and Cowley 1996, 219; their emphasis, qt. in Locke 2011: 188) Obviously, a biased approach such as this makes the deconstruction of this stereotype very difficult. But even *if* gender difference is taken as the premise for studying anger, many studies do disavow the existence of gender-stereotyped anger:

> [...] the assignment of anger to men may suggest that anger is an innate and automatic reaction toward a specific event that is shaped foremost by biological and hormonal factors. Many studies have shown that this is an incorrect representation of anger instances. [...] there is no male or female anger. This does not mean that gender is irrelevant, but it means that there is no fixed pattern that accurately describes dispositional differences in anger for males or for females. (Fischer and Evers 2010: 349 f.)

Studies that do report gender differences only do so with respect to the *expression* of anger, demonstrating that the "relationship between emotions and sex [sic] is not a psychological one, but rather a societal and cultural construct, with factors like class and ethnicity intersecting with gender" (Locke 2011: 190; cf. Reiser 1999: 140). Nevertheless, the stereotype that males are prone to acting out on their anger using violence and that females are more likely to repress anger by transforming it into other emotions such as guilt or shame remains a very lively one, not least due to its perpetuation in the picturebooks examined here. Of all the child protagonists, Max is given the most space to engage with his anger in the form of the wild things: on three consecutive wordless doublespreads, Max celebrates "the wild rumpus" with his monsters, swinging from the trees and howling at the moon. But even when he is still at home, he expresses his frustration in a very physical manner, hammering a nail into the wall and romping through the house. In contrast, Jenny, in *The Huge Bag of Worries*, fails to relieve herself because she does not dare tell anyone about her worries and when she does her concerns are brushed aside. Eventually, she sits on a wall and cries. And only then, once she displays this 'typically' feminine emotional expression, does an elderly lady offer her help by releasing the monsters from the formerly sealed up bag.

Fig. 30   *Where the Wild Things Are* (Sendak 1963)

I want to spend a little more time examining the relationship Max entertains with the wild things. Although the wild things at first appear to come out of nowhere, living in a place disconnected from the 'real' world, their behavior resembles that of Max when they "[roar] their terrible roars and [gnash] their terrible teeth and [roll] their terrible eyes and [show] their terrible claws" (Sendak 1963: np). Their body postures are a striking reflection of Max stomping down the stairs with raised wolf claws at the beginning. Their pose is threatening, but Max' facial and bodily expression betrays no sign of fear. Rather, he famously "[tames] them with the magic trick of staring into all their yellow eyes without blinking once" (ibid). This demonstration of power can also be seen as a direct reproduction of the mother's power over Max (fig. 30).

Accordingly, a popular psychological interpretation is that Max relives his dispute but with inverted roles (Swanton 1971: 38; Nodelman 1988: 127 and 2008:121; McGillis 1996: 80–82). This time he is the boss and the others have to dance to his tune. The temporary inversion of power distribution is embedded into the 'time out' period. This section of the story is introduced by a po-etic and paradox linking of chronological and spatial markers: "[…] and he sailed off through night and day [page turn] and in and out of weeks and almost over a year to where the wild things are." (Sendak 1963: np) The paradoxical impression arises from the simultaneous use of spatial prepositions (through, in, out) with

286

nouns referring to time spans (night, day, weeks, year). At the same time as it is impossible to sail through time as if time was a spatial entity (like an ocean), the amount of time (one year) that the narrator claims has lapsed between Max's departure and his arrival is equally unlikely. With this use of language, Sendak effectively marks the border between the rational world and the fantastic, somewhat dreamlike place "where the wild things are." And it is only within this fantastic setting that Max can control the wild things and order them around, his power symbolized with a crown on his head and a scepter in his hand, both of which he leaves behind before turning back home. Now, I want to return to my initial question: is the parenting attitude that shapes Max's adventures with the wild things helping him to become 'competent,' or does it undermine his competence because it consists of repression and control?

The important role of Max's mother is easily overlooked in *Where the Wild Things Are* as she is nowhere visually represented. Indeed, the narrative instance grants all the visual space to Max and the wild things which renders Max's emotional situation the most central in the book. It is perhaps for this reason that *Where the Wild Things Are* is often celebrated as a milestone for taking children and their inner worlds seriously. This appreciation often corresponds with the evaluation of the stories' ending as an empowerment for Max: having asserted his dominance over the wild things, he comes back into his room with a contented smile in his face. Because almost all of the narrative space is given to Max, the mother's importance may seem negligible. But if her words and her disciplinary interventions are taken into account, Max's journey and his adventures appear as a fantasy that is intricately interwoven with the adult world and yet sharply divided from it with regards to who gets to make the rules of that interaction. Those critics who read *Where the Wild Things Are* as a representation of a failed mother-child relationship do this on the ground of two different arguments.

The first argument is directed against the obvious lack of democracy that allows the mother to exert ultimate control over her son. Thus Kara Keeling and Scott Pollard claim that "[...] [*Where the Wild Things Are*] gives [parents] the illusion of controlling all aspects of their children's physical and imaginative lives. [It is] the perfect product of [a] rosy world [...] where there is tolerance but limited democracy" (Keeling and Pollard 1999: 130). Keeling and Pollard decisively oppose some earlier critics' interpretation of this story as scaring adults because it may undermine their authority:

> [*Where the Wild Things Are*] does not threaten [adults'] authority over their children. Moreover, Max's fantasy resolves into soporific obedience. What better way to assure the adult world that the child's emotional life is not a threat? [...] It is [the mother's] words and the fabric she has sewn [i.e. the wolf suit] that are absorbed into Max's imagination to become the fantastic embodiment of his frustration, anger, and energy. (Keeling and Pollard 1999: 130)

A different perspective, but one that leads to a similar argument, is represented via concepts of attachment parenting. Attachment theory is one of the major research fields on parenting representations (Mayseless 2006: 3). Its impact goes beyond parenting advice literature and the academic discipline of psychology. For example, Mary Galbraith has analyzed a number of picturebook classics, including *Where the Wild Things Are*, from the perspective of attachment parenting and comes to the conclusion that "the bodily relationship between parent and child characters depicted [...] is extremely deprived" (Galbraith 1998: 172). Joseph Zornado elaborates this claim to illustrate his thesis that Max, by imitating his mother and relating to the wild things "like a kind of colonialist lion tamer, [...] tells the story of Western culture in a nutshell" (Zornado 2006: 184):

> In Max's hierarchical world, negotiation does not take place, for negotiation requires two parties who recognize each other's needs as legitimate. Words are not used to make sense of the situation, for it is implied and inferred that Max is beyond words. He is a savage beast. (ibid)

According to Zornado, Western culture consists of the suppression of exuberance and any wild emotions. He describes it with reference to the established term of 'attachment parenting' as "detachment culture" that he considers synonymous with consumer culture. Because we learn to repress, control and deny our needs from an early age, Zornado argues, "we do not know what we feel or what we need, and so we *obey*" (ibid). Although Zornado's con-

Fig. 31   *Where the Wild Things Are* (Sendak 1963)

clusion seems extreme, especially considering those critics who read Max's journey as empowering, it is true that Max's mother isolates him in his room and deprives him of his food. It is the mother who later decides that Max can eat dinner after all, albeit alone in his room. Max has indeed no voice in deciding about the proceedings in his home. It is also true that Max and his mother are nowhere seen together, that their verbal exchange is short and aggressive on both sides, and that the mother decides that Max should eat his dinner alone. These interventions can be evaluated from different pedagogical angles, but I think it is important to note that the narrative instance itself does not judge or evaluate the mother's behavior. Rather the mother's actions are represented matter-of-factly. They could be seen as representative of a parental strategy that was very common in the 1960s, before the idea of democratic family politics or attachment theoretical reflections entered mainstream parenting guides. Zornado even goes a step further by arguing that nothing much has changed in terms of Western family politics – the fact that *Where the Wild Things Are* continues to be a bestselling picturebook might be used to support Zornado's claim. This would also somehow imply that purchasers of this book are more or less oblivious to the shattering criticism of parenting that this picturebook presents according to Zornado. If parents were aware of this criticism, wouldn't this mean that they somehow wanted their children to grow up with picturebooks that represent "detachment parenting" as bluntly and unremarkably as *Where the Wild Things Are*? Of course, I am oversimplifying because the social criticism in this picturebook is matched with Sendak's decided emphasis on the child character's imagination and the power of that imagination. So the bestselling quality of this picturebook might also result from its detailed portrayal of a boy's imagination, an imagination that ultimately equips him with the psychological skills to return from his battle with a contented smile in his face. As he brushes off the hood of his wolf costume he has become a little more human, a little less beast (fig. 31).

At the end, Max says goodbye to the wild things and decides to return home against their wish for him to stay: "Oh please don't go! We'll eat you up, we love you so!" The contradictory feelings Max has for his mother (frustration and aggression for being told what to do and what to be and at the same time love and affection) are here reflected in the wild things, creating a kind of *mise en abyme* that enforces the interrelatedness of Max and his mother and their emotional worlds. Although the displacement of Max's mother through the wild things is less obvious than the role reversal of Lucretzia and her parents, both picturebook narratives offer a critique of parental power.

But in contrast to the parental monsters in *Bad Habits!*, the wild things do not overpower Max. Rather, he overpowers and learns to control *them*. The sense of danger and threat that they initially emanate is outweighed by their big smiling faces, their round shape and their submissiveness to Max. Anh's anger monster is very similar in this respect: scary and threatening at first, this monster eventually dances with Anh, they "breathe together," (Silver and Krömer 2009: np) and ultimately the anger monster vanishes after nicely declining Anh's invitation to join him and his grandfather for dinner with ice-cream. In both books, the monsters are, at bottom, benevolent and supportive. Their therapeutic role consists in suggesting to the boy protagonist that he can manage them and that through managing them, the boy gains a sense of superiority and power that promises him recognition in the social world, most often through food. Max gets his dinner in the end. So does Anh – and ice cream on top. The boy protagonist Garp in the science-fiction setting in *G.E.M.* (Clarke and Parsons 2007) may not be immediately rewarded with food for getting his Green Eyed Monster under control, but his birthday party a week later with "Plutonian Pizza" and "sparkling space pod birthday cake" (ibid: np) could easily be seen as a delayed acknowledgment of his improved emotional management skills.

There are two picturebooks with female main protagonists who also struggle with their difficult emotions. Interestingly, neither of the two books puts any emphasis on control and reward, although they have a similar educational/therapeutic subtext as *Anh's Anger*, its sequel *Steps and Stones* (Silver and Krömer 2011), and *G.E.M.* Thus, in *The Huge Bag of Worries* (Ironside and Rodgers 1996), the solution to Jenny's worry-monsters arrives as an elderly lady who tells Jenny what to do (open the bag and let go of the monsters/worries). On the last page, the little monsters have all disappeared and Jenny is bouncing with joy. So here, the focus lies on confiding in an adult and letting go of the troubling emotions rather than controlling them.

When Mum Turned Into A Monster (Harrison 1996) resembles the other picturebooks in this section insofar as it is motivated to explain how negative feelings develop and transform people and to teach children what to do in such supposedly invidious situations. But here it is the mother who gets so angry at her children for ignoring her pleas to help her clean the house and for causing even more disorder and chaos that her body mutates into a green, fire-breathing monster. She only slowly recovers her human shape once her children start behaving nicely: offering her tea, vacuuming the floor, brushing their hair, and so on. What I find particularly revealing in this picturebook is that the mother's anger is very clearly and in much detail represented as the result of her children's 'misbehavior', while anger in *Where the Wild Things Are* or in *Anh's Anger*, or envy in *G.E.M.*, is suggested to be more innate, in the sense that nobody can be blamed for causing the 'ugly feelings.' If external reasons are given, such as the grandpa's call to dinner and the required interruption of playing in *Anh's Anger*, or the friend's superior material wealth in *G.E.M.*, these reasons are suggested to be irrational and unimportant. In *Where the Wild Things Are*, Max "makes mischief" for no reason at all, and readers and critics are led to believe that he is wild because he is a boy. What I find revealing, then, is that a mother's anger can only be appeased through her 'good' children's guilty collaboration and that a (male) child must deal with his anger on his own, because – this is what the picturebooks suggest – it is his responsibility and duty to be calm and composed and if he does not manage to be that he must be excluded from the family. In this respect, *When Mum Turned Into A Monster* actually works on the same premise: it is always the children who are responsible for causing and for managing troubling emotions – be it their own or their mother's.

Although I cannot claim that the representation of aggression and anger in children is gender-coded as masculine only on the basis of this small sample of picturebooks, the protagonists' *relationships* to the monsters that represent these feelings are very clearly gendered. They contribute in yet another way to the image of boys as 'naturally' drawn toward monsters; of boys having to learn to contain and control these monsters and simultaneously accept them as a part of themselves. In contrast, the two female protagonists that I have considered both relate to their monstrous feelings in purely antagonistic ways: the monsters must be expelled, disposed of, and any visible traces of them must be wiped out before normal social life can continue. In both cases, the management of the monsters can be considered as a competence and the child protagonists who learn these skills as competent. But boy protagonists learn skills and attitudes that are clearly different from those that the girl protagonist learns.

The 'lesson' for boys of mastering their ugly emotions while maintaining friendly ties with them is surprisingly consistent in all the picturebook stories I have presented here. I think this is surprising because these texts can be used to illustrate very different parenting styles. For example, Joseph Zornado and others' interpretation of *Where the Wild Things Are* as a subtly oppressive story about detachment parenting works because the disembodied representation of Max's mother or of Max's bleak room are important elements of the narrative that can convincingly be used to support this argument. Reading this book in this way promises an additional layer of satisfaction that can be derived from these critics' implicit claim to have revealed the underlying and horrible reason for Western culture's ailments: a family politics that ruthlessly disciplines and punishes children's vital expressions so that these children grow up to be cold and obedient citizens who have lost touch with their inner worlds. This argument is compelling, partly because the text and images of the book can be used to support it and partly because well-argued diagnoses about a culture's doom are always fascinating. But at the same time and quite in opposition to this argument, Max *is* bold enough to oppose his mother. Not only that: he dreams up a world complete with wild creatures that help him become even stronger and emotionally more settled. Even if detachment parenting was the hallmark of contemporary Western society – an opinion that the other books that I have discussed hardly support as they put great emphasis on adults' involvement in their children's emotional dilemmas – even if this was the horrible environment that Max has to grow up in, at least he learns how to do this and thrive. Journalist and TV host Bill Moyers relates in an interview with Maurice Sendak that literary critic and scholar Joseph Campbell once told him that *Where the Wild Things Are*, for him, constitutes one of the great moments in literature: "[…] it's only when a man tames his own demons that he becomes the king of himself if not of the world" (Sendak: interview with Moyers). Campbell's appraisal is, to me, not only the bottom line of *Where the Wild Things Are*, but also of the other picturebooks with male child protagonists: the focus lies on boys' "own demons" and on their task to tame and control them. It is essentially a solitary task and one that eventually transforms a boy into a man. Female children are by and large – as usual – left out of the picture entirely.

The child as king: 'The Boy Who Ate Around'

One reason why *Where the Wild Things Are* is so often mentioned for its empowering effects on child readers is that Max, during his fantasy journey, revels in absolute power over his subjects, his wild emotions. He becomes the king, complete with crown and scepter. Prior to his coming into power, these emotions had their grip on him by making him mischievous in the first place. The power reversal that is enforced even further when one takes into account that the wild things are a displacement of the mother[18] has sometimes been described in terms of carnival. For example, John Stephens insists that *Where the Wild Things Are* is carnivalesque for three reasons: firstly, Max's behavior is oppositional to normal socializing expectations; secondly, the wild things in the illustrations are grotesque; and thirdly, the story is built on the motif of "time out" (Stephens 1992: 135). If I apply these aspects to the rest of my corpus then picturebooks with monsters all have at least some carnivalesque quality. However, I want to employ this concept in a much stricter sense here in order to highlight a vision of the – again male – child as the supreme authority in the family that is present in two picturebooks: *The Boy Who Ate Around* (Drescher 1993) and *Monsters – An Owner's Guide* (Emmett and Oliver 2010).

In Drescher's book, a boy who does not want to eat his dinner quickly – and out of politeness as the narrator underlines – decides to eat around it, starting with his parents. In order to devour his parents and then the rest of the world, the boy Mo transforms into various monsters. Right from the beginning, Mo takes on the au-

---

[18] In an interview, Sendak explains that the inspiration for the wild things did indeed come from his adult relatives: "I remember our relatives used to come from the old country, those few who got in before the gate closed, all on my mother's side. [...] And these people didn't speak English. And were unkempt. Their teeth were horrifying. [...] [their] hair, unraveling out of their noses. And they'd pick you up and hug you and kiss you, 'Aggghh. Oh, we could eat you up.' And we knew they would eat anything, anything. And so, they're the wild things." (Sendak: interview by Moyers)

thority to rule over the dinner situation. In *Monsters – An Owner's Guide,* the constellation of protagonists and their place in the power hierarchy is relatively complex: two children, visually coded as boy and girl but verbally ungendered, are at home without any adults when a giant monster robot arrives via delivery. In the following, the children's fruitless attempts at keeping the monster under control can be read as a power reversal in two ways. On the one hand, the child figures here act in the role of the parents, and on the other hand, the monster robot, who is the 'real' child in this story, clearly dispossesses his child-parents of their authority by thwarting their parenting techniques and successfully destroying the entire house.

The protagonist whose position most resembles that of an emperor is Mo in *The Boy Who Ate Around.* He elevates himself to the heights of a king by turning into a monster and devouring his immediate superiors, his parents. Transforming into ever bigger monsters, Mo proceeds to gulp up his school, math teacher, the City Hall, the White House, complete with the President, the First Lady, the First Dog (and First Frog), North America, South America, and all the other continents and oceans of the world. These incorporations of power symbols are put in the framework of a gigantic feast, with astonishing resemblances to Mikhail Bakhtin's concept of carnival. During carnival, the power hierarchies are turned upside down and the ruling forces of society are debased and ridiculed by those who have no power during the rest of the year. The stock character of the fool very often symbolizes this group of people, assuming manners and gestures of the king with the aim of inciting laughter in the crowd. Based on this imagery, I will analyze *The Boy Who Ate Around* in the context of Bakhtin's theory of carnival and the grotesque, where laughter is seen as an instrument of power.

The image of the child as king is an old one. It can be traced back to sources of the Tanakh and the Old Testament. In Ecclesiastes 10:16 the population is told by Koheleth to beware of what is interpreted by Biblical scholars (e.g. Barnes) as childish manners, lack of control over impulses and an inclination to pleasure as characteristics in a king: "Woe to thee, O land, whose king is a child" (King James Bible). Much closer to contemporary views of this image, Maria Montessori, among other progressive pedagogues, talks of 'the child' as majestic in an admiring sense, suggesting that "the child [holds] within himself [sic] a secret of life, able to lift the veil from the mysteries of the human soul; that he [sic] represent[s] an unknown quantity, the discovery of which might enable the adult to solve *his* individual and social problems" (Montessori 1983 [1936]: 3). In Montessori's writings the image of the child as king is wrapped into her plea to adults to finally recognize the royal powers slumbering in every child. (Her consistent use of masculine pronouns for 'the child' may well be due to writing conventions at the time, but it also highlights that the generic 'child' was more or less inherently male.) Montessori's postulation comes across as serious and solemn while Drescher's picturebook story builds on humor and laughter. Despite these and other differences, both Drescher and Montessori create a world – one fictitious and the other real – where children are granted the freedom to make decisions that are usually not theirs to make – but their parents' or other carers'.

Unlike any of the other books in this chapter, the conventional order in *The Boy Who Ate Around* and in *Monsters – An Owner's Guide* is *not* reestablished at the end. Instead, readers are denied the usual satisfaction that accompanies, for example, the dissolution of Max's carnivalesque fantasy in *Where the Wild Things Are*. Readers *cannot* rest assured that it was all just a dream. The very fact that the two books in this group do not impose clear narrative limits to or dissolutions of the exaltations and transformations of their main characters elicits the question whether carnival may actually be subversive, whether it may in fact yield a potential for sustainable change in the power relations between children and adults. Such a conclusion would indeed contradict most scholars' stance toward the revolutionary capacities of carnival. On the following pages, I will trace the unfolding of the carnivalesque scenery in *The Boy Who Ate Around*, placing particular emphasis on the mechanisms of laughter and the ensuing implications for the parenting model that is represented in this picturebook.

The Boy Who Ate Around starts with a classic situation: a boy refuses to eat his dinner. Food in children's literature, including picturebooks, is a central site for power negotiations (Alston 2008: 105 ff.; McGee 2001: 15; Hunt 1996: 7). That food is a major disciplinary battle field is evident even in the small number of picturebooks that I have so far discussed in this chapter. Both *Bad Habits!* and *Where the Wild Things Are* use food and its correct handling as markers for civilization and as a criterion that paves a child's social integration into the family. In *Night of the Veggie Monster*, briefly referred to in the first section, the struggle between parents who want their child to eat vegetables and the son who feels violated by their insistence is the prosaic theme of the book, and simultaneously a reflection of many parents' and many children's real experience. In this very realistic setting, the parents decide what is eaten when, where, how and in what quantities. The parents are, very literally, the decision-makers and, on a more metaphorical level, the monarchs or, as sociologists Allison James, Chris Jenks and Alan Prout put it: "the powerful ogre of the state" (James, Jenks, Prout 1998: 11). They formulate a provocative hypothesis about the apparently inevitable consequences that a collapse of parental control would entail:

> The power of the monarch, and thus by analogy the power of the parents, is absolute and stands over and above the populace of children, who have no rights or power. The source of this parental power is knowledge, which children can only attain by eventually becoming parents themselves. The powerful ogre of the state or the parent is omnipotent and the individual is 'saved' from the worst excesses of himself or herself by contracting into the society or the family. Without parental constraint, the life of the child is anarchic. (ibid)

Bad Habits! is a fantastic illustration of this hypothesis: Lucretzia is literally 'without a ruler' (from the Greek *an* + *arkhos*) and the parents in this book are visually represented as "ogres." But just as Max and the nameless boy in *Night of the Veggie Monster*, Lucretzia is eventually tamed: she is contracted into the social laws of her family. What happens if the child character becomes the king and, more importantly, *stays* king? What if the (male) child gets to decide what food goes into his mouth? Even more: decides what counts as food in the first place, how it tastes and what role it plays in marking the borders of self and other? Henrik Drescher creates a postmodern utopia in which the usual rules about table manners and healthy food have been overridden. The story does not only start with this classic situation of a boy refusing his dinner but with a swiftly following disempowerment of the parents by devouring them. Right at the beginning, Drescher turns the usual and unequal power distribution in the family on its head. But contrary to the anarchy suggested by James, Jenks and Prout, in *The Boy Who Ate Around* the boy becomes his own and, indeed, the world's ruler. The verbal narrative starts with the familiar dinner scene I have described above:

> There once was a boy named Mo who had to eat his dinner even though he didn't like it one little bit. He took a bite of the lizard guts and bullfrog heads (actually string beans and cheese soufflé) and felt like throwing it all up, right there on the dinner table, but he was polite and didn't. Instead, he decided to eat around it. (Drescher 1994: np)

The familiarity of this scene arises from the fairy tale beginning ("There once was..."), which fosters in the reader expectations of something well-known and foreseeable, but it also arises from the conventional constellation of participating persons and objects: a child is forced to eat a kind of food that he or she finds nauseating. Here, at this point, the scene's familiarity is already broken because the usual power-holders on this scene, the parents, are well-hidden behind the verbal construction "who had to eat his dinner." Why does Mo have to eat his dinner? The most probable explanation would suggest that someone with more power must have told him to. The parents are not only hidden by the words but they are also visually absent from the first two pages of the book: the boy sits at the table alone, only joined by the dog (pink with violet patches). Not even the number of chairs would hint at the other family members. There is only one chair and it is occupied by Mo. That the parents are absent can only be deduced from the circumstance that the boy *must* eat his dinner. Hence there must be some authority behind this order. Although this order is so inconspicuous the entire plot hinges on it. Without this culinary coercion there would be no story. In other words, the story is triggered by a power conflict between a boy and his adults. But why is this conflict made invisible? Rather than being carried out between the actual adversaries, the source of conflict is transferred to the dinner plate. I will return to this question that is so central to understanding the image of parenting that is woven into this story. This image seems to depend on the concealment of the parents whose authority is further concealed through comical images.

Mo's balloon-shaped head (almost the size of the rest of his body), bent over the gruesome dish, emphatically illustrates his disgust. Particularly in light of the comic frame of the book as a whole, I think it is noteworthy that Mo's nose, which is signal red with subtle violet stripes, and his clothes (his pants are an exact color reflection of the dog's fur; Mo's shirt is yellow with orange patches) give him a clownish air that is further underlined by his apple-red cheeks, spikey hair, jug ears (also striped) and a pointy tongue sticking out of his mouth (perhaps already alluding to his monstrous transformations to come). The coloring of Mo's face as well as his gaudy clothes position him in the vicinity of the 'auguste' clown who traditionally has a lower status than, for example, the 'whiteface,' and who bears similarities with the jester and the fool – important stock characters in the carnival tradition.

> A prototypical clowning scene involves the clown's antagonist, a serious figure, going after him with a hammer or some other weapon. The clown eludes the antagonist, executing versatile evasive maneuvers despite his seeming awkwardness, and when he is finally caught and hit over the head and thrown to the ground, he always jumps up again, unhurt and invincible. Like the fool, the clown is a magician. And, like the world of folly, the world of the circus creates an oasis of enchantment within the reality of modern rationality. Most modern adults, at least those with a measure of "higher" education, are not easily amused by the antics of the circus clown. Children invariably are. (Berger 1997: 77)

Berger goes on to speculate that children's fascination with clowns is based on their knowledge of something that adults have forgotten (ibid), thus reflecting Montessori's claims about the mystical power of children. In any case, the boy Mo corresponds in many respects to the image of the clown, not only with regard to his looks: by transforming into a monster he evades the seriousness of his parents – but also the seriousness of the narrative voice that declares that the "lizard guts and bullfrog heads" on Mo's dinner plate are "actually string beans and cheese soufflé" (Drescher 1993: np). While the words disclaim the absurd notion of saurian intestines and amphibian body parts as human food, the image

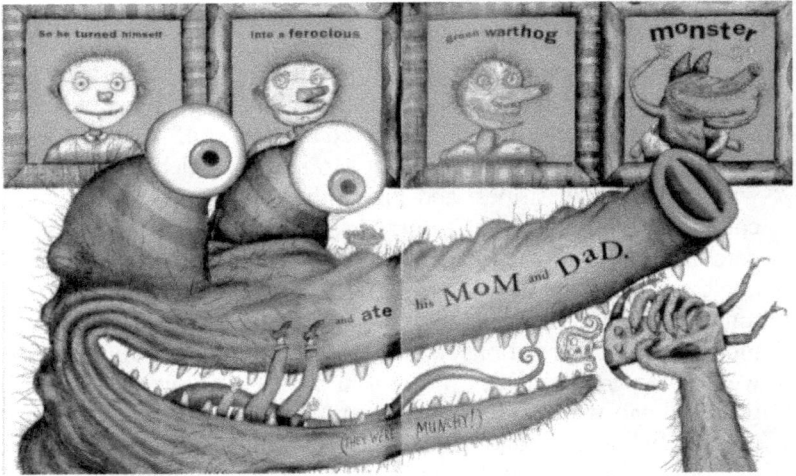

Fig. 32 *The Boy Who Ate Around* (Drescher 1993)

confirms this notion as true. The readers are left with an unsolvable puzzle that further increases the comic situation.

Right on the first opening, one of the pervading motifs of the story – and also a major motif of carnival – is put forward: an inversion of inside and outside through an opening-up of the confines of the body. Mo is supposed to insert intestines (innards) into his mouth and reacts – quite understandably – with the desire "to throw it all up." The typeset of the text is a graphical visualization of the vomit spurting out of Mo's mouth. Instead of interiorizing innards, Mo expels what has been forced upon him. This is the beginning of a massive eating binge during which Mo seems to shed off the disciplinary regimes that, according to Foucault in *Discipline and Punish*, are so deeply ingrained in every individual that it is difficult to imagine a world without these assimilated mechanisms of self-regulation (cf. Mills 2003: 44). Drescher's picturebook story can be read as a fantasy of a (brief interval of) childhood that does away with the necessity of subjection to the parents' power regime.

This fantasy is essentially carnivalesque. Thus, Mo turns into a "ferocious green warthog monster" and eats up his surroundings, starting with his parents (fig. 32). Mo interiorizes the exterior. While the devouring of parents and friends in a different setting would be disturbing – or even just the unruly farting, spitting and vomiting of Lucretzia – here the food rampage has a gay, triumphal and joyful character because it is embedded into a series of parodied actions: having to eat lizard guts and bullfrog heads – a parody of a 'sophisticated' dish (soufflé and string beans) – but eating the parents instead – a parody of the usual power relations. Here, on this second opening, Mo's parents appear very briefly, only to be immediately eaten up like little "munchy" (Drescher 1993: np) snacks. The act of eating "his Mom and Dad" (ibid) is the epitome of rule-breaking as a prerequisite of carnival. "One must know to what degree certain behaviors are forbidden, and must feel the majesty of the forbidding norm, to appreciate their transgression. Without a valid law to break, carnival is impossible" (Eco 1984: 6). And because of the comic framework of carnival, the devouring of the parents is first and foremost a funny event. But embedded into this grotesque physical humor is a dynamics of power transformations that seem to be mapped on Mikhail Bakhtin's concept of the "lower bodily stratum." There is a constant moving of opposite forces: what was high becomes low, what was inside becomes outside and vice versa. Bakhtin attests Rabelais's novels a fixation on sexual and digestive organs (Bakhtin 1984: 368 ff.). According to the Russian literary critic, it is through copulation and penetration, eating and drinking, defecating, urinating and vomiting that the most powerful institutions of early Modern France, the Church and the Crown, are continually debased throughout Rabelais' five books that chronicle the life of a giant family. The debasing serves primarily one purpose: to express the lowly man's ephemeral defiance of oppressing forces.

As might be expected of a children's picturebook, *The Boy Who Ate Around* is not obscene or pornographic – as some of Rabelais' contemporaries judged *Gargantua*, for example. Although Rabelais' verbal imagery is frequently explicitly sexual, its deeper meaning, according to Bakhtin, lies in its metaphor of death and renewal. Drescher's picturebook images clearly emphasize bodily openings, such as nostrils and mouths, and protruding body parts, most prominently tongues, noses and tails – all sexual imagery according to Bakhtin. And while *The Boy Who Ate Around* may not be about sex as such, the motif of constant transformation and renewal is extremely present. Thus, Mo's literal incorporation of his parents, followed by the rest of the house (as if the parents were household objects too), prepares Mo's next transformation from "ferocious green warthog monster" into "a very large scaly pink-eyed alligator chirper" (Drescher 1993: np). In addition to erasing the boundaries between his body and the outside world (also a recurrent motif in Rabelais' texts), Mo's monstrous incarnations symbolize perpetual death and renewal.

> These traits [of death and renewal] are most fully and concretely revealed in the act of eating; the body transgresses here its own limits: it swallows, devours, rends the world apart, is enriched and grows at the world's expense. The encounter of man with the world, which takes place inside the open, biting, rending, chewing mouth, is one of the most ancient, and most important objects of human thought and imagery. [...] Man's encounter with the world in the act of eating is joyful, triumphant; he triumphs over the world, devours it without being devoured himself. The limits between man and the world are erased, to man's advantage. (Bakhtin 1984: 281)

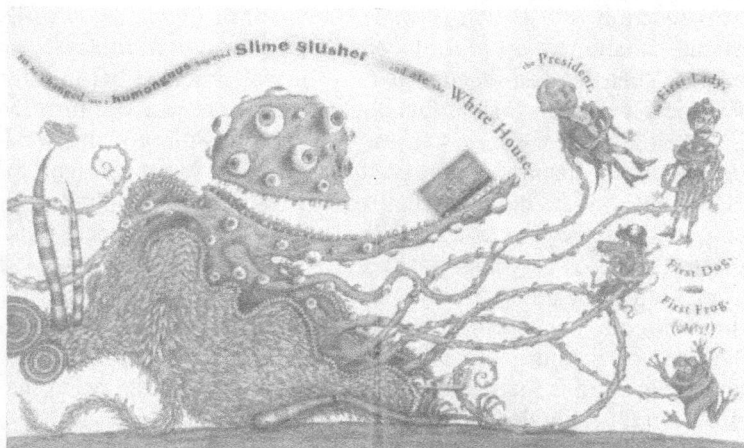

Fig. 33   *The Boy Who Ate Around* (Drescher 1993)

The topic of food, incorporation and digestion in *The Boy Who Ate Around* is fully employed for the effects here described by Bakhtin. Mo and his incarnated monsters not only symbolically but literally devour the entire world. The boundaries between Mo and the world are erased, evidently to Mo's advantage. Rabelais' theme of renewal is also quite literally transferred into this picturebook: out of every monster comes a new monster. Throughout the food rampage, not only the parents are reduced to ingested particles within the monsters' giant bellies and thereby disempowered. Other notorious symbols for power that Mo devours include various public buildings and representatives of state and national authority. The debasing of these symbols of educational, economic and political power happens on the level of physical humor (eating) but also verbal and visual humor: the "First Frog" not only rhymes with "First Dog" but also parodies the bumptious labelling of presidential pets just as it denaturalizes the undue hype that often surrounds these pets (usually dogs) in present times (fig. 33). All four represented characters (President, First Lady, dog and frog) are grimacing, expressing a kind of malaise at being seized by the tentacles of the "humongous bug-eyed slime slusher" (ibid).

This reaction is a humorous understatement of the actual severity of the situation (they look uncomfortable but far from scared to death). Their modest reaction is even further ridiculed because the President's and his wife's facial expressions are exactly mirrored in the dog's and the frog's faces. The representation of the President is clearly inspired by the picture of George Washington on the U.S. one dollar note, except that Drescher's Washington is equipped, in addition to the grimace, with a shiny red nose (reminiscent of Mo's clownish nose) and brightly colored clothes. The First Lady (not recognizably Washington's wife) on this page is draped into a dress seemingly made of the 'Star-Spangled Banner'. The humor in this picture is based to a large extent on cultural knowledge and is intensified by the degree to which the reader has access to this knowledge.

The parents are now effectively dethroned. Their dethronement is multiplied in effect by the dethronement of the ultimate 'parents' of the nation, the President and his wife (and pets). They can no longer order their son (perhaps a representative of 'the citizen') to eat what they want, for the plate with the lizard guts and bullfrog heads is skillfully avoided, although it can be detected on every single page. The remaining eating binge could in this context be read as a disintegration of educational knowledge, here mostly geography and topography, as the monsters proceed to eat up the U.S. states, and many individually named countries and continents, mountains and waters. Mo has found an ingenious solution to his initially invidious position by morphing into monsters that have the physique that is necessary to eat around the abhorred dinner dish – and to divest the usual potentates of their office.

In this context, I have already mentioned some features of the monsters' grotesque bodies. In fact, not only the bodies in Drescher's book correspond to the grotesque framework, but the graphics do too. The idea of the grotesque is, of course, central to Bakhtin's thoughts about carnival. Through the grotesque body and the grotesque aesthetics of the verbal text, the themes of eating and drinking, death and renewal, inside and outside, up and down, are effectively visualized. But what does it mean in terms of power relations if the initially powerless hero temporarily gains authority by turning into ugly, weird and ridiculous monsters? Has he now become the powerful ogre of the state – or even the world? Are these bodies gendered? Is the grotesque gendered?

Many scholars write about monsters as always inherently grotesque. Their definition of the grotesque, it seems, is based on the presence of monsters (e.g. Kelso 1999: 105–118; Webb and Enstice 1999: 91; Overthun 2009: 50). If 'grotesque' is to be used as a generic term for anything that is perceived as strange, fantastic, incongruous or weird – and what picturebook monster is not? – then talking of the grotesque in the context of monsters easily suggests itself. But although scholars agree that grotesque humor has long since become acceptable in children's literature (O'Sullivan 2005: 28) – with Lewis Carroll's *Alice's Adventures in Wonderland* (1865), if not before – I think that the underlying and contemporary definition of 'grotesque' is, in most cases, a very broad one that can only loosely be associated with Victor Hugo's conviction that "the essential aspect of [grotesque imagery] is the monstrous" (Bakhtin 1984: 43), as the children's texts that are most often cited as examples for the grotesque, such as *Alice's Adventures in Wonderland* or many of Roald Dahl's publications, illustrate: there are no actual monsters in these stories; 'the grotesque' is here primarily based on the Carroll's and Dahl's use of irreverent and nonsense humor. But even when 'grotesque' is employed as an attribute for the monsters of a picturebook, such as the wild things, the potential of such an ascription is usually not fully exploited. The word 'grotesque' is often simply used as an attribute that means several of the following: fantastic, funny, and simultaneously slightly scary. In *The Boy Who Ate Around*, the monsters' grotesqueness goes beyond a simple description of their appearance.

First of all, the idea of unity and oneness is continuously countered through the realization of transformations via a change of costume. Only the very first metamorphosis of Mo into green warthog monster shows Mo's human head turning into a monster's head over the progression of five frames. The remaining four transformations take place in the form of a costume change. The green warthog monster takes off his head and out flies the alligator chirper. The chirper's belly is zipped open by the slime slusher. The tyrannosaurus rat jumps out of the slime slusher's huge gaping mouth. And finally, Mo swings open the tyrannosaurus rat's head that is attached with a hinge-joint to the rest of the body. These

305

costume-bodies are organic, growing in size in accordance with every additional bit of the world that they ingest: "Contrary to the modern canons, the grotesque body is not separated from the rest of the world. It is not a closed, completed unit; it is unfinished, outgrows itself, transgresses its own limits." (Bakhtin 1984: 26)

As if Drescher's intention was to create a picturebook version of Bakhtin's analysis of the grotesque body in Rabelais' writing, his monsters have huge mouths, protruding noses that expel fire or brown slime, long glistening tongues, exaggeratedly protruding and countless bulgy eyes, long powerful tentacles and a strong tail that eventually, when the whole world has been eaten and the rat-monster dangles from the moon, hurls the abhorred dish into space. To no other picturebook of my corpus does the following extract from Bakhtin's description apply to such a high degree:

> The stress is laid on those parts of the body that are open to the out-side world, that is, the parts through which the body itself goes out to meet the world. This means that the emphasis is on the apertures or the convexities, or on various ramifications and offshoots: the open mouth, the genital organs, the breasts, the phallus, the potbelly, the nose. The body discloses its essence as a principle of growth which exceeds its own limits only in copulation, pregnancy, child-birth, the throes of death, eating, drinking, or defecation. (ibid)

It is all here: disproportionately large nostrils and mouths, the "ramifications and offshoots," such as forked tongues, a long and pointy beak, the muscular and agile tails, and the potbellies that grow incessantly and risk to explode just before every new trans-formation. The way in which each new monster emerges out of the old one is particularly noteworthy with reference to Bakhtin's ac-count of how Gargantua's mother, Gargamelle, gives birth to her monstrous son: "The anatomical analysis ends with the unexpected and completely carnivalesque birth of Gargantua through his mother's ear. The child does not go down, but up. This is a typical grotesque turnover." (ibid: 226) In *The Boy Who Ate Around*, the alligator chirper, the tyrannosaurus rat, and Mo in his human shape are born out of their predecessor's heads, moving up from bottom to top and thereby exemplifying the reversal of usual hierarchies.

From all these aspects only the sexual references that are so ubiquitous in Rabelais' chronicles are missing. Considering the imposing taboos in most literary texts for children, this is hardly surprising. As Peter Hunt succinctly puts it: "No sex, no violence: what are you left with? Food." (Hunt 1996: 9) So the monsters do not display any genital organs. On the other hand, it is certainly not far-fetched in my interpretation of this book as carnivalesque to ascribe the long protruding noses and the tails and tentacles phallic status. Apart from their shape, all of these body parts are shown to excrete or expel something, they are represented with phallic or digestive functions, as it were. Thus, the tyrannosaurus rat – the biggest and most powerful of all – has a fire-blowing nose, with flames dashing forward constantly, and a long pink tail that rises up between the monster's legs in the successful attempt at hurling the lizard guts and bullfrog heads into the infinite vastness of space. While the scatological references in this book, including a very graphic fart and brown slime expelled from the warthog monster's tubular nose, are not unique (cf. *Bad Habits!* or *Morris, the Mankiest Monster*), I find the emphasis on body openings and protrusions particularly dominant compared to the rest of my corpus. Although this is a union of female and male sexual 'functions' – if Drescher's imagery is, indeed, read in this way –, it is, of course, a power fantasy that I have never seen embodied by a female picturebook character and thus implicitly coded as masculine. Especially in comparison with Lucretzia in *Bad Habits!* whose behavior is also described in terms of monstrosity, the narrator's benignity in *The Boy Who Ate Around* towards Mo's rampage and blatant disrespect for table manners specifically, and his parents more generally, seems to suggest that such behavior can only be celebrated and valued in male children.

The uniting of forces that are habitually considered as separate or even opposing entities continues in the manner that Drescher interweaves his verbal text with the visual text: both become one, inseparable from one another. Thus the sentences describing Mo's desire to "[throw] it all up, right there on the dinner table…" (Drescher 1993: np) squirt forth like a reversed fountain from Mo's painfully sealed mouth and the words (and their signifieds) tumble out of the tyrannosaurus rat's hollow body. Some sentences or their fragments are wavy, some are semi-circular, but they are all formed as integral parts of the entire composition of each page opening, thereby not only making the monsters organic beings, as opposed to costumes, but also turning the text and images into an organic fabric. The bodily excretions in the images are complemented by words that are somewhat reminiscent of what Bakhtin calls the "billingsgate" or "marketplace" elements in Rabelais' texts (Bakhtin 1984: 145). Although there is no swearing in Drescher's book, there are a number of words that contain a notion of duality or of hybridity. In this sense, the attribution of the parents as "munchy!" and of the chairs and table as "crunchy!" (Drescher 1993: np) unifies two ideas that are usually kept apart: furniture and people on the one side, and food on the other. The parents as well as the dining room or kitchen furniture (as site for the initial and widespread power struggle of what goes into a child's mouth and who gets to make that decision) are literally debased: they are swallowed and subsequently move downward in the monster's/Mo's digestive system. But they are also simultaneously appreciated and loved through the basically affectionate terminology. The ridiculing, debasing and uncrowning of power symbols ultimately symbolize, according to Bakhtin, a victory over fear (Bakhtin 1994: 91). Mo has incorporated the power that usually rules his life; he has turned it into a part of his own body. It is important, I think, that the devouring of the parents and everything else is not aggressive or belligerent – as for example Max's taming of the wild things or Lucretzia's parent-monsters' party-smashing. Instead, it is a gay, triumphal and transformative gesture.

One of the important and much debated questions about carnival is whether it has any lasting transformative effects: "Most politically thoughtful commentators wonder [...] whether the 'licensed release' of carnival is not simply a form of social control of the low by the high and therefore serves the interests of that very official culture which it apparently opposes" (Stallybrass and White 13; qt. in Horlacher 2009: 38). This is, indeed, also the question that *The Boy Who Ate Around* seems to pose – and deny: Mom and Dad, who have been dumped out of the tyrannosaurus rat's belly after all the other contents, are

Fig. 34   *The Boy Who Ate Around* (Drescher 1993)

very happy to see their little rapscallion again. It was decided that string beans and cheese soufflé were off the menu forever. Then they picked up Mo's best friend, Theo, and went downtown for banana splits (WHICH IS A NICE WAY TO END A BUSY DAY). (Drescher 1993: np; [capitalized letters are handwritten in the original])

This ending is unexpected because, as Stallybrass and White imply, carnival only lasts for a certain amount of time before everyone returns to their former position in the social hierarchy. Eco explains this idea more fully:

> [...] the moment of carnivalization must be very short, and allowed only once a year [...]; an everlasting carnival does not work: an entire year of ritual observance is needed in order to make the transgression enjoyable. [...] Carnival can exist only as an *authorized* transgression (which in fact represents a blatant case of *contradiction in adjecto* [...]. (Eco 1984: 6; emphasis in the original)

Does Eco's analysis of the contradictory logic of carnival also apply to Drescher's picturebook? At first glance, at least, this does not seem to be the case. Mo might be back in his human shape, but he is still – if not even more – triumphant as he turns his face towards the readers and smirks at them (fig. 34). The handwritten relative clause "WHICH IS A NICE WAY TO END A BUSY DAY" is positioned in a semi-circle above Mo's head. Its rounded shape and highlighting with yellow crayon in addition to Mo's prominent position on this final page remind me of Lucretzia and her halo. But the effect here is opposite. Mo's 'semi-halo' is his own evaluation of the events, which are focalized through him. The most striking contrast to Lucretzia's depiction is Mo's demand-pose. Although he sits at the table with his back towards the readers, his face is turned over his left shoulder. He is smiling victoriously, even cheekily, his blue eyes are wide open, sparkling behind his glasses and directly meeting the readers' eyes, as if he was asking them to agree with him that, indeed, eating ice cream with one's parents, best friend and the family dog is a nice way to end a busy day. His body pose and facial expression as well as his position at the table are diametrically opposed to his parents' expression: they sit huddled together, fixating their cup of ice cream with slightly bent heads, looking docile and dutiful. Their visual appearance makes me wonder how happy they really are to have their son back. Considering the parents' body language, this narrative statement could also be read as a projective fantasy entertained by Mo. The power distribution continues on the level of food. Not only do the parents have to share a cup but it is also the smallest one on the table and the lowest in the composition as a whole. All the cups are highly ornamental but Mo's cup stands out because its shaft is formed as a scantily clothed servant-like figure that lifts the cup high up with both arms, making it tower above the others.

To all appearances, the boy is still king. Mo clearly dominates the scene with the hint of a halo as a symbol for his superiority. This supremacy of the child is unsettling to some commentators. Thus Kathryn Harrison, upon reviewing *The Boy Who Ate Around* in the New York Times Book Review, "wonder[s] if Mo should get to eat up his parents in lieu of green beans and then be rewarded with ice cream" (Harrison 1994: np). That parents dictate the rules to their children is so firmly rooted in many readers' experience that a reversal of positions seems inadmissible, "even within an imagined world" (ibid) of carnival. Harrison admits to "[being] one of those moms. Any tantrum, even an imaginary one, that ends with fudge and no vegetables makes me nervous" (ibid). Her nervousness derives perhaps from her impression that this carnival is not over but continues. Through the narrative voice Mo's parents even seem to appreciate their son's unruly behavior by calling him "little rapscallion." (I will leave open to debate whether or not this appreciation originates from the parents or from Mo, as I have suggested above.) According to the *Oxford English Dictionary*, 'rapscallion' is an archaic term for 'mischievous person,' probably derived from 'rascal.' The narrator's claim that Mo's parents are happy implies that they are happy (or that Mo wants them to be happy) about his mischievousness, that they approve of this character trait.

There is an interesting parallel to *Where the Wild Things Are*, particularly when considering the chronological positioning of the boy's attribution as mischievous trouble-makers. Max is declared 'mischievous' by the narrative voice only at the beginning. The kinds of mischief he is seen doing include chasing a dog with a fork and hammering a nail into the wall. Neither of these seem that bad when compared to eating up one's parents. Max only threatens his mother to eat her up and gets grounded and supper-deprived for it. The last image shows Max brushing off his bestial shell, his wolf costume's hood. His smiling face and the supper on the table in his room suggest that he is no longer mischievous. In contrast, Mo is associated with his 'mischievousness' ("little rapscallion") at the end, *after* he has eaten his parents and liberated them again. His 'naughtiness' *concludes* the story. His parents implicitly approve of his deeds by expressing their joy over his personality. Harrison's reaction seems understandable in this light, for does this ending not effectively seal the parents' dethronement?

Foucault would probably answer no to this question. He might point out to Harrison that parental power on this last double opening of *The Boy Who Ate Around* is shown to be grotesque and ridiculous, and that there is ultimately no escape from power.

> I do not think that explicitly showing power to be abject, despicable, Ubu-esque or simply ridiculous is a way of limiting its effects and of magically dethroning the person to whom one gives the crown. Ra-

ther, it seems to me to be a way of giving a striking form of expression to the unavoidability, the inevitability of power, which can function in its full rigor and at the extreme point of its rationality even when in the hands of someone who is effectively discredited. (Foucault 2003: 13)

Foucault's analysis might seem too harsh to apply to the humorous rendition of Mo's ice-cream feast, but it crystallizes the theme of this picturebook quite aptly. For although there is no evident end to the carnival in this story, the limits of carnival are still there: they exist as the material pages of this picturebook that, once read, can be closed and put back on the shelf. Countering the physical limits of the picturebook, Drescher attempts to subvert even the limits that very materiality. Because what Mo's demanding gaze also does is draw attention to the materiality and the permeability of the picturebook of which he becomes more than just a fictional character. He engages with the reader, inciting tangible reactions and transgressing not only his own physical boundaries but the readers' too. It is significant that this demand pose occurs at the end – as compared to Lucretzia's at the beginning or Max's in the middle of the book – because it reminds the reader of her role in the reading process, of opening the book in the first place. The emphasis on interaction between readers and protagonists is already evident on the dedication page where Drescher has placed a drawing of the book *The Boy Who Ate Around*, as a material thing that is, at the same time, an organic being. From within the pages, the various monstrous body limbs, scaly wings, bristly claws, reverted tubular eye sockets, and tentacles, urge out, grabbing a spoon with pink ooze dripping from it. The fork, already piercing the very book cover from which these limbs emerge, is drawn in a manner that its handle seems to reach beyond the margins of the page, ending exactly where a reader would place her right hand while contemplating this double page opening. Her hand becomes the extension of the fork which turns her into the (civilized, cutlery-using) eater of the book. Even before the story itself begins, the readers are already made accomplices, engaging in the same kind of grotesque activity as the boy Mo: eating up authority. With reference to this dedication page, Mo's direct look into the readers' eyes on the last page could be seen as a reminder of their initial complicity. Last

312

but not least, Drescher's postmodern dissolution of the material boundaries of the book, its protagonists and its readers can also be read as a contribution to the question not only "of who can govern and who is governed but also the means by which that shaping of someone else's activities is achieved " (Mills 2003: 47) in the family context.

Mo's final gaze on the last page can be read as redirecting this question at the reader. It is a way of closing a circle and of drawing attention to all the different origins of power – in this case including the power and the authority to interpret a picturebook story. This is a positive and liberating prospect of power and family politics concerning food, but also potentially other concerns of parenting and growing up. The traditional laughter divide is dissolved at the same time as the physical boundaries of book and body. According to humor theorists, the audience either laughs *at* the comic hero (and consequently with the authority representing the social norms that the hero breaks), or they laugh *with* the comic hero (and at the norms). The *laughing-at* variant corresponds to a version of the comic of derision, while the *laughing-with* model is synonymous with a version of the comic of valorization, of the affirmation of the repressed character (Horlacher 2009: 22–26). But there is another concept of laughter: the full laughter of carnival which is revitalizing and liberating, proposing another perspective to the habitual view of laughter as a social corrective of power (ibid: 25). With full laughter, the model of center and margin becomes potentially multidirectional, with laughter rippling back and forth if only the readers allow it. Mo's demand gaze at the end as well as half-title page presenting the very picturebook I am holding in my hands as another item of food – both of these images suck me into the book, urging me to join in this carnivalesque humor. Of course I could refuse to laugh, as Harrison does, and thus deny this narrative its life-affirming joyfulness. But I don't.

Instead I read this picturebook as one of very few examples in the world of picturebooks generally in which laughter is multidirectional and inclusive. When I laugh about the warthog monster's swallowing Mo's parents or about their meekness on the last page, I also laugh about myself and at my own failings at always respecting my children's boundaries. By reading this book and laughing about it *with* my children, I laugh to some extent at my own dethronement – however fictitious it may be. And by laughing at myself, I return some of my power to my children. No other book in my corpus displays a comparable kind of open laughter. In some instances, laughter is directed at the parents, as in *Not Now, Bernard*. Here Bernard parents' failure to recognize that their son has been replaced by a monster creates a comic effect, which is, however, mingled with horror and uncertainty because the situation is never resolved. In *Monsters – An Owner's Guide*, the implied readers also laugh at the child-parents' incapacity to keep their monster-robot-child under control. The monster-parents in *Bad Habits!* are also funny and somewhat ridiculous, but they ultimately invite the reader to laugh *with* them, to rejoice over their victory over the uncivilized little monster that is their daughter. In *Not Now Bernard* and in *Monsters – An Owner's Guide*, laughter can be seen as an instrument of educative and corrective power that is directed *at* the parents or other adult caregivers. But only in *The Boy Who Ate Around* are the parents as openly invited to join in. I find Stefan Horlacher's reflection on the interrelatedness of power and laughter very productive for understanding laughter in this picturebook, too:

> Laughter, […] 1) demonstrates that the ostracized is and has always been a part of the very order that excludes it and 2) proves that there is an implicit and secret identity between the power of exclusion and that which is excluded. From this perspective laughter is simultaneously criticism and affirmation. It criticizes the 'serious' world and its order and is an expression of happiness and plenitude, accepting or even celebrating the right of the excluded. (Horlacher 2009: 35)

The Boy Who Ate Around is a compelling example for this ambiguity. It reveals power mechanisms at work by representing them in their most grotesque forms of expression. The humor that permeates every page of this book is a criticism of educative and parental conventions, such as dictating ones children what to eat, but it is an inclusive criticism, one that is dominated by cheerfulness and gaiety, an affirmation of the pleasures of eating, of life – and of parenting. *Monsters – An Owner's Guide* is much less affirmative and joyful in that sense, but it shares the ambiguity of power relations by representing the parental figures as laughable. But the ultimate comedians in both books are the child figures: Mo and the monster robot respectively.

> A humorist or a comedian is a *homo ludens* who engages in cultural juggling: He or she playfully reshuffles the components of the surrounding *nomos*, turns the established order of opposites such as masculinity and femininity or good and evil around, and inverts traditional hierarchies. By doing so, special attention is paid to the ambiguities and incongruities of the human condition [...]. (Horlacher 2009: 23)

Both picturebooks construct a fictional world in which "the established order of opposites" is disrupted or simply turned upside down and none of them offers a resolution that would reestablish that order – as is usually the case in picturebooks and children's literature more generally. Although Horlacher suggests that the subversion of order can also be aimed at gender this is not a relevant issue in these two picturebooks. In *The Boy Who Ate Around*, the power to disclose the "incongruities of the human condition" and, more particularly the incongruities of power relations between parents and children, is placed into the hands of a boy. In *Monsters – An Owner's Guide*, the child figure is, as I have argued, actually represented by the "monstermatic toy" that wreaks havoc in the house and that is referred to with the gender-neutral "it" (Emmett and Oliver 2010). The verbal narrative does not mention the two children that have to take control of the monster robot because it is composed like an instruction manual that addresses its reader with a "you." Even if the visual coding of the two children as male and female is deconstructed in favor of a queer reading, thus making the short-haired cargo-pants-wearing child, who is shown as much more enthusiastic about the monster than the long-haired and pink-skirt wearing child, gender-nonconforming – even with this kind of deconstruction the power incongruities that are shown here concern the relationship between adults and children, not girls and boys. But of course, a story that does not make gender a relevant issue changes nothing about the fact that it *is* a relevant issue. The number of female versus male child protagonists respectively in this group of picturebooks is somewhat representative for my corpus as a whole: although there are more girl protagonists than in the other groups they are still underrepresented. More importantly, when they do have a main role the authors make sure that their initial bond with the monsters or any possibility of affirming that relationship is destroyed. Just as relevant and never made verbally explicit is the class and social background of all the child characters I have discussed here. Most of them live in suburban or small-town middle-class, two-level houses. The only child whose home is not represented in this way is Anh – who is also the only main protagonist of color. – Early years teachers and even Maurice Sendak himself can proclaim as often as they like that *Where the Wild Things Are* is a story that speaks to all children because Max is a universal child. There is no universal child. Max is a boy and he is white and lives in a middle-class home where he has his own room. And so are Mo, Garp and Bernard.

Conclusion

A recurrent motif in most of the books I have discussed across the three sections of this chapter is that of border crossing between human shape and monster shape, either through devouring (or the threat of devouring) or through metamorphosis. In all books, 'monster' signifies an existential state of the child characters that is both innate and irreconcilable with family life. And so these picturebook stories present ways of dealing with these monsters. Depending on the image of child that is present, the child's monstrosity, i.e., his or her 'uncivilized behavior,' is externalized and mapped onto the parents, or the monsters are represented as the child's unsocial emotions that need to be repressed and exiled, or the monsters are welcome as pranksters and humorous reminders that not only pets but kids have rights, too.

I started this chapter with the question how monsters are used within the educative process which I represented as the main theme of the picturebooks I examined here. Although fundamental ideas about education – that change historically and culturally – form the basis of almost all of children's fiction, including picturebooks, this theme is usually not made explicit on the story level. One reason for the invisibility of the educative impetus of picturebooks may be the absence or non-involvement of parental figures within the narrative. The picturebooks that I have grouped into this chapter are an exception in this respect. Although humor is present more or less subtly in all the books of my corpus, I have found it most salient in the books of this group. My task for this chapter was consequently a very complex one: identifying and analyzing the use of the monster as an educative commodity, developing a perspective on the role humor plays in the parenting styles that the books unfold, examining the representation of male and female protagonists, and evaluating this representation in the context of the corpus as a whole.

In the first section, I offered a detailed discussion of *Bad Habits!* and suggested that this picturebook parodies the image of the evil child. Here, as in the other three books of this group, monsters are simultaneously used as a measure of determent from unwanted behavior and an invitation to laughter. This simultaneity creates an ambiguity concerning the 'message' of the respective books: Although the four narratives are all built upon the assumption – however ironic – that 'the child' is 'evil,' they all tend to leave the reader in doubt as to how seriously this assumption should be taken. Despite the variety of disciplinary measures (from the complete annihilation of Judy and Paul by Beastie in *Pat the Beastie*, to a mere self-deprecating 'cautionary tale' in *Monsters Eat Whiny Children*; and from the total eradication of all monstrous traits in Lucretzia in *Bad Habits!* to the parents' sarcastic distancing from their son's looming imaginary monster transformation in *Night of the Veggie Monster*), the narrative voices in all four books are clearly biased towards an adult perspective. In all four books, the underlying question is whether the child protagonists will be bettered at the end through the adults' educational intervention – the humor that is also present in all four books just makes it difficult to decide how seriously this question must be taken. At least in *Bad Habits!* humor seems to rely mostly on its "critical, moralistic and civilizing qualities" (Brulotte 2006: 14). From the six child protagonists in this group, Lucretzia doubtlessly undergoes the most radical transformation, from "uncivilized little monster" to "civilized little angel". *Bad Habits!* suggests that a girl must be docile, silent, slim and gracious in order to be valued and liked by anyone – and that a girl who behaves in the opposite way (disrespectful, loud, fat and violent) is branded 'monster,' in a purely detrimental sense. In *Bad Habits!*, the association between child protagonist and monster is marked 'wrong' *because* the child is female. No amount of humor can downplay the sexism that is inherent in this representation – then again, without the sexism, the book would lose an important source of its humor in the first place.

The books in the second section use monsters as a supposedly suitable means to teach their (child) readers about emotions that are conceptualized as mostly difficult or problematic: anger, worry, envy, defiance. Out of eight books, only one has a female main child protagonist (*The Huge Bag of Worries*) and one has a female main adult protagonist (*When Mum Turned into a Monster*). In both of these books, monsters or the state of being a monster is considered undesirable and even fearful. This is a striking contrast to the remaining books, in which the emotion-representing monsters may exude some danger initially, but ultimately bond with the boy characters, forming a strengthening and friendly relationship with one another. I examined *Where the Wild Things Are* in greater detail. This book is not only a point of aesthetic reference for subsequent picturebook authors but it has also heavily contributed to an idea of how boys in picturebooks should ideally mature into more 'civilized' human beings. In this ideal, the realization of parental responsibility and influence is crucial, but driven into the background through numerous narrative and pictorial devices. The boy protagonist moves to the foreground, with an emphasis on his own competence to find a way out of his emotional troubles. Despite the centrality of the child character, the adult caregivers provide the normative frame, consisting of disciplinary measures such as grounding or temporary food-deprivation. These measures are represented as appropriate and effective. If humor is present at all in these books it is in the aesthetical forms of the monsters but it does not impinge on the parents' authority.

Despite otherwise vast differences, the two picturebooks that I categorized into the last group represent a parenting strategy of non-involvement, placing considerable responsibility but also authority onto the child characters' shoulders. In both books, the monster has destructive, norm-disrupting potential that the male (or visually male-coded) child characters use or try to use to their advantage. Humor is here as present as in the books of the first group. Humor also considerably shapes the image of the male 'child' as resourceful, adventurous and endowed with an admirable gift for imagination. Although the carnivalesque humor in *The Boy Who Ate Around* is unusually close to Bakhtin's theoretical concept, my analysis of this book has highlighted a number of aspects that are also relevant in *Monsters – An Owner's Guide*, which is less obviously carnivalesque. Both books present a scenario in which the mere possibility of parental authority and control is thwarted. Compared to the humor in the books of the first group, these books present the other, the dangerous side of laughter, namely its "power to free us from servitude and illusion" (Brulotte 2006: 15). The implied readers, including the adult implied readers, are compelled to laugh about their own dethronement, their own disempowerment. But the dynamics of laughter is more complex than the decision whether readers laugh *at* or *with* the comic hero. This division is sporadically dissolved, approaching Bakhtin's idea of "full laughter." In his analysis of progressive educationalist rhetoric, Marcus Reiß asks how pedagogy can present itself if it does *not* want to be authoritarian, if it wants to renounce any form of disciplinary agitation, such as corporeal or psychological punishment (Reiß 2012: 207). I think that *The Boy Who Ate Around* provides inspiration for finding answers to that question.

5 Conclusion

Monsters in picturebooks are not simply boys' funny and furry friends that lack any definitional basis for actual monstrosity. Rather, picturebook monsters fulfil a vast array of functions in the construction of gendered childhood and in the discursive establishments of the paradigms of contemporary children's consumer culture. As such, the picturebook monster can be defined in its etymological sense as a figure that shows (*monstrare*) how boys and girls are supposed to see and comport themselves in order to be recognized and valued by their social environment. The extent to which these *demonstrations* rely and depend on a dichotomous view of gender occasionally reaches disturbing dimensions, which could be linked to another original meaning of the monster as 'that which disturbs.' In this sense, I regard the picturebook monster partly as a disturbance of my ideal that these creatures contribute to the diversification of childhood subjectivities with respect to gender, sexuality, ethnicity, culture and ability. Despite their potential to do this, picturebook monsters address and represent a rather homogenous group of children. But apart from not fulfilling their idealistic potential, are picturebook monsters disturbing in any other respect?

At first glance, they certainly do not appear in this way. Indeed, the disturbing quality that monsters exude in narratives for grown-ups, most notably through their reversed representation of what is considered human in the dominant culture, is, by and large, absent in picturebooks. Here, monsters are employed as stabilizing agents for contemporary ideas about predominantly male, middle-class and white children. What might be considered disturbing, then, is the fact that the intimate association of monsters and boys is perceived (in academia and beyond) as trivial and literally unremarkable. My previous discussions of four thematic complexes, in which picturebook monsters are actively engaged, hopefully contribute to changing this view. Although these four motifs cover vastly different areas, they are nevertheless all imbued with often hidden pedagogical messages, which I want briefly to recapitulate.

Thus, the obviously didactically inspired motif of the fear of the monster is only a pseudo-therapeutic narrative, because alleviating the boy protagonist's initial fear is nothing more than a potential side effect of another process of far greater importance. It is a process of maturation during which the boy learns a set of skills that enable him to master his crisis successfully on his own and to grow into a successful and socially well-adapted adult male. In my readings, befriending the monster is a metaphor for the adaptation of characteristics and values associated with hegemonic masculinity. These values comprise both traditional attributes of boys, such as courage, politeness and loyalty, and more modern descriptions of desirable characteristics, such as care, empathy, and humor. It is perhaps the monster's hybrid nature that makes it such an ideal place holder for all these different personality traits. At the same time as the picturebook monster encourages the boy protagonists to incorporate and embrace these complex qualities, the only girl protagonist in this group activates an image of girls as passive, helpless and naïve. As extreme as this case may be, through its intertextual links with the fairy tale of *Little Red Riding Hood* it contributes to a dominant cultural narrative that treats sexism as a legitimate frame of mind.

Some very few picturebooks portray girl characters with similarly positively connoted qualities as the majority of boy characters. However, the assertiveness of two exemplary heroic girl protagonists is compromised by the necessity for these girls to position themselves towards marriage. Their involuntary involvement in the concept of romantic, heterosexual relationships suggests that strong girls, almost as a narrative requirement in children's fiction, need to hold their ground against boys and men in order to assert their power and independent minds. Their entanglement with issues of marriage transforms the explicitly feminist motivation of *Princess Smartypants* as well as Ida's heroism in *Outside Over There* into very complex narratives that have nothing in common with the typical picturebook monster story. In this light, the monsters' divergent relationship to both Ida and Smartypants, and their radically different depiction is hardly surprising.

Although monsters in adults' culture are most often employed as signifiers for different forms of 'otherness,' this motif proved less dominant in my corpus. Most striking, in my mind, was the narrative support and encouragement of boy protagonists' adoption of traditionally and stereotypically feminine (or 'non-masculine') attributes, such as tenderness, emotionality, cuteness, or artistic talent. In these picturebooks, being a 'soft' boy was represented as an ultimately admirable and certainly acceptable subject position to inhabit. The same vision of tolerance cannot be claimed for female protagonists, protagonists representing ethnic and cultural diversity or a non-normative body image. Especially ethnically/culturally diverse characters' inclusion into the dominant culture was regularly shown to be futile or illusory. Here again, gender had an additional impact on the success or failure of individuals' struggles to integrate themselves into any kind of social network, insofar as male protagonists were shown to take the initiative for solving their isolation through xenophobia much more actively than the only female protagonist in this situation. Those protagonists – all monsters – representing a physique that the narratives described as 'ugly' were all male. Although the degree of their access to interpersonal contact differed greatly, these characters' stories all ended with their contentment and happiness.

Considering that picturebooks belong to one of the first types of media that are supposed to teach children values and behaviors that help them navigate in this world, I found the scope of diversity in these books very limited. In the light of continuing efforts of making picturebooks by and about people of color more visible and more easily available, for instance through official recognition like the Coretta Scott King Award for African-American writing and illustration for children (annually awarded since 1970), the disillusioned view offered in the small number of picturebooks with this theme in my corpus is unlikely to be representative of picturebooks in general. On a more positive side, the small number of books with this theme in my corpus clearly indicates that the majority of monsters in picturebooks fulfill other functions than marking an ethnic and/or cultural minority status.

The fourth thematic group, finally, provided enough material for me to distinguish three different concepts of 'child' that are established through a use of the monster as a childrearing device. The reliance of humor for the understanding of the stories in two of these concepts (the ironic treatment of a Black Pedagogy and 'the evil child', and the carnivalesque power reversal of 'the child as king') questions the extent to which these concepts should be taken at face value. With regards to the political incorrectness of overtly labelling a child as 'evil' or to the unrealistic vision of a child as the legitimate ruler of the family, the ambiguity of these two narrative patterns seems inevitable. As ambiguous as the narratives and their pedagogical messages might be, the relationship pattern between monsters and boy protagonists in this group is practically identical with the books in the other two groups: monsters in picturebooks help boys overcome emotional crises and conflicts with parental authority, just as boys are encouraged to form and maintain friendly ties with these monsters. Monsters in picturebooks thus not only enhance an image of boyhood, they are also specifically employed as fictitious parenting aids. The efficiency of these aids, however, remains to be questioned, as the monsters' oscillation between power and its lack mirrors a widespread uncertainty among parents over what is right or wrong in childrearing and education. How exactly should power be distributed among the members of a family? Should parents monitor and control their child's practice of exerting power? What happens when a child gains absolute power in the household?

That the children in these scenarios are predominantly male aptly reflects the distribution of gender in my entire corpus. My analysis of thematic patterns is, of course, inextricably connected with the motif of the monster and the medium of the picturebook. That is to say, the various functions that I ascribe to the picturebook monster are likely to be specific for this type of children's narrative. Unlike some other cultural consumer products marketed for children, such as TV series, commercials or video games (where monsters also abound), picturebooks are addressed to largely middle-class families who put great emphasis on literature in their children's education. The dominance of white characters in picturebooks remains a problematic issue, since it impinges on the representation of ethnic diversity in children's literature and implies a predominantly white readership. This issue appeared to me especially acute in my corpus. Of course, a number of sixty-five titles can never be representative for the incredibly rich entirety of picturebooks. In this sense, my study was a very specific one and my claims, for example concerning the consolidation of (hegemonic) masculine values, can only be understood in relation with monsters in this type of literature. Similarly specific as my literary research motif is the language area on which I chose to focus my study. Thus, German or Mexican or Chinese picturebook monsters may well have quite different implications concerning gender, ethnicity, and other identity markers. The fact that picturebooks are rarely translated, some exceptions (such as *Where the Wild Things Are* and *The Gruffalo*) notwithstanding, indicates that picturebook monsters are culturally very specific.

Nevertheless, I want to suggest that this specificity be seen within a larger, global context of cultural consumer products for children, where monsters as a visual and conceptual motif play a dominant role. The link between picturebooks as a possibly marginal repository for monsters and other products, which are more clearly recognized as *consumer* products and where monsters might be even more visible, is not as remote as it might seem. Think of, for example, *Where the Wild Things Are*, a picturebook with almost unparalleled success and whose monsters are sold as plush toys and as prints on apparel and commodities. This picturebook was made into a major motion picture, directed by Spike Jonze in 2009, which further fuelled its popularity. There is one other picturebook monster that has been turned into an extremely profitable and widely recognized global brand: the Gruffalo, based on two picturebooks: *The Gruffalo* (1999) and *The Gruffalo's Child* (2004) by Julia Donaldson and Axel Scheffler. The Gruffalo's immense popularity among preschoolers in the West is certainly not due to two picturebooks alone, but must rather be attributed to their professional management by a production company (Magic Light Pictures) that works together with roughly thirty international licensees. Although the picturebook tells the story of a cunning, male mouse who outsmarts three, equally male animals of prey (a fox, a snake and an owl) and the (also male) monster, Gruffalo merchandise is marketed as explicitly unisex, as brand director Daryl Shute asserts in an interview with Licensing.biz (Shute 2014: np). This is a rare phenomenon in the world of children's consumer products, which are usually tailored towards maximizing profits by making them gender-specific.

Following up this trend, it might be possible or thinkable, then, that monsters as a recognizable and attractive figure in children's culture have more potential to address children across gender boundaries than other popular figures, such as the Disney Princess, Barbie, Star Wars or Marvel merchandise. At first glance, such a proposal seems at odds with my analysis of picturebook monsters as enforcing a gender dichotomy that relies heavily on sexist assumptions particularly about girls. But on the other hand,

these very picturebook monsters *do* encourage at least boy protagonists to embrace qualities that other popular figures in children's culture still present as typically feminine. Furthermore, once
the monster has left the monitored and carefully designed space of
the picturebook and has become, for example, a toy, children are
free to invent their own narratives. And so, the monster as a signifier for contemporary constructions of children may well work as
the harbinger of a (gender) category crisis, as which it has been
hailed by monster theorists before – only that now, it will no
longer be denied this status on the grounds that it is a children's
motif. Above all else, I hope that this research project will contribute to the recognition of monsters as relevant meaning-makers for
conceptions of boys and girls.

6 Works Cited

Illustrations

The pictures in this book have been reprinted with the friendly permission of their respective copyright holders, except where copyright has expired:

ORBIS PICTUS by Comenius 1658. Fig. 1 and 2.

THE BAD CHILD BOOK OF BEASTS by Hilaire Belloc and Lord Basil Temple Blackwood 1896. Fig.3.

LITTLE NEMO by Winsor McCay 1905. Fig. 4.

Details of copyright permissions as follows:

From WHERE THE WILD THINGS ARE by Maurice Sendak. Copyright © 1963 by Maurice Sendak, copyright renewed 1991. Used by permission of Harper Collins Publishers. Fig. 3, 29, 30, and 31.

THERE'S A NIGHTMARE IN MY CLOSET by Mercer Mayer, copyright © 1968 by Mercer Mayer. Used by permission of Dial Books for Young Readers, an imprint of Penguin Young Readers Group, a division of Penguin Random House LLC. Fig. 5.

LITTLE RED RIDING HOOD. Copyright © 1983 by Trina Schart Hyman. Reprinted by permission of Holiday House. Fig. 6.

Picturebooks

Andreae, Giles, and Sarah McIntyre. *Morris the Mankiest Monster*. Oxford: David Fickling Books, 2009. Print.

Arnold, Tedd. *Five Ugly Monsters.* New York: Scholastics, 1995. Print.

Baguley, Elizabeth, and Mark Chambers. *Pigeon Poo*. London: Little Tiger Press, 2012. Print.

Baker, Allen. *Good Night, William*. London: Andre Deutsch, 1990. Print.

Belloc, Hilaire, and Lord Basil Temple Blackwood. *The Bad Child's Book of Beasts*. London: Gerald Duckworth 1974 [1896]. Print.

Bissett, Josie, and Kevan J. Atteberry. *Tickle Monster*. Seattle: Compendium, 2010. Print.

Bright, Paul, and Hannah George. *Boris's Big Bogey*. London: Little Tiger Press, 2011. Print.

Bright, Paul, and Ben Cort. *Under the Bed*. London: Little Tiger Press, 2004. Print.

Bright, Rachel. *Love Monster*. London: Harper Collins Children's Books, 2012. Print.

Busch, Wilhelm. *Max und Moritz – Eine Bubengeschichte in sieben Streichen.* Munich: Verlag Braun und Schneider, 1906 [1865]. Project Gutenberg. Web. 12 Jan. 2015.

Caldecott, Randolph. *Hey Diddle Diddle* and *Baby Bunting*. London: George Routledge & Sons, 1882. Archive.org. Web. 16 Dec. 2014.

Child, Lauren. *Clarice Bean* series. London: Orchard Books, 1999-present. Print.

Clarke, Jane, and Garry Parsons. *G.E.M.* London: Red Fox, 2006. Print.

Comenius, Johann Amos. *Orbis Sensualium Pictus.* Syracuse: C. W. Bardeen, 1887 [1658]. Project Gutenberg. Web. 16 Dec. 2014.

Cole, Babette. *Bad Habits!* London: Puffin Books, 1999 [1998]. Print.

___. *Long Live Princess Smartypants.* London: Puffin Books, 2005 [2004]. Print.

___. *Prince Cinders.* London: Penguin, 1997 [1987]. Print.

___. *Princess Smartypants.* London: Penguin, 1996 [1986]. Print.

___. *Princess Smartypants Breaks the Rules.* London: Puffin Books, 2009. Print.

___. *The Trouble With Gran.* London: Mammoth, 1997 [1987]. Print.

___. *The Trouble With Grandad.* London: Egmont Books 2004 [1988]. Print.

___. *The Trouble With Mum.* London: Egmont Children's Books, 1999 [1983]. Print.

Deacon, Alexis. *Beegu.* London: Red Fox Books, 2004 [2003]. Print.

de Brunhoff, Jean. *The Story of Babar.* New York: Random House, 1937. Print.

Donaldson, Julia, and Axel Scheffler. *The Gruffalo.* London: MacMillan, 1999. Print.

Doyle, Malachy, and Paul Hess. *Hungry! Hungry! Hungry!* London: Andersen, 2004 [2000]. Print.

Drescher, Henrik. *The Boy Who Ate Around*. New York: Hyperion, 1996 [1994]. Print.

___. *Pat the Beastie*. London: Orion Children's Books, 1993. Print.

Dunbar, Joyce, and Jimmy Liao. *The Monster Who Ate Darkness*. London: Walker, 2009 [2008]. Print.

Edwards, Gareth, and Hannah Shaw. *The Disgusting Sandwich*. London: Alison Green Books, 2013. Print.

Emberly, Edd. *Go Away, Big Green Monster!* New York: Little, Brown and Company, 1992. Print.

Emberly, Edd, and Anne Miranda. *Sad Monster, Glad Monster*. New York: Little, Brown and Company, 1997. Print.

Emmett, Jonathan, and Mark Oliver. *Monsters – An Owner's Guide*. London and Oxford: Macmillan Children's Books, 2010. Print.

Falconer, Ian. *Olivia*. New York: Atheneum, 2000. Print.

Fardell, John. *The Day Louis Got Eaten*. London: Andersen Press, 2011. Print.

Freedman, Claire, and Ben Cort. *Monstersaurus*. London and New York: Simon and Schuster, 2011. Print.

Gerstein, Mordicai. *The Absolutely Awful Alphabet*. San Diego: Harcourt Brace & Company, 1999. Print.

Gibbs, Sarah. *Monsters Are...* London: Gullane Children's Books, 2009. Print.

Harrison, Joanna. *When Mum Turned Into A Monster*. London: Picture Lions, 1996. Print.

Hoban, Russell, and Quentin Blake. *Monsters*. New York: Scholastic, 1989. Print.

Hoffmann, Heinrich. *Der Struwwelpeter – Lustige Geschichten und drollige Bilder*. Frankfurt am Main: Literarische Anstalt, 1845. Project Gutenberg. Web. 16 Dec. 2014

Hutchins, Pat. *The Very Worst Monster*. New York: Harper-Collins Children's Books, 1985. Print.

Ironside, Virginia, and Frank Rodgers. *The Huge Bag of Worries*. London and Sydney: Hodder Children's Books, 2011 [1996]. Print.

Kaplan, Bruce Eric. *Monsters Eat Whiny Children*. New York: Simon & Schuster, 2010. Print.

Lee, Lyn, and Kim Gamble. *POG: The Monster Who Was Afraid of Children*. London and Sydney: Omnibus, 2001 [2000]. Print.

Leuck, Laura, and Mark Buehner. *My Monster Mama Loves Me So*. New York: HarpeCollins, 1999. Print.

Mayer, Mercer. *There's A Nightmare in My Closet*. New York: The Dial Press, 1968. Print.

Meyer, Stephanie. *Twilight Saga*. New York: Little, Brown and Company, 2005-2008. Print.

McAllister, Angela, and Alison Edgson. *YUCK! That's Not A Monster!* London: Little Tiger Press, 2010. Print.

McCarty, Peter. *Jeremy Draws A Monster*. New York: Henry Holt and Company, 2009. Print.

McClements, George. *Night of the Veggie Monster*. New York and London: Bloomsbury, 2007. Print.

McDonnell, Patrick. *The Monster's Monster*. New York: Little, Brown and Company, 2012. Print.

McKee, David. *The Monster and the Teddy Bear*. London: Andersen, 1989. Print.

___. *Not Now, Bernard*. London: Red Fox, 1990 [1984]. Print.

___. *Three Monsters*. London: Andersen Press, 2006 [2005]. Print.

___. *Two Monsters*. London: Andersen Press, 2009 [1985]. Print.

McNaughton. *Have You Seen Who's Just Moved In Next Door To Us?* London: Walker Books, 1993 [1991]. Print.

Miller, Edward. *The Monster Health Book*. New York: Holiday House, 2012 [2006]. Print.

Nicholson, William. *Clever Bill*. Portsmouth: Heinemann Young Books, 1999 [1926]. Print.

___. *The Pirate Twins*. Andrew Jones Art, 2005 [1929]. Print.

Noll, Amanda, and Howard McWilliam. *I Need My Monster*. Brooklyn: Flashlight, 2009. Print.

O'Keeffe, Susan Heyboer, and Lynn Munsinger. *One Hungry Monster: A Counting Book in Rhyme*. New York: Little, Brown and Company, 1989. Print.

Prelutsky, Jack, and Kevin Hawkes. *Imagine That!* New York: Alfred A. Knopf, 1998. Print.

Rex, Michael. *Goodnight Goon – A Petrifying Parody*. New York: G. P. Putnam's Sons, 2008. Print.

Riddell, Chris. *Mr. Underbed*. London: Andersen Press, 2011 [1986]. Print.

Roberts, David. *Dirty Bertie*. London: Little Tiger Press, 2003. Print.

Ross, Tony. *I'm Coming To Get You!* London: Andersen, 2008 [1984]. Print.

Sauer, Tammi, and Scott Magoon. *Mostly Monsterly*. New York: Simon and Schuster, 2010. Print.

Sendak, Maurice, Arthur Yorinks, and Matthew Reinhart. *Mommy?* New York: Di Capua, 2006. Print.

Sendak, Maurice. *Dear Mili.* New York: HarperCollins, 2004 [1988]. Print.

___. *Where the Wild Things Are.* New York: Harper Trophy, 1991 [1963]. Print.

___. *In the Night Kitchen.* London: Red Fox Books, 2001 [1970]. Print.

___. *Outside Over There.* London: Red Fox Books, 2002 [1981]. Print.

Silver, Gail, and Christiane Krömer. *Anh's Anger.* Berkeley: Plum Blossom Books, 2009. Print.

___. *Steps and Stones.* Berkeley: Plum Blossom Books, 2011. Print.

Smallman, Steve, and Joele Dreidemy. *Smelly Peter, the Great Pea Eater.* London: Little Tiger Press, 2009. Print.

Steig, William. *Shrek!* New York: Square Fish, 2009 [1990]. Print.

Stewart, Joel. *Dexter Bexley and the Big Blue Beastie.* London: Random House, 2008 [2007]. Print.

Stone, Jon, and Mike Smollin. *The Monster at the End of This Book: Starring Lovable, Furry Old Grover.* New York: Random House, 1999 [1979]. Print.

Thomas, Valerie, and Korky Paul. *Winnie the Witch* books. Oxford: Oxford University Press, 1987-present. Print.

Thompson, Kay, and Hilary Knight. *Eloise.* New York: Simon & Schuster, 1955. Print.

Vere, Ed. *Bedtime For Monsters.* London: Penguin, 2011. Print.

Waddell, Martin, and Patrick Benson. *The Tough Princess.* London: Walker Books, 2002 [1986]. Print.

Willems, Mo. *Leonardo the Terrible Monster*. London: Hyperion, 2007 [2005]. Print.

Willis, Jeanne, and Susan Varley. *The Monster Bed*. London: Red Fox Books, 1998 [1986]. Print.

Wise Brown, Margaret, and Clement Hurd. *Goodnight, Moon*. New York: HarperCollins, 2006 [1947]. Print.

Wong, Vicky, and Michael C. Murphy (meomi). *The Octonauts & the Only Lonely Monster*. London: HarperCollins, 2009 [2009]. Print.

Wormell, Chris. *The Big Ugly Monster and the Little Stone Rabbit*. London: Red Fox Books, 2004. Print.

Yolen, Janet, and Diane Stanley. *Sleeping Ugly*. New York: Paper Star, 1997 [1981]. Print.

Other Children's Books

Barrie, J. M. *Peter Pan*. Jack Zipes, ed. and intr. London: Penguin, 2004 [1902]. Print.

Baum, Frank L., *The Wizard of Oz*. Cornelia Funke, intr. London: Puffin Classics 2008 [1900]. Print.

Carroll, Lewis. *Alice in Wonderland* and *Through the Looking-Glass*. New York: Bantam Classic, 1984 [1864 and 1871]. Print.

Dahl, Roald. *Revolting Recipes*. New York: Puffin, 1997. Print.

Ende, Michael. *Neverending Story*. Trans. Ralph Manheim. London: Puffin, 1993 [1979]. Print.

Hauff, Wilhelm. *Dwarf Long-Nose*. Ill. Maurice Sendak. New York: Random House, 1960. [1826]. Print.

Hoffmann, E. T. A. *The Nutcracker*. Trans. Joachim Neugro-schel. Jack Zipes, ed. and intr. London: Penguin Clas-sics, 2007 [1816]. Print.

Lewis, C. S. *The Chronicles of Narnia*. New York: Harper-Collins, 2001 [1950-1956]. Print.

Lindren, Astrid. *Pippi Longstocking*. Trans. Edna Hurup. Ill. Tony Ross. Oxford and New York: Oxford University Press, 2012 [1945]. Print.

McCay, Winsor. *The Complete Little Nemo*. Cologne: Bene-dikt Taschen Verlag, 2014 [1905-1914]. Print.

Nesbit, Edith. *Five Children and It*. London and New York: Vintage Children's Classics, 2012 [1902]. Print.

Pullman, Philip. *His Dark Materials – Gift Edition Including All Three Novels*. New York: Everyman, 2011 [1995-2000]. Print.

Rowling, J. K. *Harry Potter – The Complete Collection*. Lon-don: Bloomsbury, 2014 [1997-2007]. Print.

Wilde, Oscar. "Birthday of the Infanta." *The Complete Fairy Tales of Oscar Wilde*. Winnetka: Norilana Books, 2007 [1891].

TV Shows, Films and Video Games

Aladdin. Dir. Ron Clements and John Musker. Walt Disney Pictures and Walt Disney Feature Animation, 1992. Film.

Barney & Friends. Created by Sheryl Leach. The Lyons Group, HiT Entertainment, Conneticut Public Televi-sion, and WNET New York, 1992-2009. TV show.

Cinderella. Dir. Clyde Geronimo, et al. Walt Disney Produc-tions. RKO Radio Pictures, Inc., 1950. Film.

The Hunchback of Notre Dame. Dir. Gary Trousdale and Kirk Wise. Walt Disney Pictures and Walt Disney Feature Animation. Buena Vista Pictures, 1996. Film.

The Jungle Book. Dir. Wolfgang Reitherman. Walt Disney Productions. Buena Vista Pictures, 1967. Film.

The Little Mermaid. Dir. Ron Clements and John Musker. Walt Disney Pictures. Buena Vista Pictures, 1989. Film.

Monsters Inc. Dir. Pete Docter. Walt Disney Pictures and Pixar Animation Studios. Buena Vista Pictures, 2001. Film.

My Neighbor Totoro (Tonari no Totoro). Dir. Hayao Miyazaki. Studio Ghibli. Toho, 1988. Film.

Pinocchio. Dir. Ben Sharpsteen, et al. Walt Disney. RKO Radio Pictures, 1940. Film.

Pokémon. Created by Satoshi Tajiri. The Pokémon Company, 1996. Video game.

Sesame Street. Created by Joan Ganz Cooney and Lloyd Morrisett. Children's Television Workshop and Sesame Workshop, 1969-present. TV show.

Shrek! Dir. Andrew Adamson and Vicky Jenson. Pacific Data Images. DreamWorks Pictures, 2001. Film.

Snow White and the Seven Dwarfs . Dir. David Hand et al. Walt Disney Productions. RKO Radio Pictures, 1937. Film.

Supernanny. Starr. Jo Frost. Ricochet Enterteinmant Shed Media, 2004-2012. TV show.

Toy Story. Dir. John Lasseter. Walt Disney Pictures and Pixar Animation Studios. Buena Vista Pictures, 1995. Film.

Whatever Works. Dir. Woody Allen. Gravier Productions and Wild Bunch. Sony Pictures Classics, 2009. Film.

Where the Wild Things Are. Dir. Spike Jonze. Legendary Pictures, Village Roadshow Pictures, Wild Things Productions, and Playtone. Warner Bros., 2009. Film.

Secondary Sources

Ahmed, Sara. *The Cultural Politics of Emotion.* Edinburgh: Edinburgh University Press, 2004. Print.

Allen, Marjorie N. *What Are Little Girls Made Of? A Guide to Female Role Models in Children's Books.* New York (NY): Facts On File, 1999. Print.

Alston, Ann. *The Family in English Children's Literature.* London: Routledge, 2008. Print.

Andriano, Joseph D. *Immortal Monster – The Mythological Evolution of the Fantastic Beast in Modern Fiction and Film.* Westport (CN) & London: Greenwood Press, 1999. Print.

Arakelian, Paul G. "Text and Illustration: A Stylistic Analysis of Books by Sendak and Mayer." *Children's Literature Association Quarterly* 10.3 (1985) 122-127. Print.

Ariès, Philippe. *Centuries of Childhood.* London: Richard Clay (The Chaucer Press), 1973. Print.

Arzipe, Evelyn, and Morag Styles. *Children Reading Pictures: Interpreting Visual Texts.* London: Routledge, 2003. Print.

Ashliman, D. L. "Changelings." 3 Sept. 1997. Web. 16 Dec. 2014.

Asma, Stephen T. *Monsters – An Unnatural History of Our Worst Fears.* Oxford and New York (NY): Oxford University Press, 2009. Print.

Atkinson, Michael. *Deconstructing Men and Masculinities.* Don Mills: Oxford UP Canada, 2011. Print.

Avery, Gillian, and Margaret Kinnell. "Morality and Levity (1780-1850)." Hunt, Butts, et al. Print.

Baglieri, Susan, and Arthur Shapiro. *Disability Studies and the Inclusive Classroom.* New York: Routledge, 2012. Print.

Baker, Sheridan. "Narration. The Writer's Essential Mimesis." *The Journal of Narrative Technique* 11.3 (1981): 155-165. Print.

Bakhtin, Mikhail. *Rabelais and His World.* Trans. Hélène Iswolsky. Bloomington (IN): Indiana University Press. 1984. Print.

Barnes, Albert. *Notes on the Bible.* Web. 16 Dec 2014.

Baumrind, Diana. "Child Care Practices Anteceding Three Patterns of Preschool Behavior." *Genetic Psychology Monographs* 75.1 (1967): 43-88. Print.

Beasley, Chris. *Gender & Sexuality – Critical Theories, Critical Thinkers.* London, Thousand Oaks, New Delhi: Sage, 2005. Print.

Beckett, Sandra L. *Recycling Red Riding Hood.* New York & London: Routledge, 2002. Print.

Benton, Michael. "Readers, Texts, Contexts – Reader-Response Criticism." Peter Hunt, 2005. 86-102. Print.

Berger, Peter L. *Redeeming Laughter: The Comic Dimension of Human Experience.* Berlin and New York: Walter de Gruyter, 1997. Print.

Bergmann, Wolfgang. "Zur Hölle mit der Disziplin." Interview by Martin Zips. *Süddeutschen Zeitung.* 20 Feb. 2009. Web. 16 Dec. 2014.

Bettelheim, Bruno. *The Uses of Enchantment: The Meaning and Importance of Fairy Tales.* New York: Knopf, 1976. Print.

___. "Little Red Cap and the Pubertal Girl." Dundes 168-191. Print.

Bigner, Jeremy. *Parent-Child Relations: An Introduction to Parenting.* New York: Macmillan, 1979. Print.

Biklen, D. "Constructing Inclusion: Lessons from Critical Disability Narratives." *International Journal on Inclusive Education* 4.4 (2000): 337-353. Print.

Blamires, David. "The Meaning of Disfigurement in Wilhelm Hauff's *Dwarf Nose.*" *Children's Literature in Education* 33.4 (2002): 297-307. Print.

Bodmer, George. "Max-Mickey-Ida – Sendak's Underground Journey." *Journal of Evolutionary Psychology* 7.3/4 (1986): 270-284. Print.

Böhn, Andreas. "Subversions of Gender Identities through Laughter and the Comic?" Pailer, et al. 49-64. Print.

Bornstein, Kate. *Gender Outlaw: On Women, Men, and the Rest of Us.* New York: Vintage, 1995 [1992]. Print.

___. *My Gender Workbook: Who to Become a Real Man, a Real Woman, the Real You, or Something Else Entirely.* Ill. Diane DiMassa. New York and London: Routledge, 1997. Print.

Bottigheimer, Ruth B. *Grimm's Bad Girls and Bold Boys: The Moral and Social Vision of the Tales.* New Haven: Yale University Press, 1987. Print.

Briggs, Julia. "Transitions." Hunt, Butts, et al. 167-191. Print.

Brooks, Wanda, and Susan Browne. "Towards a Culturally Situated Reader Response Theory." *Children's Literature in Education*. 43 (2012): 74-85. Print.

Brittnacher, Hans R. *Ästhetik des Horrors – Gespenster, Vampire, Monster, Teufel und künstliche Menschen in der phantastischen Literatur*. Frankfurt am Main: Suhrkamp, 1995. Print.

Brownmiller, Susan. *Against Our Will: Men, Women, and Rape*. London: Secker & Warburg, 1985. Print.

Brugeilles, Carole, Isabelle Cromer et al. "Male and Female Characters in Illustrated Children's Books or How Children's Literature contributes to the Construction of Gender." *I.N.E.D. Population* 57 (2002): 237-267. Print.

Brulotte, Gaëtan. "Laughing at Power." Trans. John Phillips. *Laughter and Power*. John Parkin and John Phillips, eds. Bern: Peter Lang, 2006. Print.

Bueb, Bernhard. *Lob der Disziplin. Eine Streitschrift*. Berlin: Ullstein, 2006. Print.

Burke, Peter. "Frontiers of the Monstrous: Perceiving National Characters in Early Modern Europe." Lunge Knoppers and Landes. 25-39. Print.

Burr, Vivien. *Social Constructionism*. New York and London: Routledge, 2003. Print.

Butler, Judith. *Gender Trouble – Feminism and the Subversion of Identity*. New York and London: Routledge, 2007. Print.

___. *Bodies That Matter: On the Discursive Limits of "Sex"*. New York and London: Routledge, 2003. Print.

___. "Imitation and Gender Insubordination." *Inside/Out: Lesbian Theories, Gay Theories*. Diana Fuss, ed. London and New York: Routledge, 1991. Print.

___. *Undoing Gender*. New York and London: Routledge, 2004. Print.

Cai, Mingshui. "Images of Chinese and Chinese Americans Mirrored in Picture Books." *Children's Literature in Education* 25.3 (1994): 169-191. Print.

Calabrese, Omar. *Neo-Baroque: A Sign of the Times*. Trans. Charles Lambert. Princeton: Princeton University Press, 1992. Print.

Canguilhem, Georges. *Knowledge of Life*. Trans. Stefanos Geroulanos and Daniela Ginsburg. Paola Marrati and Todd Meyers, eds. Fordham University Press: New York, 2008. Print.

Carlyon, David. "The Trickster as Academic Comfort Food." *Journal of American & Comparative Cultures* 25.1/2 (2002): 14-18. Print.

Carrellas, Barbara. "Lambda Literary Pioneer Award Talks, 2014." Web. 16 Dec. 2014.

Casson, Andrew. *Funny Bodies – Transgressional and Grotesque Humour in English Children's Literature*. Diss. Department of Literature, University of Stockholm, 1997. Print.

Chang-Kredl, Sandra. "Voicing Early Years Teachers' Subjective Experience Through Maurice Sendak's *Outside Over There*." *Children's Literature in Education* 44 (2013): 174-190. Print.

Chapleau, Sebastien. "Alterity and the Production of Books for Children: A Linguistic Approach." Vanessa Joosen and Katrien Vloeberghs. 45-54. Print.

Chodorow, Nancy. *The Reproduction of Mothering: Psychoanalysis and the Sociology of Gender, Updated Edition*. Berkley: University of California Press, 1999. Print.

Chou, Wan-Hisang. "Co-sleeping and the Importation of Picture Books About Bedtime." *Children's Literature in Education* 40 (2009): 19-32. Print.

Chua, Amy. *Battle Hymn of the Tiger Mother*. New York: Penguin Press, 2011. Print.

Clark, Christine. *Teacher's Guide for 'In the Shadow of Race' [by Teja Arboleda]: Growing Up As a Multiethnic, Multicultural, and 'Multiracial' American*. London and New York: Routledge, 1999. Print.

Clark, Roger, Heidi Kulkin, and Liam Clancy. "The Liberal Bias in Feminist Social Science Research on Children's Books." Lyon Clark and Higonnet. 71-82. Print.

Clark, Roger, Rachel Lennon, and Leanna Morris. "Of Caldecotts and Kings: Gendered Images in Recent American Children's Books by Black and Non-Black Illustrators." *Gender & Society* 7.2 (1993): 227-245. Print.

Clark, Roger. "Why All the Counting? Feminist Social Science Research on Children's Literature." *Children's Literature in Education* 33.4 (2002): 285-295. Print.

Coats, Karen. "Postmodern Picturebooks and the Transmodern Self." Sipe and Pantaleo. 75-88. Print.

Cohen, Jeffrey Jerome. *Monster Theory – Reading Culture*. Minneapolis (MN): University of Minnesota Press, 1996. Print.

Coontz, Stephanie. *The Way We Never Were – American Families and the Nostalgia Trap*. New York: Basic Books, 1992. Print.

Crisp, Thomas, and Brittany Hiller. "'Is This a Boy or a Girl?':
    Rethinking Sex-Role Representation in Caldecott
    Medal-Winning Picturebooks, 1938-2011." *Chil-
    dren's Literature in Education* 42 (2011): 196-212.
    Print.

Crisp, Thomas. "It's Not the Book, It's Not the Author, It's the
    Award: The Lambda Literary Award and the Case for
    Strategic Essentialism." *Children's Literature in Edu-
    cation* 42 (2011): 91-104. Print.

Dégh, Linda. "Zur Rezeption der Grimmschen Märchen in den
    USA." *Über Märchen für Kinder von heute – Essays
    zu ihrem Wandel und ihrer Funktion*. Klaus Doderer,
    ed. Weinheim and Basel: Beltz, 1983. 116-128. Print.

De Mause, L., ed. *The History of Childhood*. London: Souve-
    nir, 1976. Print.

Delany, Samuel R. *Shorter Views – Queer Thoughts & The
    Politics of the Paraliterary*. Hanover and London:
    University of New England Press, 1999. Print.

Delarue, Paul. "The Story of Grandmother." Dundes. 13-20.
    Print.

Delgado, Richard, and Jean Stefancic. *Critical White Studies:
    Looking Behind the Mirror*. Philadelphia: Temple
    University Press, 1997. Print.

Dobson, James C. *Temper Your Child's Tantrums – How
    Firm, Loving Discipline Will Lead to a More Peaceful
    Home*. Carol Stream (IL): Tyndale Momentum, 2012.
    Print.

Doonan, Jane. "Sharing Picture Books with Adolescent Stu-
    dents – A Training in Visual Literacy." *Siehst Du
    Das? Die Wahrnehmung von Bildern in Kinderbü-
    chern – Visual Literacy*. Verena Rutschmann, ed.
    Zürich: Chronos, 1997. 53-72.

Doonan, Jane. "The Modern Picture Book." Peter Hunt, 1996. 228-237.

Dreikurs, Rudolf. *The Challenge of Parenthood*. New York: Hawthorne, 1948. Print.

Dundes, Alan, ed. *Little Red Riding Hood: A Casebook*. Madison: U of Wisconsin P, 1989. Print.

Eco, Umberto. "The frames of comic 'freedom'." *Carnival!* Thomas A. Sebeok, ed. Berlin, New York & Amsterdam: Mouton Publishers, 1984.

Eggers, Maisha, Grada Kilomba, et al, eds. *Mythen, Masken und Subjekte – Kritische Weißseinsforschung in Deutschland*. Münster: Unrast Verlag, 2009. Print.

Ewers, Hans-Heino. "Germany." *Oxford Encyclopedia of Children's Literature*. Zipes, ed. Print.

Feustel, Elke. *Rätselprinzessinnen und schlafende Schönheiten – Typologie und Funktionen der weiblichen Figuren in den Kinder- und Hausmärchen der Brüder Grimm*. Hildesheim, Zürich & New York: Olms – Weidmann, 2012. Print.

Fiedler, Leslie. *Freaks – Myths and Images of the Secret Self*. New York (NY): Simon & Schuster, 1978. Print.

Fischer, Agneta H., and Catherine Evers. "Anger in the Context of Gender." Potegal, Stemmler, and Spielberger. 349-360. Print.

Flanagan, Victoria. *Into the Closet: Cross-Dressing and the Gendered Body in Children's Literature and Film*. New York & London: Routledge, 2008. Print.

Eberhard, Wolfram. "The Story of Grandaunt Tiger." Dundes 21-63. Print.

Foucault, Michel. *Abnormal – Lectures at the Collège de France 1974-1975*. New York (NY): Picador, 2003.

____. *Discipline and Punish: The Birth of the Prison*. Trans. Alan Sheridan. New York: Random House, 1995. Print.

____. *The History of Sexuality. An Introduction*. Trans. Robert Hurley. New York: Random House, 1990. Print.

Frosh, Stephen. *For and Against Psychoanalysis*. Milton Park, Abingdon & New York (NY): Routledge, 1997. Print.

Gannon, Susan R. "Women as Heroes. Review" *Children's Literature Association Quarterly* 8.3 (1983): 31. Print.

Galbraith, Mary. "'Goodnight Nobody' Revisited: Using Attachment Perspective to Study Picture Books about Bedtime." *Children's Literature Association Quarterly* 23.4 (1998-99): 172-180. Print.

Garber, Marjorie. *Vested Interests: Cross-Dressing and Cultural Anxiety*. New York & London: Routledge, 1992. Print.

Gardner, John. "Fun and Games and Dark Imaginings." *New York Times Book Review*. 26 April 1981. Print.

Garhart Mooney, Carol. *Theories of Childhood – An Introduction to Dewey, Montessori, Erikson, Piaget, and Vygotsky*. Upper Saddle River (NJ): Redleaf Press, 2000. Print.

Garland-Thompson, Rosemarie. *Extraordinary Bodies: Figuring Physical Disability in American Culture and Literature*. New York: Columbia University Press, 1997. Print.

Geisenhanslüke, Achim, and Georg Mein, eds. *Monströse Ordnungen – Zur Typologie und Ästhetik des Anormalen*. Düsseldorf: transcript Verlag, 2009. Print.

Goetsch, Paul. *Monsters in English Literature: From the Romantic Age to the First World War. Neue Studien zur*

Anglistik und Amerikanistik Bd. 83.: Frankfurt am Main: Peter Lang, 2002. Print.

Goldner, Virginia. 'Ironic Gender/Authentic Sex' in: *Studies in Gender and Sexuality* 4.2 (2003): 113-139. Print.

Goudreau, Jenna. "Disney Princess Tops List of the 20 Best-Selling Entertainment Products." *Forbes*, 17 Sept. 2012. Web 17 Dec. 2014.

Graham, Judith. "Creativity and Picture Books." *Literacy* 34.2 (2000): 61-67. Print.

Grauerholz, Elizabeth, and Bernice A. Pescosolido. "Gender Representation in Children's Literature: 1900-1984." *Gender & Society* 3.1 (1989): 113-125. Print.

Greenleaf, Sarah. "The Beast Within." *Children's Literature in Education* 23.1 (1992): 49-57. Print.

Grimm, Wilhelm and Jakob. *Kinder- und Hausmärchen, 2 Bände*. Berlin: Realschulbuchhandlung, 1812/1815. Web. 16 Dec. 2014.

____. *The Juniper Tree and Other Tales From Grimm*. Trans. Lore Segal and Randall Jarrell. Ill. Maurice Sendak. New York: Farrar, Straus and Giroux, 2003 [1973]. Print.

Griswold, Jerry. "Through the Window." *The Nation* 30 May 1981. Print.

Hacking, Ian. *The Construction of What?* Cambridge (MA): Harvard University Press, 2001. Print.

Halberstam, Judith. *Female Masculinity*. Durham and London: Duke University Press, 1998. Print.

____. *Skin Shows: Gothic Horror and the Technology of Monsters*. Durham and London: Duke University Press, 1995. Print.

___. "On Pronouns." *Jack Halberstam – Gaga Feminism and Queer Failure...* Aug 2008. Web. 16 Dec 2014.

Hall, Christine. "Imagination and Multimodality – Reading, Picturebooks, and Anxieties About Childhood." Sipes and Pantaleo. 130-146. Print.

Hall, David. *Queer Theories*. Basingstoke: Palgrave Macmillan, 2003. Print.

Handler Spitz, Ellen. *Inside Picture Books*. New Haven: Yale University Press, 1999. Print.

___. "Good and Naughty/ Boys and Girls: Reflections on the Impact of Culture on Young Minds." *American Imago* 51.3 (1994): 307-328. Print.

Hartland, Edwin Sidney. *The Science of Fairy Tales: An Inquiry into Fairy Mythology*. London: Walter Scott, 1891. Web. 16 Dec. 2014.

Harrison, Kathryn. "The Boy Who Came to Dinner." *New York Times Book Review*. 13 Nov. 1994. Web. 16 Dec. 2014

Hendler, Glenn. *Public Sentiments: Structures of Feeling in Nineteenth-Century American Literature*. Chapel Hill: University of North Carolina Press, 2001. Print.

Hill, Mike, ed. *Whiteness – A Critical Reader*. New York: New York University Press, 1997. Print.

Hollindale, Peter, and Zena Sutherland. "Internationalism, Fantasy, and Realism." Hunt, Butts, et al. 252-288. Print.

Honeyman, Susan. *Consuming Agency in Fairy Tales, Childlore, and Folkliterature*. New York (NY) and Abindon, Oxon: Routledge, 2010. Print.

Horlacher, Stefan. "A Short Introduction to Theories of Humour, the Comic, and Laughter." Pailer, et al. 17-47. Print.

Huck, Charlotte. "Introduction." *Beauty, Brains, and Brawn – The Construction of Gender in Children's Literature*. Susan Lehr, ed. Portsmouth (NH): Heinemann, 2001. Print.

Hunt, Peter. "'Coldtonguehamcoldbeefpickledgherkins…': Fantastic Food in the Books of Roald Dahl." *Journal of the Fantastic in Arts* 7.1 (1996): 5-22. Print.

___. "Children's literature and childhood." *An Introduction to Childhood Studies*. Ed. Mary Jane Kehily. Maidenhead (Berkshire, UK): Open University Press, 2009. Print.

___, Dennis Butts, et al. eds. *Children's Literature – An Illustrated History*. Oxford & New York (NY): Oxford University Press, 1995. Print.

___, ed. *International Companion Encyclopedia of Children's Literature*. Abingdon: Routledge, 1996. Print.

___, ed. *Understanding Children's Literature*. London and New York: Routledge, 2005. Print.

Hüther, Gerald. *Bedienungsanleitung für ein menschliches Gehirn*. Göttingen: Vandenhoeck & Ruprecht, 2013. Print.

Iser, Wolfgang. *The Act of Reading: A Theory of Aesthetic Response*. Baltimore: Johns Hopkins, 1980. Print.

___. *The Implied Reader: Patterns of Communication in Prose Fiction From Bunyan to Beckett*. Baltimore: Johns Hopkins University Press, 1974. Print.

Jacobs-Thomas, Gina. "10 Gross Things You Hope Your Kids Will Never Do (But Probably Will)." *Scarymommy*, no publication date provided. Web. 17 Dec. 2014.

Jaggar, A. M. "Love and Knowledge: Emotion in Feminist Epistemology." *Women, Knowledge, and Reality: Explorations in Feminist Philosophy*. A. Garry and M. Pearsall, eds. New York: Routledge, 1996. Print.

James, Adrian, and Allison James. "Changing Childhood in the UK: Reconstructing Discourses of 'Risk' and 'Protection'." *European Childhoods – Cultures, Politics and Childhoods in Europe*. Ed. A. James and A. L. James. Houndmills, Basingstoke and New York: Palgrave Mcmilla, 2008. 105-128. Print.

___ . *Constructing Childhood – Theory, Policy and Social Practice*. Basingstoke, Hampshire and New York: Palgrave Macmillan, 2004. Print.

James, Allison, Chris Jenks, and Alan Prout. *Theorizing Childhood*. Cambridge: Polity Press, 1998. Print.

Jatzek, Gerald. "Konrad, sprach die Frau Mama." *Wiener Zeitung*, 13 June 2009. Web. 16 Dec. 2014.

Jenkins, Henry, ed. *The Children's Culture Reader*. New York and London: New York University Press. Print.

Jenks, Chris. *Childhood*. London: Routledge, 1996. Print.

Jesch Tatjana, and Malte Stein. "Perspectivization and Focalization. Two Concepts – One Meaning? An Attempt at Conceptual Differentiation." *Point of View, Perspective and Focalization. Modeling Mediation in Narrative* (= Narratologia, Bd. 17). Peter Hühn, Wolf Schmid, Jörg Schönert, eds. Berlin: De Gruyter, 2009. 59-78. Print.

Joosen, Vanessa, and Katrien Vloeberghs. *Changing Concepts of Childhood and Children's Literature*. Newcastle: Cambridge Scholars Press, 2006. Print.

Joosen, Vanessa. "Fairy-tale Retellings between Art and Pedagogy." *Children's Literature in Education* 36.2 (2005): 129-139. Print.

Juul, Jesper. *Your Competent Child – Towards New Basic Values for the Family*. Bloomington: Balboa Press, 2011. Print.

Kane, Emily W. *The Gender Trap – Parents and the Pitfalls of Raising Boys and Girls*. New York and London: New York University Press, 2012. Print.

Keeling, Kara, and Scott Pollard. "Power, Food, and Eating in Maurice Sendak and Henrik Drescher: *Where the Wild Things Are, In the Night Kitchen*, and *The Boy Who Ate Around*." *Children's Literature in Education* 30.2 (1999): 127-143.

Kelleter, Frank, and Daniel Stein. "*Great, Mad, New*. Populärkultur, serielle Ästhetik und der frühe amerikanische Zeitungscomic." *Comics. Zur Geschichte und Theorie eines populärkulturellen Mediums*. Stephan Ditschke, Katerina Kroucheva, and Daniel Stein, eds. Bielefeld: transcript Verlag, 2009. Print.

Kelso, Sylvia. "Monster Marks: Sliding Significations of the Grotesque in Popular Fiction." Alice Mills. 105-118. Print.

Kidd, Kenneth. "Picturing the Wolf in Children's Literature" (review). *Children's Literature Association Quarterly* 36.2 (2011): 242-246.

Kiefer, Barbara. "What is a Picturebook, Anyway? – The Evolution of Form and Substance through the Postmodern Era and Beyond." Sipes and Pantaleo. 9-21. Print.

Kimmel, Michael S. "Masculinity as Homophobia: Fear, Shame, and Silence in the Construction of Gender Identity." *Privilege: A Reader*. Michael S. Kimmel and Abby L. Ferber, eds. Boulder: Westview Press, 2003. 51-74. Print.

Kortenhaus, Carole M., and Jack Demarest. "Gender Role Stereotyping in Children's Literature: An Update." *Sex Roles* 28.3/4 (1993): 219-232. Print.

Kress, Gunther, and Theo van Leeuwen. *Reading Images – The Grammar of Visual Design.* London and New York: Routledge, 2010. Print.

Kristeva, Julia. *Pouvoirs de l'horreur.* Paris: Seuil, 1980. Print.

Kümmerling-Meibauer, Bettina. "Metalinguistic Awareness and the Child's Development of Irony: The Relationships Between Pictures and Text in Ironic Picturebooks." *The Lion and the Unicorn* 23 (1999): 157-183. Print.

Lehmann, Johannes F. *Im Abgrund der Wut – Zur Kultur- und Literaturgeschichte des Zorns.* Freiburg, Berlin und Wien: Rombach, 2012.

Lesnik-Oberstein, Karín, and Stephen Thomson. "What is Queer Theory Doing With the Child?" *Parallax* 8.1 (2010): 35-46. Print.

Lesnik-Oberstein. *Children's Literature – Criticism and the Fictional Child.* Oxford: Clarendon Press, 1994. Print.

Lewis, David. *Picturing Text – Reading Contemporary Picturebooks.* London: Routledge, 2001. Print.

Lieberman, Marcia. "Some Day My Prince Will Come." *College English* 34 (1972): 383-395. Print.

Locke, Abigail. "The social psychologising of emotion and gender." *Sexed Sentiments – Interdisciplinary Perspectives on Gender and Emotion.* Willemijn Ruberg and Kristine Steenbergh, eds. Amsterdam and New York: Rodopi, 2011. 185-205. Print.

Lunger Knoppers, Laura, and Joan B. Landes, eds. *Monstrous Bodies/ Political Monstrosities in Early Modern Europe.* Ithaca and London: Cornell University Press, 2004. Print.

Lüthi, Max. *Märchen* 10. Auflage. Stuttgart: Metzler, 2004. Print.

Lyon Clark, Beverly, and Margaret R. Higonnet, eds. *Girls, Boys, Books, Toys – Gender in Children's Literature and Culture*. Baltimore and London: The Johns Hopkins University Press, 1999. Print.

Lyon Clark, Beverly. "Introduction." Lyon Clark and Higonnet. 1-10. Print.

MacDonald, Ruth. "The Tale Retold: Feminist Fairy Tales." *Children's Literature Association Quarterly* 7.2 (1982): 18-20. Print.

Maier, Karl Ernst. *Jugendliteratur. Formen, Inhalte, Pädagogische Bedeutung*. Bad Heilbrunn: Klinkhart, 1993. Print.

Mallan, Kerry. *Gender Dilemmas in Children's Fiction*. Basingstoke & New York (NY): Palgrave Macmillan, 2009. Print.

___. "Picturing the Male – Representations of Masculinity in Picture Books." Stephens, 2002. 15-37. Print.

Marshall, Elizabeth. "Girlhood, Sexual Violence, and Agency in Francesca Lia Block's 'Wolf'." *Children's Literature in Education* 40 (2009): 217-234. Print.

___. "Stripping for the Wolf: Rethinking Representations of Gender in Children's Literature." *Reading Research Quarterly* 39.3 (2004): 256-270. Print.

Mayall, Berry. *Towards a Sociology for Childhood – Thinking from Children's Lives*. Buckingham: Open University Press, 2002. Print.

Mayseless, Ofra. *Parenting Representations – Theory, Research, and Clinical Implications*. New York: Cambridge University Press, 2006. Print.

McCulloch, Fiona. *Children's Literature in Context*. London and New York (NY): Continuum, 2011. Print.

McGee, Diane. *Writing the Meal: Dinner in the Fiction of Early Twentieth-Century Women Writers*. Toronto: University of Toronto Press, 2001. Print.

McGillis, Roderick. *The Nimble Reader: Literary Theory and Children's Literature*. New York: Twayne Publishers, 1996. Print.

McNair, Jonda. "'I Never Knew There Were So Many Books About Us' Parents and Children Reading and Responding to African American Children's Literature Together." *Children's Literature in Education* 44 (2013): 191-207. Print.

McNulty, Faith. "Books: Children's Books for Christmas." *The New Yorker*, Dec. 1981. 216-124. Print.

Mendelson, Michael. "Forever Acting Alone: The Absence of Female Collaboration in *Grimms' Fairy Tales*." *Children's Literature in Education* 28.3 (1997): 111-125. Print.

Menninghaus, Winfried. *Disgust – Theory and History of a Strong Sensation*. Trans. Howard Eiland and Joel Golb. Albany: State University of New York Press, 2003. Print.

Miller, Cynthia L. "Qualitative Differences Among Gender-Stereotyped Toys: Implications for Cognitive and Social Development in Girls and Boys." *Sex Roles* 16.9/10 (1987): 473-487. Print.

Mills, Alice, ed. *Seriously Weird – Papers on the Grotesque*. New York: Peter Lang, 1999. Print.

Mills, Sara *Michel Foucault – Routledge Critical Thinkers*. London: Routledge, 2003. Print.

Mitts-Smith, Debra. *Picturing the Wolf in Children's Literature*. New York: Routledge, 2010. Print.

Moebius, William. "Introduction to picturebook codes." *Word & Image* 2.2 (1986): 141-158. Print.

Montessori, Maria. *The Secret of Childhood*. London: Sangam, 1983 [1936]. Print.

Montgomery, Heather. *An Introduction to Childhood: Anthropological Perspectives on Children's Lives*. London: Wiley-Blackwell, 2009. Print.

Moon, Michael. *A Small Boy and Others: Imitation and Initiation in American Culture from Henry James to Andy Warhol.* Durham and London: Duke University Press, 1998. Print.

Morgan, Judith, and Neil Morgan. *Dr. Seuss & Mr. Geisel.* New York: Random House, 1995. Print.

Morgenstern, John. "Children and Other Talking Animals." *The Lion and the Unicorn* 24 (2000): 110-127. Print.

Morrison-Fortunato. "Three is the New Two." *Scarymommy,* 13 Nov. 2013. Web. 17 Dec. 2014.

Müller, Ulrich, and Werner Wunderlich. *Dämonen, Monster, Fabelwesen.* St. Gallen: UVK Fachverlag für Wissenschaft und Studium, 1999. Print.

Naumann, Karl. "Klassiker der Pädagogik der frühen Kindheit." *Pädagogik der frühen Kindheit.* Lilian Fried und Susanna Roux, eds. Weinheim und Basel: Beltz, 2006. 212-214. Print.

Nell, Philip. *Dr. Seuss: American Icon.* New York (NY): Continuum, 2009. Print.

Ngai, Sianne. *Ugly Feelings.* Cambridge (MA) and London: Harvard University Press, 2005. Print.

Nicholson, Mervyn. *Male Envy – The Logic of Malice in Literature and Culture.* Lanham, Boulder, New York, Oxford: Lexington Books, 1999. Print.

Nikolajeva, Maria, and Carol Scott. "The Dynamics of Picturebook Communication." *Children's Literature in Education* 31 (2000): 225-239. Print.

___. *How Picturebooks Work.* New York: Routledge, 2006. Print.

Nikolajeva, Maria. "Fantasy." *Oxford Encyclopedia of Children's Literature.* Zipes, ed. Print.

___. *From Mythic to Linear: Time in Children's Literature.* Lanham (MD): Scarecrow, 2000. Print.

___. *Power, Voice and Subjectivity in Literature for Young Readers.* New York and London: Routledge, 2010. Print.

___. "Reading Other People's Minds Through Word and Image." *Children's Literature in Education* 43 (2012): 273-291. Print.

___. "The verbal and the visual – The picturebook as a medium." *Children's Literature as Communication.* Roger D. Sell, ed. Amsterdam and Philadelphia: John Benjamins Publishing Company, 2002. 85-110. Print.

Nodelman, Perry. *The Hidden Adult – Defining Children's Literature.* Baltimore (MD): The Johns Hopkins University Press, 2008. Print.

___. *Words About Pictures – The Narrative Art of Children's Picture Books.* Athens (GA): University of Georgia Press, 1988. Print.

___. "Making Boys Appear: The Masculinity of Children's Fiction." John Stephens, 2002. 1-14. Print.

Nussbaum, Martha. *From Disgust to Humanity: Sexual Orientation and Constitutional: Law.* Oxford and New York: Oxford University Press, 2010. Print.

Ogden, Thomas H. *This Art of Psychoanalysis: Dreaming Undreamt Dreams and Interrupted Cries.* New York (NY): Routledge. Print.

O'Malley, Andrew. *The Making of the Modern Child: Children's Literature and Childhood in the Late Eighteenth Century.* London: Routledge, 2003. Print.

Orenstein, Catherine. *Little Red Riding Hood Uncloaked: Sex, Morality, and the Evolution of a Fairy Tale.* New York: Basic, 2003. Print.

Orenstein, Peggy. "What's Wrong With Cinderella?" *New York Times*, 24 Dec. 2006. Web. 17 Dec. 2014.

O'Sullivan, Emer. *Comparative Children's Literature*. Trans. Anthea Bell. London: Taylor & Francis, 2005. Print.

___. "S is for Spaniard – The representation of foreign nations in ABCs and picturebooks." *European Journal of English Studies* 13.3 (2009): 333-349. Print.

Overthun, Rasmus. "Das Monströse und das Normale – Konstellationen einer Ästhetik des Monströsen." Geisenhanslüke and Mein. 43-80. Print.

Pailer, Gaby, Andreas Böhn, Stefan Horlacher, and Ulrich Schneck, eds. *Gender and Laughter – Comic Affirmation and Subversion in Traditional and Modern Media*. Amsterdam & New York: Rodopi, 2009. Print.

Pailer, Gaby. "Introduction." Pailer, et al. 7-14. Print.

Parr, Rolf. "Monströse Körper und Schwellenfiguren als Faszinations- und Narrationstypen ästhetischen Differenzgewinns." *Monströse Ordnungen: Zur Typologie und Ästhetik des Anormalen*. Ed. Achim Geisenhanslüke and Georg Mein. Düsseldorf: transcript, 2009. Print.

Parsons, Elisabeth. "Starring in the Intimate Space: Picture Book Narratives and Performance Semiotics." *Image & Narrative* 9 (2004): 1-12. Print.

Pattison, Darcy. "Picture Book Standards: 32 Pages." 2 Aug 2008. Web. 16 Dec. 2014.

Perl, Jed. "Where the Wild Things Are." *The New Republic*. March 18 1996. Print.

Perrault, Charles. *Histoires ou contes du temps passé*. Paris: Gallimard, 1999 [1697]. Print.

Perrot, Jean. "Deconstructing Maurice Sendak's Modern Palimpsest." *Children's Literature Association Quarterly* 16.4 (1991): 159-263. Print.

Piaschewski, Gisela. *Der Wechselbalg: Ein Beitrag zum Aberglauben der nordeuropäischen Völker*. Breslau: Maruschke & Berendt Verlag, 1935. Print.

Pinsent, Pat. *Children's Literature and the Politics of Equality*. London: David Fulton Publishers, 1997. Print.

Pollock, Linda A. *Forgotten Children: Parent-Child Relations from 1500 to 1900*. Cambridge: Cambridge University Press, 1983. Print.

Poole, L. M. *Maurice Sendak and the Art of Children's Book Illustration*. Maidstone: Crescent Moon, 1996. Print.

Potegal, Michael, Gerhard Stemmler, and Charles Spielberger, eds. *The International Handbook of Anger – Constituent and Concomitant Biological, Psychological and Social Processes*. New York, Heidelberg, London: Springer, 2010. Print.

Ptak, John. "Dr. Seuss and the 236 Words That Changed Reading Forever." Web. 16 Dec. 2014.

Pugh, Tison. *Innocence, Heterosexuality, and the Queerness of Children's Literature*. London and New York: Routledge, 2011. Print.

Reed, Michael D. "The Female Oedipal Complex in Maurice Sendak's *Outside Over There*." *Children's Literature Association Quarterly* 11. 4 (1986-87): 176-180. Print.

Rees, David. "King of the Wild Things." *San Jose Studies* 14.3 (1988): 96-107. Print.

Reiser, Christa. *Reflections on Anger – Women and Men in a Changing Society*. Westport (CN) and London: Praeger, 1999. Print.

Reiß, Marcus. *Kindheit bei Maria Montessori and Ellen Key – Disziplinierung und Normalisierung*. Paderborn: Ferdinand Schöningh, 2012. Print.

Reynolds, Kimberly. *Children's Literature in the 1890s and the 1990s*. Plymouth: Northcote House, 1994. Print.

___. *Girls Only? Gender and Popular Children's Fiction in Britain, 1880-1910*. Philadelphia (PA): Temple University Press, 1990. Print.

Rieu, D. C. H. "Introduction." *The Odyssey* by Homer. Trans. E. V. Rieu. London: Penguin, 2003. Print.

Róheim, Géza. "Little Red Riding Hood." Dundes 159-167. Print.

Rollin, Lucy, and Mark I. West. *Psychoanalytic responses to children's literature*. Jefferson (NC): Mc Farland & Company, 1999. Print.

Rose, Jacqueline. *The Case of Peter Pan or The Impossibility of Children's Fiction*. London: Macmillan, 1984. Print.

Rousseau, Jean-Jacques. *Emile or On Education*. Trans. Allan Bloom, ed. New York: Basic Books, 1979. Print.

___. *Emilius and Sophia; or, The Solitaries*. London: Gale Ecco, 2010. Print.

Roxburgh, Stephen. "A Picture Equals How Many Words? Narrative Theory and Picture Books for Children." *The Lion and the Unicorn* 7/8 (1983): 20-33. Print.

Sadler, David F. "From 'Where the Wild Things Are' to 'Wild in the World'." *Children's Literature in Education* 13 (1974): 53-67. Print.

Sandberg, Sheryl. *Lean In: Women, Work, and the Will to Lead.* New York: A. Knopf, 2013. Print.

Said, Edward. *Orientalism.* London: Routledge & Kegan Paul, 2003. Print.

Schwarcz, Joseph. *Ways of the Illustrator: Visual Communication in Children's Literature.* Chicago: American Library Association, 1981. Print.

Schweik, Susan M. *The ugly laws: disability in public.* New York and London: New York University Press, 2009. Print.

Scott, Carol. "Dual Audience in Picture Books." *Transcending Boundaries: Writing for a Dual Audience of Children and Adults.* Sandra L. Beckett, ed. New York: Garland, 1999. 99-110. Print.

Sears, Martha, and William Sears. *The Discipline Book – How to Have a Better-Behaved Child From Birth to Age Ten.* New York: Little, Brown and Company, 1995. Print.

Segdwick, Eve Kosofsky. "How to Bring Your Kids Up Gay." Henry Jenkins. 231-239. Print.

___. *Tendencies.* Durham and London: Duke University Press, 1993. Print.

Seiter, Ellen. *Sold Separately: Parents & Children in Consumer Culture.* New Brunswick: Rutgers University Press, 1995. Print.

Sendak, Maurice. "Interview: Maurice Sendak." Interview by Bill Moyers. *Now on PBS*, 2004. Web. 16 Dec. 2014.

___. "Interview: Maurice Sendak on his Work, Childhood, Inspiration." *Rosenbach Museum & Library*, 1 June 2011. Web. 16. Dec. 2014.

Shaddock, Jennifer. *"Where the Wild Things Are*: Sendak's Journey into the Heart of Darkness." *Children's Literature Association Quarterly* 22.4 (1997-98): 155-159). Print.

Shute, Daryl. "Interview: Magic Light Pictures on 15 Years with the Gruffalo." Interview by Billy Langsworthy. *Licensing.biz*, 1 April 2014. Web. 12 Jan. 2015.

Sipe, Lawrence, and Sylvia Pantaleo, eds. *Postmodern Picturebooks – Play, Parody, and Self-Referentiality*. New York and Oxon: Routledge, 2008. Print.

Sipe, Lawrence. "How Picturebooks Work: A Semiotically Framed Theory of Text-Picture Relationships." *Children's Literature in Education* 29.2 (1998): 97-108. Print.

___. "Revisiting the Relationships Between Text and Picture." *Children's Literature in Education* 43 (2012): 4-21. Print.

___. *Storytime: Young Children's Literary Understanding in the Classroom*. New York: Teachers College Press, 2007. Print.

___. "Young Children's Visual Meaning-Making in Response to Picturebooks." *Handbook of Research in Teaching Literacy Through the Visual and Communicative Arts* Vol. 2. James Flood, Shirly Brice-Heath, and Diane Lapp, eds. New York: Lawrence Erlbaum, 2008. 381-392. Print.

Smith, Vivienne. "All in a Flap About Reading: Catherine Morland, Spot, and Mister Wolf." *Children's Literature in Education* 32.3 (2001): 225-236. Print.

Smith Chalou, Barbara. *A Postmodern Analysis of the Little Red Riding Hood Tale*. Lewiston, Queenston, Lampeter: The Edwin Mellen Press, 2002. Print.

Spigel, Lynn. "Seducing the Innocent – Childhood and Television in Postwar America." Henry Jenkins. 110-135. Print

Stallcup, Jackie. "Power, Fear, and Children's Picture Books." *Children's Literature* 30 (2002): 125-58. Print.

Stearns, Peter N. *American Cool – Constructing a Twentieth-Century Emotional Style.* New York and London: New York University Press, 1994. Print.

Steinberg, Shirly R., Michael Kehler, and Lindsay Cornish, eds. *Boy Culture – An Encyclopedia.* Santa Barbara (CA), Denver (CO), Oxford: Greenwood, 2010. Print.

Stephens, John. *Language and Ideology in Children's Fiction.* Harlow: Longman, 1992. Print.

___. "Analysing texts – Linguistics and stylistics." Hunt, 1999. 73-85. Print.

___, ed. *Ways of Being Male – Representing Masculinities in Children's Literature and Film.* New York & London: Routledge, 2002. Print.

Stephens, John, and Robyn McCallum. *Retelling Stories, Framing Culture: Traditional Story and Metanarratives in Children's Literature.* New York: Garland, 1998. Print.

Stone, Kaye F. "The Misuses of Enchantment: Controversies on the Significance of Fairy Tales." *Women's Folklore, Women's Culture.* Ed. Rosan A. Jordan and Susan J. Kalcik. Philadelphia: U of Pennsylvania P, 1985. 125-45. Print.

___. "Things Walt Disney Never Told Us." *Women and Folklore.* Claire R. Farrer, ed. Austin: University of Texas Press, 1975. 42-45. Print.

Strasen, Sven. "Analyse der Erzählsituation und Fokalisierung," *Einführung in die Erzähltextanalyse – Kategorien, Modelle, Probleme.* Peter Wenzel, ed. Trier: Wissenschaftlicher Verlag Trier, 2004. 111-140. Print.

Swanton, Averil. "Maurice Sendak's Picture Books." *Children's Literature in Education* 2.3 (1971): 38-48. Print.

Taber, Nancy, and Vera Woloshyn. "Dumb Dorky Girls and Wimpy Boys: Gendered Themes in Diary Cartoon Novels." *Children's Literature in Education* 42 (2011): 226-242. Print.

Tatar, Maria. *The Hard Facts of the Grimms' Fairy Tales.* Princeton: Princeton University Press, 1987. Print.

Tepper, Clary A., and Kimberly Wright Cassidy. "Gender Differences in Emotional Language in Children's Picture Books." *Sex Roles* 40.3/4 (1999): 265-280. Print.

Tetenbaum, Toby Jane, and Judith Pearson. "The Voices in Children's Literature: The Impact of Gender on the Moral Decisions of Storybook Characters." *Sex Roles* 20.7/8 (1989): 381-395. Print.

Thomas, Gary. "A Review of Thinking and Research About Inclusive Education Policy, With Suggestions for a New Kind of Inclusive Thinking." *Educational Research Association* 39.3 (2013): 473-490. Print.

Toomey, Sarah. *Embodying an Image: Gender and Genre in a Selection of Children's Responses to Picturebooks and Illustrated Texts.* Newcastle upon Tyne: Cambridge Scholars Publishing, 2009. Print.

Trepanier-Street, Mary L., and Jane A. Romatowski. "The Influence of Children's Literature on Gender Role

Perceptions: A Reexamination." *Early Childhood Education Journal* 26.3 (1999): 155-159. Print.

Turner-Bowker, Diane M. "Gender Stereotyped Descriptors in Children's Picture Books: Does 'Curious Jane' Exist in the Literature?" *Sex Roles* 35.7/8 (1996): 461-488. Print.

Tuttle-Singer, Sarah. "When the Little Shit Is Yours." *Scarymommy*, 3 Oct. 2013. Web. 16 Dec. 2014.

Uther, Hans-Jörg. *The Types of International Folktales: A Classification and Bibliography, Based on the System of Antti Aarne and Stith Thompson*, Issue 285. Suomalainen Tiedeakatemia: Academia Scientiarum Fennica, 2004. Print.

van der Pol, Coosje. "Reading Picturebooks *as Literature*: Four-to-Six-Year-Old Children and the Development of Literary Competence." *Children's Literature in Education* 43 (2012): 93-106. Print.

Votava, Jerry. "US military to permit women to serve in combat units." *Jurist*, 24 Jan. 2013. Web. 18 Dec. 2014.

Walter, Clemens. "Sendak's Enchanted Land." *Newsweek* 18 May 1981. Print.

Wannamaker, Annette. "Reading the Gaps and Lacks: (De)Constructing Masculinity in Louis Sachar's *Holes*." *Children's Literature in Education* 37.1 (2006): 15-33. Print.

Webb, Janeen, and Andrew Enstice. "Domesticating the Monster." Alice Mills. 89-103. Print.

Weinreich, Thorben. *Children's Literature: Art or Pedagogy?* Frederiksberg: Roskilde University Press, 2000. Print.

Weitzman, Lenore, Deborah Eifler, et al. "Sex-role socialization in picturebooks for preschool children." *American Journal of Sociology* 77 (1972): 1125-1150. Print.

Wessling, Elisabeth. "Visual Narrativity in the Picture Book: Heinrich Hoffmann's Der Struwwelpeter." *Children's Literature in Education* 35.4 (2004): 319-345. Print.

Whalley, Joyce Irene. "The Development of Illustrated Texts and Picture Books." Peter Hunt, 1996. 318-328. Print.

Winterhoff, Michael. *Warum unsere Kinder Tyrannen werden. Oder: Die Abschaffung der Kindheit.* Munich: Goldmann, 2010. Print.

World Health Organization. "Disabilities." No publication date provided. Web. 18 Dec. 2014.

Wild, Inge. "Kindsein heute – zwischen Lachen und Weinen." *Veränderte Kindheit in der aktuellen Kinderliteratur.* Hannelore Daubert and Hans-Heino Ewers, eds. Braunschweig: Westermann Schulbuchverlag, 1999. Print.

Xiao, Hong. "Class, Gender, and Parental Values in the 1990s." *Gender and Society* 14.6 (2000): 785-803. Print.

Yarbrough, Wynn William. *Masculinity in Children's Animal Stories, 1888-1928: A Critical Study of Anthropomorphic Tales of Wilde, Kipling, Potter, Grahame and Milne.* Jefferson: McFarland & Company, 2011. Print.

Zelizer, Viviana A. *Pricing the Priceless Child – The Changing Social Value of Children.* New York (NY): Basic Books, 1985. Print.

Zipes, Jack. *Don't Bet On the Prince – Contemporary Feminist Fairy Tales in North America and England.* New York (NY): Routledge, 1989. Print.

___, ed. *The Oxford Encyclopedia for Children's Literature*. Oxford: OUP, 2006. Print.

___. *Fairy Tales and the Art of Subversion*. London & New York (NY): Routledge, 2012. Print.

___. *The Trials and Tribulations of Little Red Riding Hood*. South Hadley: Bergin & Garvey, 1989. Print.

Zisowitz Stearns, Carol and Peter N. Stearns. *Anger – The Struggle for Emotional Control in America's History*. Chicago and London: The University of Chicago Press, 1986. Print.

Zornado, Joseph L. *Inventing the Child: Culture, Ideology, and the Story of Childhood*. New York and London: Routledge, 2006. Print.

www.ingramcontent.com/pod-product-compliance
Lightning Source LLC
Chambersburg PA
CBHW022133020426
42334CB00015B/877